Vernon K. Robbins

Atlanta

9-13-1995

D1058638

PARABLES AS POETIC FICTIONS

PARABLES
AS POETIC
FICTIONS
The Creative Voice of Jesus

CHARLES W. HEDRICK

HENDRICKSON
PUBLISHERS

Copyright © 1994 by Hendrickson Publishers, Inc.
P. O. Box 3473
Peabody, Massachusetts 01961–3473
All rights reserved
Printed in the United States of America

ISBN 0–913573–90–6

Library of Congress Cataloging-in-Publication Data

Hedrick, Charles W.
    Parables as poetic fictions: the creative voice of Jesus   /
Charles W. Hedrick
        p. cm.
    Includes bibliographical references and indexes.
    ISBN 0–913573–90–6
    1. Jesus Christ—Parables.   2. Bible as literature.   I. Title.
    BT375.2.H38   1994
    226.8'06—dc20   94–34579
                                                                      CIP

To Mother

Harriet Eva Margaret Lettie Magnolia

A virtuous woman

Table of Contents

Foreword

THE HISTORY OF PARABLES INTERPRETATION HAS PASSED THROUGH FIVE readily recognizable phases. The first was the context of their original oral delivery in which Jesus spoke them to early first-century Palestinian Jews and other auditors. At that time there was no church to provide authoritative explanations for the stories. People understood them, or not, depending upon their own varied frames of reference. The parables' original historical context, the social context of their original delivery and audition, is irretrievably lost to modern New Testament scholarship! In a second phase the parables were claimed by the earliest Christian communities and were reperformed and interpreted orally. Later these reinterpreted stories were written down and read as examples of proper Christian behavior, as figures representing some unearthly reality, and as allegorical riddles of the resurrected "Lord of the Church" whose words spoke specifically, if differently, to the early Christian communities of faith. This second phase of parables interpretation was the exclusive way parables were read until the end of the nineteenth century. A third phase began (1888) with the pivotal work of Adolf Jülicher, who argued that the parables were intended to make a one-point comparison between an unseen referential world and the situation reflected in the parables; thus he discarded allegory's polyvalent interpretations, with its multiple points, for a single (moral) point of meaning. A fourth phase derives from the work of C. H. Dodd (1935), who argued that the parables were metaphors that intended to bring the kingdom of God to expression in vivid memorable language. A fifth phase of parables interpretation began in 1967 with Dan Via's book, *The Parables: Their Literary and Existential Dimension.* Via argued that one could appreciate the parables in the same way that one appreciated objects of art. It was, therefore, possible to analyze the understanding of human existence reflected in the narrative, with virtually no reference to a historical context. Via's insight that the

narratives have a life of their own, one that is not subject to the intention
of their inventor, has yet to be properly appreciated.

Virtually concurrent with the appearance of Via's book was the
translation and publication of the *Gospel of Thomas* (1959), an early
Christian text, a complete Coptic version of which was found with the
Nag Hammadi Library in 1945. Thomas contains two previously unknown parables of Jesus, as well as significantly different versions of
parables already known from the synoptic gospel tradition.

The availability of new source material is always justification for
reexamining issues. Accordingly, besides the traditional synoptic material, the present study also draws upon the *Gospel of Thomas*, a text that
puts the modern reader in touch with the earliest levels of the Jesus
tradition. Our study will show how noncanonical early Christian sources
can facilitate the quest for historical understanding of the parables
attributed to Jesus of Nazareth. Drawing upon the insights of Via, this
study will analyze the parables as literary narrative; but in distinction to
Via, this study regards reading the parables in the context of the culture
of first-century Palestine as crucial to their historical understanding.

Finally, this study will consciously challenge the assumption that
the place to begin reading the parables is by initially regarding them as
metaphor/symbol; that is to say, by regarding them as images that are
consciously designed to take the reader outside the story where one finds
relevant "meanings" in theological abstractions. Rather, this study contends that it is only inside the story that discoveries about oneself and
the world may be made.

Acknowledgments

THIS BOOK BEGAN BY ACCIDENT. WHEN I REALIZED THAT I HAD WRITTEN two papers on the parables (chapter 7 and Appendix A) that seemed to be taking me out of the "mainstream" of parables interpretation, I decided that a review of the entire parables corpus was in order. This led to a third paper (chapter 2 in the present volume) that took me still further out of the mainstream. The die was cast. At that point there was no alternative but to stay the course and see where it led.

Southwest Missouri State University awarded me a sabbatical leave from my teaching responsibilities during 1986–87 for the purpose of researching this book. There were several other projects then in process that had to be completed in the intervening years. In 1991 the Iraqi war caused a major disruption to my academic life when I was called to active duty for seven months as a reserve army chaplain.

I am indebted to many from whose books, articles, and lectures I have learned, but several deserve special mention, for their work has been particularly influential on this book: my Doktorvater, colleague, and friend, James M. Robinson, for his example of uncompromising critical scholarship; Amos N. Wilder, with whom I all too briefly shared poetry as well as the parables of Jesus; Norman Perrin and Robert W. Funk, whose critical thought has provided a research model for a generation of North American students of the Jesus traditions; Dan O. Via, whose little book is a watershed in parables study, the vanguard of the future; and John Dominic Crossan, whose personal quest for the historical Jesus has made him mentor to us all.

To Ms. JoAnne Brown, secretary extraordinaire of the Religious Studies Department at Southwest Missouri State University, and her staff of student workers goes my deep appreciation for originally converting my frequently indecipherable scribbling of most of the chapters of this book into comprehensible prose. To Mrs. Ann Reberry goes my appreciation for preparing the computer disk for the press from which the pages of this book were prepared. A special word of thanks is due Patrick Alexander, whose careful critical reading has contributed immeasurably to the improvement of this volume. I am grateful to my colleagues at Southwest Missouri State University. Their continued collegial support has turned a work place into a delightful academic environment. And finally I will always be indebted to my wife Peggy for her continual patience, understanding, and encouragement without which this book never would have been written.

Abbreviations

a. Hebrew Scriptures

Gen	Genesis
Exod	Exodus
Lev	Leviticus
Num	Numbers
Deut	Deuteronomy
Josh	Joshua
Judg	Judges
Ruth	Ruth
1 Sam	1 Samuel
2 Sam	2 Samuel
1 Kgs	1 Kings
2 Kgs	2 Kings
1 Chron	1 Chronicles
Ezra	Ezra
Neh	Nehemiah
Esth	Esther
Job	Job
Ps	Psalms
Prov	Proverbs
Eccl	Ecclesiastes
Isa	Isaiah
Jer	Jeremiah
Lam	Lamentations
Ezek	Ezekiel
Dan	Daniel
Hos	Hosea
Joel	Joel
Amos	Amos
Jonah	Jonah
Mic	Micah
Hab	Habakkuk
Zeph	Zephaniah
Hag	Haggai
Zech	Zechariah
Mal	Malachi

b. New Testament

Matt	Matthew
Mark	Mark
Luke	Luke
John	John
Acts	Acts
Rom	Romans
1 Cor	1 Corinthians
2 Cor	2 Corinthians
Gal	Galatians
Eph	Ephesians
2 Tim	2 Timothy
Heb	Hebrews
Jas	James
1 Pet	1 Peter
2 Pet	2 Peter
Rev	Revelation

c. Apocrypha

Ep Jer	Epistle of Jeremiah
1 Esd	1 Esdras
2 Esd	2 Esdras
Jdt	Judith
4 Kgs	4 Kings
1 Macc	1 Maccabees
2 Macc	2 Maccabees
4 Macc	4 Maccabees
Sir	Sirach

Tob	Tobit	CE	Common Era
Wis	Wisdom of Solomon	CEV	Contemporary English Version

d. Mishnah (m.), Talmud (b. Babylonian), Tosephta (t.)

'Abot	*'Abot*	cf.	*confer*, compare
'Arak	*'Arakin*	e.g.	*exempli gratia*, for example
Ber.	*Berakot*	esp.	especially
Bik.	*Bikkurim*	fem.	feminine
B. Meṣi'a	*Baba Meṣi'a*	id.	*idem*, the same
Demai	*Demai*	i.e.	*id est*, it is
Giṭ.	*Giṭṭin*	log.	logion
Ketub.	*Ketubot*	LXX	Septuagint
Ma'aś.	*Ma'aśerot*	masc.	masculine
Ma'aś. Š.	*Ma'aśer Šeni*	n.	note
Ned.	*Nedarim*	NAB	New American Bible
Nid.	*Niddah*	n.d.	no date indicated
Qidd.	*Qiddušin*	NEB	New English Bible
Sanh.	*Sanhedrin*	NIV	New International Version
Šeb.	*Šebi'it*	NT	New Testament
Tamid	*Tamid*	p(p).	page(s)
Ter.	*Terumot*	par.	parallel(s)
Yoma	*Yoma*	plu.	plural
Zer.	*Zera'im*	RSV	Revised Standard Version
		sc.	*scilicet*, namely
		s.v.	*sub verbo*, under the word

e. Other Abbreviations

BCE	Before the Common Era	TEV	Today's English Version
		vol.	volume(s)

Short Titles

AB	Anchor Bible.
Albright-Mann, *Matthew*	Albright, W. F. and C. S. Mann. *Matthew. Introduction, Translation, and Notes.* AB 26. Garden City, N.Y.: Doubleday, 1971.
Allen, *Matthew*	Allen, W. C. *A Critical and Exegetical Commentary on the Gospel According to S. Matthew.* ICC. New York: Scribner's, 1913.
Allen, *Vox Graeca*	Allen, W. S. *Vox Graeca: A Guide to the Pronouncement of Classical Greek.* Cambridge: University Press, 1968.
Anderson, *Old Testament*	Anderson, B. W. *Understanding the Old Testament.* Englewood Cliffs, N.J.: Prentice-Hall, 1975.
ANF	Ante-Nicene Fathers, 1980–82.
Ap. Jas.	*Apocryphon of James.*
Argyle, *Matthew*	Argyle, A. W. *The Gospel According to Matthew.* Cambridge Bible Commentary on the New English Bible. Cambridge: University Press, 1963.
Aristot.	Aristotle
Rhet.	*Rhetorica.*
Poet.	*Poetica.*
Hist. An.	*Historia Animalium.*
Arr. *Anab.*	Arrian, *Anabasis.*
Ash, *Columella*	Ash, H. B. *Lucius Junius Moderatus Columella On Agriculture with a Recension of the Text and an English Translation.* LCL. 3 vols. Cambridge, Mass.: Harvard University Press; London: Heinemann, 1941.

Atkins, *Literary Criticism*

Atkins, J. W. H. *Literary Criticism in Antiquity. A Sketch of its Development*. 2 vols. Cambridge: University Press, 1934.

Attridge, *NHC I*

Attridge, H. W. ed. *Nag Hammadi Codex I (The Jung Codex)*. NHS 22–23. 2 vols. Leiden: Brill, 1985.

Auerbach, *Mimesis*

Auerbach, E. *Mimesis. The Representation of Reality in Western Literature*. Trans. W. A. Trask. Princeton: University Press, 1953 [German 1946].

Avigad, *Discovering Jerusalem*

Avigad, N. *Discovering Jerusalem*. Nashville/Camden/New York: Thomas Nelson, 1980.

BA

Biblical Archaeologist.

Bailey, *Poet and Peasant*

Bailey, K. E. *Poet and Peasant and Through Peasant Eyes. A Literary Cultural Approach to the Parables in Luke. Combined Edition*. Two vols. in one. Grand Rapids: Eerdmans, 1976 and 1980.

Bauer, "Echte Jesusworte"

Bauer, J. B. "Echte Jesusworte." Pp. 108–50 in *Evangelien aus dem Nilsand*. Ed. W. C. van Unnik. Frankfurt: Schaffer, 1960.

Benner and Forbes, *Letters*

Benner, A. R. and F. H. Forbes. *The Letters of Alciphron, Aelian and Philostratus*. Cambridge, Mass.: Harvard University Press; London: Heinemann, 1979.

Betz, *Galatians*

Betz, H. D. *Galatians, A Commentary on Paul's Letter to the Churches in Galatia*. Hermeneia. Philadelphia: Fortress, 1979.

Betz, "Dead Sea Scrolls"

Betz, O. "Dead Sea Scrolls." Vol. 1.790–802 in G. A. Buttrick, et al., eds. *The Interpreter's Dictionary of the Bible*. New York/Nashville: Abingdon, 1962.

Blass-Debrunner-Funk, *Greek Grammar*

Blass, F. and A. Debrunner. *A Greek Grammar of the New Testament and Early Christian Literature*. Trans. and rev. R. W. Funk. Chicago: University Press, 1967 [9th German ed.].

Borg, "Temperate Case"

Borg, M. J. "A Temperate Case for a Non-Eschatological Jesus." *Forum* 2.3 (1986) 81–102.

Boring, "Criteria of Authenticity"

Boring, M. E. "The Historical-Critical Method's 'Criteria of Authenticity': The Beatitudes in Q and Thomas as a Test Case." Pp. 9–44 in Hedrick, *Historical Jesus and Rejected Gospels*.

Boring, *Sayings*

Boring, M. E. *Sayings of the Risen Jesus: Christian Prophecy in the Synoptic Tradition.* SNTSMS 46. London/New York/New Rochelle/Melbourne/ Sidney: Cambridge University Press, 1982.

Borowski, "Agriculture"

Borowski, O. "Agriculture in Iron Age Israel." Ph.D. diss., University of Michigan, 1979.

Boucher, *Mysterious Parable*

Boucher, M. *The Mysterious Parable: A Literary Study.* CBQMS 6. Washington: Catholic Biblical Association, 1977.

Boucher, *Parables*

Boucher, M. *The Parables.* Wilmington, Del.: Michael Glazier, 1983.

Box, *Testament of Abraham*

Box, G. H. *The Testament of Abraham Translated from the Greek Text with Introduction and Notes.* London: SPCK, 1927.

Breech, "Parables of Jesus"

Breech, J. "Kingdom of God and the Parables of Jesus." Pp. 15–40 in *The Poetics of Faith Essays Offered to Amos Niven Wilder. Part 1. Rhetoric, Eschatology and Ethics in the New Testament.* Ed. W. A. Beardslee. *Semeia* 12. Missoula, Mont.: Scholars, 1978.

Breech, *Silence of Jesus*

Breech, J. *The Silence of Jesus. The Authentic Voice of the Historical Man.* Philadelphia: Fortress, 1983.

Bright, *History*

Bright, J. *A History of Israel.* 3d ed. Philadelphia: Westminster, 1981.

Bruce, *Parabolic Teaching*

Bruce, A. B. *The Parabolic Teaching of Christ. A Systematic and Critical Study of the Parables of Our Lord.* 3d rev. ed. New York: A. C. Armstrong & Son, 1886 [1st ed. 1882].

BTB

Biblical Theology Bulletin.

Bugge, *Haupt-Parabeln*

Bugge, C. A. *Die Haupt-Parabeln Jesu.* Giessen: J. Ricker, 1903.

Bultmann, "Interpretation von Mk 4,3–9"

Bultmann, R. "Die Interpretation von Mk 4,3–9 seit Jülicher." Pp. 30–34 in *Jesus und Paulus. Festschrift für Werner Georg Kümmel zum 70. Geburtstag.* Ed. E. E. Ellis and E. Grässer. 2d ed. Göttingen: Vandenhoek & Ruprecht, 1987.

Bultmann, *Synoptic Tradition*

Bultmann, R. *The History of the Synoptic Tradition.* Trans. J. Marsh. Oxford: Blackwell, 1963 [German 1st ed. 1921].

Bultmann, *Theology*

Bultmann, R. *Theology of the New Testament.* Trans. K. Grobel. 2 vols. New York: Scribner's, 1951 and 1955.

Burney, *Poetry*   Burney, C. F. *The Poetry of Our Lord: An
                                  Examination of the Formal Elements of Hebrew
                                  Poetry in the Discourses of Jesus Christ.* Oxford:
                                  Clarendon, 1925.

Butts, "Probing the   Butts, J. R. "Probing the Polling. Jesus Seminar
    Polling"   Results on the Kingdom Sayings." *Forum* 3.1
                                  (1987) 98–128.

Byatt, "Connoisseur of   Byatt, A. S. "Connoisseur of Order." *New
    Order"   Statesman* 74 (4 August 1967) 146.

Bynum, *Daemon in the*   Bynum, D. E. *The Daemon in the Wood. A Study of
    Wood   Oral Narrative Patterns.* Publication of the Milman
                                  Parry Collection, Monograph Series One.
                                  Cambridge, Mass.: Harvard University Press, 1978.

BZNW   Beihefte zur ZNW.

Cadbury, *Method of Luke*   Cadbury, H. J. *The Style and Literary Method of
                                  Luke.* HTS 6. Cambridge, Mass.: Harvard
                                  University Press, 1920.

Cadoux, *Parables*   Cadoux, A. T. *The Parables of Jesus: Their Art and
                                  Use.* New York: Macmillan, 1931.

Cameron, "Parable and   Cameron, R. "Parable and Interpretation in the
    Interpretation"   Gospel of Thomas." *Forum* 2.2 (1986) 3–39.

Cameron, *Other Gospels*   Cameron, R. *The Other Gospels: Non-Canonical
                                  Gospel Texts.* Philadelphia: Westminster, 1982.

Cameron, *Sayings*   Cameron, R. *Sayings Traditions in the Apocryphon
    Traditions   of James.* HTS 34. Philadelphia: Fortress, 1984.

Carlston, *Triple Tradition*   Carlston, C. E. *The Parables of the Triple Tradition.*
                                  Philadelphia: Fortress, 1975.

Cary, *Dionysius*   Cary, E. *The Roman Antiquities of Dionysius of
                                  Halicarnassus with an English Translation.* LCL. 7
                                  vols. Cambridge, Mass.: Harvard University Press;
                                  London: Heinemann, 1963.

Casper, "Sense of an   Casper, L. "The Sense of an Ending." *Thought* 43
    Ending"   (Fall 1968) 443–44.

CBQ   *Catholic Biblical Quarterly*

CBQMS   Catholic Biblical Quarterly Monograph Series

Charles, *Ascension of Isaiah* Charles, R. H. *The Ascension of Isaiah.* London:
                                  Adam and Charles Black, 1900.

Charlesworth,   Charlesworth, J. H. *The Pseudepigrapha and Modern
    Pseudepigrapha   Research with a Supplement.* Septuagint and
                                  Cognate Studies 7. Chico, Calif.: Scholars, 1981.

Cic. *Sen.*	M. Tullius Cicero, *De Senectute.*
Clem. Alex. *Strom.*	Clement of Alexandria, *Stromata.*
Coleman-Norton, *Studies*	Coleman-Norton, P. R. *Studies in Roman Economic and Social History in Honor of Allan Chester Johnson.* Princeton: University Press, 1951.
Collingwood, *Roman Britain*	Collingwood, P. G. *The Archaeology of Roman Britain.* London: Methuen, 1930.
Conzelmann, *1 Corinthians*	Conzelmann, H. *1 Corinthians. A Commentary on the First Epistle to the Corinthians.* Hermeneia. Trans. J. W. Leitch. Philadelphia: Fortress, 1975 [11th German ed. 1969].
Conzelmann, *Theology of St. Luke*	Conzelmann, H. *The Theology of St. Luke.* Trans. G. Buswell. Philadelphia: Fortress, 1961 [German, 1953].
Cook, Adcock, and Charlesworth, *Cambridge Ancient History*	Cook, S. A., F. E. Adcock, and M. P. Charlesworth, eds. *The Cambridge Ancient History.* Vol. 10: *The Augustan Empire 44 B. C. –A. D. 70.* Cambridge: University Press, 1971.
Cooper, *Poetics of Aristotle*	Cooper, L. *The Poetics of Aristotle. Its Meaning and Influence.* New York: Cooper Square, 1963.
Corley, *Colloquy*	Corley, B. ed. *Colloquy on New Testament Studies: A Time for Reappraisal and Fresh Approaches.* Macon, Ga.: Mercer, 1983.
Crossan, *Cliffs of Fall*	Crossan, J. D. *Cliffs of Fall, Paradox and Polyvalence in the Parables of Jesus.* New York: Seabury, 1980.
Crossan, *Dark Interval*	Crossan, J. D. *The Dark Interval. Towards a Theology of Story.* Rev. ed. Sonoma, Calif.: Polebridge, 1988.
Crossan, "Divine Immediacy"	Crossan, J. D. "Divine Immediacy and Human Immediacy. Towards a New First Principle in Historical Jesus Research." Pp. 121–40 in Hedrick, *Jesus and the Rejected Gospels.*
Crossan, *First Act*	Crossan, J. D. *Finding is the First Act. Trove Folktales and Jesus' Treasure Parable.* Philadelphia: Fortress; Missoula, Mont.: Scholars, 1979.
Crossan, "Hermeneutical Jesus"	Crossan, J. D. "The Hermeneutical Jesus." Pp. 237–49 in *The Bible and its Traditions.* Ed. M. P. O'Connor and D. N. Freedman. Ann Arbor: University of Michigan, 1983.
Crossan, "Hidden Treasure Parables"	Crossan, J. D. "Hidden Treasure Parables in Late Antiquity." Pp. 359–79 in *Society of Biblical*

                                      Literature 1976 Seminar Papers. Ed. George
                                      MacRae. Missoula, Mont.: Scholars, 1976.

Crossan, *Historical Jesus*   Crossan, J. D. *The Historical Jesus. The Life of a
                                     Mediterranean Jewish Peasant.* San Francisco:
                                     Harper, 1991.

Crossan, *In Fragments*   Crossan, J. D. *In Fragments. The Aphorisms of
                                     Jesus.* San Francisco: Harper & Row, 1983.

Crossan, *In Parables*   Crossan, J. D. *In Parables. The Challenge of the
                                     Historical Jesus.* New York/Hagerstown/San
                                     Francisco/London: Harper & Row, 1973.

Crossan, "Review of   Crossan, J. D. "Review of Bailey, *Poet and
    Bailey"   Peasant.*" *JBL* 96.4 (1977) 606–8.

Crossan, *Sayings Parallels*   Crossan, J. D. *Sayings Parallels: A Workbook for the
                                     Jesus Tradition.* Philadelphia: Fortress, 1986.

Crossan, "Seed Parables"   Crossan, J. D. "The Seed Parables of Jesus." *JBL*
                                     92.2 (1973) 244–66.

Crum   Crum, W. E. *A Coptic Dictionary. Compiled with the
                                     Help of Many Scholars.* Oxford: Clarendon, 1939.
                                     Reprint 1962.

CTM   *Concordia Theological Monthly.*

Dana and Mantey,   Dana, H. E. and J. R. Mantey. *A Manual Grammar
    Manual Grammar   of the Greek New Testament.* Toronto: Macmillan,
                                     1927.

Danby, *Mishnah*   Danby, H. *The Mishnah.* Oxford: University Press,
                                     1933.

Davies, "Christology and   Davies, S. "The Christology and Protology of the
    Protology"   *Gospel of Thomas.*" *JBL* 3.4 (1992) 663–82.

Davies, "The Fourth   Davies, S. L. "Thomas—The Fourth Synoptic
    Synoptic Gospel"   Gospel." *BA* 46 (1983) 6–9, 12–14.

Davies, *Gospel of Thomas*   Davies, S. L. *The Gospel of Thomas and Christian
                                     Wisdom.* New York: Seabury, 1983.

Dehandschutter, "Parabole   Dehandschutter, B. "Les Paraboles de l'Evangile
    du Trésor Caché"   selon Thomas. La Parabole du Trésor Caché (log.
                                     109)." *ETL* 47 (1971) 199–219.

Dehandschutter, "Parabole   Dehandschutter, B. "La Parabole de la Perle (Mt
    de la Perle"   13, 45–46) et L'Evangile selon Thomas." *ETL* 55
                                     (1979) 243–65.

Denniston, "Assonance,   Denniston, J. D. "Assonance, Greek." P. 132 in *The
    Greek"   Oxford Classical Dictionary.* Ed. N. G. L. Hammond
                                     and H. H. Scullard. Oxford: Clarendon, 1970.

Denniston, *Greek Prose Style* — Denniston, J. D. *Greek Prose Style*. Westport, Conn.: Greenwood, 1952.

Derrett, "Unjust Judge" — Derrett, J. D. M. "Law in the New Testament: The Parable of the Unjust Judge." *NTS* 18 (1972) 178–91.

Derrett, *Law* — Derrett, J. D. M. *Law in the New Testament*. London: Darton, Longman, & Todd, 1970.

Did. — Didache.

Diod. Sic. *Historical Library* — Diodorous Siculus. *Historical Library*.

Dion. Hal. *Ant. Roma.* — Dionysius of Halicarnassus. *Antiquitates Romanae*.

Dodd, *Authority* — Dodd, C. H. *The Authority of the Bible*. London: Nisbet, 1955 [1st ed. 1928; rev. 1938].

Dodd, *Parables* — Dodd, C. H. *The Parables of the Kingdom*. Rev. ed. London and Glasgow: Collins, 1961.

Donahue, *Gospel in Parable* — Donahue, J. R. *The Gospel in Parable, Metaphor, Narrative, and Theology in the Synoptic Gospels*. Philadelphia: Fortress, 1988.

Downing, "Ambiguity" — Downing, F. G. "The Ambiguity of 'The Pharisee and the Toll-collector' (Luke 18:9–14) in the Greco-Roman World of Late Antiquity." *CBQ* 54 (1992) 80–99.

Drury, *Parables* — Drury, J. *The Parables in the Gospels: History and Allegory*. New York: Crossroads, 1985.

Duckworth, "Roman Provincial System" — Duckworth, H. T. F. "The Roman Provincial System." Pp. 171–217 in *The Beginnings of Christianity. Part I: The Acts of the Apostles*. Vol I: *Prolegomena I. The Jewish, Gentile and Christian Backgrounds*. Ed. F. J. Foakes Jackson and Kirsopp Lake. Grand Rapids: Baker, 1979.

Dupont, "Paraboles du Trésor et de la Perle" — Dupont, J. "Les Paraboles de Trésor et de la Perle." *NTS* 14 (1968) 408–18.

Eichrodt, *Theology* — Eichrodt, W. *Theology of the Old Testament*. Trans. J. Baker. 2 vols. Westminster, 1961 and 1967 [German 6th ed. 1959].

ETL — *Ephemerides theologicae lovanienses*.

Eusebius, *Eccl. Hist.* — Eusebius, *The Ecclesiastical History*. Trans. K. Lake and J. E. L. Oulton. LCL. 2 vols. Cambridge, Mass.: Harvard University Press; London: Heinemann, 1926 and 1932.

Evelyn-White, *Hesiod*

Evelyn-White, H. G. *Hesiod. The Homeric Hymns and Homerica*. LCL. London: Heinemann; New York: Putnam's Sons, 1926.

Falconer, *Cicero*

Falconer, W. A. *Cicero. De Senectute, de Amicita, de Divinatione*. LCL. Cambridge, Mass.: Harvard University Press; London: Heinemann, 1959.

Fallon and Cameron, "The Gospel of Thomas"

Fallon, F. T. and R. Cameron. "The Gospel of Thomas: A *Forschungsbericht* and Analysis." Pp. 4195–4251 in *Aufstieg und Niedergang der Römischen Welt (Rise and Decline of the Roman World)*. Ed. W. Haase and H. Temporini. Teil II: Principat, Band 25:6. Berlin and New York: De Gruyter, 1988.

Fee, *First Epistle to the Corinthians*

Fee, G. D. *The First Epistle to the Corinthians*. Grand Rapids: Eerdmans, 1987.

Ferguson, *Backgrounds*

Ferguson, E. *Backgrounds of Early Christianity*. Grand Rapids: Eerdmans, 1987.

Fergusson, "Two Perspectives"

Fergusson, F. "Two Perspectives on European Literature." *The Hudson Review* 7.1 (1954) 118–27.

Finnegan, *Oral Poetry*

Finnegan, R. *Oral Poetry. Its Nature, Significance, and Social Context*. Cambridge/London/New York/Melbourne: Cambridge University Press, 1977.

Fitzmyer, "Oxyrhynchus *Logoi*"

Fitzmyer, J. A. "The Oxyrhynchus *Logoi* of Jesus and the Coptic Gospel According to Thomas." *ThSt* (1959) 505–60.

Fitzmyer, *Luke*

Fitzmyer, J. *The Gospel According to Luke*. AB 28–28A. 2 vols. Garden City, N.Y.: Doubleday, 1981 and 1985.

Freed, "Judge and Widow"

Freed, E. D. "The Parable of the Judge and the Widow (Luke 18:1–8)." *NTS* 33 (1987) 38–60.

Freedman-Simon, *Midrash Rabbah*

Freedman, H. and M. Simon, trans. and eds. *Midrash Rabbah: Song of Songs*. London: Soncino, n. d.

Freese, *Aristotle: Rhetoric*

Freese, J. H. *Aristotle with an English Translation: The "Art" of Rhetoric*. LCL. Cambridge, Mass.: Harvard University Press; London: Heinemann, 1947.

Friedlander, *Jewish Sources*

Friedlander, G. *The Jewish Sources on the Sermon on the Mount*. New York: KTAV, 1969.

Frye, *Anatomy of Criticism*

Frye, N. *The Anatomy of Criticism: Four Essays*. Princeton: University Press, 1959.

Funk, "Beyond Criticism"　　Funk, R. W. "Beyond Criticism in Quest of
Literacy: The Parable of the Leaven." *Int* 25 (1971)
149–70.

Funk, "Good Samaritan as　　Funk, R. W. "The Good Samaritan as Metaphor."
　　Metaphor"　　Pp. 29–34 in Funk, *Parables and Presence* = "The
Good Samaritan as Metaphor." Pp. 74–81 in *The
Good Samaritan.* Ed. J. D. Crossan. *Semeia* 2.
Missoula, Mont.: University of Montana, 1974.

Funk, "How Do You Read?"　　Funk, R. W. " 'How Do You Read?' (Luke
10:25–37)." *Int* 18 (1964) 56–61.

Funk, "Parable as　　Funk, R. W. "The Parable as Metaphor." Pp.
　　Metaphor"　　133–62 in R. W. Funk, *Language, Hermeneutic, and
Word of God. The Problem of Language in New
Testament and Contemporary Theology.* New
York/Evanston/London: Harper & Row, 1966.

Funk, *Parables and Presence*　　Funk, R. W. *Parables and Presence: Forms of the New
Testament Tradition.* Philadelphia: Fortress, 1982.

Funk, "Poll on the　　Funk, R. W. "Poll on the Parables." *Forum* 2.1
　　Parables"　　(1986) 54–80.

Funk, Scott, Butts,　　Funk, R. W., B. B. Scott, and J. R. Butts. *The
　　Parables of Jesus*　　*Parables of Jesus. Red Letter Edition.* Sonoma,
Calif.: Polebridge, 1988.

Fyfe, *Aristotle*　　Fyfe, W. J. *Aristotle, The Poetics; "Longinus," On
the Sublime; Demitrius, On Style.* LCL. Cambridge,
Mass.: Harvard University Press; London:
Heinemann, 1953.

Garitte and Cerfaux,　　Garitte, G. and L. Cerfaux. "Les paraboles du
　　"Paraboles du royaume"　　royaume dans 'l'Evangile de Thomas.' " *Muséon*
70 (1957) 307–27.

Gärtner, *Theology*　　Gärtner, B. *The Theology of the Gospel of Thomas.*
Trans. E. J. Sharpe. London: Collins, 1961.

GCS　　Griechische christliche Schriftsteller.

Goodwin, *Greek Grammar*　　Goodwin, W. M. *A Greek Grammar.*
London/Melbourne/Toronto: Macmillan; New
York: St. Martin's Press, 1968.

Gos. Thom.　　*Gospel of Thomas.*

Grant, Freedman, Schoedel,　　Grant, R. M., D. N. Freedman, and D. Schoedel.
　　Secret Sayings　　*The Secret Sayings of Jesus: The Gnostic Gospel of
Thomas.* Garden City, N.Y.: Doubleday, 1960.

Gray, *Kings*　　Gray, J. *I and II Kings. A Commentary.* 2d ed. rev.
Philadelphia: Westminster, 1970.

Gundry, *Matthew*   Gundry, R. H. *Matthew. A Commentary on His Literary and Theological Art.* Grand Rapids: Eerdmans, 1982.

Guillaumont, "Sémitismes"   Guillaumont, A. "Les sémitismes dans l'Evangile selon Thomas. Essai de classement." Pp. 190–204 in *Studies in Gnosticism and Hellenistic Religions. Presented to Gilles Quispel on the Occasion of his 65th Birthday.* Eds. R. van den Broek and M. J. Vermaseren. Etudes preliminaries aux religions orientals dan l'Empire Romain 91. Leiden: Brill, 1981.

Guillaumont, *Thomas*   Guillaumont, A., H.-Ch. Puech, G. Quispel, W. Till, and Yassah 'Abd Al Masīḥ, eds. *The Gospel According to Thomas. Coptic Text Established and Translated.* Leiden: Brill; New York/Evanston: Harper & Row, 1959.

Haenchen, *Acts of the   Haenchen, E. *The Acts of the Apostles. A
Apostles*   Commentary.* Philadelphia: Westminster, 1971 [14th German ed., 1965].

Halm, *fabulae Aesopicae   Halm, C. ΑΙΣΩΠΕΙΩΝ ΜΥΘΩΝ ΣΝΑΓΩΓΗ *fabulae
collectae*   Aesopicae collectae.* Leipzig: Teubner, 1901.

Haslam, *Oxyrhynchus   Haslam, M. W. *The Oxyrhynchus Papyri Volume
Papyri*   LIII.* Graeco-Roman Memoirs 73. London: Egypt Exploration Society, 1986.

Havelock, *Literate   Havelock, E. A. *The Literate Revolution in Greece
Revolution*   and its Cultural Consequences.* Princeton: University Press, 1982.

Hawkes, *Metaphor*   Hawkes, T. *Metaphor.* London: Methuen, 1972.

Hawkins, *Horae Synopticae*   Hawkins, J. C. *Horae Synopticae. Contributions to the Study of the Synoptic Problem.* 2d ed. rev. Oxford: Clarendon, 1909. Reprint 1968.

Hedrick, "Kingdom   Hedrick, C. W. "Kingdom Sayings and Parables of
Sayings"   Jesus in the *Apocryphon of James*: Tradition and Redaction." *NTS* 29 (1983) 1–24.

Hedrick, "On Moving   Hedrick, C. W. "On Moving Mountains, Mark
Mountains"   11:22b–23/Matt 21:21 and Parallels." *Forum* 6.3/4 (1990 [appeared 1993]) 219–37.

Hedrick, "Parables and   Hedrick, C. W. "Parables and the Kingdom: The
the Kingdom"   Vision of Jesus in Fiction and Faith." Pp. 368–93 in *Society of Biblical Literature 1987 Seminar Papers.* Ed. K. L. Richards. SBLSP 26. Atlanta: Scholars, 1987.

Hedrick, "Past and Future as Ethical Exordium" — Hedrick, C. W. "Past and Future as Ethical Exordium: A Survey of Foundations for Christian Behavior in the New Testament." Pp. 93–117 in *Reaching Beyond: Chapters in the History of Perfectionism*. Ed. S. M. Burgess. Peabody, Mass.: Hendrickson, 1986.

Hedrick, "Thomas and the Synoptics" — Hedrick, C. W. "Thomas and the Synoptics. Aiming at a Consensus." *The Second Century* 7.1 (1989–90) 39–56.

Hedrick, "Treasure Parable" — Hedrick, C. W. "The Treasure Parable in Matthew and Thomas." *Forum* 2.2 (1986) 41–56.

Hedrick, "Tyranny of the Synoptic Jesus" — Hedrick, C. W. "The Tyranny of the Synoptic Jesus." Pp. 1–8 in Hedrick, *Historical Jesus and Rejected Gospels*.

Hedrick, *Apocalypse of Adam* — Hedrick, C. W. *The Apocalypse of Adam: A Literary and Source Analysis*. SBLDS 46. Chico, Calif.: Scholars, 1980.

Hedrick, *Historical Jesus and Rejected Gospels* — Hedrick, C. W. ed. *The Historical Jesus and the Rejected Gospels*. Semeia 44. Atlanta: Scholars, 1988.

Hedrick-Hodgson, *Nag Hammadi, Gnosticism, Early Christianity* — Hedrick, C. W. and R. H. Hodgson, Jr., eds. *Nag Hammadi, Gnosticism, and Early Christianity*. Peabody, Mass.: Hendrickson, 1986.

Heinisch-Heidt, *Theology* — Heinisch, P. and W. G. Heidt. *Theology of the Old Testament*. St. Paul, Minn.: Liturgical Press, 1955 [German 1952].

Hengel, *Judaism and Hellenism* — Hengel, M. *Judaism and Hellenism: Studies in their Encounter in Palestine During the Early Hellenistic Period*. Trans. J. Bowden. 2 vols. Philadelphia: Fortress, 1974.

Hennecke-Schneemelcher, *New Testament Apocrypha* — Hennecke, E. and W. Schneemelcher, eds. *New Testament Apocrypha*. Trans. and ed. R. McL. Wilson. 2 vols. Philadelphia: Westminster, 1963.

Hertzberg, *Samuel* — Hertzberg, H. W. *I and II Samuel. A Commentary*. Trans. J. S. Bowden. Philadelphia: Fortress, 1964 [German 2d rev. ed. 1960].

Herzog, *Subversive Speech* — Herzog, W. R. II. *Parables as Subversive Speech. Jesus as Pedagogue of the Oppressed*. Louisville, Ky.: Westminster/John Knox, 1994.

Hes. *Op.* — Hesiod. *Opera et Dies*.

Higgins, "Non-Gnostic Sayings" — Higgins, A. J. B. "Non-Gnostic Sayings in the Gospel of Thomas." *NovT* 4 (1960) 292–306.

Hodgson, "Testimony   Hodgson, Robert Jr. "The Testimony Hypothesis."
   Hypothesis"   *JBL* 98 (1979) 361–78.

Holtzmann, *Synoptiker*   Holtzmann, H. J. *Die Synoptiker*. Hand-Commentar
                             zum Neuen Testament 1,1. 3d ed. rev. Tübingen
                             and Leipzig: J. C. B. Mohr [Paul Siebeck], 1901.

Hooper-Ash, *Cato*   Hooper, W. D. and H. B. Ash. *Marcus Porcius Cato
                             On Agriculture; Marcus Terentius Varro On
                             Agriculture*. LCL. Cambridge, Mass.: Harvard
                             University Press; London: Heinemann, 1936.

Hopkins, *Highlands of*   Hopkins, D. C. *The Highlands of Canaan:
   Canaan*   Agricultural Life in the Early Iron Age*. Social World
                             of Biblical Antiquity Series 3. Decatur, Ga.:
                             Almond, 1985.

Hort, *Theophrastus*   Hort, A. *Theophrastus Enquiry into Plants and
                             Minor Works on Odours and Weather Signs*. LCL. 2
                             vols. London: Heinemann; New York: G. P.
                             Putnam's Sons, 1916.

Hough, "End of the World"   Hough, G. "The End of the World." *The Listener* 78
                             (5 October 1967) 430–32.

HTR   *Harvard Theological Review*.

HTS   Harvard Theological Studies.

Hunzinger, "Unbekannte   Hunzinger, C. H. "Unbekannte Gleichnisse Jesu
   Gleichnisse Jesu"   aus dem Thomas-Evangelium." Pp. 209–20 in
                             *Judentum, Urchristentum, Kirche: Festschrift für
                             Joachim Jeremias*. Ed. W. Eltester. BZNW 26.
                             Berlin: Töpelmann, 1960.

ICC   International Critical Commentary.

IDB   *Interpreter's Dictionary of the Bible*. Ed. G. A.
                             Buttrick. 4 vols. New York/Nashville: Abingdon,
                             1962.

IDBS   *Interpreter's Dictionary of the Bible Supplementary
                             Volume*. Gen. Ed. K. Crim. Nashville: Abingdon,
                             1976.

Int   *Interpretation*.

JAAR   *Journal of the American Academy of Religion*.

James, *Apocryphal New*   James, M. R. *The Apocryphal New Testament Being
   Testament*   the Apocryphal Gospels, Acts, Epistles, and
                             Apocalypses with Other Narratives and Fragments*.
                             Oxford: Clarendon, 1926.

James, *Philo*	James, M. R. *The Biblical Antiquities of Philo Now First Translated from the Old Latin Version.* New York: KTAV, 1971.
JBL	*Journal of Biblical Literature.*
Jeremias, "Gleichnis vom Säemann"	Jeremias, J. "Palästinakundliches zum Gleichnis vom Säemann (Mark iv. 3–8 par.)." *NTS* 13 (1966) 48–53.
Jeremias, *Jerusalem*	Jeremias, J. *Jerusalem in the Time of Jesus. An Investigation into Economic and Social Conditions During the New Testament Period.* Trans. F. H. and C. H. Cave. Philadelphia: Fortress, 1969 [German 3d ed.].
Jeremias, *Parables*	Jeremias, J. *The Parables of Jesus.* Trans. S. H. Hooke. Rev. ed. New York: Scribner's, 1963. [German 6th ed. 1962].
Jeremias, *Unknown Sayings*	Jeremias, J. *Unknown Sayings of Jesus.* Trans. R. H. Fuller. London: SPCK, 1964.
Johnson, "Review of Bailey"	Johnson, T. L. "Review of Bailey, *Through Peasant Eyes.*" *Int* 37.1 (1983) 102–3.
Jones, *Art and Truth*	Jones, G. V. *The Art and Truth of the Parables. A Study in their Literary Form and Modern Interpretation.* London: SPCK, 1964.
Jones, *Teaching*	Jones, P. R. *The Teaching of the Parables.* Nashville: Broadman, 1982.
Jos. Ant. Bell.	Flavius Josephus *Antiquitates Judaicae.* *Bellum Judaicum.*
JR	*Journal of Religion.*
JSOT	*Journal for the Study of the Old Testament.*
JTS	*Journal of Theological Studies.*
Jülicher, *Gleichnisreden Jesu*	Jülicher, A. *Die Gleichnisreden Jesu.* 2 volumes. Vol. 1: *Die Gleichnisreden Jesu im Allgemeinen.* Vol. 2: *Auslegung der Gleichnisreden der drei ersten Evangelien.* 2d ed. rev. Freiburg/Leipzig/Tübingen: J. C. B. Mohr, 1899.
Jüngel, *Paulus und Jesus*	Jüngel, E. *Paulus und Jesus. Eine Untersuchung zur Präzisierung der Frage nach dem Ursprung der Christologie.* 3d ed. rev. Tübingen: J. C. B. Mohr [Paul Siebeck], 1967.

Kasser, *Evangile Thomas*

Kasser, R. *L'Evangile selon Thomas*. NHS 5. Leiden: E. J. Brill, 1975.

Kasser, *Thomas*

Kasser, R. *L'Evangile selon Thomas. Présentation et commentaire théologique*. Neuchâtel, Switzerland: Delachaux & Niestlé, 1961.

Kelber, *Oral and Written Gospel*

Kelber, W. H. *The Oral and Written Gospel*. Philadelphia: Fortress, 1983.

Kermode, *Sense of an Ending*

Kermode, F. *The Sense of an Ending. Studies in the Theory of Fiction*. London/Oxford/New York: Oxford University Press, 1966.

Kermode, *Wallace Stevens*

Kermode, F. *Wallace Stevens*. Edinburgh/London: Oliver & Boyd, 1960.

King, "Kingdom in the Gospel of Thomas"

King, K. "Kingdom in the Gospel of Thomas." *Forum* 3.1 (1987) 48–97.

Kingsbury, *Matthew 13*

Kingsbury, J. *The Parables of Jesus in Matthew 13: A Study in Redaction Criticism*. Richmond: John Knox, 1969.

Kloppenborg, *Q Parallels*

Kloppenborg, J. S. *Q Parallels, Synopsis, Critical Notes and Concordance*. Sonoma, Calif.: Polebridge, 1988.

Klostermann-Gressmann, *Lukasevangelium*

Klostermann, E. and H. Gressmann. *Das Lukasevangelium*. Tübingen: J. C. B. Mohr [Paul Siebeck], 1919.

Klostermann-Gressmann, *Matthäus*

Klostermann, E. and H. Gressmann. *Matthäus*. Handbuch zum Neuen Testament. Tübingen: J. C. B. Mohr [Paul Siebeck], 1909.

Koester, "Apocryphal and Canonical Gospels"

Koester, H. "Apocryphal and Canonical Gospels." *HTR* 73 (1980) 105–30.

Koester, "Extracanonical Sayings of the Lord"

Koester, H. "The Extracanonical Sayings of the Lord as Products of the Christian Community." Pp. 57–77 in Hedrick, *Historical Jesus and Rejected Gospels*.

Koester, "GNOMAI DIAPHOROI"

Koester, H. "GNOMAI DIAPHOROI: The Origin and Nature of Diversification in the History of Early Christianity." Pp. 114–57 in Robinson-Koester, *Trajectories*.

Koester, *Introduction*

Koester, H. *Introduction to the New Testament*. Vol. 1: *History, Culture, and Religion of the Hellenistic Age*. Vol. 2: *History and Literature of Early Christianity*. Philadelphia: Fortress; Berlin/New York: De Gruyter, 1982 [German 1980].

Koester, "One Jesus and Four Primitive Gospels"	Koester, H. "One Jesus and Four Primitive Gospels." Pp. 158–204 in Robinson-Koester, *Trajectories*.
Koester and Pagels, "Introduction"	Koester, H. and E. Pagels. "Introduction." Pp. 1–17 in *Nag Hammadi Codex III, 5. The Dialogue of the Savior*. Ed. S. Emmel. NHS 26. Leiden: Brill, 1984.
Kuhn, "Lord's Supper"	Kuhn, K. G. "The Lord's Supper and the Communal Meal at Qumran." Pp. 65–93 in *The Scrolls and the New Testament*. Ed. K. Stendahl. New York: Harper, 1957.
Kümmel, *Promise and Fulfillment*	Kümmel, W. G. *Promise and Fulfillment. The Eschatological Message of Jesus*. SBT 23. Trans. D. M. Barton. 3d ed. London: SCM, n. d. [German 3d ed. 1956].
Kuntz, *Ancient Israel*	Kuntz, J. K. *The People of Ancient Israel. An Introduction to Old Testament Literature, History, and Thought*. New York/Evanston/San Francisco/London: Harper & Row, 1974.
Lake, *Eusebius*	Lake, K. *Eusebius: The Ecclesiastical Histories*. 2 vols. Cambridge, Mass.: Harvard University Press, 1932.
Lambdin, "Thomas"	Lambdin, T. O. "The Gospel According to Thomas." Pp. 52–93 in Layton, *NHC II*.
Lane, *Mark*	Lane, W. L. *The Gospel According to Mark, with English Text. With Introduction, Exposition and Notes*. NIC. Grand Rapids: Eerdmans, 1974.
Layton, *NHC II*	Layton, B. ed. *Nag Hammadi Codex II, 2–7 Together with XIII, 2*, Brit. Lib. Or. 4926(1), and P. Oxy. 1, 654, 655 With Contributions by Many Scholars*. Vol. 1 (NHS 20): *Gospel According to Thomas, Gospel According to Philip, Hypostasis of the Archons, and Indexes*. Vol. 2 (NHS 21): *On the Origin of the World, Expository Treatise On the Soul, Book of Thomas the Contender*. Leiden/New York/Copenhagen/Cologne: Brill, 1989.
LCL	Loeb Classical Library.
Lightfoot, *Notes on the Epistles*	Lightfoot, J. B. *Notes on the Epistles of St. Paul (I and II Thessalonians, I Corinthians 1–7, Romans 1–7, Ephesians 1:1–14)*. Grand Rapids: Zondervan, 1957.
Linnemann, *Parables*	Linnemann, E. *Jesus of the Parables. Introduction and Exposition*. New York/Evanston: Harper, 1966 [German 1962].

Lord, *Singer of Tales*   Lord, A. B. *The Singer of Tales*. Harvard Studies in
                                   Comparative Literature 24. Cambridge, Mass.:
                                   Harvard University Press, 1960.

Lucas, *Aristotle: Poetics*   Lucas, D. W. *Aristotle: Poetics*. Oxford: University
                                   Press, 1968.

Mack, "Kingdom Sayings"   Mack, B. L. "The Kingdom Sayings in Mark."
                                   Forum 3.1 (1987) 3–47.

MacQueen, *Allegory*   MacQueen, J. *Allegory*. London: Methuen, 1970.

Mann, *Mark*   Mann, C. S. *Mark. A New Translation with
                                   Introduction and Commentary*. AB 27. Garden City,
                                   N.Y.: Doubleday, 1986.

Manson, *Sayings*   Manson, T. W. *The Sayings of Jesus*. London: SCM,
                                   1937. Reprint 1964.

Marchant, *Xenophon*   Marchant, E. C. *Xenophon Memorabilia and
                                   Oeconomicus*. LCL. Cambridge, Mass.: Harvard
                                   University Press; London: Heinemann, 1938.

Marshall, *Luke*   Marshall, I. H. *Commentary on Luke*. New
                                   International Greek Commentary on the New
                                   Testament. Grand Rapids: Eerdmans, 1978.

McFague, *Speaking in*   McFague, S. *Speaking in Parables*. Philadelphia:
   Parables   Fortress, 1975.

Ménard, *Thomas*   Ménard, J. -E. *L'Evangile selon Thomas*. NHS 5.
                                   Leiden: Brill, 1975.

Metzger, *Textual*   Metzger, B. *A Textual Commentary on the Greek
   Commentary*   New Testament*. London/New York: United Bible
                                   Societies, 1971.

Meyers-Strange,   Meyers, E. M. and J. F. Strange. *Archaeology, the
   Archaeology   Rabbis, and Early Christianity*. Nashville:
                                   Abingdon, 1981.

Michaels, *Servant and Son*   Michaels, J. R. *Servant and Son: Jesus in Parable
                                   and Gospel*. Atlanta: John Knox, 1981.

Miller, *Complete Gospels*   Miller, R. J. ed. *The Complete Gospels. Annotated
                                   Scholars Version*. Sonoma, Calif.: Polebridge, 1992.

Minot, *Three Genres*   Minot, S. *Three Genres. The Writings of Fiction,
                                   Poetry, and Drama*. Englewood Cliffs, N.J.:
                                   Prentice-Hall, 1965.

Montefiore, *Synoptic Gospels*   Montefiore, C. *The Synoptic Gospels*. 3 vols.
                                   London: Macmillan, 1909.

Montefiore and Turner, *Thomas and the Evangelists*   Montefiore, H. and H. Turner. *Thomas and the Evangelists*. SBT 35. London: SCM, 1962.

Moulton and Milligan, *Vocabulary of the Greek Testament*   Moulton, J. H. and G. Milligan. *The Vocabulary of the Greek Testament Illustrated from the Papyri and other Non-Literary Sources*. London: Hodder & Stoughton, 1930. Reprint 1972.

Muscatine, "Review of Auerbach"   Muscatine, C. "Review of Auerbach, *Mimesis.*" *Romance Philology* 9.4 (1956) 448–57.

Myers, *1 Chronicles*   Myers, J. M. *1 Chronicles. Introduction, Translation, and Notes*. AB 12–13. 2 vols. Garden City, N.Y.: Doubleday, 1965.

Naumann, "Review of Auerbach"   Naumann, W. "Review of Auerbach, *Mimesis.*" *Modern Philology* 45 (1947/48) 211–12.

Neusner, *Philosophical Mishnah*   Neusner, J. *The Philosophical Mishnah. Volume Two. The Tractates' Agenda. From Abodah Zarah Through Moed Qatan*. Atlanta: Scholars, 1989.

Neusner, *Talmud of Babylonia*   Neusner, J. *The Talmud of Babylonia. An American Translation. XXIII A: Tractate Sanhedrin Chapters 1–13*. Brown Judaic Studies 81. Chico, Calif.: Scholars, 1984.

NHLE   Robinson, J. M. gen. ed. *The Nag Hammadi Library in English*. 3d rev. ed. New York: Harper & Row, 1988.

NHS   Nag Hammadi Studies.

von Nordheim, "Zitat des Paulus in 1 Kor 2,9"   von Nordheim, E. "Das Zitat des Paulus in 1 Kor 2,9 und seine Beziehung zum koptischen Testament Jakobs." *ZNW* 65 (1974) 118–20.

Noth, *Leviticus*   Noth, M. *Leviticus. A Commentary*. The Old Testament Library. Trans. J. E. Anderson. Philadelphia: Westminster, 1965 [German 1962].

Noth, *Pentateuch*   Noth, M. *The Laws in the Pentateuch and Other Studies*. Trans. D. R. Ap-Thomas. London: SCM, 1967 [German rev. ed. 1960].

NTS   *New Testament Studies.*

Oesterley, *Gospel Parables*   Oesterley, W. O. E. *The Gospel Parables in the Light of their Jewish Background*. London: SPCK; New York: Macmillan, 1936.

Oppenheimer, *'Am Ha-aretz*   Oppenheimer, A. *The 'Am Ha-aretz. A Study in the Social History of the Jewish People in the Hellenistic-Roman Period*. Arbeiten zur Literatur und Geschichte des hellenistichen Judentum 8. Leiden: Brill, 1977.

Origen,
    hom. in Jer.
    hom. in Luc.
    comm. in Matt.

Origen
    homiliae in Jeremiam.
    homiliae in Lucam.
    commentarii in Mattheum.

P. Oxy.

Oxyrhynchus Papyrus.

Parry, *Homeric Verse*

Parry, M. *The Making of Homeric Verse. The Collected Papers of Milmann Parry.* Ed. A. Parry. Oxford: Clarendon, 1971.

Patte, *Semiology*

Patte, D. *Semiology and Parable. An Exploration of the Possibilities Offered by Structuralism for Exegesis.* Pittsburgh: Pickwick, 1976.

Patterson, *Gospel of Thomas*

Patterson, S. J. *The Gospel of Thomas and Jesus.* Sonoma, Calif.: Polebridge, 1993.

Payne, "Order"

Payne, P. B. "The Order of Sowing and Ploughing in the Parable of the Sower." *NTS* 25 (1979) 123–29.

Peabody, *Winged Word*

Peabody, B. *The Winged Word. A Study in the Technique of Ancient Greek Oral Composition as Seen Principally Through Hesiod's Works and Days.* Albany, N.Y.: SUNY Press, 1975.

Perkins, *Gnosticism and the New Testament*

Perkins, P. *Gnosticism and the New Testament.* Minneapolis: Fortress, 1993.

Perkins, "Kingdom Sayings"

Perkins, P. "The Rejected Jesus and the Kingdom Sayings." Pp. 79–94 in Hedrick, *Historical Jesus and Rejected Gospels.*

Perkins, "Pronouncement Stories"

Perkins, P. "Pronouncement Stories in the Gospel of Thomas." Pp. 121–32 in *Pronouncement Stories.* Ed. R. C. Tannehill. *Semeia* 20. Chico, Calif.: Scholars, 1981.

Perkins, *Parables*

Perkins, P. *Hearing the Parables of Jesus.* New York/Ramsey, N.J.: Paulist, 1981.

Perrin, *Kingdom of God*

Perrin, N. *The Kingdom of God in the Teaching of Jesus.* Philadelphia: Westminster, 1963.

Perrin, *Language of the Kingdom*

Perrin, N. *Jesus and the Language of the Kingdom: Symbol and Metaphor in New Testament Interpretation.* Philadelphia: Fortress, 1976.

Perrin, *Rediscovering*

Perrin, N. *Rediscovering the Teaching of Jesus.* New York/Evanston: Harper & Row, 1967.

Perrin, "Secret" Perrin, N. "Secret, Messianic." Pp. 798–99 in *IDBS*.

Perrin-Duling, *New Testament Introduction* Perrin, N. and D. Duling. *The New Testament. An Introduction*. 2d ed. New York: Harcourt/Brace/ Jovanovich, 1982.

Perrine, *Sound and Sense* Perrine, L. *Sound and Sense. An Introduction to Poetry*. 3d ed. New York: Harcourt/Brace/World: 1969.

Perry, *Babrius and Phaedrus* Perry, B. E. *Babrius and Phaedrus. Newly Edited and Translated into English, Together with An Historical Introduction and a Comprehensive Survey of Greek and Latin Fables in the Aesopic Tradition*. Cambridge, Mass.: Harvard University Press; London: Heinemann, 1965. Reprint 1984.

PG Migne, J. *Patrologia Graeca*.

Plin. *Hist. Nat.* C. Plinius Secundus. *Naturalis Historia*.

Plummer, *Luke* Plummer, A. *A Critical and Exegetical Commentary on the Gospel According to St. Luke*. ICC. New York: Scribner's, 1920.

Pol. *Phil.* Polycarp to the Philippians.

Q-Thomas Reader Kloppenborg, J. S., M. W. Meyer, S. J. Patterson, M. G. Steinhauser. *Q-Thomas Reader*. Sonoma, Calif.: Polebridge, 1990.

Quint. *Inst. Orat.* M. Fabius Quintilianus. *Institutio Oratoria*.

Rackham, *Pliny* Rackham, H. *Pliny Natural History with an English Translation in Ten Volumes*. LCL. 10 vols. Cambridge, Mass.: Harvard University Press; London: Heinemann, 1950.

Rauer, *Origenes Werke* Rauer, M. *Origenes Werke. Neunter Band. Die Homilien zu Lukas in der Übersetzung des Hieronymus und die Griechischen Reste der Homilien und des Lukas-Kommentars*. GCS 35. Leipzig: J. C. Hinrichs, 1930.

Rauschenbusch, *Social Gospel* Rauschenbusch, W. *A Theology for the Social Gospel*. New York/Nashville: Abingdon, 1945.

Resch, *Agrapha* Resch, A. *Agrapha: Aussercanonische Schriftfragmente*. TU n. f. 15.3–4. 2d ed. Leipzig: Hinrichs, 1906.

Rhodes, "Narrative Criticism" Rhodes, D. "Narrative Criticism and the Gospel of Mark." *JAAR* 50 (1982) 411–34.

| Roberts, "Bringing Pathos into Focus" | Roberts, P. "Bringing Pathos into Focus." *Motive* 14 (1953) 7–10, 15. |

Roberts, "Theory of Dramatic Tragedy" — Roberts, P. "A Christian Theory of Dramatic Tragedy." *JR* 31 (1951) 1–20.

Roberts, *Greek Rhetoric* — Roberts, W. R. *Greek Rhetoric and Literary Criticism.* New York: Cooper Square, 1963.

Robertson, *Word Pictures* — Robertson, A. T. *Word Pictures in the New Testament.* 6 vols. Nashville: Broadman, 1930.

Robinson, "Bridging the Gulf" — Robinson, J. M. "On Bridging the Gulf from Q to the Gospel of Thomas (or *vice versa*)." Pp. 127–75 in Hedrick-Hodgson, *Nag Hammadi, Gnosticism, Early Christianity.*

Robinson, "LOGOI SOPHON" — Robinson, J. M. "LOGOI SOPHON. On the Gattung of Q." Pp. 71–113 in Robinson-Koester, *Trajectories.*

Robinson, "Study of the Historical Jesus" — Robinson, J. M. "The Study of the Historical Jesus after Nag Hammadi." Pp. 45–55 in Hedrick, *Historical Jesus and Rejected Gospels.*

Robinson-Koester, *Trajectories* — Robinson, J. M. and H. Koester. *Trajectories Through Early Christianity.* Philadelphia: Fortress, 1971.

Sabourin, "Parables" — Sabourin, L. "Parables of the Kingdom." *BTB* 6 (1976) 115–60.

Safrai and Stern, *Jewish People in the First Century* — Safrai, S. and M. Stern, eds. *The Jewish People in the First Century. Historical Geography, Political History, Social, Cultural and Religious Life and Institutions.* Compendia rerum Iudaicarum ad Novum Testamentum. 2 vols. Philadelphia: Fortress, 1974 and 1976.

Sanders, *Paul and Palestinian Judaism* — Sanders, E. P. *Paul and Palestinian Judaism. A Comparison of Patterns of Religion.* Philadelphia: Fortress, 1977.

Sandmel, *First Christian Century* — Sandmel, S. *The First Christian Century in Judaism and Christianity.* New York: Oxford, 1969.

Sandmel, *Judaism* — Sandmel, S. *Judaism and Christian Beginnings.* New York: Oxford, 1978.

Sarason, *Law of Agriculture* — Sarason, R. S. *A History of the Mishnaic Law of Agriculture. Section Three: A Study of Tractate Demai.* Leiden: Brill, 1979.

Sauerberg, *Fact into Fiction* — Sauerberg, L. O. *Fact into Fiction. Documentary Realism in the Contemporary Novel.* New York: St. Martins, 1991.

SBLDS	Society of Biblical Literature Dissertation Series.
SBLSP	Society of Biblical Literature Seminar Papers.
SBT	Studies in Biblical Theology.
Schoedel, "Parables"	Schoedel, W. R. "Parables in the Gospel of Thomas: Oral Tradition or Gnostic Exegesis." *CTM* 43 (1972) 548–60.
Schrage, *Verhältnis*	Schrage, W. *Das Verhältnis des Thomas-Evangeliums zur synoptischen Tradition und zu den koptischen Evangelien-übersetzungen: Zugleich ein Beitrag zur gnostischen Synoptikerdeutung.* BZNW 29. Berlin: Töpelmann, 1964.
Schweitzer, *Quest*	Schweitzer, A. *The Quest of the Historical Jesus. A Critical Study of its Progress from Reimarus to Wrede.* Trans. W. Montgomery. New York: Macmillan, 1968.
Scott, "Essaying the Rock"	Scott, B. B. "Essaying the Rock: The Authenticity of the Jesus Parable Tradition." *Forum* 2.1 (1986) 4.
Scott, *Hear Then the Parable*	Scott, B. B. *Hear Then the Parable. A Commentary on the Parables of Jesus.* Minneapolis: Fortress, 1989.
Scott, *Symbol-Maker*	Scott, B. B. *Jesus, Symbol-Maker for the Kingdom.* Philadelphia: Fortress, 1981.
Scott and Dean, "Sound Map"	Scott, B. B. and M. E. Dean. "A Sound Map of the Sermon on the Mount." Pp. 672–725 in *Society of Biblical Literature 1993 Seminar Papers.* Ed. E. H. Lovering, Jr. SBLSP 32. Atlanta: Scholars, 1993.
Scruton, "Apocalypse and Fiction"	Scruton, J. "Apocalypse and Fiction." *The Christian Century* 84 (21 June 1967) 814–15.
Scullard, *Roman Britain*	Scullard, H. H. *Roman Britain. Outpost of the Empire.* London: Thames & Hudson, 1979.
Sharrock, "Review of Auerbach"	Sharrock, R. "Review of Auerbach, *Mimesis.*" *The Kenyon Review* 50 (1955) 61–62.
Smallwood, *Jews Under Roman Rule*	Smallwood, M. E. *The Jews Under Roman Rule from Pompey to Diocletian.* Leiden: Brill, 1976.
Smith, *Parables*	Smith, B. T. D. *The Parables of the Synoptic Gospels. A Critical Study.* Cambridge: University Press, 1937.
SNTSMS	Society for New Testament Studies Monograph Series

Sparks, "1 Kor 2⁹"

Sparks, H. F. D. "1 Kor 2^9 a quotation from the Coptic Testament of Jacob?" *ZNW* 67 (1976) 269–76.

Speiser, *Genesis*

Speiser, E. A. *Genesis. Introduction, Translation, and Notes.* AB 1. Garden City, N.Y.: Doubleday, 1964.

Stanford, *Sound of Greek*

Stanford, W. B. *The Sound of Greek. Studies in Greek Theory and Practice of Euphony.* Berkeley/Los Angeles: University of California Press, 1967.

Stein, "Criteria for Authenticity"

Stein, R. "The Criteria for Authenticity." Pp. 225–63 in *Gospel Perspectives: Studies of History and Tradition in the Four Gospels.* Eds. R. T. France and D. Wenhem. Sheffield: *JSOT*, 1980.

Stein, *Introduction*

Stein, R. H. *An Introduction to the Parables of Jesus.* Philadelphia: Westminster, 1981.

Stevens, "Noble Rider"

Stevens, W. " The Noble Rider and the Sound of Words." Pp. 968–79 in *Critical Theory Since Plato.* Ed. H. Adams. New York/Chicago/San Francisco/Atlanta: Harcourt/Brace/Jovanovich: 1971.

Stevenson, "Imperial Administration"

Stevenson, G. H. "The Imperial Administration." Pp. 182–217 in Cook, Adcock, and Charlesworth, *Cambridge Ancient History.*

Stevenson, "Provinces and their Government"

Stevenson, G. H. "The Provinces and their Government." Pp. 461–68 in *The Cambridge Ancient History.* Vol. 9: *The Roman Republic 133–44 B. C.* Ed. S. A. Cook, F. E. Adcock, and M. P. Charlesworth. Cambridge: University Press, 1971.

Stevenson, *Roman Provincial Administration*

Stevenson, G. H. *Roman Provincial Administration till the Age of the Antonines.* London: Blackwells, 1949.

Stevenson and Momigliano, "Rebellion within the Empire"

Stevenson, G. H. and A. Momigliano. "Rebellion within the Empire." Pp. 840–65 in Cook, Adcock, and Charlesworth, *Cambridge Ancient History.*

Stone and Strugnell, *Books of Elijah*

Stone, M. E. and J. Strugnell. *The Books of Elijah Parts 1 & 2.* SBL Texts and Translations Series 18; Pseudepigrapha Series 8. Missoula, Mont.: Scholars, 1979.

Stoskopf, *Cereal Grain Crops*

Stoskopf, N. C. *Cereal Grain Crops.* Reston, Va.: Reston, 1985.

Strack-Billerbeck

Strack, H. and P. Billerbeck. *Kommentar zum Neuen Testament aus Talmud und Midrasch.* 4 vols. in 5. 5th ed. Munich: C. H. Beck, 1924 and 1926.

Stroker, "Extracanonical Parables"	Stroker, W. D. "Extracanonical Parables and the Historical Jesus." Pp. 95–120 in Hedrick, *Historical Jesus and Rejected Gospels.*
SUNY	State University of New York.
Talbert, *Reading Luke*	Talbert, C. H. *Reading Luke. A Literary and Theological Commentary on the Third Gospel.* New York: Crossroads, 1982.
Taylor, *Mark*	Taylor, V. *The Gospel According to St. Mark. The Greek Text with Introduction, Notes, and Indexes.* London: Macmillan; New York: St. Martins, 1959.
TDNT	*Theological Dictionary of the New Testament.* 10 vols. Ed. G. Kittel and G. Friedrich. Trans. G. W. Bromiley. Grand Rapids: Eerdmans, 1964–1976.
Tenney, *Economic Survey*	Tenney, F. gen. ed. *An Economic Survey of Ancient Rome.* 6 vols. Baltimore: Johns Hopkins, 1933–1940. Reprint. New York: Octagon Books, 1975. Vol. 1: F. Tenney, *Rome and Italy of the Republic.* Vol. 2: A. C. Johnson, *Roman Egypt to the Reign of Diocletian.* Vol. 3: R. G. Collingwood, J. J. Van Nostrand, V. M. Scramuzza, A. Grenier, *Roman Britain, Roman Spain, Roman Sicily, La Gaule romaine.* Vol. 4: R. M. Haywood, F. M. Heichelheim, J. A. O. Larsen, T. R. S. Broughton, *Roman Africa, Roman Syria, Roman Greece, Roman Asia.* Vol. 5: F. Tenney, *Rome and Italy of the Empire.* Vol. 6: T. R. S. Broughton, L. R. Taylor, *General Index to Volumes I–V.*
ThSt	*Theological Studies.*
Thuc. *Hist.*	Thucydides. *History of the Peloponnesian War.*
Till, *Dialektgrammatik*	Till, W. C. *Koptische Dialektgrammatik mit Lesestücken und Wörterbuch.* 2d ed. rev. Munich: C. H. Beck, 1961.
Till, *Koptische Grammatik*	Till, W. C. *Koptische Grammatik (Saïdischer Dialekt) mit Bibliographie, Lesestücken und Wörterverzeichnissen.* Lehrbücher für das Studium der orientalischen und afrikanischen Sprachen 1. Leipzig: VEB Verlag Enzyklopädie, 1966.
Tolbert, *Perspectives*	Tolbert, M. A. *Perspectives on the Parables: An Approach to Multiple Interpretations.* Philadelphia: Fortress, 1979.
Tristam, *Eastern Customs*	Tristam, H. B. *Eastern Customs in Bible Lands.* 2d ed. London: Hodder & Stoughton, 1894.

TU   Texte und Untersuchungen.

Vaihinger, *As if*   Vaihinger, H. *The Philosophy of 'As if.' A System of the Theoretical, Practical and Religious Fictions of Mankind.* New York: Harcourt, Brace & Company; London: Kegan Paul, Trench, Trubner & Co., 1925 [German 6th ed. 1920].

VC   *Vigiliae christianae.*

Vermes, *Scrolls*   Vermes, G. *The Dead Sea Scrolls in English.* 2d ed. Middlesex: Penguin, 1975.

Via, *Parables*   Via, D. O. *The Parables. Their Literary and Existential Dimension.* Philadelphia: Fortress, 1967.

Weiss, *Kingdom of God*   Weiss, J. *Jesus' Proclamation of the Kingdom of God.* Trans. and ed. R. H. Hiers and D. L. Holland. Philadelphia: Fortress, 1971.

Weiss, *Schriften*   Weiss, J. ed. *Die Schriften des Neuen Testaments.* 2 vols. Göttingen: Vandenhoeck & Ruprecht, 1907 and 1908.

Wellek, "Auerbach's   Wellek, R. "Auerbach's Special Realism." *Kenyon*
Special Realism"   *Review* 16 (1954) 299–307.

Wettstein, *Novum*   Wettstein, J. J. *Novum Testamentum Graecum.* 2
Testamentum Graecum   vols. Amsterdam: ex officina Dommeriana, 1751. Reprint. Granz, Austria: Akademische Druck, 1962.

Wharton, "Shema"   Wharton, J. M. "The Shema." Vol. 4.321–22 in *IDB.*

White, *Content of the Form*   White, H. *The Content of the Form. Narrative Discourse and Historical Representation.* Baltimore and London: Johns Hopkins, 1987.

White, *Metahistory*   White, H. *Metahistory. The Historical Imagination in Nineteenth-Century Europe.* Baltimore and London: Johns Hopkins, 1973.

White, *Tropics of Discourse*   White, H. *Tropics of Discourse. Essays in Cultural Criticism.* Baltimore and London: Johns Hopkins, 1978.

White, "Parable of the   White, K. D. "The Parable of the Sower." *JTS* 15
Sower"   (1964) 300–307.

White, *Roman Farming*   White, K. D. *Roman Farming.* Ithaca, N.Y.: Cornell University Press, 1970.

Wilder, *Bible and Literary*   Wilder, A. N. *The Bible and the Literary Critic.*
Critic   Minneapolis: Fortress, 1991.

Wilder, *Rhetoric*

Wilder, A. N. *Early Christian Rhetoric. The Language of the Gospel.* Rev. ed. Cambridge, Mass.: Harvard University Press, 1971 [1st edition 1964].

Wilder, *War of Myths*

Wilder, A. N. *Jesus' Parables and the War of Myths. Essays on Imagination in the Scripture.* Philadelphia: Fortress, 1982.

Williams, "The Apocryphon of James"

Williams, F. E. "The Apocryphon of James." Vol. 1.13–53 in Attridge, *NHC I.*

Wilson, "Review of Schrage"

Wilson, R. McL. "Review of Schrage, *Das Verhältnis des Thomas-Evangeliums zur Synoptischen Tradition.*" *VC* 20 (1966) 118–23.

Wimsatt-Beardsley, "Intentional Fallacy"

Wimsatt, W. K. Jr. and M. C. Beardsley. "The Intentional Fallacy." *Sewanee Review* 54 (1946) 468–88.

Wimsatt-Beardsley, *Verbal Icon*

Wimsatt, W. K. Jr. and M. C. Beardsley. *The Verbal Icon. Studies in the Meaning of Poetry.* Lexington: University of Kentucky Press, 1954.

Winer-Lünemann, *Grammar*

Winer, G. B. and L. Lünemann. *A Grammar of the Idiom of the New Testament. Prepared as a Solid Basis for the Interpretation of the New Testament.* Ed. J. H. Thayer. 7th ed. enlarged and improved. Andover: Draper, 1892.

Wrede, *Messianic Secret*

Wrede, W. *The Messianic Secret.* Trans. J. C. G. Greig. Cambridge/London: James Clarke, 1971 [German 1901].

Wright-Filson-Albright, *Historical Atlas*

Wright, G. E., F. V. Filson, and W. F. Albright. *The Westminster Historical Atlas to the Bible.* Philadelphia: Westminster, 1956.

Xenoph. *Oec.*

Xenophon. *Oeconomicus.*

Yadin, *Masada*

Yadin, Y. *Masada: Herod's Fortress and the Zealots' Last Stand.* London: Sphere, 1973.

Young, *Jewish Parables*

Young, B. H. *Jesus and His Jewish Parables. Rediscovering the Roots of Jesus' Teaching.* New York/Mahwah: Paulist, 1989.

ZNW

Zeitschrift für die neutestamentliche Wissenschaft.

PART I
PROLEGOMENON

1

Introduction: Assumptions and Methods

THE APPROACH TAKEN IN THIS BOOK IS SUFFICIENTLY DIFFERENT TO WAR-rant a brief summary of the principal assumptions and a succinct statement of methodology. The subjects of the study are the stories of Jesus—commonly described as "parables." Currently there is no consensus as to how Jesus used his brief stories. Hence they are variously interpreted in contemporary study as metaphors/symbols for the kingdom of God, example stories, stories teaching a brief moral, stories transmitting a particular view of human existence, and even as allegories. The assumption of this study, however, is that they are ordinary stories, brief fictions realistically portraying aspects of first-century Palestinian life. A reader is not authorized to go outside the world of the story or to use non-story "referential" language in "interpreting" the story, unless it is mandated by particular semantic markers in the story itself.

Only the stories originate with Jesus of Nazareth. The literary settings in early Christian gospel literature constitute their earliest extant interpretations. Frequently the evangelists' literary settings lead readers astray and hamper their engagement of the story as a pre-ecclesiastical first-century fiction.

Early Christian gospel literature provides the modern reader with data that open access to the historical man, Jesus of Nazareth. But the gospels are themselves also part of the problem and hinder recovery of the historical figure in that they push on the reader particular ecclesiastical interpretations. This is clear from the different literary settings in which they have embedded the traditional sayings and the frequent summary meanings they derive from them.

THE GOSPEL OF THOMAS

Thomas represents an early Christian tradition that is independent of the canonical gospels. It is ultimately derived from the same oral sources available to John and the Synoptic Gospels. Thomas gives the modern reader access to the Jesus tradition in a pre-synoptic form, i.e., before its shaping by the synoptic kerygma. Hence where they appear in Thomas, the parables provide modern scholarship with the means to critique the synoptic versions of the same parable. Parables preserved in the *Gospel of Thomas* (and the *Apocryphon of James*) but not in the Synoptic Gospels may well be stories that originated with the historical Jesus. As with all Jesus material, the origin of a parable in the life of the historical man Jesus must be demonstrated and not assumed.

PARABLES AND THE KINGDOM OF GOD

Early Christians first associated Jesus' parables with the kingdom of God in an attempt to make sense of stories that they found to be no longer relevant as ordinary stories. Their strangeness is due to the church's rapidly changing cultural situations. What may have been understandable as a story by Jesus to Palestinian peasants in pre-church rural Galilee would have seemed obscure in the post-resurrection Hellenistic church that expected spiritual enlightenment from the words of the Lord. Hence we should begin reading the parables on their own terms, as ordinary stories, rather than for what we imagine they might "reveal" about the kingdom of God, morality, human existence, or some other value.

REALISM AND POETICS

If the parables realistically portray life in first-century Palestinian antiquity, then where they deviate from our understanding of Palestinian antiquity becomes significant for how they are read. Their realism, character as deliberately created fictions, and their appeal to ordinary human experience leads one to Aristotle's *Poetica*. It provides a cogent method for analyzing the poetics of a brief narrative that is a deliberate artistic invention. A poetic analysis focuses on the narrative and examines its construction, provides an analysis of its plot, examines the development of characters and the way language is used in the narrative. Read as poetic fictions the stories of Jesus do not inevitably produce a single specific summary "meaning," but rather legitimize a limited range of plausible readings. Summary meanings tend to dispense with the polyvalence of the story. Read thus the stories have the potential to affirm or subvert a reader's views, but they offer few obvious clues that would lead a reader to a specific summary meaning that supposedly captures the intention of Jesus in creating and telling them.

PARABLES AS FREELY INVENTED FICTIONS

These stories as brief fictions have an integrity that, for the most part, has protected them from the vagaries of the church's changing historical circumstances, and hence they can, and should, be analyzed apart from their literary context. In this volume I will analyze parables as freely invented fiction narratives in the historical context of first-century Palestinian Judaism. They would initially have been heard in the context of the fictional narrative constructs that Palestinian Judaism developed for making sense of its own existence. Jesus' stories would have competed with, subverted, or affirmed those constructs, and offered to auditors/readers new ways of viewing reality, and new ways for them to make discoveries about themselves.

OLD STORIES AND NEW READINGS

In part two I work toward providing new "readings" of certain parables, beginning with their earliest interpretations in early Christian literature. These literary settings show how the stories were read and understood in the first-century church. The next step is to show how the stories are currently being interpreted in modern scholarship. The diversity of interpretations by modern scholars is sometimes surprising and verifies the judgment that the polyvalence of the stories encourages a range of readings. Modern interpretations range from simplistic ecclesiastical propositions that do not do justice to the polyvalence of the stories to jargon-laden explanations that in their complexity would scarcely have been comprehended in that way by an average Palestinian peasant.

The next step is to analyze the poetics of the narrative (i.e., its structural design and prosodic values) in terms of Aristotle's *Poetica*. The analysis will show what the innate construction of the narrative implies for its reading. A fourth step is a historical analysis of the story as a first-century fiction phrase by phrase, i.e., in its smallest narrative units. Then in some cases will follow a discussion of how the story worked as first-century fiction, i.e., to describe the action, to clarify events in terms of the first-century world, and to show how the parts fit together to make a comprehensible and engaging first-century story.

Only then do I provide my own "reading" of the story. A "reading" is different from an "interpretation" in that, on the one hand, an "interpretation" collapses the polyvalence of the story into a "meaning," i.e., a propositional summary generally described in other than story language. A "reading," on the other hand, describes a reader's engagement of and interaction with the story. In one sense it is putting the reader inside the story. Hence a "reading" is a reader's response to the story.

Finally, I consider how the story *might* have been heard against the background of the narrative constructs in terms of which first-century Jews understood themselves. This must always be tentative since it will never be possible to recapture first-century reader's responses with absolute certainty. There are potentially as many responses as readers. But one can, with some degree of confidence, describe how one fictional construct (the parables) "resonates" in the context of other fictional constructs, in this case Hebrew religious literature.

2 🌿

The Parables of Jesus and the Kingdom of God[1]

INTRODUCTION

NEW TESTAMENT SCHOLARSHIP HAS, IN THE MAIN, BEEN QUITE POSITIVE about two aspects of the Jesus tradition: it affirms that the proclamation of the kingdom of God is an essential feature of the message of Jesus and that Jesus announced his message in "parabolic" stories.[2] Any discussion of the "historical Jesus"[3] will include, therefore, a consideration of sayings about the kingdom of God and the parables of Jesus.[4]

Because a number of the parables are formally associated by the synoptic evangelists with the kingdom,[5] it has usually been assumed that all of the parables are "full of the secret of the Kingdom of God."[6] Of

---

[1] An earlier version of this chapter appeared in the SBL 1987 Seminar Papers: "Parables and the Kingdom." It was subsequently in that earlier form critiqued by Wilder, *Bible and Literary Critic*, 126–31.

[2] Recently the attitude toward Jesus' use of the term "kingdom," particularly in an apocalyptic sense, has been challenged; see Borg, "Temperate Case"; Mack, "Kingdom Sayings"; and Butts, "Probing the Polling." The parables, however, have fared much better as original sayings of Jesus; see Funk, "Poll on the Parables."

[3] The term "historical Jesus" is actually a misnomer, if one assumes that the figure that is reconstructed from sayings validated by current "criteria for originality" is Jesus as he "actually was." What is accomplished in applying these criteria rigorously is a reconstruction of a rather radical figure who has little in common with early Christianity or first-century Judaism. Norman Perrin, who was first to set out these criteria as such (though he was certainly not the first to use them for judging the originality of the tradition), clearly recognized this (Perrin and Duling, *New Testament Introduction*, 405). Perhaps the better term is "scholars' Jesus." For the most thorough survey of the criteria for originality see Boring, "Criteria of Authenticity."

[4] See Perrin, *Rediscovering*, 47.

[5] See Dodd, *Parables*, 27–28.

[6] The statement is quoted with approval by Jeremias, *Parables*, 230. The association of the parables with Jesus' proclamation of the kingdom of God has

course how the parables and the kingdom are related is far from clear even in early Christian literature, and that lack of clarity is responsible for the lengthy history of diverse interpretations of the parables that commences with the earliest level of the Jesus tradition. Not even the gospels themselves uniformly agree on how they read the parables they have in common.

It is somewhat surprising to realize that critical study of the parables is only one hundred years old,[7] and that since Jesus first teased a group with one of his stories (going on 2000 years now) parables interpretation has experienced essentially five (overlapping) phases. The earliest interpretive phase of parables originally spoken by Jesus was the context of his public ministry in Palestine a little past the first quarter of the first century CE. Individual auditors made sense of them (or did not!) in the social context of their lives as Palestinian Jews. (The church as a social institution lay before them in the not too distant future.) The specific circumstances of their narration in the life of Jesus is irretrievably lost to modern scholarship.

The second phase, documented as early as 70 CE in Mark's theory of parables (Mark 4:3–20), began earlier than Mark with the emergence of the church as a social organism. Parables were read in this context as allegories for the church. This essentially anti-historical way of reading the parables was the only way parables were read until the end of the nineteenth century. It still survives today, however, as the most popular way of reading the parables in the church, because of the high regard in which the canonical gospels are held as oracular literature (i.e., they are regarded as divine "oracles").

The third phase, the modern critical study of parables, began at the end of the nineteenth century (1886) with the publication of Adolf Jülicher's *Die Gleichnisreden Jesu*. Jülicher's pivotal study liberated the parables from the tyranny of the allegorical method, at least for critical New Testament scholarship. Jülicher's study reduced the stories to a single point of meaning that derived from reading them against a hypothetical "historical" background in the life of Jesus. For Jülicher the one point scored by the parable was a general moral principle in line with

---

routinely been made by modern scholars. Indeed such an association may be said to be one of the primary assumptions of the modern study of the parables of Jesus. Compare for example: Boucher, *Parables*, 59; Breech, *Silence of Jesus*, 66–74; Crossan, *In Parables*, 23–36; Funk, *Parables and Presence*, 3; McFague, *Speaking in Parables*, 78–79; Michaels, *Servant and Son*, 89–91; Scott, *Hear Then the Parable*, 56–62; id., *Symbol-Maker*, 5–22; Stein, *Introduction*, 82–147; Tolbert, *Perspectives*, 116; Via, *Parables*, 95, 104–105.

[7] See the excellent brief review of the history of parables interpretation by Perrin, *Language of the Kingdom*, 89–181 and also the study by Jones, *Art and Truth*, 3–54.

nineteenth century German idealism.[8] Even today the parables are still read as stories that teach a specific, if frequently different, moral.

A fourth phase of study began with the insights of C. H. Dodd (*The Parables of the Kingdom*, 1935). Drawing upon the work of Albert Schweitzer (*Quest of the Historical Jesus*, 1906), Dodd argued that the point of a parable (following Jülicher) was to be derived by reading it against a background of Jewish apocalyptic thought: for Dodd the parables were metaphors of the kingdom of God.[9] "At its simplest the parable is a metaphor or simile drawn from nature or common life, arresting the hearer by its vividness or strangeness, and leaving the mind in sufficient doubt about its precise application to tease it into active thought."[10] J. Jeremias (*The Parables of Jesus*, 1947) following Dodd's stress on the parables as teaching about the kingdom of God, wrote the definitive history of the parables tradition and argued their one-point meaning (following Jülicher) against a hypothetical setting in the first-century context of Jesus' preaching to the masses and his debates with the Jewish religious authorities.[11]

Drawing specifically from Dodd, current critical study of the parables proceeds from the assumption that parables are metaphors and symbols.[12] As it is currently employed, however, the metaphor/symbol school differs dramatically from the one-point approach of Dodd and Jeremias, and it also has a strong affinity with the older allegorical approach, although utilizing the insights of modern literary criticism and social theory.

The distinctive literary/existential approach of Dan Via's book, *The Parables: Their Literary and Existential Dimension*, opened a fifth phase of study in 1967. Throughout the second, third, and fourth phases of

---

[8] Perrin, *Language of the Kingdom*, 92–96. Jülicher gets the credit for this innovation, although a similar approach and rejection of allegory had been taken some four years earlier by A. B. Bruce in his book *Parabolic Teaching*. Jülicher said of Bruce (*Gleichnisreden Jesu*, 1.300): "A decided turn for the better was first made by Glasgow professor A. B. Bruce. His knowledge of earlier learned works, German and English as well as Latin and Greek, is even more comprehensive than Trench's. He has broken with bias consistently advancing intrinsic meanings [for the parables] out of the images." Jülicher did not, however, approve of his attempt to construct a three-tiered approach to the parables corpus.

[9] See the preface to Dodd, *Parables*. In particular see page 28: "I shall try to show that not only the parables which explicitly referred to the Kingdom of God, but many others do in fact bear upon this idea, and that a study of them throws important light upon its meaning."

[10] Dodd, *Parables*, 16.

[11] Jeremias, *Parables*, 115–229. The principle of interpreting the parables against their first-century Palestinian background (if known) is correct, if one is interested in Jesus of Nazareth, but we scarcely know the actual historical context of any of the sayings. Compare pp. 128–32, however, where Jeremias accepts Luke's setting for the parable of the Prodigal Son/Elder Brother as the "historical context."

[12] See, for example, Funk, "Parable as Metaphor," 133, and the discussion by Crossan, *In Parables*, 7–36.

parables study it remained a canon of parables research that the parables of Jesus are primarily (though not exclusively) concerned with the kingdom of God. Prior to Jülicher's work parables were thought to contain hidden secrets about the kingdom of God.[13] In the work following Dodd it was assumed that the parables were metaphor/symbol, and that they have the kingdom of God (itself a symbol!) as their referent. Via, in contrast, argued that one can read the parables as "aesthetic art" and that therefore it is possible to analyze the understanding of human existence reflected in the narratives with virtually no reference to their original historical context and without requiring that they be read against the background of an ancient historical context or without going outside the stories to a hypothetical referent.[14] Hence, Via analyzes them as refractions of human existence and not as reflections of the kingdom of God.[15] Via's method is essentially ahistorical. Throughout all these phases of study, parables have been variously regarded, being treated as allegories, metaphors, symbols, stories with a specific moral, or stories reflecting a specific understanding of existence.[16]

What are parables, and how did they function in early Christian literature? These two questions, while different, are nevertheless related. This chapter will survey the evidence from early Christian literature for formulating answers to the questions, and it will consider the significance of the survey for developing a hermeneutic for the parables.

AN INVENTORY OF PARABLES IN EARLY CHRISTIAN LITERATURE

This section will survey early Christian texts whose date of origin may reasonably be assigned to the first century CE. Apart from the Synoptic Gospels, there are actually few sources for sayings of Jesus that may be assigned to the first century. Although the Gospel of John is a

---

[13] See Hedrick "Treasure Parable," 48–49.

[14] See Via, *Parables*, 73–88, and the discussion of this point by Perrin, *Language of the Kingdom*, 146–48. Via stops just short of declaring that the parables are non-referential (esp. pp. 86–88): "In a truly aesthetic piece of narrative fiction the centripetal interlocking of the parts will keep the attention focally on the work itself. But the reader will be subsidiarily aware—aware at lower levels of consciousness—of various kinds of pointing outward to the world outside the narrative" (p. 87). But compare: "The peculiar function of language used aesthetically is that through its centripetal interlocking of content into form it grasps the attention of the beholder as a total psychosomatic unity—including conscious and unconscious aspects—in an intransitive or non-referential way" (p. 79).

[15] But compare *Parables*, 104–5 where Via does associate the stories with the kingdom of God.

[16] See n. 7.

first-century text, it is not a source for the story (plot) parables of Jesus. It does not use the word parable, παραβολή, and it does not report any of the story parables that are found as a hallmark of the teaching of the synoptic Jesus.[17] Even expanding the data base to include the noncanonical texts increases the number of story parables only slightly.

What should one include in a list of parables? There is general agreement on what comprises the corpus of Jesus' "parabolic" discourse. For convenience—and precision—a distinction is usually made between types of sayings in the "parabolic" discourse. For example, modern scholars regularly distinguish on formal grounds between parables, similes, similitudes, metaphors, aphorisms, and example stories. Unfortunately these neat distinctions are not made by the synoptic evangelists; they do not agree that a particular literary type is to be designated as parable. For example, Luke calls the story about the Lost Sheep a parable (15:3), but Matthew (18:10–14) does not. Luke also calls the figures of the "unshrunk cloth" and the "new wine in old wineskins" (5:36–39) *a* (i.e., one) parable but Matthew (9:16–17) and Mark (2:21–22) do not use the term parable to describe these two figures. The *forms* of these two literary units (the story of the Lost Sheep and the figures of the unshrunk cloth/new wine in old wineskins) are quite different. The sheep saying is a "story" with narrative "plot" (i.e., a structural plan having beginning, middle, and end), while the sayings about the unshrunk cloth and new wine in old wineskins are images, which Crossan defines as aphorisms.[18] In any case, while they trade in metaphor, they are not stories having a "plot" (i.e., beginning, middle, and end); they more closely resemble John's figures of the good shepherd and the sheepfold, rather than Luke's story of the Samaritan.

In this chapter, I propose to inventory[19] the "stories" of Jesus. I will include those units that have "plots," which I take to mean a structural plan consisting of beginning, middle, and end.[20] In Appendix B I have

---

[17] See the discussion below, pp. 21–22. For translations of other early Christian texts see Cameron, *Other Gospels*, and Miller, *Complete Gospels*.

[18] Crossan, *In Fragments*, 121–27.

[19] Compare the inventories by Jeremias, *Parables*, 247–48; Crossan, *Sayings Parallels*, 2–20; and Scott, *Hear Then the Parable*, 460 (and his table of contents). My inventory will differ somewhat from these lists. For example, I do not include in my inventory of parables the following listed by Jeremias: the Budding Fig Tree (Mark 13:28–29; Matt 24:32–33; Luke 21:29–31), the Children in the Marketplace (Matt 11:16–19; Luke 7:31–35), the Servant Supervisor (Matt 24:45–51; Luke 12:42–46), the Last Judgment (Matt 25:31–46), the Closed Door (Luke 13:24–30), and the Children in a Field (*Gos. Thom.* log. 21a [36,35–37,6]). Nor do I include another listed by Crossan: the Grain of Wheat (*Ap. Jas.* 8,16–23). Scott does not include the Date Palm Shoot (*Ap. Jas.* 7,24–28) and the Ear of Grain (*Ap. Jas.* 12,22–27), which I do.

[20] The criterion is taken from Aristot. *Poet.* 7.1–7: Fyfe, *Aristotle*, 29–31. See Crossan (*Sayings Parallels*, xi) who uses the same criterion.

set out all versions of the stories attributed to Jesus appearing in (plausibly) first-century Christian texts. Appendix B indicates the various versions of the individual stories by literary source; my citations to the stories consciously exclude what I take to be early Christian interpretation, or "enhancement," appended as a conclusion to each. Hence the appendix identifies only those verses considered a part of the plot of the story. For convenience I have adopted the usual titles for these stories as they appear in the inventories of Jeremias and Crossan, except where I felt it necessary to change.[21]

Although both Crossan and I follow the same criterion for identifying the stories, we have arrived at different results. I have designated as stories six narrative units that Crossan does not include. They are "the Unclean Spirit," "On Settling out of Court," "the Two Houses," "the Two Sons," "the Two Debtors," "the Persistent Friend," and "the Servant."

Of these additional stories the Unclean Spirit (Matt 12:43–45a = Luke 11:24–26a), the Two Houses (Matt 7:24b–27 = Luke 6:47b–49), the Two Sons (Matt 21:28a–30), and the Two Debtors (Luke 7:41–42a) are clearly stories with a beginning, middle, and end and need no further justification for their inclusion in the inventory. The other three (On Settling out of Court, the Persistent Friend, and the Servant), while not cast in story form in their extant versions, nevertheless, give clear evidence of plot, i.e., they are more story than simple figure. These narrative units may be abbreviated versions of stories whose more complete forms no longer exist. Nevertheless, in their present form there exists enough of a plot to qualify them as "story"; hence I include them in my inventory.

On Settling out of Court (Matt 5:25–26 = Luke 12:58–59) concerns an individual ("you") who has been sued by another party (a nameless accuser) over a debt. The reader is not given the beginning of the story where the loan is made, or the circumstances that led to the court action, but readers naturally assume these lacking elements. The story picks up at its middle part, i.e., as the case is being called before the bench. The conclusion is presented proleptically as two possibilities. Either reconciliation is made and the story ends before a trial takes place, or the case goes before the bench and the story ends tragically. But in either case, an anticipated conclusion to the story "exists" proleptically before the reader, who is called on to "finish" the story.

---

[21] The whole issue of titles for the stories should be rethought in the light of an analysis that focuses on the story, rather than on the basis of its perceived "meaning." Scott (*Hear Then the Parable*, 4) has retitled all of them using the first words of each parable as a title. For example he titles "The Good Samaritan" as "From Jerusalem to Jericho." See Appendix E below for my attempt to redirect a reading focus for the stories.

The story of the Persistent Friend (Luke 11:5–8)[22] describes a house-holder who has an unexpected guest who arrives after a journey. The householder discovers that there is no food in the house to serve the unexpected guest. This "beginning" of the story exists only in the extant middle part of the story in the householder's explanation (Luke 11:6) of why he disturbed the neighbor. An auditor/reader will, however, naturally "evoke" that beginning retroactively as the required circumstance from which the middle part of the story necessarily derives. The house-holder, therefore, goes to his friend and requests three loaves for the unexpected guest. It is at this (middle) point that the reader actually enters the story. At such a late hour, the sleeping neighbor refuses the house-holder's request and tells him not to bother him, since he has retired for the night. The story ends with the narrator's promise that the insistent person *will receive* the loaves he requested because of his persistence. Although that concluding event is not actually "shown" as a part of the story, an auditor/reader naturally infers it, and that inference satisfies the reader's sense of closure.

The Servant (Luke 17:7–9) describes a wealthy farmer ("you") who has a servant/slave, δοῦλος, tasked with plowing, tending sheep, and waiting tables. Although this information is not formally stated as the circumstance from which the action in the story proceeds, it will naturally be inferred by a reader who consents to enter the story. I take this natural inference as the beginning of the story. A reader enters the story at its middle part as the servant comes in from the field at meal time. Again the conclusion to the story is presented as two possibilities, and it is left to an auditor/reader to fill in an "actual" conclusion from these two potential endings. Is the servant invited to the table to dine with the master of the house, or is he directed to prepare the master's meal? The narrator implies that it is the latter, and that implication satisfies the reader's sense of closure. In each of these three "narratives" there appears to be sufficient evidence of plot to justify including them in the inventory of story parables.

WHAT ARE PARABLES IN EARLY CHRISTIAN LITERATURE?[23]

The Literary Classification "Parable" παραβολή

The Synoptic Gospels. The Synoptic Gospels are scarcely consistent in what they designate by the term parable. All three designate the following stories as parables: a Sower (Matt 13:3, 10, 18; Mark 4:2, 10, 13,

---

[22] Also described as parable by Scott, *Hear Then the Parable*, 87.

[23] For the following discussion refer to Appendixes C and D.

33–34; Luke 8:4, 9–10), a Vineyard (Matt 21:33, 45; Mark 12:1, 12; Luke 20:9, 19), and the Fig Tree (Matt 24:32; Mark 13:28; Luke 21:29). The Fig Tree parable is not a story (so Scott and Crossan); it is a simple image lacking plot. All three of the evangelists report the Mustard Seed, but only Matthew (13:31) and Mark (4:2, 30, 33–34) describe it as a parable. Luke (13:19) gives it no formal literary designation. The synoptic evangelists are also divided on the Leaven. Matthew (13:33) calls it a parable, but Luke (13:21) does not, and Mark does not report it.

In the Matthean special material only the Good Seed and Weeds (13:24) is designated as a parable in its introductory frame. Matthew's broader literary frame (13:53), however, implies that the following are parables: the Hid Treasure (13:44), a Merchant in Search of Pearls (13:45), and a Net Thrown into the Sea (13:47–48), although they are not each separately given that designation.

In the Lukan special material the following are designated as parables: the Rich Man (12:16), the Barren Fig Tree (13:6), the Unjust Judge (18:1), and the Pharisee and the Toll Collector (18:9). In the Markan special material a Sprouting Seed is not in its own introductory frame designated as a parable, although Mark's broader literary frame (4:2, 33–34) implies that it is a parable.

In the material that Matthew and Luke share (Q), the evangelists are divided on the following stories: Luke calls the Lost Sheep (15:3) and the Entrusted Money (19:11) parables, but Matthew does not. Matthew calls the Leaven (13:33) and the Feast (22:1) parables, but Luke does not. Neither Matthew nor Luke calls the following stories parables: the Unclean Spirit, On Settling out of Court, and the Two Houses.

Finally, all three synoptic evangelists use the term parable to include units of material that are not narratives. The image of the householder, regarded by Crossan as an aphorism,[24] is called a parable by Luke (12:41), but not by Matthew (24:43) or Thomas (log. 21b). Matthew (15:10–20) and Mark (7:15–17) regard the aphorism about "things coming out of a man defiling him" as being a parable. All three gospels (Mark 13:28 = Matt 24:32 = Luke 21:29–30) regard the image of the fig tree as a parable. Luke (6:39) regards the aphorism of the blind man leading a blind man as a parable but Matthew (15:10–20) apparently does not. While Matthew (9:16–17) and Mark (2:21–22) know the twin aphorisms of the new patch on an old garment/new wine in old wineskins, only Luke (5:36–38) describes them as a parable. Mark, on the other hand, apparently regards the aphorisms in 4:21–22 as parables since they are included in the literary frame Mark 4:2, 33–34, and Mark even concludes them with the "floating" saying (4:23) inviting the reader to reflect on their significance as cryptic sayings, just as was done after the

---

[24]Crossan, *In Fragments*, 58–61.

story of the Sower (4:9). Likewise Mark regards the Beelzebul controversy (3:23–26) with its appended aphorisms (3:27–29) as parabolic speech, although Matthew (12:25–32) and Luke (11:17–23) do not share this understanding of the pericope. Luke even regards Jesus' teaching on seating etiquette at a marriage banquet (14:8–10) as parable (14:7), and follows it with a moralistic conclusion (14:11), the same moral that Luke used for the Pharisee and the Toll Collector (18:14b). Luke likewise designates the traditional proverb at 4:23 as parable.

Thus, early Christian canonical literature appears to lack any consensus as to what the term parable should designate. Parables may be stories with plot, aphorisms, proverbs, simple figures or images, or even common discourse that seems to reflect no imagery at all. The synoptic writers do, nonetheless, either agree that parables are difficult to understand or regard them as so banal that they could not have possibly meant what they said. In either case, however, they concluded that they surely must have had some esoteric meaning. In this latter respect they agree with the Gospel of John where the common discourse of Jesus is regarded as cryptic, and hence difficult to understand (16:16–30).

The Gospel of Thomas and the Apocryphon of James. The *Gospel of Thomas* does not use the word παραβολή; hence Thomas does not identify any of its stories, or any other literary form, by the designation parable. The *Apocryphon of James*, however, is aware of the parables as a special literary tradition in the church. Not even the canonical gospels are as self-conscious of parables as a formal tradition. The *Apocryphon of James* lists a collection of seven titles (I,2:8,1–10) but does not describe their contents; apparently the author assumed that readers were completely familiar with the parable designated by the title. Citing the parables by specific title is enough in itself to lead to the conclusion that by the time of the *Apocryphon of James* individual parables were widely recognized as distinctive narrative units in the tradition (e.g., like "the Lord's Prayer"). But it is the apparent assumption of the author of the *Apocryphon of James* that the reader will evoke the contents of the parables from the title alone that confirms the parables collection behind Mark 4 as an identifiable independent tradition, like other sayings collections (Q and *logoi sophon*) and the early Christian *testimonia*.[25]

It is all the more interesting that the *Apocryphon of James* narrates two new stories that are attributed to Jesus, neither of which is designated in an introductory frame as parable. The author of the *Apocryphon of James*, however, clearly regards them as a type of obscure discourse that must be explained; note the contrast between "speaking in parables" and "speaking openly" in *Ap. Jas.* I,2:7,1–10. The fact that Jesus must remain on earth another eighteen days "for the sake of the parables"

---

[25] On the testimony lists see Hodgson, "The Testimony Hypothesis."

(8,1–4) suggests that the titled parables too are a type of obscure discourse (cf. 7:1–10) and had by the time of this text become a problem for the church.

Do Parables (Stories) Call for a Comparison?

Some stories do not call for a comparison. On the surface this may appear to be a question with an obvious answer. After all, the very meaning of the word parable as a "thing cast alongside" something else, suggests comparison. The Greek word can even be translated by various other comparative words, such as figure and symbol. Indeed the whole history of scholarship has treated parables as image language of one sort or another.

Today the stories of Jesus are regarded in North American New Testament scholarship as metaphors, or symbols, that evoke a broader conceptual reality. Again the evidence from early Christian literature is mixed. Surprisingly there are nineteen stories whose introductory frames in all versions do not make a comparison between the story and some other reality outside the story. These are a Sower,[26] a Vineyard, the Unclean Spirit, On Settling Out of Court, the Prodigal Son/Elder Brother, the Two Sons, the Two Debtors, the Samaritan, the Persistent Friend, the Rich Man, the Barren Fig Tree, the Tower Builder, the Warring King, the Lost Coin, the Dishonest Steward, a Rich Man and Lazarus, the Servant, the Unjust Judge, and the Pharisee and the Toll Collector.

Some stories differ as to whether a comparison is to be made. There are four stories where the evidence with regard to a comparative introductory frame is divided among the various versions. Some do introduce the story with a literary frame that calls for a comparison to be made by the reader, but other versions do not: the Lost Sheep (Thomas compares the story to the kingdom, but Matthew and Luke have no introductory frame calling for a comparison), a Sprouting Seed (Mark compares the story to the kingdom of God, but Thomas does not call for a comparison), the Feast (Matthew compares the story to the kingdom of heaven, but Luke and Thomas do not call for a comparison), the Entrusted Money (Matthew compares the story to the parousia [25:10, 13–14?], but Luke has no call for a comparison [though Luke does associate the story with the kingdom of God, 19:11]).

Some stories call for a comparison with the kingdom. There are thirteen stories where a comparison is made in all extant versions between

---

[26] This is true in all three versions. In the Synoptic Gospels, however, it is treated as figurative language by the inclusion of allegorical interpretations. The Thomas version, however, has no interpretation or contiguous comparative frame.

the kingdom of God (heaven, Father) and the story: a Mustard Seed (Matthew, Luke, and Thomas—kingdom of heaven; Mark—kingdom of God), the Good Seed and Weeds (Matthew—kingdom of heaven; Thomas—kingdom of the Father), the Leaven (Matthew—kingdom of heaven; Luke—kingdom of God; Thomas—kingdom of the Father), the Hid Treasure (Matthew—kingdom of heaven; Thomas—the kingdom), a Merchant in Search of Pearls (Matthew—kingdom of heaven; Thomas—kingdom of the Father), a King Settling Accounts (Matthew—kingdom of heaven), the Wage of the Workmen (Matthew—kingdom of heaven), the Lamps of the Maidens (Matthew—kingdom of heaven), the Empty Jar (Thomas—kingdom of the Father), the Killer (Thomas—kingdom of the Father), the Date Palm Shoot (James—kingdom of heaven), the Ear of Grain (James—kingdom of heaven), a Net Thrown into the Sea (Matthew—kingdom of heaven; but cf. Thomas—the Man).

Some stories are compared to something other than the kingdom. Four stories are compared to something other than the kingdom of God (heaven, Father): In the story of a Net Thrown into the Sea Thomas makes a comparison to the "Man"; Matthew and Luke compare the Two Houses to one who hears and does the words of Jesus; Matthew compares the Entrusted Money to the return of the Son of Man; Mark compares a Man Going on a Journey to the return of the Son of Man; Luke compares it to the "disciples" in view of the return of the Son of Man.

EARLY CHRISTIAN USE OF THE STORIES

Mark

The earliest extant discussion of the function of the stories attributed to Jesus of Nazareth is found in the Gospel of Mark (4:1–34). According to Mark's "theory of parables" (4:10–12), the stories function as ciphers whose secrets are intended by Jesus for the enlightenment not of the masses but only of the disciples,[27] the inner group around Jesus. Indeed, according to Mark, Jesus generally speaks enigmatically in order to keep outsiders from understanding, for if they understood they would "turn and be forgiven" (4:12).[28] Mark 4:11–12 and 34, the heart of the theory, is probably a pre–Markan tradition describing one view of Jesus' teaching by a group of early Christians that flourished between the death of Jesus and the writing of Mark (i.e., 30–70 CE).[29] But it is nevertheless

---

[27] Cf. Rhodes, "Narrative Criticism," 424–25.

[28] Mark's parable theory has been treated to extensive discussion. See in particular Jeremias, *Parables*, 13–18, and Carlston, *Triple Tradition*, 97–109.

[29] Jeremias (*Parables*, 15) and Carlston (*Triple Tradition*, 101) agree that the tradition is pre-Markan.

true that Mark agrees with this theory of parables and interprets Jesus'
"parabolic" (i.e., story-telling) discourse in its light.

All but two of Mark's story parables appear in Mark 4: a Man Going
on a Journey (13:34) and the allegory of a Vineyard (12:1b–9). An analysis
of Mark's treatment of these stories demonstrates that Mark regarded
them as "allegories"; that is to say, they are stories that say one thing
but mean something quite different. In a true allegory one subject is
described under the guise of another suggestively similar subject. The
elements of the allegory are conceived and cast so as to have a one-to-one
correlation between the allegorical figure(s) and the "real" subject(s)
being described.[30] When one "allegorizes" an already existing story that
was not deliberately cast as an allegory, one brings a different subject to
the story and attempts to correlate elements of the already existing story
to the different reality or realities existing outside the story proper in the
mind of the allegorist. This appears to be what has been done with the
story of a Sower. Compare Mark 4:9, where Mark invites his reader to
hear "more" in the story than it actually says. For example, the Sower/
Seeds/Ground story (Mark 4:3–8) realistically describes the difficulty of
farming in first-century Palestine. Yet Mark's "explanation" (4:14–20)
makes a one-to-one correlation of most elements of the farming story to
the difficulties of ecclesiastical evangelism in the first century. This
"interpretation" is the real subject of Mark's interest in narrating the
Sower/Seeds/Ground story. Once the interpretation is stated, the story
actually becomes an embarrassment, since, when they are closely compared, the story subverts the interpretation. Allegorical interpretations
are parasitic and narrativorous: they consume and dispense with the
"stories" to which they are appended.

The collection of sayings (4:21–25) appended as "discourse" following the "interpretation" to the story of a Sower supports the view that
the stories in Mark's understanding are really ciphers, or riddles, whose
concealed meaning is open only to a select group. Mark's calculated
literary frame (4:10–11 and 4:33–34) and the model interpretation of the
story of a Sower (4:14–20) lead the reader to see all of these stories (and
sayings!) as having a hidden meaning. Mark 4:21: In this context, the
lamp/bushel, bed/stand image suggests that these stories do contain the
secret of the kingdom of God (4:11) intended only for the disciples. One
does not conceal the light, for the lamp is intended to illuminate. Mark
4:22: That which is concealed in the stories is intended to be revealed.
Mark 4:23 (cf. 4:9) invites the disciple to seek that secret meaning
concealed in the stories. Mark 4:24–25 affirms the inner group of disciples
as the only ones who can understand the concealed message(s) about the
kingdom of God. Hence Mark 4:26–29 and 4:30–32 are stories that

---

[30] See the discussion by MacQueen, *Allegory.*

conceal information about the kingdom of God. In the light of Mark's interpretation to the story of a Sower (4:14–20) and the allegory of a Vineyard (12:1b–9) it seems clear that Mark takes these two stories as having an ecclesiastical significance, although Mark does not provide the reader with any formal interpretation.

Matthew

Matthew agrees with Mark that the stories are allegories containing secrets about the kingdom of God[31] that must be explained (though Matthew scarcely accepts Mark's "hardening" theory; cf. 13:10–17). And accordingly in Matthew one finds two fully developed allegorical explanations relating to early Christian eschatology (13:37–43, 49–50) in addition to Matthew's use of Mark's explanation of a Sower (Matt 13:19–23). In these explanations can be noted both the detailed one-to-one correlation between the story and the experience of the church and the lack of consistency when each feature of the story cannot be fitted into Matthew's rather whimsical explanation.[32] Of course Matthew's briefer explanations of other stories, appended as a short "moral" to each story, also assume that the stories relate to the life and faith of Matthew's church. In that sense the stories "mean" to Matthew something quite different from what they actually say.[33]

A Vineyard (21:33b–40) is a story-become-allegory of Jesus' rejection by Israel (21:42–43). The possessed man in Jesus' story of the Unclean Spirit (12:43–45a) functions as a Matthean allegorical figure for "this evil generation" (12:45b). On Settling out of Court (5:25–26) has no appended explanation, since it is not in the form of a story; but in Matthew it becomes an example of how the church ought to worship (5:23–24). The Two Houses (7:24b–27) also lacks an appended interpretation since Matthew offers it as an example (7:24a) of the lifestyle of the Christian scribe (to 7:24a, "wise man" [not in Luke] cf. 13:52). The Lost Sheep (18:12–13) is an allegory on preserving the Christian disciple in the church (18:14). A King Settling Accounts (18:23–34) is an allegory on judgment (18:35). In the Wage of the Workmen (20:1–15) Matthew employs a floating saying (cf. 19:30; Mark 10:31; Luke 13:30) to indicate that the story is intended to illustrate reversal of rank at the last judgment (20:16).[34] The Two Sons (21:28–30) has no appended explanation since Matthew uses it to illustrate the rejection of Israel at the last

---

[31] See Hedrick, "Treasure Parable" for a redactional analysis of Matthew 13.
[32] See in particular Jeremias, *Parables*, 66–89.
[33] I do not discuss here Matt 13:33b, 44, 45–46. They are allegorically interpreted by Matthew as being secrets about the kingdom of God. See note 31 above.
[34] See Jeremias, *Parables*, 35.

judgment (21:31).[35] And finally, the Lamps of the Maidens (25:1–10) is an allegory on the parousia (25:13).[36]

Luke

While Luke, like Matthew, also does not subscribe to Mark's "hardening" theory of parables (and hence omits the offensive phrase, "lest they should turn and be forgiven"—to Mark 4:12 cf. Luke 8:10), Luke nevertheless does present the stories as allegories, i.e., concealed secrets about the kingdom of God that must be explained to the disciples (8:9–10a, 11) and concealed from outsiders (8:10b). Hence, Luke also, adopting Mark's explanation, offers a detailed "interpretation" (8:11b–15) to the story of a Sower (8:5–8a), followed by the cryptic statements about concealing and revealing (8:16–18) discussed above in connection with Mark 4:21–25. The result is the same; the message of the "allegorical" stories is still meant for the insider, although one may argue that Luke is more optimistic about the potential ability of the outsider to understand. For example, Luke resists the sharp insider/outsider contrast present in Mark. Luke does not have the following: Mark 4:10, the statement about the outsiders in Mark 4:11, and the offensive "hardening" statement in Mark 4:12b. Moreover, Luke 8:18 stresses that one should take care "how" one "hears," a statement suggesting that one may be able to understand if one listens carefully.

Luke follows Mark's allegorical interpretation (20:16b–19) to the allegory of a Vineyard (20:9b–16a). Luke also takes the story of a Man Going on a Journey (12:36–38) as an allegory of the church's expectation of the parousia (12:40). In Luke there is no appended interpretation to On Settling out of Court (12:58–59), since it is cast not as a story but as an admonition to judge correctly about proper human behavior (12:57) in light of the fact that the parousia could occur at any moment (to judge from the eschatological nature of the context—12:35–56). Likewise Luke casts the Two Houses (6:48–49) as an example of what it means to be obedient to the Lord (6:46–47). The stories of the Lost Coin (15:8–9), the Lost Sheep (15:4–6), and the Prodigal Son/Elder Brother (15:11–32) are presented as allegories concerning the conversion of sinners, i.e., bringing the lost (cf. 15:24, 32) into the church (15:1–2, 7, 10).

Luke is quite conservative in the explanation (14:24) to the story of the Feast (14:16–23), but the story's context (14:7–14, 25–27) suggests that Luke understands it as an allegory of the church's mission activities.

---

[35] See Jeremias, *Parables*, 80–81. The association of the figure with John the Baptist (21:32) was probably made before Matthew.

[36] I take Matt 25:11–12 to be Matthew's intensification of the story's conclusion that appears in 25:10. The sayings in 25:11–12 are "floating" sayings; to Matt 25:11 compare Luke 13:25a; to Matt 25:12 compare Matt 7:23 and Luke 13:25b, 27.

The Entrusted Money (19:12b–24) conceals teaching about the church's expectation of the parousia (19:11). Hence the story's interpretive expansion (19:25–27) relates to final judgment. The Two Debtors (7:41–42a) is not given as story, but functions for Luke as an example clarifying the gratitude of sinners at the forgiveness of God (7:36–39, 42b–50). The story of a Samaritan (10:30–35) serves Luke as an example story illustrating what it means to act as a neighbor (10:25–29, 36–37). The Persistent Friend (11:5–8) becomes an example of how one ought to pray (11:2–4, 9–13). The Rich Man (12:16b–20) functions as an example, warning against the dangers of wealth (12:21) and covetousness (12:13–15). Luke offers no explanation for the following stories: a Mustard Seed (13:19), the Leaven (13:21), the Barren Fig Tree (13:6b–9), and a Rich Man and Lazarus (16:19–31). The strange story of the Unclean Spirit (11:24–26a) seems to function as an example of the dangers of demon possession (11:26b); and in this case, for Luke, demon possession seems to be a figure for those who do not heed the "word of God" (11:27–28), i.e., this evil generation (11:29–32). The Tower Builder (14:28–30) and the Warring King (14:31–32) Luke uses as examples of the kind of personal assessment that is required of those who would become disciples of Jesus. Compare the explanation of the two stories (14:33) and the context in which the stories are used (14:25–27).

The Dishonest Steward (16:1b–7) is an example story with a series of four different appended interpretations: 16:8—an example of shrewdness; 16:9—an example of "worldly wisdom" (?); 16:10–12—an admonition to a faithful use of "mammon"; 16:13—a warning that one can serve either God or "mammon" but not both.[37] Luke reads the Servant (17:7–9) as an example of Christian discipleship. Doing all that the Lord demands does not qualify one for praise; it was the least that one could do (17:10). The Pharisee and the Toll Collector (18:10–13) serves Luke as an example story illustrating the Christian ideal of humility (18:9, 14). The Unjust Judge (18:2–5) illustrates persistence in prayer (18:1) and faithfulness in view of the parousia (18:6–8).

John

One of the interesting and provocative differences between the Synoptic Gospels and the Gospel of John is that John does not have any of the stories that Mark (4:34) indicates were a characteristic feature of Jesus' teaching. The word παραβολή does not even appear in the Gospel

---

[37] The questionable moral character of the "hero" in this story apparently created problems for a church that regarded the stories as allegories about the kingdom of God, or as moral examples of proper human behavior for the community of faith. In both cases the stories are taken as talking about something "religious" under the guise of something quite different.

of John! John does, however, employ figurative language: for example, the figures of the vine and the branches (15:1–8), the sheepfold (10:1–5, 7–10), and the good shepherd (10:11–18). The author of John refers to this kind of image language as παροιμία, a word that can be translated as proverb, maxim, figure, comparison, or even by the word parable. But the point to note here is that John does not use the word παραβολή, nor does John use the stories with narrative plot that are the characteristic of Jesus' teaching in the Synoptic Gospels. John, apparently, quite deliberately uses παροιμία (figure). Compare, for example the reaction of the crowd to Jesus' image of the sheepfold (10:6): it was regarded as a "figure" that they did not understand. In John παροιμία carries the idea of obscure language. The assumption of John is that "figures" need explanation.[38]

Indeed, "figures," or obscure language, in John contrast with plain or open παρρησία language (7:4, 13, 26; 11:54 [public versus private]; 18:20–21; cf. 16:16–30). For example, compare the use of this language in John chapter 11. John 11:14 understands the figure (sleep for death) in John 11:11 as cryptic language that confuses the disciples (11:12), while the unraveling of the cryptic language is described as open or plain language (παρρησίᾳ, 11:14).

Hence both the Synoptic Gospels and the Gospel of John agree that the language of Jesus was, in certain aspects, at the very least, unclear or cryptic, and this was particularly the case in John's use of images.

The *Gospel of Thomas*

The *Gospel of Thomas* preserves thirteen narratives (logia 8, 9, 20, 57, 63, 64, 65, 76, 96, 97, 98, 107, 109) and one Markan story (i.e., it appears in Mark in story form) in the form of a logion (a Sprouting Seed—log. 21d = *Gos. Thom.* II,2:37,15–18). Two of the stories in Thomas were unknown in the canonical gospel literature prior to the discovery of the *Gospel of Thomas*: the Killer (log. 98–*Gos. Thom.* II,2:49,16–20) and the Empty Jar (log. 97–*Gos. Thom.* II,2:49,8–14).[39] One of the unusual features of the stories in Thomas is the virtual lack of contiguous allegorical interpretation, which figures so prominently in the canonical gospels. The absence of such interpretations in Thomas may be the best

---

[38] The "explanation" (10:7–10) to the figure of the sheepfold is equally obscure, however.

[39] The Great Fish (log. 8 = II,2:33,28–34,2) is an earlier version of Matthew's Net Thrown into the Sea (Matt 13:47–48). Both appear to be variants of Aesop's fable, "The Fisherman and the Fish." Aesop describes a small fish (ὁ λεπτός) escaping through the net, while the "large fish" (ὁ μέγας) was caught (Perry, *Babrius and Phaedrus*, 8–11).

evidence that Jesus did not originally cast his stories as allegories as the Synoptic Gospels portray him as doing.[40]

Thomas's use of the stories is also striking. Seven have no contiguous interpretations whatsoever (a Sower—log. 9, a Mustard Seed—log. 20, the Good Seed and Weeds—log. 57, the Empty Jar—log. 97, the Killer—log. 98, the Lost Sheep—log. 107, the Hid Treasure—log. 109). And one of the stories (the Feast—log. 64) has a brief anti-business interpretation (viz., "tradesmen and merchants [shall] not [enter] the places of my father," 44, 34–45; Guillaumont, *Thomas*, 37).[41]

One story (a Merchant in Search of Pearls—log. 76) may have more extensive interpretation; it depends on how one understands the introductory frames for the sayings in Thomas. The editors of the *editio princeps* of the *Gospel of Thomas*[42] judged it to have 114 individual sayings, assuming that each saying is introduced by a schematic "Jesus said," or "he said." In certain instances, however, they emended the text to provide the introductory frame, "Jesus said," apparently because they felt that they could clearly distinguish the beginning of another different and separate logion (logia 27, 93, 101). In other cases they felt that a new logion had begun because they recognized a different introductory frame (logia 6, 12, 18, 20, 21, 22, 24, 37, 43, 51, 52, 53, 79, 91, 99, 100, 104, 113, 114). Logion 69 they divide into two separate macarisms (69a and 69b), even though 69b is not introduced by an introductory frame. And on one occasion they emend the text to begin a new logion with "they saw" (log. 60). When one recognizes that many of the numbered sayings of the *editio princeps* include sayings that can be found separately in the canonical gospels, the modern numbering system for Thomas seems suspiciously arbitrary. Or put another way, the numbering system of Thomas in the *editio princeps* is a modern convenience and does not necessarily reflect the ancient scribal understanding of what constituted a logion. Therefore what the ancient scribe understood as the limits of a given logion must be argued in each individual case.

For example, when one compares log. 21 to the synoptic tradition, it appears to be comprised of four different logia: the simile of the children in a field (36,35–37,6), the image of the householder (37,6–10), an interpretation to the image of the householder (37,10–15), and a logion on a "man of understanding" (37,15–18). Is the image of the householder intended as an interpretation of the "children in a field," or have they simply been collected together, or were they conflated into and conceived as one saying in antiquity? On the one hand, while it seems clear that

---

[40]See Stroker, "Extracanonical Parables."

[41]The lack of such interpretations is unusual in the light of the opening lines to Thomas (32,10–19) where it is indicated that the "author" had in mind hidden meanings.

[42]Guillaumont, *Thomas*.

the householder and the "logion" immediately following are related as saying and interpretation, such a connection is not as obvious for a "man of understanding." On the other hand, log. 76b (46,19–22) does appear to interpret the story of a Merchant in Search of Pearls.

What is more significant for understanding Thomas's use of these stories is that at the end of five of them (logia 8, 63, 65, 96, 21d [here it appears to serve as a conclusion for log. 21]). Thomas has added a floating saying ("He that has ears to hear, let him hear") as an invitation to the reader to reflect on the story. This invitation, suggesting that the reader should "hear" more in the story than is actually stated, corresponds to the introductory frame of the *Gospel of Thomas* where the reader is encouraged to reflect on, and to seek, the cryptic significance of all the sayings (32,10–19). In other words, with one or two exceptions (log. 64 and log. 76), Thomas does not openly tell the reader the point(s) the story is intended to score, but rather solicits all readers to search for the "explanation" that provides eternal life. In this respect, Thomas openly conflicts with Mark's exclusivism, i.e., Mark's contrast between insider and outsider.

The same floating saying inviting the reader to reflect on the meaning of the stories in Thomas is also used in connection with four of the canonical stories. It ends a Sower (Matt 13:8; Mark 4:9; Luke 8:8) as its earliest extant conclusion. It comes at the end (13:43b) of Matthew's explanation (13:37–43a) of the Good Seed and Weeds (13:24b–30). Mark uses it at 4:23 following the lamp/bushel, bed/stand saying (4:21–22). And Luke employs it at 14:35b (turning the banal saying about salt [14:34–35a] into a cryptic saying) following the double stories of the Tower Builder (14:28–30) and the Warring King (14:31–32).

The association of this floating saying with these stories suggests that Thomas finds some hidden significance in them. In its use of a general invitation to any reader, however, Thomas contrasts rather dramatically with the allegorical interpretations of the Synoptic Gospels. If the floating saying used in the synoptic tradition in connection with the stories should prove to be an early pre-synoptic interpretation,[43] then Thomas also is probably utilizing an earlier pre-synoptic tradition.

The *Apocryphon of James*

The *Apocryphon of James* clearly knows a parables tradition and even uses the "titles" of some: the Shepherds, the Seed, the Building, the Lamps of the Virgins, the Wage of the Workmen, the Didrachmae, and the Woman (*Ap. Jas.* I,2:8,1–10). Whether or not these titles correspond to the

---

[43] So Kingsbury, *Matthew 13*, 145, n. 50, and Jeremias, *Parables*, 14, n. 8, and 109–10.

canonical stories is not completely certain.[44] The Wage of the Workmen and the Lamps of the Virgins, however, do appear to be early Christian titles for "the Workers in the Vineyard" (Matt 20:1–15) and "the Ten Virgins" (Matt 25:1–10). The similarity seems too close to be accidental.[45]

In addition to mentioning these titles, the *Apocryphon of James* also narrates two "stories," each of which is followed by a fully developed interpretation. The interpretation (I,2:7,29–35) to the Date Palm Shoot (I,2:7,24–28) is allegorical as well as cryptic and obscure. The story of the Ear of Grain (I,2:12:22–27) takes it to refer to the kingdom of God, which appears to be a cipher for a certain kind of knowledge that brings wisdom (I,2:12:27–31). The Grain of Wheat (I,2:8,16–23) is so heavily allegorized that one despairs of reconstructing any story from which it may have derived.[46] Its allegorical interpretation (I,2:8,23–27) is likewise cryptic, hence, it is not included in the present inventory.

PARABLES IN EARLY CHRISTIAN LITERATURE: ANALYSIS AND CONCLUSIONS

The general conclusion of contemporary scholarship from this rather surprisingly diverse and fluid use of the parables has been: (1) The parables of Jesus are intended to present the kingdom of God/heaven in various images. They are symbolical or metaphorical stories that intentionally point outward to the kingdom. This includes even those stories without an introductory comparative frame.[47] (2) The allegorizing and moralizing of the parables by the evangelists have been rejected in principle because such interpretations derive from the life setting of the early church.[48] (3) The example stories, contrary to the understanding of early Christianity, were not really example stories that make moral points about some aspect of proper human behavior; they are actually figurative, i.e., symbolical and/or metaphorical.[49] (4) Indeed scholars have essentially rejected[50] the early Christian understanding of the

---

[44]See the discussion by Williams, "The Apocryphon of James."

[45]It seems less certain that "the Seed" is to be associated with the story of the Mustard Seed in Mark 4:31–34 = Matt 13:31b–32 = Luke 13:19 = Thomas II,2:36,28–33 (log. 20).

[46]See Cameron, *Sayings Traditions*, 12–16.

[47]For example, compare Jeremias' interpretation to the story of a Sower, a story having no introductory comparative frame: *Parables*, 149–51, the interpretation by Kingsbury, *Matthew 13*, 35–37, and that by Scott, *Hear Then the Parable*, 56–62, 343–62.

[48]Jeremias, *Parables*, 66–89.

[49]Compare the treatment of the story of the Samaritan by Funk, "Good Samaritan as Metaphor."

[50]Cf. Jeremias (*Parables*, 31), who occasionally accepts the synoptic literary setting of the parable as its setting in the life of the historical Jesus.

parables as to meaning but have largely accepted without question the
early Christian use of the parables as to function. Scholars *assume* that
the stories were intended by the historical Jesus to compare a known area
of human experience with the kingdom of God. Jeremias' reconstruction
of an Aramaic *Vorlage* for the introductory comparative frame to the
parables (viz., it is the case with the kingdom of God as it is with . . .)[51]
has been without serious question attributed to the historical Jesus,
although it could equally well derive from early Palestinian Jewish
Christianity.

The evidence from early Christian literature, however, challenges
the assumption that Jesus used the stories figuratively. The early Christian understanding of these stories as figurative could derive equally as
well from the early Christian difficulty with understanding the language
of Jesus (i.e., from the necessity that early Christianity sensed for deriving
relevant meanings from the sayings of Jesus that related to its own life
situation) as it could from the historical Jesus himself.

Indeed, on balance, it seems more probable that early Christianity
resorted to allegory and moralizing to make sense of Jesus' stories than
it is that early Christianity was led to allegory by the historical memory
that Jesus' stories were figures. The diversity in the way the same stories
are utilized in early Christian literature suggests that the use of the
stories by the church hinged on the interpreter's skill in making sense
out of them, rather than on some clearly recognizable and innate
metaphorical/symbolical quality in the story. Some distance from the
historical Jesus and the concrete historical setting of his teaching, and
in the new context of the post-resurrection worshiping church, the
sayings and stories of Jesus are suddenly strange and require explanation
in terms of the new faith.[52] Hence any argument that the symboli-
cal/metaphorical/allegorical use of the stories originated with the historical Jesus must show why such an assumption is more plausible than the
argument that such use of the stories derives from the frustration of early
Christians over the lack of an appropriate and up-to-date ecclesiastical
meaning for the stories in the crisis of the church's changing historical
situation.

To put the matter differently, one must show why the following
historical reconstruction is less plausible than current assumptions about
the stories of Jesus: Jesus told stories (that may or may not have been
deliberately metaphorical or symbolical). The early church turned them
into allegories and example stories because the stories had little evident
significance for the changed, and continually changing, historical situation of the church. In time the sayings tradition was treated as obscure

---

[51] Jeremias, *Parables*, 100.
[52] This was recognized by Cadoux, *Parables*, 24.

or cryptic language, if an initial reading could not produce an ecclesiastical interpretation appropriate to the faith of the community. Vestiges of a hermeneutical evolution in parables' interpretation are attested in (a) Thomas's invitation to the reader to hear more in the stories than appears on the surface, (b) the allegorical, moral, and example-story interpretations of the synoptic evangelists, (c) the cryptic Jesus of John whose every word is heard as a cryptic utterance, and (d) the Markan parables theory that formally distinguishes between "insiders" and "outsiders."[53]

If scholars reject Mark's understanding of the stories as allegories, why should they continue to assume that Mark is correct about the deliberate figurative character of the stories? That characteristic likewise could have originated with the difficulty the church had extracting an appropriate religious significance from the stories. Our own modern assumption that the stories are figurative could well derive from the same frustration the early church felt: If his stories and figures are not more religiously significant than they appear to be on the surface, then Jesus is open to the charge of banality!

Jeremias' identification of an Aramaic *Vorlage* for the comparative frame that introduces some of the stories proves only that the loss of understanding occurred quite early, in the context of the Palestinian Jewish-Christian communities of faith. For example, one can easily imagine an early Christian prophet trying to make sense of the story of a Sower. Unless it is a figure that contains some hidden "spiritual" meaning, it sounds like an inane (although accurate) description of farming practices in first-century Palestine. But since Jesus was believed to be the resurrected Son of God, such an interpretation was by definition an inadequate understanding of the story. Therefore, because of who Jesus was in the faith of the church, the story must be construed as having some latent, concealed meaning that related to the church, or the kingdom of God—so the reasoning must have gone. Under the inspiration of the resurrected Christ, who dwelled in and among his people, significant prophetic interpretations for the stories were inevitable!

The way that the *Gospel of Thomas* treats the stories may reflect an earlier (pre-canonical gospels) stage in a development from simple story (with possible metaphorical or symbolical significance) to enigmatic saying. Thomas employs a comparative frame, but has virtually no contiguous interpretations, apart from the general invitation to look for a deeper meaning in the story (which is a tacit admission that the "meaning" of the stories by the time of Thomas was no longer self-evident).

---

[53] I do not assume that I have reconstructed a historical cause and effect sequence among these particular texts, but have only identified an early Christian hermeneutical trajectory. Specific points on the trajectory are visible in these texts.

The fact that some of these stories in all versions have neither comparative frame nor contiguous interpretation that treats them comparatively requires explanation by anyone who assumes that Jesus intended to make comparisons with his stories. The following stories have neither comparative frame nor contiguous interpretation that treats them figuratively: a Sower (Matthew, Mark, Luke, Thomas), the Barren Fig Tree (Luke), the Two Debtors (Luke), On Settling out of Court (Matthew, Luke), the Prodigal Son/Elder Brother (Luke), a Rich Man and Lazarus (Luke). And some of the stories that do have comparative frames and/or appended interpretations in some versions, in other versions have neither, such as a Vineyard (Thomas) and the Rich Man (Thomas).

Along with these must also be considered stories without an introductory comparative frame, but that nevertheless draw a simple moral lesson or were used as examples illustrating proper Christian behavior: the Unclean Spirit (Matthew, Luke), the Two Sons (Matthew), the Persistent Friend (Luke), the Servant (Luke), the Lost Sheep (Matthew, Luke), the Feast (Luke, Thomas), the Entrusted Money (Luke), the Rich Man (Luke), the Tower Builder and Warring King (Luke), the Lost Coin (Luke), the Dishonest Steward (Luke), the Unjust Judge (Luke) and the Pharisee and the Toll Collector (Luke).

James Breech is thus correct: it is more likely that the introductory comparative frames to these stories derive from the early Christian community and should not be used as the crucial interpretive principle for understanding them as figurative.[54] The introductory comparative frames indicate that the early church had problems making sense out of Jesus' stories as they were preserved. On the other hand, it is the early church's difficulty with understanding the stories that may be the very best historical evidence for the oblique character of Jesus' language, rather than the comparative frame itself, but that does not mean they were deliberately cast as metaphor.

THE FICTIONAL INTERNAL WORLD OF THE STORY VERSUS A REFERENTIAL WORLD

The parables of Jesus are basically realistic stories with narrative plot that may or may not have been told by Jesus of Nazareth. Scott begins with the premise that Jesus was a parabler, because of the relative lack of parables in the Greek and Jewish traditions. What is perhaps more significant is that he begins with the premise that the stories of Jesus, like the *mashal*, "reference a transcendent symbol."[55] That is to say, he

---

[54] Breech, *Silence of Jesus*, 66–74.
[55] Scott, "Essaying the Rock," 4.

assumes that Jesus used stories like the rabbis did.[56] And, it should also be noted, he assumes that these stories have an innate metaphorical quality! I am inclined to agree that Jesus was a "teller of tales," since that is reflected in virtually all strands of our literary sources for Jesus of Nazareth: Q, Mark, M, L, Thomas, and the *Apocryphon of James* (and there may even have been a story at the basis of the images of the sheepfold and good shepherd in John, as well as behind some of the other sayings in early Christian literature, viz., the allegory of the grain of wheat [*Ap. Jas.* I,2:8,16–23] and the good and wicked servants [Matt 24:45–51a and Luke 12:42–46]). But that such stories have deliberate referential (i.e., metaphorical or symbolical) quality is not to be *assumed* from an introductory comparative frame. Such metaphorical or symbolical quality must be shown to exist in particular semantic markers within each story.

In his treatment of the story of the Leaven[57] Robert Funk finds semantic markers that in his judgment lend the story a metaphorical quality and point him to a world outside the story. Interpreters must ask themselves what is the particular semantic marker in the story that "flips" the mind out of the concrete specificity of the story's world into a particular referential world. Usually it is a surprising twist or some anomaly, something that does not fit well, or exactly, the world of the story.[58] Funk finds three "clues" that trigger his imagination in the story of the Leaven.

> The proximity of the three terms, "leaven," "hide," "three measures of meal," within the confines of the brief sentence that comprises the parable, thus reverberate against each other and against the sedimented language tradition in such a way that the parable as a whole becomes plurisignificative. The terms are so subtly arranged that the unwary may well read it as a commonplace illustration of a commonplace bit of wisdom. But for the alert the parable triggers the imagination: The terms and the whole are set free to play against one another and against the tradition. Those who have ears hear strange voices.[59]

The problem encountered in the study of parables is not unique to parables' study; it is endemic to language itself. Language, all language, is subject to ambiguity and a potential range of meanings—including even language that aims at clarity. This is particularly true of oral

---

[56] See also Young, *Jewish Parables*, 55–128.

[57] Funk, "Beyond Criticism."

[58] The form in which we have the stories derives from the faith experience of early Christianity. Hence one must be careful first to reconstruct the transmission history of the story, since without such reconstruction the "trigger" may derive from early Christian allegorizing of the story. In this regard, however, care must be taken to distinguish early Christian allegorizing features from a deliberate caricature originally built into the story.

[59] Funk, "Beyond Criticism," 162.

communication, but no less true of written texts. Some language is deliberately ambiguous and partakes of irony, metaphor, and symbol.

What is unique about the parables is that they present themselves as transparent actions of first-century Jewish life, yet they have regularly been construed as opaque and mysterious conduits that transport a reader to somewhere else and something quite different. If this "sense" about the stories of Jesus is correct, they are probably to be related to poetry, since poetry functions in similar ways. Some poems present themselves as transparent narratives, clearly understandable at one level of language as accurate, though fictive, descriptions of reality, but they have broader symbolical and metaphorical ranges. Of course the literary critic should not simply assume this. Rather the critic is mandated to show by the internal semantic markers how it is that a poem presenting itself as a transparent narrative deliberately references the broader ranges. Some of the internal markers may be extremely subtle, as for example the poem "My Star" by Robert Browning.[60]

> All I know
>   Of a certain star
> Is, it can throw
>   (Like the angled spar)
> Now a dart of red,
>   Now a dart of blue;
> Till my friends have said
>   They would fain see, too,
> My star that dartles the red and the blue!
> Then it stops like a bird; like a flower, hangs furled:
>   They must solace themselves with the Saturn above it.
> What Matter to me if their star is a world?
>   Mine has opened its soul to me; therefore I love it.

Laurence Perrine in his discussion of this poem (in connection with a discussion of figurative language) finds that there is really nothing obvious in the language of the poem that causes one to think that the poem has any symbolical significance. It is only the importance of the star to Browning "that makes us suspect that he is talking about something more [than just a star]."[61] Perrine "suspects" that the poem has symbolical significance, but his only clue is the unusual and unexpected feeling the poet expresses for the star: stars do not have souls and one does not normally "love" stars. Though this may be only heightened poetical language, it is the esteem for the star that such language communicates that causes the reader to think that perhaps something more is intended.

---

[60] As quoted in Perrine, *Sound and Sense*, 84–85.
[61] Perrine, *Sound and Sense*, 85.

If the stories of Jesus are found to have deliberate metaphorical or symbolical quality, such quality must be particularized in the language of the story itself, i.e., internal semantic markers must be specified. Otherwise the metaphorical/symbolical "leap" is an imposition on the story. Hence, the interpreter must specify what in the story triggers a specific figurative understanding.

The interpreter, therefore, should not assume that Jesus' stories are symbols that reference the kingdom of God or some other transcendent reality. This is not to deny that the message of Jesus may have been concerned in some degree with the kingdom of God.[62] Rather it is to affirm that we do not know how he used the stories, nor can we tell from the evidence in early Christian literature. We must start with the story itself rather than with the kingdom of God, for even that expression itself is a symbol.[63]

These stories, if original with Jesus, are freely contrived and realistic fictions deriving from observations of first-century Palestinian life and the creative energies of Jesus' imagination.[64] They show a sharp economy in the presentation of characters/agents and plot. Most of them deal with realistic human activity, although a few treat nature subjects, and some even concern superhuman activity.[65] Like poetry they appear to be a product of Jesus' personal vision. A poem is a mimetic fiction, a product of the poet's imagination and keen observation of world. According to Aristotle, the poet has the option of re-presenting in the poetic fiction things as they are or were, as they are believed to be, or as they should be.[66] Hence the "imagination" of the poet produces a *mimesis* (i.e., a representation, a narrative "image") that derives from the poet's imaginative vision. This "image" may be performed "realistically" (Aristotle = the way things are or were) or "idealistically" (Aristotle = the way things are believed to be or should be).

What we have in the realistic *mimesis* of the stories of Jesus is, in short, a marriage of common reality and imagination that has the potential of igniting the imaginations of those who consent to enter his fictional world. And in that sense his stories are very close to the nature of poetry as Wallace Stevens described it:[67]

---

[62] Compare, for example, Jesus' aphorisms about the kingdom of God: Crossan, *In Fragments*. But see n. 2 above.

[63] Perrin, *Language of the Kingdom*, 15–32.

[64] See Via, *Parables*, 96. However, compare Michaels, *Servant and Son*, 101–4, who affirms their "visionary" character but rejects a description of the parables as products of the creative imagination of Jesus: "he did not create or invent them. He *experienced* them" (p. 104).

[65] For example, the Unclean Spirit (Matt 12:43–45a = Luke 11:24–26a).

[66] Aristot. *Poet.* 25.1–3.

[67] Stevens, "Noble Rider," 977–78.

It [i.e., the nature of poetry] is an interdependence of the imagination and reality as equals.

What is his [i.e., the poet's] function?. . . . I think that his function is to make his imagination theirs [i.e., the readers'] and that he fulfills himself only as he sees his imagination become the light in the minds of others. His role, in short, is to help people to live their lives.

If we have this experience [i.e., of imagination invoked against the pressure of reality] we know how poets help people to live their lives. . . .

There is, in fact, a world of poetry indistinguishable from the world in which we live, or, I ought to say, no doubt, from the world in which we shall come to live, since what makes the poet the potent figure that he is, or was, or ought to be, is that he creates the world to which we turn incessantly and without knowing it and that he gives to life the supreme fictions without which we are unable to conceive of it.

Hence the fictions of Jesus are occasional partial "descriptions" of his "world," his view of reality. Each story is related to the whole of the collected stories, as each is also related to an inaccessible complete narrative construct of Jesus' view of the world.[68]

The stories of Jesus *may* deliberately direct our minds to another world and to another place, but until one identifies, and particularizes, a *certain* trigger in the story itself, these stories should be read "poetically"—as freely created fictional narratives of Jesus' poetic vision of reality. Hence, these tales of Jesus mean exactly what they say—and maybe more.

READING PARABLES AS STORIES

The stories may well have metaphorical or symbolical quality, and they may deliberately reference something outside themselves, but at the same time, the interpreter cannot merely assume that to be the case. They most certainly are products of Jesus' creative imagination, and hence constitute his fictive vision in narrative form, as Amos Wilder long ago pointed out.[69] Indicators of referentiality, if any, should be specified as a separate step of exegesis (as Funk has done with the Leaven) so that others can evaluate whether it is the internal force of the language of the narrative that deliberately propels the mind outward in a specific direction, or whether it is the reader's own imagination that "creates" the trigger and the target. For example, one may agree with Funk that

---

[68] See the description of the poetry of Wallace Stevens by Kermode, *Wallace Stevens*, 95.

[69] Wilder, *Rhetoric*, 85.

the word "hid" in the Leaven is metaphorical and yet challenge his assumption that the word deliberately targets the kingdom of God and is designed to take the reader out of the story.

In this regard, one must recognize that there is a substantial difference between a story's *evoking* horizons more distant than the narrow confines of the world in the story and a story's deliberately *referencing* some other specific "thing" outside the story. The former instance describes a range of reasonable subjective responses controlled by a critical reading of the story. The latter describes a conscious strategy of the story that derives from its creation. It is the latter instance that must be capable of identification in the language of the story. The former derives from a personal engagement with the story, from which perspective one's field of vision is increased. At one end of the range lies a wooden repeating of the story; at the other end, the whimsy of allegory.

As a caution, I note there are few stories of Jesus that unquestionably use referential language, i.e., places where the narrative unambiguously uses metaphorical or nonliteral language. For example, in the stories of the Leaven, the Prodigal Son/Elder Brother, the Unjust Judge, and the Samaritan, language is used that deliberately expands or resonates beyond itself: leaven is "hidden"; the son wasted his livelihood in "loose living," was "dead" and is "alive"; the judge was worried about a "black eye"; a man "fell" among thieves. Undoubtedly there are more that will become evident in closer readings of the narratives. Such uses of metaphor may simply enhance the language of the stories, a use noted by Aristotle (*Poet.* 21.7–22.17).

A symbol actually exists as the psychological response of people in a particular community to some concrete entity. On the one hand, community participants recognize the entity for what it is perceptively, but they also clearly see its broader "significance." For example, a black cat is one thing, but a black cat crossing your path is something considerably more. The cat is still a cat, but in a particular context its "significance" resonates beyond itself. On the other hand, outsiders who do not participate in the fictions of the community miss any broader significance. For them it does not exist. Hence symbols are culturally bound concepts and are neither universal nor timeless.

The internal semantic markers of symbol in the story may be extremely subtle, if evident at all. One would almost be forced to validate the symbolical quality from outside the story, and then argue the story's compatibility with the reconstructed symbol. In any case, objective control may be lost.

A deliberate twist that can be validated as a spin on a common or expected theme could function as a "trigger" to reference something outside the story. But if it is *like* that, it also *is* that. Hence one should describe the "new world" in terms of the language of the story itself. The situation and the language of the story cannot be dispensed with in favor of an interpretation that talks about other completely different things, such as finding a "value" in the first-century story that is described in terms of twentieth-century language and situations. At no time should the center of focus shift to a supposed referential world, as is the case in the early Christian interpretations of the stories of Jesus. The center of focus *must remain* Jesus' fictive vision of reality. Careful analysis of the stories utilizing the insights of literary and historical criticism and carefully reconstructing the social world of early Christianity will shed light on how the stories may have resonated in the context of first-century Palestinian Judaism.

One is not required to develop interpretations, i.e., assigning a particular contemporary significance, or meaning, to the story. This is just another way of closing off, or controlling, the story. Leaving the story open-ended without an "authoritative" interpretation affords the modern audience/reader the same advantage (or disadvantage) as the first audience to interact with the story. If the story was originally open-ended in order to involve the audience, as appears to be the case, then providing an authoritative interpretation will subvert the strategy of the story.

Another way of treating the story is (a) to reconstruct the narrative world in the context of which Jesus' stories were told—i.e., to reconstruct Israel's own fictive view of reality and then (b) to let the story speak for itself in its own way, as it resonates in the context of that reconstructed first-century Jewish view of reality. It can then be observed how a given story "resonates" (i.e., how it subverts, affirms, or challenges) in the context of a particular reconstruction of reality. The story—as indeed all language—can "resonate" in such a way that one's field of vision is raised beyond the narrow specific circumstances of the story; that is, the story can lift an auditor's horizon of understanding. But that is not the same thing as the narrative strategically referencing something different outside itself; nor is it the same thing as extrapolating a particular meaning from the story, as if such a particularized extrapolation author-itatively exhausted the story. It is in the context of, through, and by means of the story that one's field of vision is raised. Frank Kermode said that "fictions are for finding things out";[70] that is to say, makers and readers of fiction make discoveries about life. And it is likewise true that the fictions of Jesus sometimes raise the readers' field of vision and some readers thereby glimpse a broader range of life's possibilities and potential.

Is there any valid reason why the story, after historical analysis and reconstruction of the earliest form, could not be played off against any view of reality deriving from any culture or any period? Hence rather

---

[70]Kermode, *The Sense of an Ending*, 39.

than an authoritative "interpretation"—whether it be metaphorical, symbolical, allegorical, or moral—the proper conclusion after analysis of the strategies of both views of reality (i.e., the view reflected in the story and that view contrasted with it) simply is "what do you think?"—thus inviting participation in the story (cf. Matt 18:12 and Luke 10:36). Or perhaps, as was also attributed to Jesus: "Whoever has ears, let that one hear." This approach assumes that each story by the way it is fabricated defines the number and breadth of potential horizons that may reasonably be evoked (I am indebted to Amos Wilder for this insight). Any attempt to *force* meaning out of the story, whether figurative, moral, or referential, in its own way consumes and dispenses with the story. Any one "point" derived from the story simply cannot exhaust the story, as Luke's reading of the story of the Samaritan graphically attests (see below ch. 6).

An emphasis on a "referential world" is simply another way of taking a reader out of the story. And it is the story, i.e., Jesus' own fictive vision, that should remain the focus of study—no matter how banal the narrative may seem without resorting to metaphor, symbol, or allegory. In fact, all we have are the stories; we do not know how Jesus used them individually and collectively. The issue is, do we have to assume that the stories deliberately reference something mysterious and inexpressible beyond themselves in order to experience the shock of Jesus' creative vision? Mark thought so: "To you has been given the μυστήριον of the kingdom of God, but for those outside everything is in parables" (Mark 4:11).

Jesus may have been an image-maker who always deliberately referenced something outside the story, as parables in the Hebrew and Jewish tradition did,[71] but it is equally plausible that he may not have used the stories that way. He most certainly "made up"—created—fabricated—stories. But that they were designed to be metaphorical, and deliberately reference something outside themselves, is not to be assumed. Such a quality must be shown as a separate step in the study of the story. And it must be specified how the language of the narrative itself sanctions the particular direction the reader is led "away-from-here." To assume that the stories were designed to take the reader away to a specific point of reference outside the story, treats the story as an allegory and ultimately reduces the narrative to a discardable husk.

It is possible to read these stories as brief poetic fictions that subverted, affirmed, and confronted the broader fictional views of reality on the basis of which other first-century human beings conducted their lives. And in that sense they are simply fictional descriptions of Jesus' poetic vision! They mean what they say—and maybe more. τί ὑμῖν δοκεῖ?

---

[71] See Scott, *Hear Then the Parable*, 7–19, and Young, *Jewish Parables*, 55–128.

PART II
PARABLES AS FICTIONS

3 🌿

Realism, and Literary Criticism of the Parables

REALISM AND THE STORIES OF JESUS

IT IS A CONSENSUS AMONG NEW TESTAMENT SCHOLARS THAT THE STORIES of Jesus realistically imitate life in first-century Palestine,[1] although some recent studies seem unaware of this feature and its significance for reading the stories.[2] Perrin's brief statement perhaps best describes the realism of the stories.

> The parables of Jesus are pictures and stories drawn from *petit-bourgeois* and peasant life in Palestine under the early Roman emperors. They are not myths employing archetypal symbols; they are not fables exploiting the universal features of the human condition; they are not folk tales appealing to the collective experience of people as a people. They are vivid and concrete pictures and stories drawn from the details of a particular situation at a given time and in a given place. They are occasional, transitory, essentially fleeting snapshots of life.[3]

Realism generally operates for Hollywood at the level of believability. Each film is made in the context of a given "world" (i.e., particular

---

[1] Dodd, *Authority*, 147–52; Jeremias, *Parables*, 11–12; Linnemann, *Parables*, 3–4; Wilder, *Rhetoric*, 81; Via, *Parables*, 98–99; Jones, *Art and Truth*, 112–14; Breech, "Parables of Jesus," 31; Smith, *Parables*, 61–62; Stein, *Introduction*, 36–41.

[2] Carlston, *Triple Tradition*; Crossan, *Cliffs of Fall*; id., *In Parables*; Boucher, *Mysterious Parable*; Scott, *Symbol-Maker* and id., *Hear Then the Parable*; Patte, *Semiology*. Tolbert (*Perspectives*, 89–91) specifically challenges the realism of the stories. She points to four things that argue against their realism: the fact that realism in Western literature does not begin until the nineteenth century, the presence of exaggeration and extraordinary features in the stories, the typicality of characters (i.e., not three dimensional), and the indefinite tone of the stories. These observations suggest to her that the stories are a blend of illustrative/symbolic and representational features. On the issue of realism in Western literature, however, see Auerbach, *Mimesis*.

[3] Perrin, *Language of the Kingdom*, 104.

set of cultural circumstances). The success of the film depends on whether or not the audience finds the film believable in terms of the rules of the film "world." When the viewer engages the world of the film, he or she consents to evaluate the story by the contextual rules of that world and poses the question: is it "real" in terms of *that* world depicted in the film? The same is true of literary fictions; otherwise no one would purchase science fiction novels. Hence a film or a novel could be strange or bizarre by the standards of commonly experienced reality, but the viewer, or reader, can engage it as "real," if the rules of its contextual world can be inferred. In these instances realism is evaluated on the basis of the rules of that fictional world rather than the viewer/reader's own personal world view. The continued use of early Christian gospel litera-ture is a good example of the modern reader's ability to adapt to strange and foreign worlds. The world view of the gospels incorporates demons, evil spirits, exorcisms, magic, miracles, etc. But many (most?) modern readers simply do not apply the "rules" of their own commonly experi-enced reality when reading these texts; rather they apply the "rules" of the world projected by the gospel writers.

Except for three stories having a mythical character (see Appendix E below), the stories of Jesus have none of the bizarreness that can be found throughout the canonical gospels, Acts, and other early Christian literature. Rather the stories Jesus told seem to operate at the level of commonly experienced reality—much like a modern world view. The realism of these stories derives not from their being objective and detailed historical descriptions of life in first-century Palestinian villages, but rather from their representation of action, both human and the natural processes, in that context; in other words, realism derives from their "plots," μῦθοι. Hence the focus is not on *mimesis* in a narrator's detailed description, but rather on *mimesis* in the action, i.e., the plot. Character description and setting, while minimal, support the realism of the action. Granted, the plots are minimal—almost a plot summary. Nevertheless, there remains in each story a first-century social consciousness, even in the nature stories, that resists further reduction—if one wishes to retain their first-century quality.

ERICH AUERBACH AND REALISM IN LITERATURE

The portrayal of realism in literature has been extensively studied by Auerbach.[4] He analyzes selected texts in the history of Western literature for their features of realism. At no point in the book, however, does he summarize the essential character of realism. He does, however,

---

[4]*Mimesis.*

cite instances—and even offers a definition of sorts[5]—of the charac-teristics of realism. The following features constitute the nature of realism according to Auerbach.

> In our study we are looking for representations of everyday life in which that life is treated seriously, in terms of its human and social problems or even of its tragic complications.[6]

> [realism is] a serious representation of contemporary everyday social reality against the background of a constant historical movement.[7]

In various ways Auerbach elaborates these basic definitive state-ments regarding realism throughout the book. Literary representation of life is "realistic" when:

1. It is fraught with background; in other words, as much of the narrative as possible is left in the background (pp. 11, 12, 17, 23, 26, 101).

2. It is a "serious" action, i.e., involving everyday customs and institutions of life taking place among common people rather than the elite (in classical literature common folk appear only in comedy) (pp. 31, 42, 246, 248, 318, 327–28, 331, 342, 345, 365, 382, 384, 399, 431, 457, 518).

3. It is imitative: characters are built up before the reader out of their own premises; characters feel, act, and speak in their own natural language consonant with their nature (pp. 39, 56).

4. It uses direct discourse (pp. 45–46, 88–89).

5. It is a description of random, everyday occurrences, and hence reflects the random contingencies of life (pp. 44, 294, 302, 309, 310, 413, 432).

6. It possesses a history; its changing and developing are the very essence of reality (p. 191).

7. It is not stylized but shows life in its entirety, complete with blemishes and life's baser aspects (pp. 47, 321, 404, 411, 421, 443, 518).

---

[5] See the review of Auerbach by Fergusson, "Two Perspectives," 123, but compare Sharrock, "Review of Auerbach," 61: Auerbach "is concerned only with that realism which 'combines the everyday with tragic seriousness' (p. 282)"; Wellek, "Auerbach's Special Realism," 303: "Realism must not be comic, didactic, ethical, or idyllic. It must not even only be tragic; it must be tragic with a peculiar concreteness and historical peculiarity. It reflects an existence that combines two elements: tragic depth and historical concreteness"; Muscatine, "Review of Auerbach," 449: "Reality means 'objective life,' the random everyday event. It is related to practical purposes and is sensory in quality. Its essential characteristic is change and development. . . . To be realistic in Auerbach's terms a work must embody a sense of history; it must deal with social forces underlying the facts and conditions presented, rather than static ethical concepts. It must be able to deal with the common people and with everyday life and to deal with them seriously. It must be problematic or tragic but not comic." Naumann, "Review of Auerbach," 211: Realism combines everyday occurrences and tragic seriousness.

[6] *Mimesis*, 342.

[7] *Mimesis*, 518.

8. Like life, it has an abundance of actions; many things are happening (p. 189).

9. It describes life as complete in itself; the presentation of life is not made a representation or figure for another unearthly reality (p. 310).

10. It gives the appearance of spontaneity; the representation does not appear to be pre-thought, planned, and schematized (pp. 423, 428).

11. It reflects life in historical perspective. Hence events and characters are not cast anachronistically (pp. 321–22).

12. It reflects a multiplicity of viewpoints; the representation does not show life, characters, etc. from the perspective of unipersonal subjectivism that allows only one view of reality (p. 536).

The stories attributed to Jesus generally[8] reflect Auerbach's features of realism and represent the serious everyday actions of common people. For example, they describe a farmer and his day-laborers arguing over wages, a pearl merchant searching for fine pearls, a woman looking for a lost coin, a man planning to build a tower, a father with an irresponsible son. Surprisingly only four stories mention powerful national figures: a king (Matt 18:23; 22:2; Luke 14:31, but cf. *Gos. Thom.* log. 64 "a man"), a nobleman going to receive a kingdom (Luke 19:12, but cf. Matt 25:14–15 "a man"). In every other story the "hero" is one of the common people.

Personae in the stories speak, think, and act "in character"; for example, compare the complaint made by day laborers that people who worked less than they were paid the same wage (Matt 20:1–15). Or consider the woman so happy about finding a valuable lost coin she cannot help telling her neighbors (Luke 15:8–9), or the rehearsed confession of the returning "ne'er-do-well" son, who wanted to make his best case with his father (Luke 15:11–32). Further, compare the practically-minded dishonest steward who finds still another way to defraud his employer (Luke 16:1–7).

Care should be taken in evaluating the realism of the stories, however, since realism does not require that the actions of characters be predictable. Indeed, reality is usually quite unpredictable. Thus it is within the givens of reality that a Samaritan can act humanely, that a servant totally forgiven of an unrepayable debt refuses to forgive another of a small obligation, and that a thoroughly honest judge can suddenly decide a case for his own convenience.

One striking feature of the stories is their use of soliloquy and direct speech rather than third-person narration.[9] Characters speak in their

---

[8]The mythical stories in the parables corpus do have unrealistic features, and the realism of certain other stories is questionable; for example, the shepherd who leaves his 99 sheep in the wilderness, (the Lost Sheep), or the father who sends his son to collect rent from tenants after the tenants had previously slain the father's servant (a Vineyard).

[9]This is true of the stories reflecting societal relationships. See Linnemann, *Parables*, 15.

own voices rather than having their dialogues described by the narrator. Furthermore, the stories present random occurrences reflecting the contingencies of life, such as losing a sheep, building a watch tower, purchasing a field, sowing a field, pleading a court case, building larger storage facilities, a mugging on a lonely road, and planning a murder.

In their economy of description and their brevity almost by necessity the stories are "fraught with background."[10] Like life itself, the stories of Jesus reveal only fragments of the thoughts, motives, history, and personalities of their characters.[11] For example, in the story of the Samaritan the reader learns nothing personal about the "man going down from Jerusalem to Jericho" (Luke 10:30) and only the barest details about the other three main characters. Only their role in society and, by implication, nationality are given, but personal motivation for their actions is lacking.

Some of the stories do highlight conflicting perspectives on life. In the story of the Wage of the Workmen the employer and the complaining workers disagree on wage policies. Similarly the Pharisee and toll collector reflect distinct views on life.

These stories imitate life in a first-century Palestinian environment[12] and hence do portray life in "historical perspective." Seemingly inappropriate features lend a spontaneity to some of the stories, such as a toll collector praying in the temple, the unexpected discovery of a hidden treasure, the sudden death of a wealthy investor on the eve of an important business venture, a woman carrying home an empty jar she mistakenly thought was full.

It must be admitted, however, that the stories do not reflect "an abundance of actions," number 8 of Auerbach's features of realism listed above. The stories are highly schematic. In their brevity they could hardly be otherwise.[13] And while they do not graphically portray the baser side of life, they do reflect some of its blemishes (viz., the corruption of an honest judge, a killer, a dishonest steward). There is usually a single uniform action,[14] and everything unnecessary to that action is eliminated.[15] This is likely due to the brevity of the stories; they are scarcely more than plot summaries.

Finally, whether or not the stories make human life a figure for some more important reality depends on how one reads them. If they were created as allegories, or if they deliberately reference an unearthly reality, then according to Auerbach, they forfeit their realism.

---

[10] See, e.g., Auerbach's comparative analysis of the stories in Homer and Genesis: *Mimesis*, 3–23, esp. p. 11.

[11] See Linnemann, *Parables*, 13–15.

[12] See the discussion above, pp. 39–40.

[13] See Linnemann, *Parables*, 13–15.

[14] The story of the Prodigal Son/Elder Brother is one exception.

[15] See Linnemann, *Parables*, 12, 14–15.

K. E. BAILEY AND MODERN MIDDLE EAST CULTURE

One innovative approach to parables, beginning precisely with a recognition of their realism,[16] was made by Kenneth Bailey,[17] who correctly argues that the parables should be studied against the cultural background of first-century Palestine. He contends that "internal aspects of relationship" and "attitude" reflected in the parables have not been clearly recognized. These features are best clarified by a knowledge of Palestinian culture.[18] Of course that culture, the peasant culture of first-century Palestine, has long since disappeared as a living culture, and scholars have been forced to reconstruct it primarily from first-century literary and archaeological sources that derive from the same general geographical region. Bailey, however, proposes to expand the data base for reconstructing the cultural milieu of first-century Palestine "by discussing the cultural aspects of the parables with [contemporary] Middle Easterners."[19]

While this approach is innovative, it is not novel. Others have also sought an understanding of the first-century stories on the basis of modern Middle Eastern customs.[20] But Bailey is the first to make the culture of contemporary Middle Eastern peasants into a major method-ological principle for recovering the original setting (and intention) to the parables of Jesus.[21] He, in effect, substitutes contemporary Middle Eastern peasant culture where ancient literary and archaeological evidence is lacking. Of course he realizes that one cannot simply make a blanket substitution since "the lingering question remains . . . How can we be sure the Middle Eastern peasant has not changed his culture and attitudes across the intervening centuries?"[22] It is severely damaging to Bailey's approach that he cannot answer this question. His concession in the face of his inability to answer that question is that "insight gained from the contemporary peasant must *always* be rejected if we have a more ancient or in any way more authentic alternative."[23] He feels that his approach is justifiable, since anyone who interprets the parables makes "a series of culturally influenced judgments," and that the Middle Eastern

---

[16] Bailey, *Poet and Peasant* 1.15: "The culture reflected in the Dominical parables is that of first-century Palestine."

[17] Bailey, *Poet and Peasant*, 1.27–43.

[18] Bailey, *Poet and Peasant*, 1.15, 27.

[19] Bailey, *Poet and Peasant*, 1.27.

[20] For example, Jeremias, *Parables*, 133: "Among the Bedouin the size of a flock varies from 20 to 200 head . . . "; "a Palestinian shepherd counts his flock before putting them in the fold at night"; "experts on Palestinian life all agree that a shepherd cannot possibly leave his flock to itself. . . . "

[21] Bailey, *Poet and Peasant*, 1.27–37.

[22] Bailey, *Poet and Peasant*, 1.37.

[23] Bailey, *Poet and Peasant*, 1.37.

culture is closer to the culture of first-century Palestine[24] than is modern culture. Therefore, since all interpreters make culturally influenced judgments anyway, for Bailey the only issue is "*whose* culture shall we allow to inform the text for us?"[25]

I have several reservations about his methodology.[26] One issue Bailey raises himself: We simply cannot be sure that contemporary Middle Eastern culture is identical to first-century Palestinian life. And even if we find cultural practices and other vestigial cultural remains whose survival through the centuries can be validated beyond question, that simply does not ensure that modern Middle Eastern cultural practices are survivors from the first century. We can only be certain that a cultural feature survives from antiquity when it can be validated by first-century literary and archaeological evidence. If it cannot be so validated, any interpretation based on it may equally well be a modernizing of the text.

The areas that Bailey is studying are geographically distant from Palestine.[27] This raises the question, to what extent may one generalize that cultural features in one area can be identified with those in another Middle Eastern area? To be more specific: to what extent may modern Syrian or Egyptian cultural practices be transplanted to ancient Palestine without a separate argument that there was a uniformity between the ancient Palestinian culture and the geographically distant cultural practices?

Further Bailey does not address the extent to which Islamization of Middle Eastern culture since the eighth century CE has affected the modern Middle Eastern peasant culture. While it may be true, for example, that technology has not changed much in most isolated Upper Egyptian villages since the time of the pharaohs, it seems highly uncritical to think that the peasant culture of the Middle East would not have been influenced to some degree by Islam.

Bailey's method of working in the village areas is also a problem. In general he engages select individuals in discussion on the parables. His primary group of discussion partners consists of twenty-one named resource persons from Egypt (9); the Sudan (2); Lebanon, Syria, Palestine (8); Iraq (1); Iran (1). Most of these persons are Christian Arab pastors "who themselves have wrestled with the text."[28]

---

[24] Bailey, *Poet and Peasant*, 1.30–32.

[25] Bailey, *Poet and Peasant*, 1.37.

[26] See Crossan, "Review of Bailey," and Johnson, "Review of Bailey."

[27] Bailey, *Poet and Peasant*, 1.31. "In the south of Egypt, in the mountains of Lebanon and in the isolated communities of upper Syria and Iraq. . . . "

[28] Bailey, *Poet and Peasant*, 1.36. He claims 25 but identifies only 21 by name. All but two of the resource persons are Christian pastors. See Bailey's appendix B, pp. 213–16.

His sample group of discussion partners are all people whom he has known for five years in order "to guard against receiving the stylized answers of the Easterner responding to foreigners."[29] But what is more problematical is that virtually all of the principal discussion partners are Christian clergymen. He argues that this is a plus since "the resource person with whom [he talks] must know enough about the biblical witness to understand the question put to him."[30] This feature is actually a minus, however, since he has ensured that the discussion group will have been trained in Christian biblical interpretation, informed in Christian values, and would therefore have heard the stories from a Christian perspective. First-century Palestinian Jewish peasants, on the other hand, would have heard the stories from the perspective of their Jewish culture. Bailey would have been better served by developing a broader base and by consciously omitting Christian discussion partners. In short, I seriously question that Bailey's methodology has put us in touch with first-century Palestinian culture through his study of modern Middle Eastern culture. He may enhance the realism of the stories, but it is questionable that the enhancement improves our grasp of how the stories were heard and appreciated in the first century.

ARISTOTLE'S *POETICA*

Generally, the realism of the stories is attributed to Jesus' keen observation of human life: "drawn from the daily life of Palestine" (Jeremias); "drawn from the details of a particular situation at a particular time" (Perrin); "drawn from nature or common life" (Dodd). And recent study has added the following feature: "human life . . . shaped by the creative imagination" (Jones); "freely composed stories" (Linnemann); "a freely invented story" (Via). These are not traditional universal stories that solicit readership on the basis of common human wisdom; they are deliberate and novel creations, and solicit their readership because of their novelistic character, i.e., their plots that treat the actions of typical first-century commoners.

Via calls attention to the usual distinction between the similitude and the parable: "The similitude gets its force from its appeal to what is universally acknowledged, while the parable achieves its power by making the particular credible and probable."[31] While it is a proper distinction to make, Via nevertheless obscures some of the appeal of the story to common human experience. The story shows first-century Palestinian folk in ordinary, everyday activities. In short, in its original

---

[29] Bailey, *Poet and Peasant*, 1.35.
[30] Bailey, *Poet and Peasant*, 1.35.
[31] Via, *Parables*, 11–12.

performance the story appeals to common human (i.e., first-century Palestinian) interests. While everyone who heard the story initially in its oral period, may not have experienced that particular circumstance unfolded in the action, all would have been able to conceive that action as being possible, or even probable, in the world that he or she knew. To that extent, the story *does* appeal to "common human experience." In fact, the appeal of the societal stories has persisted in spite of shifts in culture and translation into different languages.

These three elements of the stories, their *mimesis* of first-century Palestinian life, their character as created fictions, and their appeal to ordinary human experience, suggest that Aristotle's *Poetica* might help to clarify aspects of their character. Aristotle's critical analysis of poetry (i.e., dramatic tragedy) provides a cogent method for analyzing a brief narrative that has been deliberately created as a work of art as opposed to traditional folk narrative that is a community product. That Aristotle was concerned with the character of deliberate literary creations shows that such sensitivities are not only a modern concern but an ancient one as well.

Aristotle was a fourth-century BCE Greek philosopher whose treatise on poetics (*Poetica*) is the first extensive systematic treatment of the subject that has been preserved.[32] He divides poetry into three types: tragedy, comedy, and epic; and he focuses his discussion on tragedy, which he considers the highest form of poetry. His analysis of the nature and forms of poetry, therefore, derives from an analysis of Greek tragedy. Many of his literary critical insights, his methodology, and his terminology, however, provide convenient tools for analyzing the stories of Jesus. For example, Aristotle described the "poet" as a maker, ποιεῖν, or fashioner, of plots, μῦθοι; that is to say, one who invents and represents human beings doing or experiencing something (*Poet.* 9.9; 2.1). He contrasts the work of poet and historian: the historian narrates things that actually happened, while the poet describes what a certain kind of person may do or say. The historian, then, treats particular facts, while

---

[32] Plato was Aristotle's teacher, and one also finds in Plato's writings a concern for literary criticism, as well. In the *Ion* and *Phaedrus* he discusses the work of the poet favorably. Yet in the *Respublica*, when he develops his theory of the ideal state, he banishes the poet whose writings, he argued, undermined community morality and hence subverted the state. The first extant *systematic* treatise on literary criticism in Western literature must nevertheless be attributed to Aristotle. The *Poetica* was lost from the time of Aristotle until the fourth century CE: Lucas, *Aristotle: Poetics*, xxii–xxiii; at least there are no extant manuscripts or direct quotes from the *Poetica* prior to the fourth century, though the works of Aristotle were published in Rome in the first century BCE, and it has been noted that Horace's *Ars Poetica* is related to the *Poetica*: Lane Cooper, *Poetics of Aristotle*, 87–88. Even before Aristotle, however, Gorgias was also concerned with such poetic techniques as alliteration, assonance, and rhyme: Diod. Sic. *Historical Library*, 12.53 (see Roberts *Greek Rhetoric*, 36–40; and Atkins, *Literary Criticism*, 1.19–21).

the poet deals in "general truths"; and it is the poet, according to
Aristotle, that has the higher calling (*Poet.* 9.1–3).

The stories attributed to Jesus are precisely that—brief fictions (i.e.,
"made up" [ποιεῖν] imaginary happenings). They describe what a certain
kind of person might do under certain circumstances. I do not mean to
imply that Jesus' stories are dramatic tragedies, but only to suggest that
Aristotle's literary criticism of tragedy does provide a productive approach to the "stories" of Jesus.

The earliest extant systematic literary criticism of poetry and poetic
language is Aristotle's *Poetica* in which he analyzes Greek tragedy.[33] As
a basis for the discussion of the stories of Jesus, I would like to describe
briefly those parts of Aristotle that provide a clarifying literary context
for a discussion of the stories of Jesus. According to Aristotle, the "poet"
is an inventor, ποιητής, of plots (9.9), or one might say a "maker" of
stories. Poetry, that which the poet creates, constitutes the re-presentation
or μίμησις of an action that is heroic (i.e., that has a "hero" or a main
persona), complete, and of a certain "magnitude." Poetry (i.e., tragedy)
represents human action,[34] and by playing on pity and fear (and similar
such emotions) it seeks to effect the release of these emotions (6.2–4).[35]
Every tragedy has six parts: plot, character, diction, thought, spectacle,
and song (6.9–13). Two of these parts have little significance for a study
of Jesus' stories: spectacle (= stage effects, 6.28) and song (12.1–10), but
according to Aristotle the tragedy should have the same effect even if
read (14.2).

The most important element in "poetry" is the plot (μῦθος, 6.13), which
is the re-presentation (μίμησις) of the action in the arrangement of the
incidents (6.7–8; 9.12). Indeed, for Aristotle poetry is the re-presenting of
human activity that is whole or complete; i.e., in an action consisting of
beginning, middle, and end (7.1–7). The action, or plot, should approxi-
mate reality, since it is represents people experiencing something. If the
plot lacks concord with reality, it could spoil the effect (17.1).

Of course the poet is not a historian, and it is not expected that the
poet should tell "what actually happened," but the poet should describe
what could and would happen either probably or inevitably (9.1–3); so,
a poet represents life as an artist does. Poets represent "things as they
were or are; or things as they are said and seem to be; or things as they
should be" (25.1–3). Hence Aristotle regards the poets' invention as more
important than the historians' description, for the poet deals in a

---

[33] For the terms used in this discussion I have used the translation of Fyfe,
Aristotle, 4–118. For a brief survey of Aristotle's literary criticism of poetry see Atkins,
Literary Criticism, 1.71–119.

[34] On representation of human actions, see also 1.2; 7.1–3; 8.4.

[35] Aristotle discusses the "effects" (like pity, fear, anger, etc.) of language in his
Rhetorica (19.2–4).

"general truth," the sort of thing one may do or say either probably or inevitably (9.4). This means that the historian can only tell the reader what happened, but the poet can create a situation in which one can "discover" things about oneself and others. The historian deals in the particular and specific of what has already happened, and the poet trades in possibility, for the poet represents what could or would happen under certain circumstances (9.3).

In order of importance, the first principle of writing tragedy is the development of plot; character is the second; and thought is the third (6.19–23). The character of an individual in the poem is revealed in the choices that are made, for character is revealed in what is chosen, or avoided (6.24). Hence people must be shown in the exercise of will choosing between one line of conduct and another. The "hero's" character should be good and appropriate to the action, like persons in the traditional stories from which the tragedies are drawn. The representation of character should be consistent (15.1–10). The main character presented as the hero should not be particularly virtuous or just; nor should the hero fall into misfortune through villainous acts or deeds of his own doing. The hero should be of high station and good fortune (13.5–6).

The change that takes place for this individual should not be from bad to good fortune, but rather from good fortune to bad. Further, the fall should be due to some flaw in the hero's character. Aristotle is not explicit as to the nature of the flaw, but it is clear that the individual should be portrayed as undeserving of such a tragic fate (13.1–13). In short, the story represents someone slightly "better" than the average person (15.11). One should not show worthy persons passing from good to bad fortune, nor describe wicked persons passing from bad to good fortune, nor thoroughly bad characters from good to bad fortunes (13,2–4).

By "thought" Aristotle means that the individual has the ability to say in the action what is possible and appropriate (6.22). "Thought" concerns the effects of language (see *Rhet.* 19.1–6). "Diction" involves the various modes of speech appropriate to the rhetorician (*Poet.* 19.7). It is to be clear but not commonplace (22.1). His discussion of poetic language is detailed (19.7–22.20), and not all of the discussion has significance for the stories of Jesus. His discussion of metaphor is relevant, however. Poetry (tragedy) contains metaphor (21.8–15), but if a poem is made up entirely of metaphorical language it becomes a "riddle," which he defines as describing a fact by an impossible combination of words (22.4). The use of metaphor, however, gives great distinction to diction (22.16–17).

When Aristotle refers to the "magnitude" of the plot, he means that the plot should be easily remembered (7.10). Beauty consists in magnitude and ordered arrangement; if a plot is too brief its individual elements cannot be distinguished (7.8–10). Aristotle prefers the plot to be longer, but one must be able to grasp its entirety at once (7.11–12). Further, it should be of a magnitude that admits a change from bad fortune to good or good fortune to bad in a sequence of events whose order is either inevitable or probable (7.12).

The purpose of the poetics is to provide for release of emotions through fear and pity (6.2; 13.2). Hence auditor response is an important goal of the poem. Such emotions are produced when incidents are unexpected and when one incident is the result of the other, as for example in providential occurrences (9.11–13). Two of the most important elements in the production of fear and pity are reversals and discoveries (6.17–18). A reversal is a change in a situation from good to bad fortune, or bad to good (11.1–3), and a discovery is a change from ignorance to knowledge as to some aspect of plot by one of the actors (11.4–7; 16.1–12). A third element of change is calamity, a destructive or painful occurrence, such as death on the stage, and acute suffering (11.9–10).

There are two types of plots, simple and complex (10.1–4). A simple plot involves single and continuous action with beginning, middle, and end. A complex plot utilizes reversal and/or discovery to bring about change (11.1–7). The best tragedy involves a complex plot (13.2) containing incidents arousing fear and pity.

Every tragedy has a complication (i.e., a "tying") and a denouement (i.e., a "loosing") (18.1–2). The complication incorporates all the action from the beginning to just before the denouement, i.e., the change. The denouement incorporates the change to the end of the action. The denouement should be the natural result of the plot and not be produced mechanically (16.1–12). The "god in the chair"[36] should explain only what is outside the action, i.e., what happened earlier or what will happen later and therefore needs to be foretold (15.10–11). In other words, the resolution of the plot should be the natural unfolding of the action and not superimposed on it by extraneous features outside the story.

LITERARY CRITICISM OF THE PARABLES

Early literary critics of the sayings tradition did not extend their analysis to the "plot" parables. For example, Burney, who analyzed the sayings tradition in the canonical gospels from the perspective of Hebrew poetry, did not treat even one of the "plot" parables.[37] Cadoux did recognize the "artistic" character of the parables[38] and described them as "unquestionably a form of art, though not one of its highest forms."[39] Nevertheless, he asserted that "no one in the art of parables stands near

---

[36] See the note by Fyfe, *Aristotle*, 56.
[37] Burney, *Poetry*.
[38] Cadoux, *Parables*, cf. 11–13, 38, 60, 72, 127.
[39] Cadoux, *Parables*, 11.

Jesus."[40] It does not appear, however, that Cadoux understood "art" as a creation to be appreciated only for itself. Rather, the parables "are the work of an artist devoting himself to the answer of demands more humanly imperative than the call of beauty."[41] Since, according to Cadoux, the parable becomes a weapon in Jesus' arsenal for debate, it is "not shaped like a sonnet in undisturbed concentration but improvised in conflict to meet an unpremeditated situation."[42] It does, however, like other art, reflect "the imagination and sensitiveness of the poet. . . . "[43] Cadoux did not systematically analyze the artistic quality of the stories, but instead focused on their use in controversy and hence on "the penetration, rapidity, and resourcefulness of the protagonist. . . . "[44]

While Cadoux did not produce a comprehensive literary criticism of the stories, he did establish one "criterion" for determining that form of the story in the synoptics that is more likely original with Jesus. The criterion is literary in nature:

> Because the parable is a work of art, we have a criterion of authenticity when we find two different versions of the same parable. The story that is better as a story, more convincing [as a story] and self-consistent, will probably be nearer to what Jesus actually said.[45]

Amos Wilder is another of the few scholars who have described the parables as an "art form."[46]

> A work of art has a life of its own apart from its reporters. It remains itself and goes on testifying or celebrating, independently of its interpreters and their various versions and deformations of its communication. So it is with a parable or other literary form in Scripture. Its *telling* is ever and again to be heard naively and afresh.[47]

Hence according to Wilder, to understand the parable one must seek "an understanding of its language structure, its poetic," and also analyze "how this language dynamically evokes response, its semantic."[48]

According to Wilder, some parables serve as example stories that function didactically and polemically, and hence are not "symbolic," while others are extended images that reveal.

---

[40]Cadoux, *Parables*, 11.

[41]Cadoux, *Parables*, 12.

[42]Cadoux, *Parables*, 13.

[43]Cadoux, *Parables*, 13.

[44]Cadoux, *Parables*, 13. Note that the topics under which he discusses the parables reflect this conflict setting.

[45]Cadoux, *Parables*, 60. See his discussion in the chapter entitled: "Form as a Criterion of Authenticity," 60–79.

[46]See his discussion in *Rhetoric*: "The Parable," 71–88 = "Scenarios of Life and Destiny," 71–87 in Wilder, *War of Myths*.

[47]Wilder, *War of Myths*, 89–90.

[48]Wilder, *War of Myths*, 90.

This is particularly clear in the so-called parables of the Kingdom like those of the sower and the mustard seed, in which Jesus mediates his own vision and his own faith.[49]

The parables are striking in their realism, naturalness, and secularity. While they may have some unusual features, such as hyperbole,[50] they do have according to Wilder "an immediate realistic authenticity."[51] While Wilder thinks that one is able to identify the authenticity of parables by the tests of verisimilitude, force, relevance, and dependence on other parables, the "acid tests" for him are focus and depth; "there is no blurring in them or incongruity. Moreover they are not discursive."[52] Further, "as in folktales and children's stories, we find brevity, unity of perspective, limitation of the number of figures or agents, use of direct discourse, serial development, the 'rule of three,' repetition of elements and formulas, binary opposition, and resolution often by reversal."[53]

Wilder associates the parable and the poem as follows:

The characteristic design, the tight form, of these utterances helped to guarantee them against change and supplementation. A coherent image-story is resistant to change. One can press putty into different shapes but not a crystal. A crystal can pick up foreign matter, but we can recognize the difference. Here especially if a thing is well said, there is only one way to say it, as in a poem.[54]

As with a poem, the parable form as a distinctive kind of voice, and by its architecture, reveals rather than persuades. So far as it persuades, it is not by an induction, but by a visionary recognition.[55]

As Frost said of the genre of the poem, "Read it a hundred times: it will forever keep its freshness as a petal keeps its fragrance. It can never lose its sense of a meaning that once unfolded by surprise as it went." So the parable should be allowed to evoke its own horizon and its meaning in that horizon, independently of its interpreters. It should be allowed to awaken its own corresponding registers in our hearing, and even to create these. In this untrammeled exposure to it, we are captured by the primordial wonder that existence emerges out of, and prevails over, nothingness.[56]

Wilder also graphically notes the relationship between the parable and the imagination of Jesus:

---

[49] Wilder, *Rhetoric*, 72.
[50] Wilder, *Rhetoric*, 77.
[51] Wilder, *Rhetoric*, 73–74.
[52] Wilder, *Rhetoric*, 83.
[53] Wilder, *War of Myths*, 92.
[54] Wilder, *War of Myths*, 82.
[55] Wilder, *War of Myths*, 96.
[56] Wilder, *War of Myths*, 99.

Here lies the power and fatefulness of art. Jesus' speech had the character not of instruction and ideas but of compelling imagination, of spell, of mythical shock and transformation.[57]

His evaluation of poetry is much the same and hence it is surprising that Wilder did not make a formal analysis of parables as poetry:

When we thus admit the wide variety of poetic styles our difficulties in defining poetry will be all the greater, and our difficulties in distinguishing it from prose. The one test that we can rely on will be that of rhythm and the associated state of excitement or enhancement of consciousness, which often comes to expression as vision or seeing. As Goethe said, poetry is *Schauen*.[58]

Another scholar, who actually preceded Wilder in applying specific literary criticism to the parables, is G. V. Jones. Jones described his study of the parables as "a pointer to the way in which the parables, as a form of art, may be read as pictures of the human situation: an interpretation which may be considered as 'existential.' . . . "[59] Because the parables are rooted in the Hebrew art form (*mashal*), it is legitimate to study them as "disclosures, in particular images, of the general human condition."[60] The literary character of the stories is, however, admirably expressed by Jones:

Taking into account the character of the parables as a whole it is more probable that they are fiction. The parables, then, are, in the main, very short stories, given point and pungency, as has been remarked, by surprise and risk.[61]

The art of the story-teller . . . reveals to us what we would not have otherwise known, and exposes facets of experience which might well have remained hidden from us. It possesses, in a phrase, the quality of inspired-ness, the imaginative insight, the illumination, the ability to transfigure experience so that, in its recreated form, it assumes a kind of universal quality and thereby makes a particular moment, incident, or experience available to all through imaginative participation. It achieves this by means of the technique of narrative and by the pressure of the style behind the form.[62]

Because there is in the greatest of the parables the "pressure" both of vision and of style, converting the raw material of daily life into an artistic form, and expressing the resultant creation in a memorable manner, the world

---

[57] Wilder, *Rhetoric*, 84.

[58] Wilder, *Rhetoric*, 92.

[59] Jones, *Art and Truth*, ix.

[60] Jones, *Art and Truth*, x; see part three of his book for his "existentialist" interpretation (pp. 135–222) of the parable of the Prodigal Son.

[61] Jones, *Art and Truth*, 119.

[62] Jones, *Art and Truth*, 130–31.

of illusion (which in a sense most fiction is bound to be) is presented to us in a manner which gives to it a significant reality. . . . [63]

There is a reality that is not identical with that of the empirical world. It has its own laws and constitutions. This reality is the creation of the author's vision; it is given form and symbol by the imagination. Its medium and instrument is art, which is the world of illusion made real, and of reality transformed into symbol.[64]

Jones' analysis of the parable of the Prodigal Son/Elder Brother seeks an understanding of the general "human condition" that is communicated in the story, utilizing insights from an analysis of modern fiction literature. His interpretation of the story is essentially ahistorical.

In 1967 Dan Via,[65] drawing on the work of Northrop Frye,[66] applied to the stories of Jesus the two basic types of "plot movement" in the history of Western literature: i.e., the tragic and the comic. The comic plot is one that moves upward "toward well-being and the inclusion of the protagonist in a new or renewed society,"[67] or as Frye says "from threatening complications to a happy ending."[68] The tragic plot falls "toward catastrophe and the isolation of the protagonist from society,"[69] or in Frye's words, "falling from innocence toward hamartia . . . to catastrophe."[70] Via goes on to classify the parables of Jesus on the basis of these two types of plot movement.[71] In the *Poetica* Aristotle had already described both of these movements as basic to tragedy (7.12; 11.1–3). Via also appropriates from Frye (who developed it from Aristotle; see *Poet.* 2.1) a way of categorizing literature based on an analysis of the "hero's power of actions."[72] Via determines that Jesus' heroes, or protagonists, fall consistently in Frye's fourth category: the low mimetic mode, which

---

[63] Jones, *Art and Truth*, 131.

[64] Jones, *Art and Truth*, 132.

[65] Via, *Parables*, 96–97.

[66] Frye, *Anatomy of Criticism*.

[67] Via, *Parables*, 96.

[68] Frye, *Anatomy of Criticism*, 162.

[69] Via, *Parables*, 96.

[70] Frye, *Anatomy of Criticism*, 162.

[71] Via, *Parables*, 110–44 (= the tragic); 145–76 (= the comic). Frye (*Anatomy of Criticism*, 162) finds four narrative pregeneric elements of literature: tragedy, comedy, romance, and irony.

[72] Frye, *Anatomy of Criticism*, 33–35: 1. If superior in kind to other men and the environment, the hero is a god and the story is myth. 2. If superior in degree to other men and the environment, the hero is the typical hero of romance, and the story is legend and folktale. 3. If superior in degree to other men but not to the environment, the hero is a leader. This figure is the hero of the high mimetic mode of tragedy. 4. If superior neither to other men nor environment, the hero is of the low mimetic mode and "one of us." 5. If inferior in power and intelligence to ourselves so that we sense we are looking on "bondage, frustration, or absurdity," the hero is cast in an ironic mode.

is the literary character of realism. The only time the hero is cast in the high mimetic mode is when the hero is a king.[73] For Via the plots of the stories fall into two formal classes: low mimetic realistic tragedy moving downward toward catastrophe, and low mimetic realistic comedy moving upward toward well-being.[74]

Via is primarily interested in the understanding of human existence in the story, but he also moves on to see what he calls the "divine impingement" in the stories (i.e., in the fact that figures in the story point "subsidiarily to God").[75] The basic focus of Via's analysis is the plot of the story, but he insists that one should not overlook the "themes" of the stories. He defines the "theme" as "plot at a standstill."[76] It is not clear that Aristotle would agree with this definition, since, for Aristotle, plot is representation of an *action* (*Poet.* 1.2; 6.2; 7.2–7).[77] Via characterizes his own approach in the following way:

> Our grasp of a work's existential understanding grows out of being attentive to the interrelationships of the elements within the aesthetic object and not out of speculations about the author's original theological intentions nor out of any allegorical pointing outward in the story.[78]

He, therefore, draws on the three different views of human possibilities as developed in the work of Preston Roberts[79] in order to help illuminate the existential themes of the stories. Hence he really is not interested in the stories *as story*, but rather in the stories of Jesus as "illuminating models for a literary representation of the Christian view of man. . . ." [80]

For study purposes scholars generally group the stories of Jesus in various ways. James Breech, focusing on the action of the stories, groups them under the headings of "photodramatic" and "phonodramatic":

---

[73] Via, *Parables*, 98. Stories that cast the protagonist in the high mimetic mode Via limits to the Unforgiving Servant and the Wedding Garment (Matt 22:11–14). I think, however, that it is possible to understand the Pharisee (Pharisee and Toll Collector) and the rich man (Rich Fool) as cast in the high mimetic mode. There may be others.

[74] Via, *Parables*, 99.

[75] Via, *Parables*, 99–100.

[76] Via, *Parables*, 100–101.

[77] Theme (θέμα) in Greek is something "laid down," something quite different from Aristotle's plot (μῦθος). Via probably means by it "major idea"; surely he does not mean "proposition," since this evokes Jülicher's one-point moral that Via rejects (*Parables*, 2–3). Via's distinction between plot and theme in the light of Aristotle strikes me as the difference between a "movie" and a "slide show." While it is possible to discuss themes in a poem/drama, one is not thereby discussing the plot/action.

[78] Via, *Parables*, 102.

[79] Via, *Parables*, 102–3: Roberts, "Theory of Dramatic Tragedy," and "Bringing Pathos into Focus."

[80] Via, *Parables*, 103.

Both groups describe what human beings *do*; hence, their dramatic character (from the etymology of the Greek word for "drama," which means "to do"). One group limits itself to the external description of what men and women do, and so I call them photodramatic because they report *visible* actions. The other group describes what people *do* and what they *say*, and so I call them phonodramatic because they report *visible* actions and *audible* words.[81]

Breech's grouping of the stories in terms of human action is refreshing when compared to the subjective theological and thematic categories into which the stories tend to be cast.[82] Breech's groups, however, fail to accommodate all of the stories. For example, the story of the Unclean Spirit involves no *human* activity but rather the activity and speech of "unclean spirits." It is a phonodramatic story by Breech's categories, but not phonodramatic of human activity. It involves both mythical action and speech, i.e., superhuman activities.[83] Furthermore, several stories that he describes as photodramatic do not describe what men and women do at all: a Sprouting Seed, a Mustard Seed, the Date Palm Shoot, the Ear of Grain. To these one should also add a Sower and the Leaven, where the focus is on a process of nature rather than on human activity, although to be sure there is a minimal human activity involved.

We can further distinguish between stories about individual human activity (e.g., the Killer, the Warring King, and the Two Houses) and stories involving the activity of more than one individual (e.g., a Vineyard, a King Settling Accounts, the Wage of the Workmen). The stories about individual action tend to be photodramatic/monologic, whereas the stories involving more than one character (i.e., stories about the human community [society]) tend to be phonodramatic/dialogic. Hence Breech should have categorized the stories thus: (1) stories about nature, i.e., stories describing the natural processes; (2) stories about individual human action (photodramatic/monologic); (3) stories about society, i.e., stories having more than one character (phonodramatic/dialogic); and (4) mythological stories, i.e., stories involving superhuman activity (both monologic and dialogic).[84]

---

[81] Breech, *Silence of Jesus*, 66. The distinction is a good one. One group is characterized by action and speech (phonodramatic) and the other is characterized by action alone (photodramatic). But Breech does not carefully sort out the stories, perhaps because his categories are not sharp enough. For example, he characterizes the Lost Sheep and the Lost Coin as photodramatic (p. 66). And while it is true that the focus in these stories is primarily on what is done, it is also true that both have monologues.

[82] See for example Jeremias, *Parables*, 115–229.

[83] There are two additional stories involving superhuman activity; see Appendix E.

[84] Compare Appendix E. Perhaps the most sensible arrangement of the parables corpus is that by Scott (*Hear Then the Parable*), who arranges the stories in terms of Palestinian village life (p. 79).

4 🌿

Toward the Development of a Poetics for the Stories of Jesus

MEANING

IN CHAPTER 2 I NOTED THAT THE STORIES OF JESUS MEAN EXACTLY WHAT they say, and maybe more. What these stories "mean" has probably been the major focus of most studies of the parables. The goal has been to "explain" (i.e., to deduce a contemporary significance for) the parables, as though they could be reduced to propositions or summaries. Scholars generally understand that the goal of this kind of "propositional" study is to produce a definitive once and for all statement of the stories' intention or significance. Their unconscious assumption is that the narrative can be reduced to timeless specific significants.

In one sense this attempt to reduce the stories to a propositional meaning treats the stories much as an allegorical method might—as though the stories can be reduced or distilled to a specific abstract concept, idea, summary, or value. At bottom, such an approach focuses not on the story, but behind the story, on the mind of the inventor. Once the interpreter has "successfully explained" the story, the story may be discarded. And the "explanation," as long as it is regarded as "authoritative," will thereafter control both the story and the hearing of the story. The story itself then is no longer able, as Wilder said, to create new "meanings," but is ever subservient to its authoritative explanation(s).

This is not to deny that in the historical context of the story's first audition particular meanings were associated with the story, by both the original narrator and the multiple auditors. The meanings of narrator and auditors, however, may not have been identical, since once spoken the story immediately takes on a life of its own. Its original intended purpose, if there was a specific one clearly defined in the mind of the narrator, may not be that meaning the auditors derived. Both specific and general life situations of individual different auditors influence the "meaning" evoked in the mind of an auditor upon hearing the story. People hear and understand different things.

Even determining the general "intent" of the "author" is a problem. Scholars control the specific historical contexts of the stories and the life situation of the period only in the most general way. Further, between the time of their first hearing in the ministry of Jesus (if original with Jesus) and their earliest scribal performance, at least the earliest we possess, lie 40 or so years involving at least three different settings in life through which the stories were transmitted: the ministry of Jesus, the Aramaic-speaking Palestinian Christian communities, and the Hellenistic-Christian communities. The stories themselves have been shaped by the early Christian quest for meaning in all of these periods.

Surprisingly, only a few of the stories preserve (inside what is generally conceded to be their earliest form) original conclusions that quantify the stories in terms of authoritative meanings. The stories are constructed so as to require response, or put another way, to evoke meaning, by an auditor/reader. Their narrative structure teases an unspecified "response" that would usually be associated with meaning.[1] In short, the stories themselves do not really tell or even hint about how they are to be understood.

Only the following stories evaluate positive and negative features for the reader: a King Settling Accounts (Matt 18:23–34), a Man Going on a Journey (Luke 12:36–38; but not in Mark 13:34), the Rich Fool (in Luke 12:16–20; but not the Rich Man in *Gos. Thom.* log. 63), the Two Houses (Matt 7:24–27; but not Luke 6:48–49), the Entrusted Money (Matt 25:14–28; Luke 19:12b–24), and a Vineyard (Mark 12:1b–9; Luke 20:9b–16a; possibly Matt 21:33b–40[41]; but not *Gos. Thom.* log. 65). One of the stories actually concludes with an invitation to the auditor/reader to make a decision: the Wage of the Workmen (Matt 20:15). Seven other stories use an interrogative form so as to solicit response. While the extant form of the stories must be attributed to the evangelist, the interrogatives may preserve a historical memory of the original open-ended character of the stories: the Lost Sheep (Matt 18:12–13; Luke 15:4–6; but not *Gos. Thom.* log. 107), the Tower Builder (Luke 14:28–30), the Warring King (Luke 14:31–32), the Lost Coin (Luke 15:8–9), the Two Sons (Matt 21:28–30), the Persistent Friend (Luke 11:5–8), and the Servant (Luke 17:7–9). The rest of the stories present the narrative in a neutral way, and no attempt is made inside the story to sort out proper

---

[1] See the discussion (pp. 32–35) in chapter 2 above. One may also compare Crossan's *Sayings Parallels*, 2–20 where the story is printed in bold letters and the later extraneous interpretations appear in lighter print.

from improper action or to quantify positive and negative features of the action. The story is told without any value judgments.

Were one to draw conclusions about the stories from this survey, one would have to say the stories possess the potential to subvert or affirm a given understanding by an auditor/reader, but they offer no clues as to an innate purpose or intention, and therefore a specific (original) "meaning" is unclear. And more than one hundred years of critical study of these stories have failed to provide generally accepted, definitive, and enduring meanings.

While the stories are certainly not "meaningless," they do not conceal a particular exclusive "ur-meaning" or proposition into which the plot may be collapsed. That kind of meaning does not derive from the text; it is not an innate part of the story. Rather specific meanings arise from the interplay of the story with the historical circumstance and individual imaginations of auditors and readers. Therefore the stories have a potential for many meanings. Since the stories were originally open ended, calling for closure by the response or judgment of an auditor/reader, and since their original social context cannot be precisely determined, the most we can expect to determine is how the parables subvert or affirm reconstructed world views from the ancient past and the present.

PROSE AND POETRY

As two discrete literary forms, prose and poetry are easily identified in their classic forms. Frequently, however, only an extremely fine line distinguishes poetry from prose. Amos Wilder once remarked that (contemporary) poetry is distinguished from prose by its rhythm,[2] but in other instances it may simply be the arrangement of lines that distinguishes them.[3] Rhythm not only has a calculated measured quality but is more narrowly defined as a systematic movement or variation in the flow of sound.[4]

Aristotle argues that in oratory the work ποίημα should not be "metrical" but "rhythmical" (*Rhet.* 3.8.3) in a way that does not call attention to its rhythm (*Rhet.* 3.8.1–2). It is best, he concludes, to use the rhythm of paean (i.e., choral song, hymn, or chant), a structuring of the narrative that actually appears to have metrical qualities, as Aristotle describes it. Either one long syllable followed by three shorts, or three

---

[2] Wilder, *Rhetoric*, 92. Even Aristotle thought poetry should make use of rhythm: *Poet.* 6.3–4 (ῥυθμὸν καὶ ἁρμονίαν).

[3] Minot, *Three Genres*, 115–22.

[4] Minot, *Three Genres*, 116.

short syllables followed by one long characterizes the metrics of paean (*Rhet.* 3.8.4–7).

The style of the oratorical work may be either continuous, united by connecting particles, or what Aristotle calls "periodic" (*Rhet.* 3.9.1). His discussion of the periodic style (*Rhet.* 3.9.3–10) has some immediate significance for analyzing the parables. It is comprised of periods, i.e., well-rounded sentences that have beginnings and endings (*Rhet.* 3.9.3). A period is "a complete sentence, distinct in its parts and easy to repeat in a breath . . . when it is taken as a whole" (*Rhet.* 3.9.5). It may be composed either of two clauses (i.e., a part of a period) or of a single clause (what Aristotle calls a "simple" sentence).

The clauses of the periodic style may be either divided or opposed. The divided period appears to be a sentence involving two clauses (*Rhet.* 3.9.7). Opposed clauses contrast with one another as antitheses (*Rhet.* 3.9.8), but he notes that there appear to be false antitheses, which reflect the style of opposed clauses (*Rhet.* 3.9.10), yet they are actually equal clauses.

Clauses may also be "exactly balanced," παρίσωσις. Such balanced clauses have rhythmical qualities, assonance, and even rhyme:

> The similarity of the final syllables of each clause [is] paromoiosis. This must take place at the beginning or end of the clauses. At the beginning the similarity is always shown in entire words; at the end, in the last syllables, or the inflexions of one and the same word, or the repetition of the same word[5] (*Rhet.* 3.9.9–10).

Note the rhythm, balance, and rhyme of the following two examples offered by Aristotle (*Rhet.* 3.9.9):

1. Ἀγρὸν γὰρ ἔλαβεν   For he received land,
   ἀγρὸν παρ' αὐτοῦ   untilled land from him.
2. δωρητοί τ'ἐπέλοντο   They were ready to accept gifts
   παράρρητοί τ'ἐπέεσσιν   and to be persuaded by words.[6]

The stories of Jesus may not be "poems" in a narrow modern sense, but in a general sense they are "poetic." Like the dramatic tragedies that Aristotle evaluated in his *Poetica*, they employ plot—i.e., they tell a story, and they are imaginative creations—i.e., they are works, ποίημα, deliberately made or fashioned (ποιεῖν). Hence it would be reasonable to assume that one could identify their "poetic" features, i.e., the characteristic or stylized features that reflect their manufacture.

One should therefore be open to the rhythm of the narrative and to its use of sound devices, such as alliteration, assonance, consonance, and

---

[5] Translation by Freese, *Aristotle: Rhetoric*, 393.
[6] Freese, *Aristotle: Rhetoric*, 394–95; see the other examples offered by Aristotle at the same location.

onomatopoeia,[7] as well as to the use of metaphor and other images within the narrative.

The stories do not have to fit any particular poetic model in antiquity. As imaginative creations, they have their own "poetics," i.e., their own distinctive marks of manufacture. Hence care should be taken not to force them into any particular mold. Their fabrication may or may not have followed any particular ancient model. Of course, if they are stories Jesus invented, the form in which one analyzes their poetics will not be the language or the form of their original audition. While the form in which they now exist as "works of art," to use Via's designation, may tell us little about the form of their original audition, it will certainly tell us about their character as they now appear in early Christian literature.

THE POETICS OF THE LEAVEN

The poetics (i.e., a description of its construction) of the brief story of the Leaven provides an example of how such an approach may be applied. The Leaven is identical in the Greek of both Matthew and Luke (Matt 13:33 = Luke 13:21):

1.	ζύμη	to leaven
2.	ἣν λαβοῦσα γυνή	which a woman having taken
3.	ἐνέκρυψεν εἰς ἀλεύρου	and concealed into of flour
4.	σάτα τρία	three measures
5.	ἕως οὗ	until
6.	ἐζυμώθη ὅλον	the whole was leavened

Greek, with its inflected forms, lends itself to assonance, consonance, rhyme, and rhythm. One might expect, therefore, to find that the Greeks to some degree capitalized on this aspect of their language.[8] While there is no distinctive metrical pattern to the story as I have divided up the lines above, one is immediately struck by the extensive and deliberate use of assonance and consonance in this brief story of only one period:

Assonance (repetition of similar vowel sounds)

η,υ	ζύμη	line 1
	ἣν . . . γυνή	line 2
	ἐνέκρυψεν	line 3
	ἐζυμώθη	line 6

---

[7] On euphony in Greek, see the discussion by Stanford, *Sound of Greek*, esp. 48–121; Denniston, *Greek Prose Style*, 124–39, and id., "Assonance, Greek."

[8] See Stanford's survey (*Sound of Greek*, 7–19) of the ancient Greek rhetoricians' sensitivities to the euphonic character of their language. Also note (pp. 2–4) his observation that even texts were intended to be read aloud. On the sound of ancient Greek see Allen, *Vox Graeca*. I have opted to distinguish between all vowels and diphthongs, although it is clear that sounds could be confused.

α	λαβοῦσα	line 2
	ἀλεύρου	line 3
	σάτα τρία	line 4

ε	ἐνέκρυψεν	line 3
	ἕως	line 5
	ἐζυμώθη	line 6

ου, ευ	λαβοῦσα	line 2
	ἀλεύρου	line 3
	οὖ	line 5

Consonance (repetition of similar consonantal sounds)

σ	λαβοῦσα	line 2
	ἐνέκρυψεν εἰς	line 3
	σάτα	line 4
	ἕως	line 5

λ	λαβοῦσα	line 2
	ἀλεύρου	line 3
	ὅλον	line 6

Note the very close similarity in sound between:

εἰς ἀλεύρου	line 3
ἕως οὖ	line 5

Note also the euphonic: ζύμη . . . γυνη in lines one and two. Also the beginning (line one) and ending (line six) of the story are balanced off with the euphonic ζύμη ἐζυμώθη. The concentrated use of so many similar sounds in such a story of only 13 words lends a prosodic quality to the narrative: the similarity in sound gives it a rhythmical quality, draws attention to the words that share similarities in sound, and hence helps to structure the narrative.[9]

This story is one of only a few of the stories of Jesus that deliberately use metaphor within the narrative.[10] In line three above, the word "hid," ἐνέκρυψεν, is clearly a metaphor for mixing the leavening agent into the dough. It is the use of an expression normally associated with a clandestine act for an act that is rather neutral in and of itself.[11]

THE POETICS OF A MUSTARD SEED

Similar features are also found in the slightly longer story of a Mustard Seed. There are three performances of this story in the gospels.

---

[9] See the brief discussion by Perrine, *Sound and Sense*, 134–47.
[10] See chapter 2, pp. 29, 33 above.
[11] This is the point on which the story turns for Funk ("Beyond Criticism," 156–58, 162).

Mark 4:31–32

PERIOD I

1	κόκκῳ σινάπεως,	to a grain of mustard seed
2	ὃς ὅταν σπαρῇ	which when sown
3	ἐπὶ τῆς γῆς,	upon the ground
4	μικρότερον ὂν	is smaller
5	πάντων τῶν σπερμάτων	than all the seeds
6	τῶν ἐπὶ τῆς γῆς,	of those upon the ground;

PERIOD II

1	καὶ ὅταν σπαρῇ,	yet when sown
2	ἀναβαίνει καὶ γίνεται	it grows up and becomes
3	μεῖζον πάντων τῶν λαχάνων	greater than all garden vegetables
4	καὶ ποιεῖ κλάδους μεγάλους,	and puts forth large branches
5	ὥστε δύνασθαι	so that they are able
6	ὑπὸ τὴν σκιὰν αὐτοῦ	under its shadow
7	τὰ πετεινὰ τοῦ οὐρανοῦ	the birds of heaven
8	κατασκηνοῦν.	to make nests.

The story falls naturally into two major units, and I have accordingly divided it into two periods for analysis. Between the two periods, one notes the repetition of the identical phrase ὅταν σπαρῇ (I,2; II,1) and the balanced rhyme between μικρότερον ὂν πάντων τῶν σπερμάτων (I,4–5) and μεῖζον πάντων τῶν λαχάνων (II,3). There is also a subtle rhyme in σκιὰν αὐτοῦ (II,6) and -σκηνοῦν (II,8). The repetition of the phrase ἐπὶ τῆς γῆς at the conclusion (I,3,6) of both clauses (I,1–3,4–6) of the first period gives the period balance and affects how one reads period two. Because of the repetition of phrases in period I a reader tends to evoke in the mind a line lacking in period two immediately following line one as follows: καὶ ὅταν σπαρῇ [ἐπὶ τῆς γῆς].

For the listing of assonance/consonance that follows because of the slightly longer length of the narrative (42 words) I note occurrences of four or more similar sounds.

PERIOD I
Assonance

o	κόκκῳ	line 1
	ὃς ὅταν	line 2
	μικρότερον ὂν	line 4
η	σπαρῇ	line 1
	τῆς γῆς	line 3
	τῆς γῆς	line 6
ω	κόκκῳ σινάπεως	line 1
	πάντων τῶν σπερμάτων τῶν	line 5/6

α	σινάπεως	line 1
	ὅταν σπαρῇ	line 2
	πάντων . . . σπερμάτων	line 5

| ο | κόκκῳ | line 1 |
| | ὃς ὅταν | line 2 |

Consonance

σ	σινάπεως	line 1
	ὃς . . . σπαρῇ	line 2
	τῆς γῆς	line 3
	σπερμάτων	line 5
	τῆς γῆς	line 6

π	σινάπεως	line 1
	σπαρῇ	line 2
	ἐπὶ	line 3
	πάντων . . . σπερμάτων	line 5
	ἐπὶ	line 6

ν	σινάπεως	line 1
	ὅταν	line 2
	μικρότερον ὄν	line 4
	πάντων τῶν σπερμάτων τῶν	line 5/6

PERIOD II
Assonance

αι	καὶ	line 1
	ἀναβαίνει καὶ γίνεται	line 2
	καὶ	line 4
	δύνασθαι	line 5

α	ὅταν σπαρῇ	line 1
	ἀναβαίνει	line 2
	πάντων . . . λαχάνων	line 3
	κλάδους μεγάλους	line 4
	δύνασθαι	line 5
	σκιὰν	line 6
	τὰ πετεινὰ . . . οὐρανοῦ	line 7
	κατασκηνοῦν	line 8

ου,υ	κλάδους μεγάλους	line 4
	δύνασθαι	line 5
	ὑπὸ . . . αὐτοῦ	line 6
	τοῦ οὐρανοῦ	line 7
	κατασκηνοῦν	line 8

ε,ει	ἀναβαίνει . . . γίνεται	line 2
	μεῖζον	line 3
	ποιεῖ . . . μεγάλους	line 4

	ὥστε	line 5
	πετεινά	line 7

Consonance

σ	σπαρῇ	line 1
	κλάδους μεγάλους	line 4
	ὥστε δύνασθαι	line 5
	σκιὰν	line 6
	κατασκηνοῦν	line 8

τ	ὅταν	line 1
	γίνεται	line 2
	πάντων τῶν	line 3
	ὥστε	line 5
	τὴν . . . αὐτοῦ	line 6
	τὰ πετεινὰ τοῦ	line 7
	κατασκηνοῦν	line 8

π	σπαρῇ	line 1
	πάντων	line 3
	ποιεῖ	line 4
	ὑπὸ	line 6
	πετεινά	line 7

ν	ὅταν	line 1
	ἀναβαίνει . . . γίνεται	line 2
	μεῖζον πάντων τῶν λαχάνων	line 3
	δύνασθαι	line 5
	τὴν σκιὰν	line 6
	πετεινὰ . . . οὐρανοῦ	line 7
	κατασκηνοῦν	line 8

The parallels in Matthew and Luke are different. Hence in order to appreciate the distinctiveness of Mark (or for that matter Matthew and Luke) a comparison must be made contrasting the other versions of the story in Matthew and Luke.

Matthew 13:31–32

PERIOD I

1	κόκκῳ σινάπεως,	to a grain of mustard seed
2	ὃν λαβὼν ἄνθρωπος	which a man having taken
3	ἔσπειρεν ἐν τῷ ἀγρῷ αὐτοῦ·	sowed in his field.

PERIOD II

1	ὃ μικρότερον μέν ἐστιν	On the one hand, it is smaller
2	πάντων τῶν σπερμάτων,	than all seeds.
3	ὅταν δὲ αὐξηθῇ	But, on the other hand, when it has grown,

4	μεῖζον τῶν λαχάνων ἐστὶν	it is larger than garden vegetables
5	καὶ γίνεται δένδρον,	and it becomes a tree
6	ὥστε ἐλθεῖν τὰ πετεινὰ τοῦ οὐρανοῦ	so that the birds of heaven come
7	καὶ κατασκηνοῦν	and nest
8	ἐν τοῖς κλάδοις αὐτοῦ.	in its branches

With the tight μέν . . . δέ contrast between the small grain and the remarkably larger plant it produces (i.e., a tree), the balance of the narrative's structure is changed. In Matthew the statement about a man sowing seed in his field is preliminary to the contrast of the seed and its product. The act of sowing has no relationship to the comparison among the seeds. In Mark, however, it is only the act of sowing the seed upon the ground that allows the comparison to be made. Unlike Matthew, the sowing in Mark is not preliminary to the contrast but the contrast is made at the time of sowing. Hence Mark focuses attention on the sowing (note Mark's repetition of σπαρῇ in I,2 and II,1).

Further, one misses in Matthew the repetition of phrases and words (Mark: I,2 = II,1; I,3 = I,6 [and is evoked following II,1]; I,5 [πάντων] = II,3 [πάντων]) that gives the Markan narrative a certain prosodic quality that is not clearly evident in Matthew. In Mark the repetitions provide a rhythm to the story and serve to stylize, structure, and please.

PERIOD I
Assonance

ω	κόκκῳ σινάπεως	line 1
	λαβὼν ἄνθρωπος	line 2
	τῷ ἀγρῷ	line 3
α	σινάπεως	line 1
	λαβὼν ἄνθρωπος	line 2
	ἀγρῷ	line 3
ε	σινάπεως	line 1
	ἔσπειρεν ἐν	line 3

Consonance

σ	σινάπεως	line 1
	ἄνθρωπος	line 2
	ἔσπειρεν	line 3
ν	σινάπεως	line 1
	ὃν λαβὼν ἄνθρωπος	line 2
	ἔσπειρεν ἐν	line 3

PERIOD II
Assonance

ε	μικρότερον μέν ἐστιν	line 1
	σπερμάτων	line 2

	δὲ	line 3
	ἐστὶν	line 4
	γίνεται δένδρον	line 5
	ὥστε ἐλθεῖν . . . πετεινὰ	line 6
	ἐν	line 8
ι	μικρότερον . . . ἐστιν	line 1
	ἐστὶν	line 4
	γίνεται	line 5
α	πάντων . . . σπερμάτων	line 2
	ὅταν	line 3
	λαχάνων	line 4
	τὰ πετεινὰ οὐρανοῦ	line 6
	κατασκηνοῦν	line 7
	κλάδοις	line 8
ο	ὃ μικρότερον	line 1
	ὅταν	line 3
	μεῖζον	line 4
	δένδρον	line 5
ω	πάντων τῶν σπερμάτων	line 2
	τῶν λαχάνων	line 4
	ὥστε	line 6
ου	τοῦ οὐρανοῦ	line 6
	κατασκηνοῦν	line 7
	αὐτοῦ	line 8

Consonance

τ	μικρότερον . . . ἐστιν	line 1
	πάντων τῶν σπερμάτων	line 2
	ὅταν	line 3
	τῶν . . . ἐστὶν	line 4
	γίνεται	line 5
	ὥστε . . . τὰ πετεινὰ τοῦ	line 6
	κατασκηνοῦν	line 7
	τοῖς . . . αὐτοῦ	line 8
ν	μικρότερον μὲν ἐστιν	line 1
	πάντων τῶν σπερμάτων	line 2
	ὅταν	line 3
	μεῖζον τῶν λαχάνων ἐστιν	line 4
	γίνεται δένδρον	line 5
	ἐλθεῖν . . . πετεινὰ . . . οὐρανοῦ	line 6
	κατασκηνοῦν	line 7
	ἐν	line 8
σ,ξ,ζ	ἐστιν	line 1
	σπερμάτων	line 2
	αὐξηθῇ	line 3

μεῖζον . . . ἐστὶν	line 4
ὥστε	line 6
κατασκηνοῦν	line 7
τοῖς κλάδοις	line 8

Luke 13:19

1. κόκκῳ σινάπεως,	to a grain of mustard seed
2. ὃν λαβὼν ἄνθρωπος	which a man having taken
3. ἔβαλεν εἰς κῆπον ἑαυτοῦ,	sowed in his garden
4. καὶ ηὔξησεν	and it grew
5. καὶ ἐγένετο εἰς δένδρον,	and became a tree
6. καὶ τὰ πετεινὰ τοῦ οὐρανοῦ	and the birds of heaven
7. κατεσκήνωσεν ἐν τοῖς κλάδοις αὐτοῦ.	made nests in its branches.

Luke's version is noticeably more condensed by comparison to those versions in Matthew and Mark; it is so brief, in fact, that it constitutes only one period. Luke lacks Mark's structuring, repetition of phrases, and rhyme. The conscious contrast between the small seed and large shrub that one finds in Mark, and between the small seed and tree that one finds in Matthew, is completely lacking in Luke's version. Here the story is simply about the sequential process of nature: sowing, growing, maturing.

Assonance

o	κόκκῳ	line 1
	ὃν . . . ἄνθρωπος	line 2
	κῆπον	line 3
	ἐγένετο . . . δένδρον	line 5
α	σινάπεως	line 1
	λαβὼν ἄνθρωπος	line 2
	ἔβαλεν	line 3
	τὰ πετεινὰ . . . οὐρανοῦ	line 6
	κατεσκήνωσεν . . . κλάδοις	line 7
ω	κόκκῳ σινάπεως	line 1
	λαβὼν ἄνθρωπος	line 2
	κατεσκήνωσεν	line 7
ε	σινάπεως	line 1
	ἔβαλεν . . . ἑαυτοῦ	line 3
	ηὔξησεν	line 4
	ἐγένετο . . . δένδρον	line 5
	πετεινὰ	line 6
	κατεσκήνωσεν ἐν	line 7
ου,υ	ἑαυτοῦ	line 3
	ηὔξησεν	line 4

| | τοῦ οὐρανοῦ | line 6 |
| | αὐτοῦ | line 7 |

Consonance

ν	σινάπεως	line 1
	ὃν λαβὼν ἄνθρωπος	line 2
	ἔβαλεν . . . κῆπον	line 3
	ηὔξησεν	line 4
	ἐγένετο . . . δένδρον	line 5
	πετεινὰ . . . οὐρανοῦ	line 6
	κατεσκήνωσεν ἐν	line 7

π	σινάπεως	line 1
	ἄνθρωπος	line 2
	κῆπον	line 3
	πετεινὰ	line 6

σ	σινάπεως	line 1
	ἄνθρωπος	line 2
	εἰς	line 3
	ηὔξησεν	line 4
	εἰς	line 5
	κατεσκήνωσεν . . . τοῖς κλάδοις	line 7

τ	ἑαυτοῦ	line 3
	ἐγένετο	line 5
	τὰ πετεινὰ τοῦ	line 6
	κατεσκήνωσεν . . . τοῖς . . . αὐτοῦ	line 7

κ	κόκκῳ	line 1
	κῆπον	line 3
	καὶ	line 4
	καὶ	line 5
	καὶ	line 6
	κατεσκήνωσεν . . . κλάδοις	line 7

Of course the assonance and consonance in the versions by Matthew and Luke do not really compare to the rhythm and rhyme in Mark's version of the narrative, features that do not appear in either Matthew or Luke. That is to say, one cannot simply count repetition of sound; it is how those features are used that produces the prosodic quality in a work. For example: note the prosodic quality of the following lines from Mark:

I,1–2	σινάπεως ὃς ὅταν σπαρῇ
	σινάπεως . . . σπαρῇ
I,4–5	μικρότερον ὂν πάντων τῶν σπερμάτων τῶν
I,5–6	πάντων τῶν σπερμάτων των
II,2–3	ἀναβαίνει καὶ γίνεται
	ἀναβαίνει . . . μεῖζον
II,3	μεῖζον πάντων τῶν λάχανων

II,4   κλάδους μεγαλους (note κλα/γαλ)
II,7   τὰ πετεινὰ τοῦ
II,7–8   τοῦ οὐρανοῦ κατασκηνοῦν
          τοῦ οὐρανοῦ κατασκηνοῦν

While there are prosodic units to be found in the versions of Matthew and Luke, they are not as extensive and do not compare to the prosodic manufacture of Mark's narrative; by comparison Matthew and Luke appear prosaic:[12]

Matthew:

I,2   ὃν λαβὼν ἄνθρωπος
I,3   ἔσπειρεν ἐν
II,4   μεῖζον τῶν λαχάνων ἐστὶν
II,6   τὰ πετεινὰ τοῦ οὐρανοῦ [but derived from Mark or Q]

Luke:

2   ὃν λαβὼν ἄνθρωπος
6   τὰ πετεινὰ τοῦ οὐρανοῦ [but derived from Mark or Q, and LXX]

The story of the Mustard Seed in Mark, as I have analyzed it above, is comprised of two contrasting periods. The first period (I,1–6) describes the small size of the seed. The second period (II,1–8) describes the contrasting large size of the shrub it produces. The lines of these periods may be further divided into equal clauses as follows:

A.   I,1–6
1   I,1–3   κόκκῳ σινάπεως, ὃς ὅταν   σπαρῇ   ἐπὶ τῆς γῆς,
2   I,4–6   μικρότερον ὃν πάντων τῶν σπερμάτων τῶν ἐπὶ τῆς γῆς,

B.   II,1–8
1   II,1–3   καὶ ὅταν σπαρῇ, ἀναβαίνει καὶ γίνεται μεῖζον πάντων
                τῶν λαχάνων
2   II,4–8   καὶ ποιεῖ κλάδους μεγάλους, ὥστε δύνασθαι ὑπὸ τὴν
                σκιὰν αὐτοῦ τὰ πετεινὰ τοῦ οὐρανοῦ κατασκηνοῦν.

---

[12] Matthew and Luke agree with one another against Mark in the following:
The Beginning:

Matthew	Luke
ὃν λαβὼν ἄνθρωπος	ὃν λαβὼν ἄνθρωπος
γίνεται δένδρον	ἐγένετο εἰς δένδρον

The Conclusion:

Matthew	Luke
ἐν τοῖς	ἐν τοῖς
κλάδοις αὐτοῦ	κλάδοις αὐτοῦ

This close agreement causes most scholars to postulate a version of the story in Q (Kloppenborg, *Q Parallels*, 148–51).

In the first period (I,1–6) the two clauses end with an identical expression (I,3 = I,6: ἐπὶ τῆς γῆς) and the second line of each three-lined clause in period I (see above p. 63) concludes with different inflections of similar words: σπαρῇ (I,2) and σπερμάτων (I,5). Certain final syllables are also euphonic: viz., I,1 (-ω); I,4 (-ὄν); I,5 (-ων); I,2 (-ῇ); I,3 (-ῆς); I,6 (ῆς).

In the second period (II,1–8) the first verbal forms of each clause have similar endings: ἀναβαίνει (II,2) and ποιεῖ (II,4), and so do the second verbal forms of each clause: γίνεται (II,2) and δύνασθαι (II,5). The first word of each clause, καί II,1 and II,4, is the same. In the second clause of the second period the endings of its 1st, 3rd, 4th, and 5th lines (II,4: -ους; II,6 and 7: -οῦ; II,8: -οῦν) are euphonic. There is rhyme in II,4 (κλάδους/μεγάλους) and between II,6 and II,8 (σκίαν αὐτοῦ/-σκηνοῦν).

The balance between the two periods is most striking. The second line of the first period (I,2 ὅταν σπαρῇ) is repeated in the first line of the second period (II,1 ὅταν σπαρῇ) and the concluding line of each clause of the first period (ἐπὶ τῆς γῆς: I,3,6) is evoked following the ὅταν σπαρῇ in II,1, although it is not present in the text. Lines I,4–5 in the second clause of the first period are antithetically paralleled by line 3 of the first clause of the second period as follows:

I,4–5   μικρότερον ὂν πάντων τῶν σπερμάτων
II,3   μεῖζον πάντων τῶν λαχάνων

Such prosodic features, where they can be identified throughout the parables, attest a deliberate artistic manufacture. Further if they are like this at the Greek level of the tradition, it suggests that their present form probably does not derive from the creative formation of Jesus.[13] Rather the present artistic features, particularly of Mark's version, are probably due to shaping in the oral Greek period; that is to say, these features are characteristics of their orality, since they appeal primarily to the ear rather than to the eye.[14] This kind of evidence can lead to the conclusion that the more prosodic the story, the closer it is to an oral period of transmission; and the more didactic and prosaic the story, the further it is from the oral period. Patterning, repetition, rhythm, and rhyme are features that appeal to one's aural senses. Hence stories exhibiting these

---

[13] See Crossan's argument that in the aphorisms the most we have preserved from the historical Jesus is an aphoristic core, a structure that is transmitted in various performances (*In Fragments*, 37–66). This may be true of the stories of Jesus as well.

[14] See Finnegan, *Oral Poetry*, 88–133. Kelber has argued that Mark's gospel reflects an oral heritage: *Oral and Written Gospel*, in particular pages 44–89. Recently Scott and Dean have argued that the Sermon on the Mount has been structured on the basis of its aural features; see Scott and Dean, "Sound Map," particularly pp. 678–719.

features are more likely to have been crafted for an oral performance. On the other hand, texts lacking such features are more likely to stand further away from a point in time when they were orally presented.[15] In any case, Matthew and Luke reflect fewer of these oral/aural features in the story of a Mustard Seed, and are probably separated further in time from a true oral/aural context.[16]

---

[15] See Stanford, *Sound of Greek*, 2–4: in ancient Greece even the written text was intended for reading aloud.

[16] While these prosodic features in Mark are clearly characteristic of oral literature (see Finnegan, *Oral Poetry*, 88–133), they do not prove that this story was originally orally composed. Such proof would usually be determined by the presence of formulaic expressions in the narrative on the basis of the studies of Milman Parry (*Homeric Verse*). See for example the brief statement by Lord (*Singer of Tales*, 130): "An *oral* text will yield a predominance of clearly demonstrable formulas, with the bulk of the remainder 'formulaic,' and a small number of nonformulaic expressions. A *literary* text will show a predominance of nonformulaic expressions with some formulaic expressions and very few clear "formulas" (cf. pp. 124–38). For a brief statement of the theory and how it works see Bynum, *Daemon in the Wood*, 3–31. Berkley Peabody (*Winged Word*, 3–5) argued for five tests that allow one to identify a given text as the product of an oral tradition (see also the review by Havelock, *Literate Revolution*, 150–65). Kelber (*Oral and Written Gospel*, 78–79) is of the opinion that one may not too quickly draw a parallel between Homer and the gospels.

5 ≈

The Parables of Jesus and the Clash of Fictions

TURNING ORDINARY STORIES
INTO STORIES FOR THE CHURCH

IN ORDER TO AVOID THE "AFFECTIVE FALLACY"[1] (I.E., IDENTIFYING THE "meaning" of the story with its effect on the reader) New Testament scholars rely on historical reconstruction of the ancient world in the context of which, for example, a saying of Jesus, a gospel, or a segment of a Pauline letter is to be read and understood. The reconstructed cultural context, involving all pertinent aspects of the ancient world (historical, sociological, religious, etc.), functions as a "brake" to the imaginations of modern readers, many of whom read all texts exclusively for a "meaning" in the contemporary world. Modern readers tend to exploit ancient religious texts in order to extract some relevance for understanding their own lives in the modern world (a similar use is made of fiction literature). For example, consider how the early ecclesiastical communities of the synoptics read the stories of Jesus. Their character as commonplace representations of life prompted the church to read them as deposits of esoterica. Since they were sayings of the resurrected Lord, the stories, it was reasoned by the church, must have had some deeper religious significance. Reading the parables merely as stories apparently did not provide adequate guidance for communities of faith trying to make religious sense of them in their changed and changing historical situation. In short, the loss of the parables as mere stories, like the anticipation of the Lord's immediate return, was one of the casualties of the church's historicizing of its eschatological faith.[2] The Jesus traditions

---

[1] See Via, *Parables*, 73–88, and in particular Wimsatt-Beardsley, *Verbal Icon*, 3–18, and "Intentional Fallacy."

[2] The eschatological shift can already be seen in Paul's letters. Compare 1 Cor 7 where Paul clearly anticipates the end of the age as an immediate occurrence

became for the church resources for shaping Christian faith and for answering specific religious and existential questions provoked by the church's new cultural situations.

One issue that concerned some early Christians was the kingdom of God. The frustrating and bitterly disappointing statement that Luke places on the lips of the disciples at the conclusion of the gospel is, of course, Luke's representation of the situation that Luke understood to pertain at the death of Jesus, but the disappointment was undoubtedly shared by Christians who looked for the kingdom of God (cf. Mark 9:1; 14:25; Matt 25:34; Luke 21:31): "But we had hoped that he was the one to redeem Israel" (Luke 24:21). The "redemption of Israel" in this context should not be understood in a political sense, at least not so far as Luke is concerned.[3] The "redemption of Israel" expected by these disciples in Luke was the fulfillment of the end-time expectation; it was the coming of God's kingdom. This is made clear in Luke's second book, Acts, where the disciples ask the ascending Christ: "Lord will you at this time restore the kingdom to Israel?" (Acts 1:6 RSV).[4] Synoptic Christianity had a serious preoccupation with the future kingdom of God, a preoccupation that is simply not a prominent feature of Pauline or Johannine Christianity; nor for that matter is it a major focus of the faith of Thomas, early Q, the deutero-Paulines, Pastorals, and the General letters.

That the kingdom of God was a part of the message of the historical Jesus until recently has been a common assumption of New Testament scholarship.[5] But what Jesus may have meant by that expression is, and probably always will be, a matter of continuing debate.[6] The major reason that critical scholarship has been unable to reach a consensus on the nature of the kingdom as proclaimed by Jesus stems from the con-

---

pressing itself upon his own day: "in view of the present distress" (7:26), "the appointed time has grown very short" (7:29), "for the form of this world is passing away" (7:31). Nevertheless Paul has to contend in the same context with "historical" problems, as well. The issue is graphically focused in his advice to slaves (7:20–24): because of the immediacy of the end, people should remain as they are (cf. 7:29–35), and this includes slaves; nevertheless, if the slave can secure freedom, the slave should take advantage of that opportunity. See Hedrick, "Past and Future as Ethical Exordium," 93–117.

[3] The messianic implications of the statement seem clear enough in the light of 1:32–33 and 22:30; see Klostermann-Gressmann, *Lukasevangelium,* 605. But cf. Fitzmyer, *Luke,* 2.1564, who takes it to refer to political redemption.

[4] So Haenchen, *Acts of the Apostles,* 143.

[5] See, e.g., Perrin, *Kingdom of God* and Scott, *Symbol-Maker,* 6–11, and id., *Hear Then the Parable,* 56–62. This is because scholars generally construct their historical portraits of Jesus out of the Synoptic Gospels; see Hedrick, "Tyranny of the Synoptic Jesus." The consensus that Jesus was an apocalyptist who announced the advent of an otherworldly kingdom has recently been challenged, see chapter 2 note 2 above.

[6] Perrin, *Language of the Kingdom,* 15–88.

flicting reports in early Christian literature.[7] Understanding the nature of the kingdom was apparently no less a problem for the early Christians themselves, as early Christian literature reflects diverse expectations.

The kingdom is a reality of the imminent future:

Mark 9:1: "Truly, I say to you, there are some standing here who will not taste death before they see that the kingdom of God has come with power" (RSV).

Mark 1:15: "The time is fulfilled, and the kingdom of God is at hand; repent and believe in the gospel" (RSV).

The kingdom is realized in the present:

Luke 17:20–21: "The kingdom of God is not coming with watching; nor will they say, 'Behold here!' or 'There!' for behold the kingdom is within you [ἐντὸς ὑμῶν]."

Gospel of Thomas log. 3 (II,2:32,25–26): "But the kingdom is within you [ⲤⳘⲠⲉⲦⲚ̄ϨⲞⲨⲚ], and it is outside of you [ⲤⳘⲠⲉⲦⲚ̄ⲂⲀⲖ]."

The kingdom is conceived concretely as a hope of Israel's future:

Luke 22:29–30: "I assign to you, as my Father assigned to me, a kingdom, that you may eat and drink at my table in my kingdom, and sit on thrones judging the twelve tribes of Israel" (RSV).

The kingdom is a "spiritual" reality:

Rom 14:17: "For the kingdom of God is not food and drink, but righteousness and peace and joy in the Holy Spirit" (RSV).

John 18:36: "My kingship is not of this world; if my kingship were of this world, my servants would fight, that I might not be handed over to the Jews; but my kingship is not from the world" (RSV).

John 3:3: "Truly, truly, I say to you, unless one is born anew, he cannot see the kingdom of God" (RSV).

Ap. Jas. I,2:13,17–19: "Do not make the kingdom of Heaven a desert within you" (NHLE).

One receives the kingdom:

Mark 10:15: "Truly, I say to you, whoever does not receive the kingdom of God like a child shall not enter it" (RSV).

---

[7] Because it is ultimately a symbol, its substance is "filled in" by the interpreter. Compare, e.g., the "other worldliness" in the interpretation of Weiss, *Kingdom of God*, and the "this worldliness" in the understanding of Rauschenbusch, *Social Gospel*.

One enters the kingdom:

| Mark 10:23: | "How hard it will be for those who have riches to enter the kingdom of God" (RSV). |
| John 3:5: | "Truly, truly, I say to you, unless one is born of water and the Spirit, he cannot enter the kingdom of God." |

The signs of the kingdom's presence are exorcisms by Jesus:

| Luke 11:20: | "But if it is by the finger of God that I cast out demons, then the kingdom of God has come upon you" (RSV; cf. Matt 12:28). |

There is no evident sign of the coming of the kingdom:

| Luke 17:20: | "The kingdom of God is not coming with watching; nor will they say, 'Behold, here!' or 'There!' " |

The kingdom comes as the result of God's activity:

| Luke 12:32: | "Fear not, little flock, for it is your Father's good pleasure to give you the kingdom" (RSV). |
| Matt 6:10: | "Thy kingdom come. Thy will be done" (RSV). |

Human beings can have an effect on the kingdom:

Matt 11:12:	"From the days of John the Baptist until now the kingdom of heaven has suffered violence, and men of violence take it by force" (RSV).
Matt 16:19:	"I will give you the keys of the kingdom of heaven, and whatever you bind on earth shall be bound in heaven, and whatever you loose on earth shall be loosed in heaven" (RSV).
Ap. Jas. I,2:13,17–19:	"Do not make the kingdom of Heaven a desert within you" (*NHLE*).
Matt 23:13:	"Woe to you, scribes and Pharisees, hypocrites! because you shut the kingdom of heaven against men; for you neither enter yourselves, nor allow those who would enter to go in" (RSV).

These rather rich and contrasting traditions underline the vagaries of the early Christian conceptualizations of the kingdom, but at the same time they closely tie the preaching of Jesus to the announcement of the kingdom of God.

Hence inevitably early Christian preoccupation with the kingdom of God led them to sift the sayings tradition for information about, and a better understanding of, the nature of the kingdom. Equally understandably, early Christian prophets under the inspiration of the indwelling spirit of Christ would produce sayings on the kingdom of God.[8] In

---

[8] See Boring, *Sayings of the Risen Jesus*, esp. pp. 230–38. For an example of an early Christian prophet producing sayings of the resurrected Lord see Rev 1:1–3:22.

such a climate it is therefore not surprising that the stories of Jesus handed on by the tradition were exploited for insights about the kingdom of God, whether they originally had that focus or not. In my judgment, the varieties of understanding of the "kingdom" within early Christianity demonstrate that it was a problem, and that problem provides a plausible historical context for the association of the stories of Jesus with the kingdom of God. This explanation is at least as plausible as the argument that the historical Jesus himself associated his stories with the kingdom.

There was a type of early Christianity that can be characterized as "synoptic"; that is, these Christians shared a similar oral and written tradition. Those who shared this cycle of traditions tried to make sense out of their changing historical situation using these traditions. In the process they "invented" explanations out of the traditions to provide concords among (1) what they understood their beginning to have been, (2) a new vision of their future end, and (3) their present.[9] The "secrecy" features in the Gospel of Mark illustrate one such literary invention necessitated by the passage of time and a changing social situation. The earlier understanding (Wrede) of these "injunctions to silence" made by Mark's Jesus to demons, disciples, and persons he healed, held that it was Mark's "literary fiction" to accommodate the tension between the early Christian belief that Jesus was the Messiah and the historical memory that his ministry had been nonmessianic.[10] Later scholarship modified Wrede's view. Current explanations for secrecy features attributable to Mark (as opposed to traditional features that Mark appropriated) contend that Mark used them to correct a traditional Christology depicting Jesus as a wonderworking Son of God. Mark thus deliberately modified traditional Christology by incorporating the motif of suffering into the way Jesus had been traditionally understood.[11] Both explanations, however, agree that the author of the gospel both created certain of the commands to silence and then used them in the construction of a new Christology.[12]

Another issue that faced those early Christian communities expecting an early return of the Lord was the comportment of life in the unanticipated present, i.e., the unexpected historical situation in which

[9] See the discussion below, pp. 81–87.

[10] Wrede, *Messianic Secret.*

[11] See the brief review article with bibliography by Perrin, "Secret."

[12] A similar hermeneutical use is made of the stories of Jesus in certain other early Christian communities sharing aspects of the gnostic vision, although their interpretations are slanted in a different direction. Gnostic Christians also associated the "meaning" of the stories with Jesus' preaching of the kingdom, as appears, e.g., in the *Apocryphon of James.* Compare the interpretations to the parables of a Sower (Mark 4:14–20 = Matt 13:18–23 = Luke 8:11–15), Good Seed and Weeds (Matt 13:37–43), and a Net Thrown into the Sea (Matt 13:49–50) with the interpretations of the parables of the Grain of Wheat (*Ap. Jas.* I,2:8,23–27), the Date Palm Shoot (*Ap. Jas.* I,2:7,29–35), and the Ear of Grain (*Ap. Jas.* I,2:12:27–30).

they found themselves after the expected end did not occur. The nonappearance of the parousia raised a wide range of social and organizational issues for the church, and one may even read early Christian literature as specific responses to those unanticipated issues. For example, Paul's letter to the Galatians concerned the nature of the gospel: did God intend that the gospel go to the Gentiles as Gentiles or did God expect that Gentiles must first come into the community of faith through Judaism?[13] First Corinthians clearly reflects a diversity of problems faced by one early community at Corinth[14] and graphically depicts the social adjustments the church was required to make in coming to terms with both new cultural settings and the nonappearance of Jesus. The Pastorals deal with the establishment of church order and governance by a church forced to deal with its continued existence in the world. The canonical gospels set forth a narrative account of both the "foundation" of the kerygma and the community, and so on. Hence in a community that looked to both its past and its future for making sense out of its present, the stories the church traced to Jesus would inevitably be exploited for guidance in its present life. This can be distinctly seen in Matthew's organization of the sayings tradition into "discourses," one dealing with church order (Matt 18) and another with Christian discipleship (Matt 5–7).

Under similar pressures some stories became parables of the kingdom of God, while others were read as examples of proper conduct; still others served as evangelistic illustrations, eschatological warnings, or ecclesiastical admonitions.[15] And because the church believed itself to be "inspired" by the Spirit of God (cf. Acts 2:4; Rev 2:7, 11, 17, 29; 3:6, 13, 22) in its understanding of the stories, even the forms of the stories, i.e., the oral or written forms received by the evangelists, could be modified to fit whatever interpretation the evangelist under the inspiration of the Spirit felt "led" to make. The authority was not the story, but rather the story as interpreted and explicated by the Spirit.[16] Compare the different performances of the story of a Vineyard in Mark (12:1–11), Matthew (21:33–43), Luke (20:9–18), and the *Gospel of Thomas* (log. 65) where one can see different early Christian performances of the same story.

THE STORIES OF JESUS AS "AESTHETIC OBJECTS"

What we have, therefore, in the parables of Jesus are ordinary stories that may, once one has written their tradition history, provide an access to Jesus of Nazareth. In this sense recent research is correct that we

---

[13] See Betz, *Galatians*, 5–9.
[14] Conzelmann, *1 Corinthians*, and Fee, *First Epistle to the Corinthians*.
[15] Jeremias, *Parables*, 23–114.
[16] Jeremias, *Parables*, 23–114.

must focus on the language-world of the story,[17] since it is only the story that would, if original, be the product of Jesus' creative imagination.[18]

D. O. Via, Jr., was really the first systematically to analyze the stories of Jesus as "aesthetic objects," worthy of being studied for themselves alone. He was first to apply the criteria of narrative fiction to the study of the stories, although others had used the terminology.[19] Rejecting Jülicher's one-point moralizing approach to the stories[20] as well as the contention of Jeremias and Dodd that the stories are typical recurring incidents in the life of first-century Palestinian peasants, Via asserts that a parable is:

> a freely invented story told with a series of verbs in a past tense. The parable is not concerned with what everyone typically does but narrates a particulate thing. . . . The similitude gets its force from its appeal to what is universally acknowledged, while the parable achieves its power by making the particular credible and probable.[21]

Via recognizes that parables may be multifaceted, and he resists reducing the parable to a one-point meaning:

> There is more than one important element in a parable, and all of these features must be given consideration, but they do not relate primarily and in the first place to an event, events, or ideas outside of the parable. They relate first of all to each other within the parable, and the structure of connections of these elements is not determined by events or ideas outside of the parable but by the author's creative composition. . . . Neither one nor many of the elements point directly and individually out of the story.[22]

While Via does not completely reject the importance of the "historical setting," the historical context of the story and its historical function are clearly not of primary significance for understanding the story.[23] Via does not read the stories against a reconstruction of the first-century

---

[17] For example, cf. the similar approach taken in Via, *Parables*, and Crossan, *First Act*. Both in different ways emphasize the literary character of the story.

[18] See Crossan, *In Fragments*, who argues that it is only the structure that goes back to Jesus. The particular formal expression of the stories that we have in early Christian literature derives from the preference of the individual gospel "author."

[19] See the discussion above pp. 50–56.

[20] Via, *Parables*, 70–107.

[21] Via, *Parables*, 11–12. By insisting that parables do not reflect "typical life" but narrate a "particulate thing" Via seems to be trying to avoid Jülicher's extraction from the story of a generalizing one-point summary. Note, however, that Aristotle says that poetry gives general truths while history gives particular facts (*Poet.* 9.1).

[22] Via, *Parables*, 25.

[23] Via, *Parables*, 91. But cf.: "While one would not want to argue for a methodology which completely ignored the life setting, some modification of the present tendency [i.e., what Via calls the severely historical approach] seems called for" (p. 21).

world, but instead focuses on their language by means of what he calls "literary criticism and theological-existential exegesis."[24] His analysis of the stories as brief fictions draws minimally on historical insights.[25]

Via is decidedly correct, in my opinion: the stories are brief fictions, freely contrived from the creative imagination of Jesus, if original with him. Since they have plot, they can be analyzed as any other piece of fiction literature. This insight has far-reaching consequences for their study. Via's rigorous avoidance of the historical context, however, limits the success of his approach. He rightly recognizes that a severely histori- cal approach has distracted scholars from appreciating the story as story. The historical approach as it has been applied, like allegory, does tend to focus outside the story and reduce it to existential and moral signifi- cance. Scholars have been so busy trying to get something out of the story, to determine "its meaning," that they have overlooked the story itself. Via's interpretations of the stories, however, have a distinctly modern ring to them! They were probably never heard in antiquity like he explains them today.[26] For this reason he is probably subject to what he calls the "affective fallacy."[27]

Via makes pointed use of Aristotle's *Poetica* in analyzing the stories:

> The primacy of plot in the parables makes the Aristotelian literary approach especially pertinent, for the heart of Aristotle's famous definition of tragedy is that it is the imitation of a serious action.[28]

What Via does not stress is that tragedy is precisely a representation (μίμησις) of an action.[29] The plot (μῦθος) is a movement, or action, showing the kind of thing that "could or would happen either probably or inevitably."[30] Tragedy also involves character, diction, and thought, and all of these elements are to be expressed appropriate to the action. In other words, there is an element of realism in the imitation of the action, since human beings engaged in life are the subjects of the tragedy.[31]

If Jesus' stories are fictive representations of actions that happened, or may have happened, in the past, then it would seem that their *mimesis*,

---

[24] Via, *Parables*, 95.

[25] Via, *Parables*, 93–107.

[26] Via would probably agree with that, since he is not analyzing the parables as a Jewish peasant, Pharisee, or toll collector, etc. might have heard them; he is focusing instead on the parables as artistic creations and deposits of a particular view of existence.

[27] Via is, of course, aware of the problem (*Parables*, 79–88), and would probably deny that this is the case.

[28] Via, *Parables*, 100.

[29] Aristot. *Poet.* 6.2, 21.

[30] Aristot. *Poet.* 9.2–3.

[31] Aristot. *Poet.* 2.1–5; 4.1–13, and, in particular, 25.1–3.

as *mimesis*, is likewise capable of analysis. This inevitably raises the issue of what is being represented, and how true it is to human life. In any case, the examination of the realism of the stories in their historical context is a valid part of a literary analysis,[32] and that involves analysis of Jesus' stories specifically in their historical context.

I will analyze the stories of Jesus precisely as "first-century narrative fictions." Hence while the focus of the study is on the narratives as invented first-century fictions (i.e., it does not try to abstract from them a summary "meaning" or to pursue some supposed outside referent), it is also concerned with their historical character. Jesus was a first-century human being who would have invented plots, designed characters, and composed diction—all out of his own language and culture. The creative genius of Jesus' stories derives from his historically conditioned imagination, whether affirming, rejecting, or being indifferent to, his world; and hence the raw materials for plot, character, and diction originated in first-century Palestinian Judaism.[33]

"HISTORY" AS A FICTIVE "MENTAL CONSTRUCT"

Almost thirty years ago (1966) Frank Kermode published a series of lectures delivered at Bryn Mawr College in a book entitled: *The Sense of an Ending: Studies in the Theory of Fiction*.[34] The book was, in general, favorably reviewed by literary critics, who did, however (justifiably), chide Kermode for his difficult to read style.[35] The volume, however, received scant attention from biblical scholars. Kermode associated apocalyptic expectations of the end of the world with the character of the modern novel. He argued that both the apocalyptist and the novelist try to bring order out of chaos, to impose form on the essentially formlessness of reality, to convert *chronos* (an endless succession of unrelated events) into *kairos* (significant time):

> Men, like poets, rush "into the middest," *in medias res*, when they are born; they also die *in mediis rebus*, and to make sense out of their span they need fictive concords with origins and ends, such as give meaning to lives and to poems.[36]

---

[32] See in particular Auerbach's analysis of the Fortunata episode in Petronius, *Mimesis*, 24–49.

[33] This seems clear enough, in general, from the nature of the stories. They are not modern inventions and do reflect their antiquity in every sense of the word.

[34] The Mary Flexner lectures, London: Oxford, 1966.

[35] See, e.g.: Byatt, "Connoisseur of Order"; Hough, "End of the World"; Casper, "Sense of an Ending"; Scruton, "Apocalypse and Fiction"; and *Yale Review* 57 (October 1967) xxviii–xxix. Kermode has never revised the book.

[36] Kermode, *Sense of an Ending*, 7.

The necessity of an end for making sense out of where we live, i.e., the present (what Kermode calls the middest), emerges in the tendency for individuals and groups to invent new apocalyptic ends, when the old end-expectations are disconfirmed. Indeed, as "often as the predicted end of the world has been disconfirmed, the sense of an ending itself has never been discredited."[37]

> What it seems to come to is this. Men in the middest make considerable imaginative investments in coherent patterns which, by the provision of an end, make possible a satisfactory consonance with the origins and with the middle. That is why the image of an end can never be *permanently* falsified.[38]

That is to say, humans need "ends" to make sense out of the present. But with the emergence of modernity human beings are not, in general, given to naive apocalyptic expectations and mythological ends; consequently, Kermode argues that we have invented "critical time" by which the mythic beginning, and the apocalyptic temporal end that loomed imminently "out there," have become immanent:

> We give ourselves meaning by inventing critical time. . . . The free imagination makes endless plots on reality, attempts to make our proportionals convenient for our equations in everything. . . . So here we are in the middest, . . . reinventing the world. . . . [39]

Kermode notes that our skepticism about the "beginning" and the "end" (as it has been taught in Judeo-Christian tradition) has been accompanied by the rise of modern fiction:

> It is worth remembering that the rise of what we call literary fiction happened at a time when the revealed, authenticated account of the beginning was losing its authority. Now that changes in things as they are change beginnings to make them fit, beginnings have lost their mythical rigidity. There are, it is true, modern attempts to restore this [mythical] rigidity [i.e., to the way the world began]. But on the whole there is a correlation between subtlety and variety in our [literary] fictions and remoteness and doubtfulness about ends and origins. There is a necessary relation between the fictions by which we order our world and the increasing complexity of what we take to be the "real" history of that world.[40]

Novels and poems become ways of making sense out of the world; we use them as "working models . . . to interpret our world and our history to ourselves."[41] In short, literary fiction is part of the general theory of fictions by which human beings make sense out of their world:

---

[37] Casper, "Sense of an Ending," 443.
[38] Kermode, *Sense of an Ending*, 17.
[39] Kermode, *Sense of an Ending*, 164.
[40] Kermode, *Sense of an Ending*, 67.
[41] Byatt, "Connoisseur of Order," 146.

So my suggestion is that literary fictions belong to [Hans] Vaihinger's category of "the consciously false." They are not subject, like hypotheses, to proof or disconfirmation, only, if they come to lose their operational effectiveness, to neglect. They are then thrown, in [Wallace] Steven's figure, on to the "dump"—"to sit among mattresses of the dead." In this, they resemble the fictions of science, mathematics, and law, and differ from those [fictions] of theology only because religious fictions are harder to free from the mythical "deposit." I see no reason why we cannot apply to literary fictions what Vaihinger says of fictions in general, that they "are mental structures. . . . "[42]

Even "history," as Kermode notes, belongs to the category of fiction:

The recognition, now commonplace, that the writing of history involves the use of regulative fictions, is part of the same process. World history, the imposition of a plot on time, is a substitute for myth.[43]

"World history" is thus essentially a "constructed" fiction, a mental construct, and it must be kept as a fiction—at the level of a consciously "constructed fiction" (i.e., according to Kermode: "consciously false")—if we want to avoid turning our "histories" into myths and to continue finding out about ourselves.[44] Kermode distinguishes between myth and fiction (i.e., a mental construct) perhaps too rigidly,[45] but the distinction is instructive:

We have to distinguish between myths and fictions. Fictions can degenerate into myths whenever they are not consciously held to be fictive. . . . Myth operates within the diagrams of ritual, which presupposes total and adequate explanations of things as they are and were; it is a sequence of radically unchangeable gestures. Fictions are for finding things out and they change as the needs of sense-making change. Myths are the agents of stability, fictions the agents of change. Myths call for absolute, fictions for conditional assent. Myths make sense in terms of a lost order of time . . . ; fictions, if successful, make sense of the here and now. . . . [46]

I do not understand Kermode's use of the word "fiction" to mean "untrue," as the word is popularly taken. "Fiction" derives from the Latin *fingere*, to form, mold, devise. Hence, *fictum*, past participle of *fingere*, describes a thing devised or formed, and a *fictor* is a maker of "constructs." A "fiction," as I am understanding and using the word, and as I understand Kermode to use it, is a creation or an invention, or as Kermode says "a mental construct." When Kermode (following Vaihinger) talks about such constructions being "consciously false," I understand

---

[42]Kermode, *Sense of an Ending*, 40. See also Vaihinger, *As if.*
[43]Kermode, *Sense of an Ending*, 43.
[44]Kermode, *Sense of an Ending*, 40, 43.
[45]Hough, "End of the World," 431–32.
[46]Kermode, *Sense of an Ending*, 39.

him to mean that they are always found to be "inadequate and temporary constructions" that can be replaced once their usefulness is past.

Kermode's book forms a theoretical basis for an understanding of history and literature in terms of which the stories of Jesus are most reasonably explicable. Historians, like novelists, also impose "plots" on raw data. It is the informed and disciplined imagination of the historian that "creates" a given history by sifting the raw data and deciding the facts, their order, and their relationship that comprise the most plausible construct.

> Facts do not speak for themselves, but . . . the historian speaks for them, speaks on their behalf, and fashions the fragments of the past into a whole whose integrity is—in its *re*presentation—a purely discursive one. Novelists might be dealing only with imaginary events whereas historians are dealing with real ones, but the process of fusing events, whether imaginary or real, into a comprehensible totality capable of serving as the *object* of a representation is a poetic process. Here the historians must utilize precisely the same tropological strategies, the same modalities of representing relationships in words, that the poet or novelist uses. In the unprocessed historical record and in the chronicle of events which the historian extracts from the record, the facts exist only as a congeries of contiguously related fragments. These fragments have to be put together to make a whole of a particular, not a general, kind. And they are put together in the same ways that novelists use to put together figments of their imaginations to display an ordered world, a cosmos. . . . [47]

Historians who assume that their reconstructions of "history" have produced knowledge of an "objective" reality outside their reconstructions, "a knowledge as certain as anything offered by the physical sciences and as objective as a mathematical exercise,"[48] are dangerously close to myth.

What Kermode has argued about the evolution of narrative from fiction into myth is readily the case with Jewish literature. The sacred literature of Judaism (Tanak, Mishna, and Talmud) is a chronicle of human experience; the collections represent early Hebrew and later Jewish understandings of reality. From these writings they have sought, and still seek, to "find out about themselves." Tanak, as it is presently organized, tells a "story" beginning with the creation of all things in Genesis. It traces the origins of the people and the development of community, kingship, and loss of kingdom. It preserves the Hebrew struggle for self-understanding in prophetic, legal, and devotional literature. It reflects a sense of an ending in the form of a hope for an ideal future kingdom under the reign of Yahweh.[49]

---

[47] White, *Tropics of Discourse*, 125; see also Sauerberg, *Fact into Fiction*, 40–45, and White, *Content of the Form*, 1–25, 83–103, 169–213; id., *Metahistory*, 1–42.

[48] White, *Tropics of Discourse*, 125.

[49] See Eichrodt, *Theology*, 472–511; and Heinisch-Heidt, *Theology*, 311–70.

The linear concept of time that Israel created out of ideal beginning and end, and incorporated into the design of its sacred writings, is unique in ancient literature.[50] Tanak, in effect, contains the basic elements of plot: beginning, middle, and end. In short, what Hebrew faith has done is to "impose a plot on time," to create a middle by "inventing" a beginning and an end. Mishna and Talmud constitute new fictions invented by later Judaism to establish concords for their new "middest." Jewish apocalyptic literature may be seen as failed endings.

Was the "story," i.e., Israel's literary construct, ever held to be fictive? Probably not in the sense that Kermode would have it, i.e., in the sense of people consciously creating experimental models for understanding reality. Rather, in Israel's story the origin of all things is mythical; Israel's national epic is mythical; ideal kingship is mythical; Israel's devotional literature is immersed in myth, and so on. But Israel's authors were projecting a "plot" on the world precisely in the sense that Kermode would have it. The Pentateuch periodized history; apocalyptic literature, of which only vestiges remain in Israel's canon, periodized history. These texts effectively created small epochs on a national, universal/cosmic scale that led up to, and anticipated, the end.[51] The "stories" were mental constructs, "fictive" attempts to make sense out of the human condition in the middest.

What Kermode has argued is that human beings create fictions out of which they try to understand themselves. This is as true, if not more so, for cultures, societies, and nations, as for individuals; otherwise human beings could not live in community. Each "community" has a certain mental construct of reality, "a worldview," that unites the community and establishes concords of meaning for individuals in that community. And people generally make sense out of their lives in terms of these concords of meaning. Certain individuals in the community may invent other fictions that affirm or subvert the common community fiction, since some may not be able to live totally out of the common community fiction. An example of this is an individual reinterpretation of an overly literal, or mythical, religious confession. The new inventions make it possible for an individual to continue living in the community even when the old fictions are no longer functional. This is particularly true of religious communities, but no less true of nations and cultures in general.

Religions have tended to express in narrative their mental constructs, and these narratives rapidly assume the role of authoritative fictions or fall into myth around which other fictions emerge. For example, Christianity affirms the Bible, Judaism affirms Tanak-Mishna-Talmuds, and Islam affirms the Qur'an. The Greeks had Homer; America

---

[50] See, e.g., the introduction in Anderson, *Old Testament*, 1–14.
[51] See Noth, *Pentateuch*, 194–214 and Hedrick, *Apocalypse of Adam*, 66–79.

has the Constitution, and so on. The making of such narratives seems endemic to the human condition, if Kermode and others are correct. It was no less true of first-century Palestinian Judaism.[52]

Obviously not every first-century Jew categorically affirmed every element of Israel's "fiction," but there was, in fact, a common "community story" in the context of which first-century Jews lived and found meaning for themselves, whether in affirmation of, or over against, the construct. A sharp definition and extensive elaboration of the story are not as important for my purposes at this point as is the recognition that such a "cover story" or fiction existed and formed a basis for life in first-century Palestine.

The stories of Jesus may have been intended as metaphor or symbol, i.e., consciously composed in order to refer the reader outside themselves to an unearthly reality, as early Christianity's difficulty with the language of Jesus attests. But if they were so intended, then the interpreter ought to be able to point to some semantic marker in the story to show what it is that deliberately moves the mind outside the story. Based on the analysis in chapter 2 above, it seems methodologically improper to blindly *assume* that all the stories of Jesus are by definition metaphorical or symbolical, i.e., that they are consciously self-effacing. One must specify the internal markers of metaphor; otherwise one may be mistaking the subjective "effect" of the story on an individual reader as its "significance." One must begin with the assumption that the stories are what they appear to be and mean exactly what they say, unless there is a compelling reason to regard them as metaphorical gestures.

Whether they were metaphorical or not, however, the stories would have been heard, at least initially, in the context of Judaism's narrative fictions about itself. Just as early Christianity later heard them in the context of its own fictions. Hence the stories would have been grasped as affirmation, assault, or subversion of Judaism's shared "mental construct" about itself.[53] Because they were "stories," a listener would first have been caught up in the story; i.e., in the plots. Upon entering the story world, an individual may have recognized elements of the story as subversive or affirmative, since the story would have been heard against the backdrop of the listener's own mental constructs.

In one sense the story might have been heard in a variety of ways, since each individual brought unique distinctive constructs to the com-

---

[52] For such discussions the reader is referred to the standard texts on first-century Palestinian Judaism. For example: Meyers and Strange, *Archaeology*; Sandmel, *Judaism*; id., *First Christian Century*; Sanders, *Paul and Palestinian Judaism*; Hengel, *Judaism and Hellenism*; and Koester, *Introduction*, vol. 1.

[53] Jeremias' sensitivity that the stories precipitated a clash between Jesus and the Jewish leaders is therefore, in my opinion, fundamentally correct. For example, see Jeremias, *Parables*, 38, 124, 127, 128, 132, 145.

mon story. In another sense, however, the story would have played itself off against the general Jewish construct of reality. Therefore by taking this approach one misses the multifaceted response of individuals to the story. Of course one can always invent those responses by creating a hypothetical context or auditor, as has been done so often in the study of the parables. But it is at least possible to know how Jesus' general fictive vision, represented by the stories, resonated with first-century Judaism's general fictive understanding of itself.

Kermode notes: "Sex, time, liberal thought, are all enemies of paradigmatic rigidity. . . . "[54] It is one assumption of this study that the novel thought of Jesus as reflected in these stories would have clashed with the "paradigmatic reality" of Judaism in much the same way that the community at Qumran, for example, clashed with the temple authorities. I therefore approach the stories of Jesus as potentially radical poetic fictions that competed with Judaism's paradigmatic narrative rigidity.

The stories of Jesus tend to compete with the fictions of Israel, and at the same time they offer in themselves new fictions for understanding reality, new fictions for finding things out. In this way one can make sense of the stories without resorting to allegory, as the early church did, and without assuming a deliberate metaphorical or symbolical quality to the stories, as most current exegesis promotes, and without employing a timeless ahistorical interpretation.

EXAMPLES OF THE CLASH OF FICTIONS IN HEBREW AND EARLY CHRISTIAN LITERATURE

The "clash of fictions" refers to the tension created by the differences between (or among) the mental constructs out of which human beings live. It relates to the essentially different ways that an individual, a community, or a people conceptualize and express in narrative the fictive constructs out of which they live their lives, and in the context of which meanings and concords for living are sought and found. It is not necessary that there exist open warfare between competing mental constructs, such as it is classically portrayed, for example, between Athens and Sparta in the funeral oration of Pericles (Thuc. *Hist.* 2.35–46). Nor is it even necessary that texts have a historical continuity, in the sense that they derive from the same historical context and time period. Texts of any culture or time period can be compared to disclose how their views of reality "clash" or "resonate." But when texts are in proximate temporal continuity, one is closer to describing an actual historical "resonation," than simply one potential "resonation."

---

[54] Kermode, *Sense of an Ending*, 110.

The clash of fictions is evident by comparing narratives that express essentially different mental constructs. The distinctives of a given "plot" become apparent by comparing that plot with other plots. The legal codes of Deuteronomy, for example, have a different "tone" when compared to the Sermon on the Mount than they do when read against the Code of Hammurabi. In the same way, played off against first-century Palestinian Judaism, the parables of Jesus "resonate" with subtleties that are lacking when one ignores historical considerations.

Examples of such clashes in Hebrew and early Christian literature are many. Because the framers of Tanak adeptly blended Israel's stories, the clash of fictions is not always immediately evident, until the competing stories are set side by side. Compare, for example, the two Genesis accounts of creation (Gen 1:1–2:4a and Gen 2:4b–3:24). They are unquestionably similar, and yet each clearly promotes a different story of the creation.[55] The conquest of Canaan by Israel is described in two essentially different ways by Josh 1–21 and Judg 1:1–2:5. Each account derives from an essentially different view of Israel's origin.[56] The narratives concerning the origin of kingship are equally competitive. First Samuel 11 describes Saul's appointment as king with the approval of the Lord as a result of Saul's defeat of the Ammonites; 1 Sam 10:17–27 describes Saul's selection as king by lot; 1 Sam 9:1–10:16 reflects Saul's secret selection and private anointing as king; but 1 Samuel 8 is essentially antimonarchical—the selection of a king is a rejection of Yahweh as king.[57] One of the best examples in Tanak is, of course, the rewriting of Israelite history by the Chronicler (1, 2 Chronicles, Ezra, and Nehemiah) in which, among other things, the Chronicler favorably revises the images of David and Solomon.[58] Another excellent example that reflects the clash of fictions and the influence of "narrative" on the way people comport their lives is the story of the religious reformation that took place under the reign of Josiah when the book of the law was discovered in the temple (2 Kgs 22:3–23:7).[59]

Examples also surface in early Christian literature. The vision of the nature of Christian faith of Paul's opponents in Galatians appears to differ radically from Paul's, to judge from the demands Paul accuses them of making upon Gentiles entering the church. Paul insisted that Gentiles did not have to become Jews in order to become Christians. His opponents, however, insisted that obedience to Torah was a prerequisite to Christian faith.[60] A similar clash is discernible in 1 and 2 Corinthians in

---

[55] Speiser, *Genesis*, 3–28.
[56] Bright, *History*, 129–33.
[57] Hertzberg, *Samuel*, 70–95.
[58] Myers, *1 Chronicles*, 1.xv–xciv.
[59] Gray, *Kings*, 713–46.
[60] See Betz, *Galatians*, 5–9.

the issues related to the nature of a Christian lifestyle that Paul debated with the congregation. Note in the gospels how Matthew and Luke edit the Gospel of Mark, particularly with respect to improving the image of Jesus.[61]

A final example will be given here. Paul describes his participation in an early church conference concerning the character of the Christian gospel (Gal 1:18–2:10) and notes the agreement reached by the parties in Gal 2:9–10. Some years later Luke also describes the conference (Acts 15:1–29) but depicts a remarkably different conclusion to the conference (Acts 15:19, 28–29).[62]

Other examples could be given, but these demonstrate that there existed in the Hebrew scriptures and in early Christian texts differences in the way a group/individual gave narrative expression to particular constructs of reality. In each case a different "cover story" was operating; the different narratives derived from different ways of viewing a given reality. In each case it is not necessary to project a specific historical situation to understand how the "fictions clash." One can understand the stories Jesus told functioning in the same way in the context of the narrative expression of Israel's faith. And now this study turns to readings of specific stories of Jesus, against the background of the narrative fictions of first-century Judaism.

---

[61] See Hawkins, *Horae Synopticae*, 114–53.
[62] See Betz, *Galatians*, 81–84.

PART III
READINGS OF THE PARABLES
AS POETIC FICTIONS

6 🌿

The Samaritan

IT IS ONLY RECENTLY THAT THE SAMARITAN HAS BEEN DESCRIBED AND interpreted as metaphor. Generally it has been regarded as a story that teaches or instructs by example. I begin with the assumption, however, that it is simply a story. While its original literary setting in Luke tells readers how Luke read the Samaritan, Luke's setting is not part of the story proper and hence is disregarded as the key for reading the story. This assumption is based on the fact that the story antedates Luke and circulated in the oral tradition without Luke's setting, which is scarcely the original social setting, but rather a literary setting. My first engagement with the Samaritan in this chapter is not with the story but rather with the narrative. Basic to any reading of the story is first a description of how the narrative has been constructed, i.e., one must first examine the poetics of the narrative. Its construction will give a reader clues as to how it was designed to work. I then proceed to a detailed analysis of the elements of the story of the Samaritan as first-century fiction, and address how the story may have worked in the first-century world, given our present understanding of it. Then my own modern reading of the story is proposed, and finally I raise the historical question: How might this story have been heard in the first century in the context of general Jewish fictions about Israel as the people of God?

THE SETTING OF THE STORY:
AN EARLY CHRISTIAN READING

This story, known generally as "the Good Samaritan," appears only in Luke's Gospel (10:30b–35). Hence, the only version we possess derives from Luke's performance; there are no parallels for comparative study.

The text of the story has remained stable through the textual history of Luke's Gospel.[1]

Luke takes "parables" to be esoteric and cryptic discourse that contain "secrets" about the kingdom of God. To Luke 8:9–10 compare Mark 4:10–12, for example, where Mark reads "secret," but Luke reads "secrets." Luke does not, however, interpret all parabolic language as a referent to the kingdom.[2]

Luke gives no formal designation to the narrative, and the moralizing interpretation of the story does not find it full of hidden secrets about the kingdom. On the contrary, Luke regards it simply as an "example story" (Luke 10:36–37) intended to illustrate the existential truth of Lev 19:18, i.e., being a neighbor means showing mercy to others.

Luke uses the story as Jesus' response to a question of an expert on Torah (Luke 10:25) in the context of a debate that focuses on the interpretation of Lev 19:18.[3] Playing off Lev 19:18, the lawyer (νομικός) asks, "Who is my neighbor?"[4] In response Jesus tells a story about a man who fell among robbers (10:29–35). At the conclusion of the story, Jesus

---

[1] Of the few minor textual variations, none are really significant for the story. The reading γενόμενος (10:32) appears to be the most problematical. See Metzger, *Textual Commentary*, 152–53.

[2] See above chapter 2. Note in particular Luke 14:7–11, where Luke regards Jesus' instructions on "table etiquette" as "parable" from which Luke draws an appropriate (for Luke) moralizing interpretation.

[3] The setting of the story in Luke is routinely taken as Luke's *literary* setting rather than as reflecting a historical memory of an original setting in the life of Jesus. The dispute also appears in Mark 12:28–34 (= Matt 22:34–40) as a debate about which "commandment" took precedence over all others. Luke, however, narrates the situation as a debate over "inheriting eternal life" (10:25, 28), though the substance of the discussion remains the two "great commandments." Each of the evangelists concludes the segment differently. Mark ends with Jesus' statement that the scribe was not far from the kingdom of God (12:34); Matthew concludes with a summarizing response by Jesus on the two greatest commandments (22:37–40). Luke ends the segment like Mark with Jesus' affirmation of the lawyer's statement (10:28), but in Luke the debate is continued and expanded by the story of the Samaritan (10:29–37). But cf. Stein, *Introduction*, 74–75, who argues for the unity of the passage Luke 10:25–37, and Jeremias (*Parables*, 203), who takes Luke's setting to reflect a historical memory of the life of Jesus.

[4] It is not really clear to me how Luke intends the reader to understand 10:29a (ὁ δὲ θέλων δικαιῶσαι). The lawyer did not need to "justify himself," since Jesus had agreed with his response (10:27) and commended him for it (10:28). For 10:29a to make reasonable sense one must assume that the lawyer makes a correct verbal response to Jesus' question (10:26), but that his lifestyle does not match his judicial judgment and that the lawyer himself is aware of the inconsistency between his knowledge of the law and his personal behavior and knows that Jesus is also aware of it. It is probably best to understand 10:29a as a weak connective between story and setting that derives from Luke's bias against these experts in the law (νομικός: Luke 7:30; 11:45, 46, 52; 14:3). Except for one questionable appearance in Matthew, νομικός appears only in Luke. See Metzger, *Textual Commentary*, 59.

poses his own question to the lawyer: "Which of these three characters in my story was a neighbor to the unfortunate victim of the robbery?" (10:36). The lawyer replies: "The one who showed mercy on him" (10:37). Jesus then draws the moral: "Go and do likewise" (10:38).

While the lawyer's question ("Who is my neighbor?") concerned identifying one's neighbor, Jesus' response appears to be designed to provide an example of what it means to *be* a neighbor; that is to say, to demonstrate what it means practically "to love one's neighbor." This is precisely the issue of Lev 19:18, 33–34, but the lawyer as Luke portrays him focuses on a pedantic issue, i.e., "Who is my neighbor?"[5] Hence Luke portrays the lawyer as ironically missing the point of the text in dispute (Lev 19:18) in his question (Luke 10:29b), but as coming to the true understanding of it in his final response to Jesus (10:37a).[6] If this is correct, Luke 10:37a constitutes both a Lukan interpretation of Lev 19:18 and a Lukan interpretation to the story of the Samaritan; in Luke's view showing mercy is the essence of what it means to love one's neighbor, as Lev 19:33–34 already suggests.[7] In short, the story provides a concrete example of "loving one's neighbor," which Luke takes to mean "showing mercy on others."[8]

MODERN INTERPRETATIONS

As Crossan has demonstrated, most modern interpreters take the story to be an example story,[9] virtually as Luke would have it. This view of the narrative has remained a popular one.[10]

There is really nothing unique in the concept of loving the neighbor, as Luke's setting clearly shows. It is a part of the Torah requirement

---

[5] This was apparently a social issue in Judaism; see *TDNT* πλησίον, 6.315.

[6] To explain Luke 10:37a as the lawyer's circumlocution for "Samaritan," because he could not bring himself even to utter the name of the despised "race" is in my opinion a historicizing and romanticizing of the text. One simply cannot know the lawyer's inner motivations apart from Luke's telling the reader what they are. The statement is best understood as Luke's interpretation of the incident that he ironically places on the lips of the lawyer. At best it gives us an insight into a Lukan prejudice. But cf. Crossan, *In Parables*, 63–64.

[7] Breech (*Silence of Jesus*, 160) suggests that the description of the Samaritan's compassion (10:33) derives from Luke, since it "reflects Luke's own view that the story is about someone who is an example of what it means to be a neighbor."

[8] See Breech, *Silence of Jesus*, 160. Luke has included other parables without a context in a controversy setting in order to interpret them.

[9] See Crossan, *In Parables*, 57. Crossan provides statements from Jeremias, Linnemann, Jones, Perrin, Via.

[10] Smith, *Parables*, 181; Boucher, *Parables*, 128; Stein, *Introduction*, 20, 77, 79; Oesterley, *Gospel Parables*, 165 (but to Oesterly cf. Prov 24:17 [LXX]).

(Lev 19:18, 33–34), and rabbinic material likewise deals with the issues of concern and care for others.[11] Love for the neighbor may even be described as the essence of early Christian morality (cf. Matt 5:43; 19:19; 22:39 [= Mark 12:31]; Rom 13:8–9; Gal 5:14; Jas 2:8).[12] Further, not only does Luke's interpretation (10:36–37) say nothing new, it stands somewhat in tension with the story and ultimately dispenses with it. The story says nothing about neighbors, nor is there anything in Luke's interpretation about robbery, travelers, priests, or Samaritans.[13] Luke's interpre-

---

[11] See Oesterley, *Gospel Parables*, 166–68, and 2 Chron 28:8–15 (as noted in Crossan, *In Fragments*, 65).

[12] On the other hand, the injunction to "love your enemies" in Matt 5:44b specifically clashes with this bit of typical Jewish/Christian piety. Gundry (*Matthew*, 97) argues, however, that Matt 5:44b is a creation of Matthew. Gundry assumes that the Q text used by Matthew read as does the current text of Luke (6:27–28) and that there existed in Q an original double couplet for Matthew to manipulate,

Love your enemies; do good to those who hate you;
bless those who curse you; pray for those who abuse you.

But that this was the situation in Q seems far from certain. The only common agreement between Matthew and Luke at this point is precisely Matthew's formulation of 5:44b. How likely is it that Luke has expanded a single couplet into a double couplet? Luke's double couplet appears to be constructed from an originating concept ("love your enemies") followed by three hermeneutical expansions (do good, bless, pray for) of the original concept. They are not really parallel. Hence, "do good," and "pray for" tells what it means "to love," while "hate you," "curse you," "abuse you" interprets what it means to be "enemy." The Didache (1:3ac) has added an additional hermeneutical expansion, "fast for those who persecute you." But how the Didache treats the Lukan material demonstrates the true relationship among the terms in the double couplet by treating them as interchangeable. (Note that Didache has retained Luke's "bless those who curse you.")

Luke:	*Love* your enemies; do good to those who *hate you.*
Didache:	*Love* those who *hate you.*

This is true of the other parallels to Luke:

Luke:	Pray for those who *abuse you*
P.Oxy. 1224, 2:	Pray for your *enemies*
Pol. *Phil.* 1:23:	Pray for those who *persecute and hate you*
Didache:	Pray for your *enemies*

The originating nucleus that produces all these various hermeneutical performances is the statement, "love your enemies." Already in Q the statement has given rise to one hermeneutical variation ("pray for those who [persecute] you") and is transmitted as a couplet into Matthew. Most of the parallels that are cited for the saying "love your enemies" deal with some practical positive *actions* toward people with whom other individuals stand at odds, but they do not deal with the attitude (see Friedlander, *Jewish Sources*, 72–73, for the parallels). Hence the conceptual idealistic nucleus "love your enemies" does contrast well with the Torah's "love your neighbor" (Lev 19:18). And this Jewish/Christian moral, "love your neighbor," also contrasts with Jesus who focused on the naked absolute: "Love your enemies."

[13] Most commentators have noted the discrepancy between the lawyer's question, "who is my neighbor," and the story. The story actually responds to an

tation focuses solely on Luke 10:33 (ἐσπλαγχνίσθη)[14] and dispenses with the rest of the narrative, as do most modern interpretations that focus on the actions of the Samaritan to the exclusion of the rest of the story.

Others, correctly ignoring Luke's setting, read the story not as allegory, example story, or didactic story with a moral, but as metaphor that specifically references the kingdom of God.[15] Robert Funk has championed the nature of parable as metaphor,[16] particularly with reference to this parable.[17]

The word "metaphor" (μεταφέρειν) is a standard figure of speech that literally means "to carry over" or "to transfer." As it has been understood since the time of Aristotle,[18] metaphor defines a way of speaking about something that likens one thing to another unlike thing by speaking of the one as if it were the other. In other words A is likened to B by using terms and expressions normally applied to B in order to describe A. That is to say, appropriate characteristics of B are transferred to A.[19] For example in the statement "An aged man is but a paltry thing, a tattered coat upon a stick" (W. B. Yeats, "Sailing to Byzantium"), one is speaking of the aged man (A) as if he were a scarecrow (B). The "aged man" is the principal subject and the "tattered coat on a stick" (the scarecrow) is the vehicle. In other plainer words, scarecrow characteristics are attributed to the aged man.

Metaphor does not mean literally what it says, but its image language helps the auditor/reader capture the spirit, soul, or vision the maker of the metaphor finds in the principal subject.[20] For metaphors to work, the principal subject must draw on the vehicle and the vehicle must reference the principal subject. According to Funk "parables" constitute the metaphorical language of Jesus that references the kingdom of God.[21] Funk carefully distinguishes between a "reading" of the story that stays within its verbal horizons[22] and a reflection "on the parable

---

unspoken question, "how is a neighbor supposed to act?" But the problem is simply glossed over, and Jesus is made to be a shrewd disputant with his answers.

[14] Breech (*Silence of Jesus*, 159–60) argues that this one element was in fact Luke's adjustment of the story so that it would fit Luke's interpretation better.

[15] For example, Scott, *Symbol-Maker*, 12–17, 25–32; Crossan, *In Parables*, 10–19, 65–66; Scott, *Hear Then the Parable*, 42–62, 200–202.

[16] See Funk, "Parable as Metaphor," 133–62. See Perrin (*Language of the Kingdom*, 132–41, 155–68) for an excellent brief analysis of this approach.

[17] See Funk, "How Do You Read?"; id., "Good Samaritan as Metaphor."

[18] Aristot. *Poet.* 21–22.

[19] See Perrine, *Sound and Sense*, 65; Minot, *Three Genres*, 159.

[20] See Hawkes, *Metaphor*.

[21] Funk, "Parable as Metaphor," 133–62; particularly 146–47. Funk never really addresses the issue of how he knows the story deliberately references the kingdom of God, but simply assumes it.

[22] Funk, "Good Samaritan as Metaphor," 31–34.

as metaphor" (a separate and distinct step) that seeks "to raise its meaning into discursive language."[23] About his "reading" he says:

> The parable is therefore also an invitation to comport oneself as the story indicates: it does not suggest that one behave as a good neighbor like the Samaritan, but that one become the victim in the ditch who is helped by an enemy. Indeed, the parable as metaphor was meant to be permission to so understand oneself. The metaphor is permission because it gives reality that shape.[24]

One cannot be more specific about the meaning of the story because, according to Funk, the story is nonliteral language (i.e., metaphor). But one can reflect on the story to attempt to raise its figurative language to discursive speech, but, as he notes, the abstraction is quite different from the language of the story itself:[25]

(1)   In the kingdom of God mercy comes only to those who have no right to expect it and who cannot resist it when it comes.

(2)   Mercy always comes from the quarter from which one does not and cannot expect it.

An enterprising theologian might attempt to reduce these two sentences to one:

(1)   In the kingdom mercy is always a surprise.[26]

Funk summarizes the story in the language of the story and then as a second and distinct step he offers an abstraction of the story in other terms. Others who follow Funk are not as careful and obscure their reading and their abstraction of the story's "meaning." For example, Crossan writes of this parable:

> If we abandon finally and completely the idea of an example, as deriving from the tradition and not from Jesus, we must see this as a parable and so suggest the leap from literal point to the metaphorical point which is the real purpose of the literary creation. The literal point confronted the hearers with the necessity of saying the impossible and having their world turned upside down and radically questioned in its presuppositions. The metaphorical point is that *just so* does the Kingdom of God break abruptly into human consciousness and demand the overturn of prior values, closed options, set judgments, and established conclusions. . . . The hearer struggling with the contradictory dualism of Good/Samaritan is actually experiencing in and through this the inbreaking of the Kingdom. Not only does it happen like this, it happens in this.[27]

---

[23] Funk, "Good Samaritan as Metaphor," 34.

[24] Funk, "Good Samaritan as Metaphor," 34.

[25] It is significant that Funk recognizes that his abstraction will take him out of the story, and that he senses a need to stay as close as possible to the language used by the story.

[26] Funk, "Good Samaritan as Metaphor," 34.

[27] Crossan, *In Parables*, 65–66.

And Scott:

> As parable the story subverts the effort to order reality into the known hierarchy of priest, Levite, and Israelite. Utterly rejected is any notion that the kingdom can be marked off as religious: the map no longer has boundaries. The kingdom does not separate insiders and outsiders on the basis of religious categories.[28]

Perrin has argued that the parables are best understood as symbol.[29] In brief a symbol is one thing that "stands for," or represents, another thing. It derives from the Greek συμβάλλειν, to cast, to throw together, to unite; and hence σύμβολον is a sign or token by which one stated thing evokes something else. Thus a "symbol" is something that stands for or represents another thing. Symbol and metaphor are quite similar, and yet also different. While a metaphor is one thing that means something else, a symbol means what it is and something more beyond that.[30]

> The symbol is the richest and at the same time the most difficult of the poetical figures. Both its richness and its difficulty result from its imprecision. Although the poet may pin down the meaning of his symbol to something fairly definite and precise . . . more often the symbol is so general in its meaning that it is able to suggest a great variety of more specific meanings. It is like an opal that flashes out different colors when slowly turned in the light. The choice in "The Road Not Taken" [a poem by Robert Frost], for instance, concerns some choice in life, but what choice? . . . We cannot determine what particular choice the poet had in mind, if any. . . . [31]

It is in this sense that Perrin understands the parables. They are "tensive symbols," and as such "have a set of meanings that can neither be exhausted nor adequately expressed by any one referent. . . ."[32] Although Perrin did not make a detailed analysis of the story of the Samaritan, his approach to the story is in line with the metaphorical approach offered by Funk, Crossan, and Scott:

> [The parables] challenge the hearer to explore the manifold possibilities of the experience of God as king, and they do so in ways which constantly remind the hearer that, on the one hand, God is to be experienced in the historicality of the world of everyday, while on the other hand, they claim that God is to be experienced precisely in the shattering of that everyday world.[33]

---

[28] Scott, *Hear Then the Parable*, 201–2 and cf. id., *Symbol-Maker*, 29.
[29] See *Language of the Kingdom*.
[30] Perrine, *Sound and Sense*, 82–108.
[31] Perrine, *Sound and Sense*, 85.
[32] Perrin, *Language of the Kingdom*, 30. A "tensive symbol" is loaded with a multiplicity of potential meanings. On the other hand, a "steno-symbol" has a one-to-one relationship to that which it represents, such as mathematical symbols.
[33] Perrin, *Language of the Kingdom*, 199.

One writer who takes a different approach is James Breech.[34] Arguing that the comparative frames introducing the stories of Jesus in early Christian literature derive from early Christian attempts to understand them, he treats the parables as "stories" that "disclose dimensions of reality."[35]

Hence in the story of the Samaritan, Breech finds that Jesus:

> directly addresses the problem of evil, in the form of death which threatens to terminate the [wounded] man's story.[36]

> The story functions in order to focus attention on the fact that the third man's activity is opposed to the robbers' activity, that it is oriented to enabling the beaten man to continue his story. . . . [37]

> The *ultimate* force grasped by Jesus' vision in the parable is not evil, but rather the superabundant power out of which the third man lives, and which he communicates to the innkeeper.[38]

Breech does not read the Samaritan as metaphor, symbol, or example story, but rather as an existentialist or a structuralist might. All historical indicators are ultimately disregarded,[39] and the story is read as a timeless narrative dealing with the possibilities and depravities of human existence bounded by death and life. Breech has universalized an occasional incident.[40]

THE POETICS OF THE STORY

In this section I will divide the narrative into appropriate periods and clauses, and examine its assonance and consonance, as was done in chapter 4. The goal is to determine what the poetics of the narrative imply for a reading of the story. Since Luke's story is the only extant version, no comparison with other versions is possible.

PERIOD I	1	ἄνθρωπός τις κατέβαινεν ἀπὸ Ἰερουσαλὴμ εἰς Ἰεριχὼ
	2	καὶ λῃσταῖς περιέπεσεν,
	3	οἳ καὶ ἐκδύσαντες αὐτὸν καὶ πληγὰς ἐπιθέντες ἀπῆλθον ἀφέντες ἡμιθανῆ.
PERIOD II	1	κατὰ συγκυρίαν δὲ ἱερεύς τις κατέβαινεν ἐν τῇ ὁδῷ ἐκείνῃ
	2	καὶ ἰδὼν αὐτὸν ἀντιπαρῆλθεν·

---

[34] Breech, *Silence of Jesus*, 158–83.

[35] Breech, *Silence of Jesus*, 10, 74, 166.

[36] Breech, *Silence of Jesus*, 173.

[37] Breech, *Silence of Jesus*, 178.

[38] Breech, *Silence of Jesus*, 180.

[39] Breech, *Silence of Jesus*, 162–63.

[40] Breech, *Silence of Jesus*, 181.

PERIOD III   1   ὁμοίως δὲ καὶ Λευίτης κατὰ τὸν τόπον ἐλθὼν
2   καὶ ἰδὼν ἀντιπαρῆλθεν.

PERIOD IV   1   Σαμαρίτης δέ τις ὁδεύων ἦλθεν κατ' αὐτὸν
2   καὶ ἰδὼν ἐσπλαγχνίσθη,
3   καὶ προσελθὼν κατέδησεν τὰ τραύματα αὐτοῦ
4   ἐπιχέων ἔλαιον καὶ οἶνον,
5   ἐπιβιβάσας δὲ αὐτὸν ἐπὶ τὸ ἴδιον κτῆνος
6   ἤγαγεν αὐτὸν εἰς πανδοχεῖον
7   καὶ ἐπεμελήθη αὐτοῦ.

PERIOD V   1   καὶ ἐπὶ τὴν αὔριον
2   ἐκβαλὼν ἔδωκεν δύο δηνάρια τῷ πανδοχεῖ
3   καὶ εἶπεν, ἐπιμελήθητι αὐτοῦ,
4   καὶ ὅ τι ἂν προσδαπανήσῃς
5   ἐγὼ ἐν τῷ ἐπανέρχεσθαί με ἀποδώσω σοι.

One notes immediately the structural balance and verbal similarity that exists among periods I–IV:

I,3	καὶ	ἐκδύσαντες	αὐτὸν	
	καὶ πληγὰς	ἐπιθέντες		ἀπῆλθον
		ἀφέντες	ἡμιθανῆ	
II,2	καὶ	ἰδὼν	αὐτὸν	ἀντιπαρῆλθεν
III,2	καὶ	ἰδὼν		ἀντιπαρῆλθεν
IV,2	καὶ	ἰδὼν		ἐσπλαγχνίσθη

And there is great similarity in expressing the subjects of periods I–IV:

I,1	ἄνθρωπός	τις
II,1	ἱερεύς	τις
III,1	Λευίτης	[τις is also evoked by ὁμοίως δὲ καὶ]
IV,1	Σαμαρίτης	τις

In order to examine the assonance and consonance of the story I list here all occurrences of four or more repetitions in a given period. Because the story is considerably longer than the Leaven, one might expect considerably more euphony, but this is not necessarily the case.

PERIOD I

Assonance	α = 9	ε = 15	ο = 4
	ι = 6	η = 6	αι = 5
Consonance	ν = 10	τ = 7	ρ = 4
	θ = 4	κ = 5	σ = 11
	π = 7		

PERIOD II

| Assonance | α = 6 | ε = 7 | ι = 5 |
| Consonance | κ = 5 | ν = 9 | τ = 6 |

PERIOD III

Assonance	o = 4	α = 4
Consonance	τ = 5	ν = 6

Periods IV and V are considerably expanded in the text in comparison to the first three periods; hence one would expect to find increased euphony in consonants and vowels. And so we do.

PERIOD IV

Assonance	α = 12	ε = 15	αι = 4
	ι = 9	o = 11	
	η = 8	αυ = 6	
Consonance	σ = 10	ν = 18	π = 7
	τ = 13	λ = 5	
	δ = 7	κ = 7	

PERIOD V

Assonance	αι = 4	η = 5	ω = 7
	ε = 13	o = 6	
	ι = 6	α = 9	
Consonance	κ = 5	τ = 6	δ = 6
	π = 8	ν = 11	σ = 6

Aside from the fact that in proportion to the amount of text the number of repetitions is quite small, there does not seem to be in either period IV or V a conscious use of euphony or a stylized structuring of the story beyond what was noted in periods I–IV. The few euphonic phrases are not nearly enough to overcome the basic prosaic quality of the narrative.[41]

What is significant in the narrative is what the third traveler does. Periods I–III are set apart from periods IV and V by their economy of description, similarity in form, and even verbal repetition. Periods IV and V are linked to periods I–III by the formula in clauses 1 and 2 of period IV: "and a certain . . . seeing . . . was moved to compassion." By comparison to the first three periods the unexpected elaboration of the behavior of the third traveler throws the focus of the story on him.

Most of period IV and all of period V are devoted to his behavior. The first half of the story ends with IV,2: καὶ ἰδὼν ἐσπλαγχνίσθη. IV,3 through V,5 is clarification of what it means to "have compassion" (ἐσπλαγχνίσθη). Until this point the story has been spiraling downward

---

[41] For example:

I,1   Ἰερουσαλὴμ εἰς Ἰεριχὼ
I,3,   ἐπιθέντες . . . ἀφέντες
III,1/2   κατὰ τὸν τόπον ἐλθὼν/καὶ ἰδὼν
IV,1/2   ὁδεύων . . . κατ᾽ αὐτὸν/καὶ ἰδὼν
IV,3/4   προσελθὼν . . . /ἐπιχέων ἔλαιον καὶ οἶνον

toward tragedy. But the compassion of the Samaritan reverses an expected tragic conclusion with a comic ending.

THE STORY: LUKE 10:30b–35

A certain man. The auditors know virtually nothing about the figure traveling from Jerusalem to Jericho. He could have been of any nationality: Greek, Roman, Jew, Samaritan, or something else. Most interpreters simply ignore the anonymity of this shadowy figure as apparently insignificant for the story;[42] or if they note the anonymity of the man, they simply assume he is Jewish.[43] That identification likely stems from one of the following three assumptions: (1) the designation of priest and Levite as characters in the story imply it; (2) being misled by Luke's emphasis on the designated character of the third man as Samaritan, they assume the story does not work without the injured man being Jewish;[44] (3) they assume that Jesus told the story to Jews, and hence the auditors would assume that the injured man was Jewish. But precisely because social labels are deliberately given to three of four characters in the story,[45] the anonymity of the fourth character must be taken seriously.[46] The anonymity of the injured man may likewise be a deliberate non-designation. It adds a universal quality to the story that makes identification with this character that holds the story together much easier for any auditor.

---

[42] Compare, e.g., Talbert, *Reading Luke*, 123–25; Stein, *Introduction*, 72–81; Jeremias, *Parables*, 202–6; Boucher, *Parables*, 125–29; Crossan, *In Parables*, 57–66; Linnemann, *Parables*, 51–58. But on the other hand, see Bruce who specifically calls attention to the wounded man's anonymity (*Parabolic Teaching*, 347).

[43] Oesterley, *Gospel Parables*, 161; Bailey, *Poet and Peasant*, 2.42; Scott, *Hear Then the Parable*, 194; Funk "Good Samaritan as Metaphor," 32.

[44] Jüngel (*Paulus und Jesus*, 172), e.g., calls attention to the rabbinic tradition that a Jew who accepts aid from a non-Jew will delay Israel's redemption.

[45] Breech, *Silence of Jesus*, 162–63, assumes that the social labels have been added to the original story of Jesus, because such social labeling is not typical of the stories of Jesus. But the stories of Jesus do deal with social functions, and the functions are designated as such. For example, servants, householder, merchant, fisherman, shepherd, tenants, farmer, vinedresser, steward, hired men, judge, Pharisee, toll collector.

[46] Of course it may be as Smith (*Parables*, 180) has pointed out: the man was unidentified because the popular story tends to omit irrelevant details. My point, on the other hand, is that the conscious identification of the three other characters focuses attention on the injured man, thereby making his lack of identification significant. Bailey (*Poet and Peasant*, 2.42) points out that the fact that he is stripped of his clothing deprives him of his "distinctive traditional dress" which would have identified his ethnic group. If this is correct, it confirms that the man's anonymity is essential to any reading of the story.

Hence the story begins with a completely anonymous man, who was in fact nobody in particular; in short, he was anyone. Any characterization attributed to the injured man apart from what the story says of him constitutes interpretation of the story by the modern exegete or auditor/reader. Such characterization of the injured man is an attempt to control the horizons of the story. Should one insist that the story must have been told to Jews, and hence the injured man would naturally be identified in such a context as Jewish, one can only reply that understanding the situation in this way is an assumption. The injured man can be whoever any auditor wants him to be—if the interpreter does not violate the givens of the story and identify him for the auditor/reader. That the injured man was Jewish is simply not validated by the givens of the story.

Went down from Jerusalem to Jericho. This is one of two stories that preserve a geographical allusion. Jerusalem is located in the Central Highlands of Palestine at an elevation of about 2500 feet above sea level, while Jericho, lying seventeen miles to the northwest, is situated in the Jordan valley at an elevation of about 800 feet below sea level. Hence the descent from Jerusalem to Jericho is about 3300 feet in seventeen miles, almost 200 feet per mile.[47]

He fell among thieves who stripped him, beat him, and left him half dead. In antiquity the road going from Jerusalem to Jericho was known to be dangerous,[48] and even today it is desolate. What these particular thieves did to the traveler was quite vicious. They robbed him,[49] stripped him, and, *then* while he was completely helpless and nude before them, they beat him. The loss of his clothes that may have distinguished his race and village[50] further strongly underlines the man's anonymity. He is left lying on one side of the road (cf. Luke 10:31–32; "on the other side") "half dead," and hence as Scott notes, he could very well have been taken for dead.[51]

---

[47] See Breech's note *Silence of Jesus*, 162, n. 1, though Breech challenges the originality of the location. Compare, however, the specificity of the location (i.e., temple) in the story of the Pharisee and toll collector.

[48] For sources see Scott, *Hear Then the Parable*, 194; Oesterley, *Gospel Parables*, 161; Bailey, *Poet and Peasant*, 2.41–42; Plummer, *Luke*, 286.

[49] Breech is technically correct that the story does not pointedly say the man was "robbed," i.e., that the thieves took what goods and money he may have had (*Silence of Jesus*, 166). But "falling among robbers" could scarcely mean anything other than "being robbed." The stripping and the beating are vicious acts above and beyond the robbing, and are hence mentioned apart from the robbery. See Bruce (*Parabolic Teaching*, 347), who notes that καὶ before ἐκδύσαντες implies a previous act of violence.

[50] Bailey, *Poet and Peasant*, 2.42.

[51] Scott, *Hear Then the Parable*, 194.

"*By chance*" (κατὰ συγκυρίαν). Few commentators have paid any attention to this phrase.[52] It is a rather remarkable expression that creates all kinds of havoc with the plot of the story. How seriously is one to regard the narrator's affirmation that it was merely "by chance" that it was a priest, Levite, and Samaritan who happened to pass that way, in the light of the fact that the narrator has deliberately bothered to identify them with these specific social labels?[53] The pure secularity of the expression "by chance" grates against any attempt to read the events of the story within a traditional Christian or Jewish frame of reference.[54] With these words the story has suddenly been invaded with the randomness of a complete secularity in which nothing is predetermined. There is no wise, benevolent, overarching divine providence that assures a happy ending to the story. Its outcome, as this expression assures the reader, is far from certain. The next travelers by the spot where the injured man lies could have been anyone. Frankly, the expression κατὰ συγκυρίαν renders any interpretation of the story that turns on the social labels of priest, Levite, or Samaritan highly unlikely.

A certain priest went down that road, and looking at him, passed by on the other side. Priests, of course, were major functionaries in the Jerusalem temple who, during their shift in the temple, performed daily and special sacrifices.[55] As a priest, this traveler would have held a position of prestige in the community. There was, however, nothing special about this particular priest; he was only one of the several thousand who served periodically in the temple during the time of Jesus.[56] For anyone familiar with temple worship, the appearance of the priest would have evoked the image of the temple cultus. In a sense, though not formally, the priest would have represented the temple.

Some commentators have argued that the priest had proper religious grounds for avoiding what he thought was a dead body beside the road, since defilement by touching a dead body would require the priest

---

[52] Both Plummer (*Luke*, 287) and Oesterley (*Gospel Parables*, 161–62) want to reduce the "accidental" character of the expression and bring it under the umbrella of divine providence, but without good reason. But see Scott (*Hear Then the Parable*, 195), who correctly notes the random character of the expression.

[53] That all three subsequent travelers fall under the influence of κατὰ συγκυρίαν in 10:31 is suggested by (1) ὁμοίως . . . καὶ (10:32), (2) the string of δὲ connectives (10:31, 32, 33), and (3) the similar language used of each traveler in 10:31, 32, 33. But see Bruce (*Parabolic Teaching*, 344), who seems to reject this possibility.

[54] κατὰ συγκυρίαν may be simply irony if the narrator says, "now by chance . . . " and "winks" at his audience at the same time. So everyone hearing the statement understands it is not a serious statement. I think this is not the case, however, because of the general economy of language in these stories. See n. 79.

[55] See 1 Chron 24:1–19 and Luke 1:5, 8–9.

[56] Jeremias (*Jerusalem*, 147) reports that at the time of Jesus there were 7,200 priests that periodically served in the temple.

to go through a period of cleansing before he could offer sacrifice again.[57] Others, however, have noted that the direction the priest was traveling— from Jerusalem to Jericho—suggests that he was returning home follow- ing his shift in the temple. Hence defilement would not have disrupted his temple ministrations.[58] Scott, however, shows from the Mishnah and Talmud that the priest (and the Levite, as well) were not excused from burying a "neglected corpse," which is precisely what the wounded man would have appeared to be. It was required that a corpse neglected on the road must be buried, and the holy man may perform this task without threat of uncleanness.[59] The story, however, portrays the priest and Levite as not even bothering to verify whether or not he was dead.[60]

Others have speculated that the priest's behavior may have been motivated by fears that the robbers might still be lingering in the location. Hence, out of fear for his own safety the priest quickly scurries past the man and continues his journey.[61]

But the fact is that readers simply do not know why the priest was traveling or what went through his mind when he saw the man beside the road. All a reader knows for certain is that he, like the injured man, was traveling between Jerusalem and Jericho. A reader may be shocked by his behavior, but there is simply not enough information at this point in the story to pass judgment on his actions. The story is not done yet, and readers do not know what kind of story it is. Perhaps the behavior of the priest is typical of the people who live in the make-believe world of this narrative. So, for the moment, the wise auditor/reader will reserve judgment—and wonder.

And likewise also a Levite coming to the place and looking, passed by on the other side. Levites were also temple functionaries, lesser in rank and responsibility than priests; they performed chores other than sacrifice.[62] Like the priest, a Levite would have been understood to "represent" the temple and its services. Again the narrative tells practically nothing about this figure. He is presented simply as a temple functionary who also comes to the place where the injured man is lying. The direction he is traveling is not even made clear. But he, like the priest, sees the injured man and without closer investigation passes by on the other side of the road. And as in the case of the priest, no explanation is given for his behavior. The auditor/reader knows only that, for whatever reason, his

---

[57] See Scott, *Hear Then the Parable*, 195–96, for the literature.

[58] See, for example, Scott, *Hear Then the Parable*, 195, n. 29.

[59] Scott, *Hear Then the Parable*, 196.

[60] The priest and Levite saw him and passed by on the far side of the road, but the Samaritan went up to him, saw him, and was moved to compassion.

[61] Scott, *Hear Then the Parable*, 195.

[62] See 1 Chron 23. Jeremias reports that at the time of Jesus there were 9,600 Levites engaged in temple service (*Jerusalem*, 147).

behavior reinforces that of the priest. The auditor may be shocked at, or applaud, the behavior of the Levite, but the fact that two figures of social standing have acted in similar fashion leads to the suspicion that there may be a perfectly "logical"[63] explanation for the behavior of both men. In short, the Levite's behavior reinforces that of the priest, at least for the purposes of this story.

And a certain Samaritan . . . The hostility between Judah and Samaria is well documented and widely known.[64] The tension between the two regions runs from the early settlement of the area from the conquest through New Testament times.[65] Samaritans identified themselves as the descendants of the Northern Kingdom of Israel (from the half tribes of Ephraim and Manasseh) who survived the Assyrian deportation in 722 BCE. When forced out of the city of Samaria by Alexander the Great ca. 332 BCE, they fled to Shechem and on nearby Mount Gerizim built a temple that would have clearly competed with the Jerusalem temple, only a short distance away.[66] The Samaritan temple was destroyed in 128 BCE by the Hasmonean king, John Hyrcanus. Although the temple was never rebuilt, the Samaritans continued to worship at Gerizim, as they did in the time of Jesus (John 4:5, 20). They accepted the Pentateuch as scripture and claimed descent from Abraham. They are called "Samaritans" after the name of the chief city of the district, Samaria.

The inhabitants of the area south of Samaria, Judah (from which the designation "Jew" is derived), on the other hand, regarded the Samaritans as descendants of the colonialists imported into the region by the Assyrian conqueror Shalmaneser (2 Kings 17:21–41). Jews regarded the Samaritan knowledge of the Hebrew faith as both limited and corrupted by syncretism.[67] Jews, therefore, grouped them with Gentiles and did not regard them as true descendants of Abraham.[68] During the

---

[63] By this I mean either "logical" according to the canons of the story, or "logical" according to the conventions of the social world of first-century Palestine.

[64] See Linnemann, *Parables*, 54; Talbert, *Reading Luke*, 123; Bailey, *Poet and Peasant*, 2.48, and Oesterley, *Gospel Parables*, 162.

[65] Wright-Filson-Albright, *Historical Atlas*, 61b–62a.

[66] There was, of course, nothing *de facto* sectarian about building another temple. In the ancient world there were Jewish temples at Elephantine in Upper Egypt, Leontopolis in Lower Egypt, and at one time in the Transjordan; see Koester, *Introduction*, 1.248.

[67] *IDB* 4.191, s.v. "Samaritans." In this regard see the discussion by Koester, *Introduction*, 1.247–49.

[68] See Linnemann, (*Parables*, 54) who, citing Bugge (*Haupt-Parabeln*, 395), writes of the Samaritans: Between the Jews and the Samaritans "there reigned implacable hatred. On the Jewish side it went so far that they cursed the Samaritans publically in the synagogues, and prayed God that they should have no share in eternal life; that they would not believe the testimony of a Samaritan nor accept service from one." See also Oesterley, *Gospel Parables*, 162.

first century, hostility between the two religious groups was particularly tense due probably to an incident in which Samaritans were thought to have scattered human bones throughout the temple at Jerusalem (6–9 CE) during a Passover season.[69]

It seems, however, quite unlikely that the two religious communities were totally isolated. Mount Gerizim was only about 30 miles from Jerusalem with no natural barriers intervening. And if Jews went through Samaria when traveling from Galilee to Jerusalem, as they did,[70] it is highly likely that Samaritans would also have been found in and around Jerusalem. Just a few years before the defilement of the temple by Samaritans, Herod had taken a Samaritan wife,[71] and Jewish religious injunctions against Samaritans verify that Jews and Samaritans had social interaction.[72] Hence I am not persuaded by the argument that finds the Samaritan's presence on the Jerusalem/Jericho road a threat to the reality of the story.[73]

As he journeyed, came to him, and looking, was moved to compassion. Here we have, for this story, radically unexpected behavior. Until this point the custom in the story has been that people can be abused with impunity, and abused people are avoided, but it is not made clear to the auditor/reader why this is the case. The third traveler, the Samaritan, however, goes directly to the man beside the road and examines him (10:33). But the priest and the Levite had just looked at him from a distance[74] and then avoided him. When the Samaritan saw the wounded man's condition, he was moved to compassion.[75] It is the extraordinary behavior of the Samaritan (that is to say, extraordinary in this particular story) that gives the auditor/reader pause to reflect on the behavior of the priest and Levite. The attention given to the behavior of the third traveler is a tacit criticism by the narrator of the actions of priest and Levite.

---

[69] Jeremias, *Jerusalem*, 352–58.

[70] According to Jeremias (*Jerusalem*, 353) harsh treatment of Jews by Samaritans while Jews were traveling through Samaria was one of the reasons for the Jewish hostility.

[71] Jeremias, *Jerusalem*, 353.

[72] See the references in Mishnah that show Jews and Samaritans in social interaction: *Ber.* 7.1, 8.8; *Demai* 3.4, 5.9, 6.1, 7.4; *Ter.* 3.9; *Ketub.* 3.1; *Ned.* 3.10; *Giṭ.* 3.10; *Qidd.* 4.3; *Nid.* 4.1.

[73] See Scott, *Hear Then the Parable*, 199, n. 50. I agree that the story is fictional, but it is realistic fiction.

[74] The same expression is used of all three travelers when they see (ἰδών, 10:31, 32, 33) the wounded man beside the road, but their perspective is radically different. It is pointedly said of the Samaritan that he went to him (ἦλθεν κατ' αὐτόν) and then looked at him. Clearly the story depicts the men examining the wounded man from different perspectives.

[75] See n. 14 above; Breech, I think incorrectly, takes ἐσπλαγχνίσθη to be Luke's adjustment to the story.

And approaching, he bound up his wounds, pouring on oil and wine, and putting him upon his own beast he brought him to an inn and cared for him. On the next day . . . he gave two denarii to the innkeeper and said, "care for him and whatever more you may spend in addition, I will pay you when I return." Luke 10:34–35 emphasizes the Samaritan by focusing attention on specific details of his behavior. The Samaritan cared for the man by treating his wounds "medically" in the field with oil and wine.[76] Taking him to an inn, he continues care, and then he arranges with the innkeeper to care for him further. This triple concrete expression of compassion starkly contrasts with the double "by-pass" behavior of the priest and Levite.

He pays the innkeeper the equivalent of two days' wages for a laborer.[77] And finally in a remarkable act of charity the Samaritan tells the innkeeper that "whatever more he may spend" in caring for the man, he, the Samaritan, will reimburse him when he returns. In short, there is apparently no limit to the Samaritan's personal obligation on behalf of the wounded man![78]

HOW DOES THE STORY WORK?
SOME POSSIBLE EXPLANATIONS

Although the narrator claims (10:31) that it was merely coincidence that a priest, Levite, and Samaritan happened along that road in that particular sequence, the deliberate selection of these three characters for parts in the drama may actually be significant after all. κατὰ συγκυρίαν could be read as the narrator's irony. Hence with a "twinkle in his eye," a shrug of his shoulder, and a slight wink at the audience the narrator describes the travelers, but both he and the audience realize he really does not mean what he says. In short, if one regards κατὰ συγκυρίαν as irony, then the selection of priest, Levite, and Samaritan is absolutely essential to how the story functions and is hence essential to the story's design.[79]

---

[76] See Scott *Hear Then the Parable*, 199, n. 52.

[77] Cf. Matt 20:2, 9.

[78] The story is silent on a whole range of questions that would help the auditor/reader put this final aspect of the Samaritan's actions in better perspective. For example, was he a man of means who could afford to make such a commitment? Was he a frequent traveler on this road and known to the innkeeper?

[79] I do not take the statement to be irony. The economy of language in these stories is well known. If the expression was made as irony it would, in my opinion, long before have dropped out of the narrative, since its presence in a written narrative adds nothing to the story and actually, once noticed, works against a Christian reading of the story. Readers do tend to take the social functions of priest, Levite, and Samaritan as essential to the story, and this little bit of secularity in the story grates on modern interpretations, since it undermines the social roles of priest, Levite, and

If the characters are essential to the functioning of the story, the story may hold an anti-temple motif, on the basis of which the story would then turn. Read from this perspective the priest and the Levite represent the Jerusalem temple and are cast in the narrative as opponents of the healing of the wounded man. The Samaritan, on the other hand, representing a competing temple and religious system, is cast as a helper that facilitates the injured man's healing. On the basis of this kind of reading, one must assume that the audience will recognize the innate humanity of the Samaritan's behavior and the basic inhumanity of the behavior of priest and Levite.[80] The story is therefore told at the expense of the priest and Levite. It is not so much that the Samaritan is the hero, but rather that the priest and Levite are villains, and their villainy is underscored in that a despised Samaritan fulfills the spirit of Torah.

Had the injured man been Jewish,[81] it is possible that the story may have turned on the basis of an anti-Jewish motif. One rabbinic tradition asserts that a Jew who accepts alms and aid from a Samaritan will delay the redemption of Israel.[82] Read from this perspective, the story directly evokes and plays off of the religious hostility between Jews and Samaritans. In this case, it is not specifically the temple cultus that is at issue, but rather the legalistic character of Jewish religion. Under this reading the story turns on the absurdity of such a religious attitude.[83] The injured

---

Samaritan, and that it should not do as irony. Its challenge to the popular reading may be the reason it was omitted in the Old Latin manuscripts. If it is intended seriously, it undermines the significance of priest, Levite, and Samaritan. If it is irony it pointedly affirms the selection of these characters as essential to the story, while appearing to discount them.

[80] It seems unlikely to me that the story in its present form is simply anti-clerical. If that were the case the third traveler down the road would have been better cast as an "Israelite." The three classes of people in Israel were Priest, Levite, and Israelite (See Scott, *Hear Then the Parable*, 198–99). In this latter case the auditor/reader would have been confronted with the basic inhumanity of clerics contrasted by the layman who acted in the spirit of Torah. But the selection of the Samaritan as the helper of the injured man is clearly excessive for such an interpretation to function easily. The "Samaritan" brings associations to the story that do not contribute to a clear anti-clerical thrust. Indeed it subverts the anti-clerical interpretation since it draws attention to the religious hostility of Jews for Samaritans and invokes a competing religious system. See Crossan (*In Parables*, 64) for the distractions the use of the Samaritan adds to the story.

[81] See the discussion above. The identification of the injured man as Jewish is not part of the conscious design of the story, but rather an assumption about the story.

[82] Jüngel, *Paulus und Jesus*, 172.

[83] Scott, (*Hear Then the Parable*, 195–97) has shown that the argument depicting the priest and Levite as bound by Torah to avoid defilement from association with dead bodies is simply no longer a viable position, either as an excuse for their behavior or as the point on which the story turns. It is not a story that criticizes Jewish ritual restrictions. Hence it could not be an anti-Torah story.

man could have done nothing to aid himself. For him to refuse the aid of the Samaritan (even if he had been capable of it) would have been absurd under the conditions represented in the story.

On the other hand, it may be a simple example story with a universal moral after all. If one is not misled by the social codes priest, Levite, Samaritan, the story may simply emphasize proper human behavior: one human being humanely extending care and concern to a second human being in need, preceded by two examples of how not to behave: the priest and the Levite who fail to extend compassion and care.[84] But such an interpretation misses the point of the Samaritan's behavior; he went beyond being kind, even to the extent of risking all. The story clearly affirms the behavior of the Samaritan, but his behavior is more than that of a good neighbor.[85]

Robert Funk has argued that the story turns on the auditor's identification, or non-identification, with the man "in the ditch."[86] The "man in the ditch" as Funk calls him, is after all the one coherent element in the story. He holds the story together in that the narrative proceeds with narrator and auditor standing beside the injured man at all points in the story. Hence, as Funk argues: "If the auditor as Jew, understands what it means to be the victim in the ditch in this story, he/she also understands what the kingdom is all about."[87] For "in the Kingdom of God mercy comes only to those who have no right to expect it and who cannot resist it when it comes."[88]

Funk is correct in his stress on the wounded man. The auditor/ reader is indeed forced to identify with the anonymous man beside the road, since the story is narrated from the wounded man's perspective. The auditor/reader travels from Jerusalem with him to the point of the robbery; observes the robbery, stripping, and beating (10:30); stands beside him on his side of the road as priest and Levite pass him by (10:31–32), watches the unexpected behavior of the Samaritan (10:33–34); and travels to the inn with him.[89] Hence the auditor/reader sees the story and experiences it alongside the injured man. If the auditor/reader

---

[84] But see Crossan (*In Parables*, 63), who points out that if Jesus had wanted to teach a general moral there would have been no need to use three travelers with these particular social associations. Instead he would have simply talked of three travelers.

[85] See the discussion below.

[86] Funk, "Good Samaritan as Metaphor," 32; he is followed by Scott, *Symbol-Maker*, 27, and id., *Hear Then the Parable*, 200–201.

[87] Funk, "Good Samaritan as Metaphor," 33.

[88] Funk, "Good Samaritan as Metaphor," 34.

[89] Luke 10:35 is the only place in the story where the perspective of the narrator may have changed, since the action could have taken place away from the injured man. Though, to be sure, the injured man is still the focus of the action.

stays with the story, he/she has no alternative except to identify with the injured man since that is the design of the story.[90]

ANOTHER READING OF THE STORY

Standing beside the injured man at one side of the road, I am most struck by the magnificent grace of the Samaritan. At great personal risk[91] (remember that there had already been one robbery/assault at that location!), he goes to the aid of a faceless, nameless nobody. He offers immediate aid in the field at the scene of the robbery and assault, and assumes personal responsibility and liability for the injured man. He pays for the man's care for the immediate future (10:35a) and gives the innkeeper a "blank check" on his personal account for the man's long term care (10:35b).[92] By comparison the priest and Levite appear mean, little, and self-centered (to say the least), whatever their reason for not giving aid to the injured man.

It is only the grace of the third man that condemns the behavior of the first two travelers. Had the third man been a wealthy merchant who, upon stopping to render aid, was himself also robbed and beaten, a reader might well have viewed the actions of the first two travelers differently. In such a situation, a reader might have applauded the worldly wisdom of priest and Levite, who were too shrewd to be caught in such a trap, and then criticized the "merchant" for his naiveté. Or had the third traveler left clothing and food for the injured man and then continued on his journey leaving the injured man beside the road, a reader might well have been critical even of the third traveler who offered only superficial aid.

It seems to me that the story condemns the first two travelers, not as priest and Levite, but rather as human beings. What is at issue in this story is not their status in Jewish society, but their behavior in the human community. They could have borne any social code and we

---

[90] Scott (*Symbol-Maker*, 27) may be correct that the auditor/reader has the option of identifying with the priest and Levite (which they would not do) and the Samaritan (which they could not do); from the standpoint of reader response criticism can one also add the "robbers" as another alternative? But from the way the story is designed, like it or not, they are forced to "identify with," i.e., stand beside, the injured man and see things from his viewpoint. The auditors/readers do not actually "participate" in the story. They must remain where the narrator places them and critique the story or ignore the narrator and opt out of the story.

[91] This is at least potentially true for the Samaritan, regardless of how one reads the story.

[92] This unexpected "abundance" at the end of the story has parallels in the stories of a Sower and a King Settling Accounts.

would still condemn them precisely because the story condemns them through the extraordinary behavior of the third traveler.

I know very few people like the Samaritan in this story. I know a lot of "kind" people, but the Samaritan went beyond being kind—or even beyond being a "good neighbor." Were I to try to identify with (i.e., examine myself in terms of) the characters in the story, I find that I am always the injured man beside the road, i.e., I am always the recipient of the kindness, or pettiness, of others. On occasion I have been a "priest" or a "Levite," but candidly I have never been a "Samaritan." I do rejoice at the idealism of the Samaritan's benevolence, but my common sense says that one cannot conduct one's life as the Samaritan. One simply must be more practical. There may be a time to act like the Samaritan, but it is never when one travels the "Jericho road"; that is, to act as he did in such a potentially dangerous situation.

At this point in my analysis of the story, it becomes apparent that the horizons of the story have receded considerably. I am still reading the story from the inside and thinking about the story using the story's language. But I am beginning to catch a glimmer of a quite different view of reality, one that is very discomfiting; for now I am thinking not only about specific characters in the story, but also about the possibilities of human existence open to anyone. The story has suddenly invaded my objectivity and become a story about the possibilities of my own life. I find that its vision of the possibilities for human existence is frighteningly idealistic. The outlandish, unexpected, and radical behavior of the Samaritan challenges my own acts of charity. It assaults the delicate balance I have established between formal religious acts and life in the world. To respond with the excessive grace of the Samaritan to every faceless, nameless nobody I meet who lies at the extremities of existence will simply exhaust me and my resources. I simply do not have the resources or the time for such behavior, nor do I dare risk all as the Samaritan did. In short, the story challenges an auditor/reader to a radical selfless response in the face of every human need. By its very design the story undermines the objectivity of auditor/reader.

Any auditor or reader staying with the story faces only two possible responses to the injured man: callous indifference or outlandish benevolence. In the light of the second, the first is clearly wrong; while the second is an impossible ideal that condemns auditor/reader for failure to live at risk.

HOW MIGHT THE STORY HAVE BEEN HEARD IN THE CONTEXT OF ISRAEL'S FICTIONS ABOUT ITSELF

It is a rather complex story, and to judge by the diversity of modern readings, it could have been heard—as it has been read—in many different ways. Many, perhaps even most, readers might have aborted the story, being derailed by its social coding. Priests and Levites, along with certain devout Jews, who ignored the narrator's κατὰ συγκυρίαν could easily have been offended by finding themselves cast in such a callous role. Others may have aborted the story on the basis of the initial helpfulness of the Samaritan (10:33) without ever having reached the dramatic conclusion of the story, being offended that a despised Samaritan was cast in the role of helper. Because of the social coding, the common peasant may likely have heard it as an anti-temple or anti-clerical story.

But for those not derailed by the social codes, in what kind of context might they have heard the story: The broad context of the events of the story invokes "deeds of righteousness" that were required by Torah of all Jews (and also Samaritans!). These deeds were usually stated with specific reference to the sojourners, orphans, and widows. The concept of "deeds of righteousness" (Tob 2:9, 14) is quite broad and incorporates even the traditional background for the story of the Samaritan (i.e., Lev 19:18, 33–34) as well as "righteous behavior" in the treatment of the poor, in giving loans (cf. Sir 29:1–20) and alms (Sir 3:30–4:10; Acts 10:2, 4; 24:17). The appeal to "righteous deeds" as a part of the Israelite's ethical response to God is made on the basis of the facts (a) that God acts righteously (Tob 3:2) and so expects his people to act righteously (Sir 7:10; 17:22; 40:24; Isa 1:17; Hos 6:6; cf. Dan 4:27); (b) that Israel itself suffered while in Egypt (Deut 24:17–18, 19–22); (c) that charitable acts are tied to redemption (Prov 11:21; 14:21, 31; 16:16; 19:27; 21:12–13; Isa 1:27; Dan 4:24; Sir 3:14–15, 30; 29:19; Tob 4:10; 12:8; 13:6); and (d) that God rewards the righteous man (Prov 11:18; Tob 4:7–11). In fact no good can come to a man who does not give alms (Sir 12:3). The focus of the charitable deed is the fellow Israelite (Deut 15:7–11), but in particular it has to do with the poor (Deut 15:11; 24:10–15; Ps 112:9; Prov 21:13), the sojourner (Exod 22:21–27; 23:9; Lev 19:33–34; Deut 10:17–19; 14:28–29; 24:14–22; 26:11–15; 29:10–13; Ps 94:3–7; 146:9; Jer 22:3; Zech 7:10; Mal 3:5),[93] the widow and orphan (Exod 22:21–27; Deut 10:17–19; 24:17–22; 27:19; Isa 1:17; Ezek 22:7; Zech 7:9–10; Mal 3:5; Wis 2:10).

There is also a kind of international or universal quality to the righteous deeds expected of the Israelite. Compare in this regard Elijah's healing of the Syrian Naaman (2 Kgs 5:1–19) and Elisha's kindness to the widow of Zarephath (1 Kgs 17:8–24). There is also a contrast between

---

[93] The sojourner/proselyte according to Torah was to be regarded as Jewish (Num 9:14; 15:15–16; Exod 12:49; Lev 17:8–9, 15; 24:16, 22) and care was to be exercised for non-Jews living nearby (see *IDB* 4.397, s.v. "Sojourner"). The stranger was a non-Israelite who lived among Israelites. The sojourner could have been a non-Israelite or poverty stricken Israelite who brought himself under the protection of Israelites on whose property he had become a squatter.

formal ritual acts, such as fasting and sacrifices, and "righteous deeds" in which "housing for the homeless" and "clothing for the naked" (Isa 58:6–9; cf. Mic 6:6–8) are extolled over ritual acts. Job's protestations of innocence rested primarily on his "righteous deeds" that consisted of care for orphans, widows, the poor, blind, lame, and oppressed (Job 29:11–17; 31:16–21).

The righteous man is a liberal giver and lender and is rewarded for such behavior (Ps 37:26; 112:5; Prov 3:28; cf. Sir 40:17). One aspect of the character of the ideal wife in Israel is that she opens her hand to the poor and reaches out her hand to the needy (Prov 31:20). The Essenes required their members to contribute two days' wages every year for the orphan, poor, needy, aged, sick, the homeless, captive, the virgin with no near kin, and the maid for whom no man cares.[94]

Of course there were limits to what was expected of the righteous man. He should know the one to whom his kindness was extended; and his kindness was to be extended to the godly and humble but not the ungodly (Sir 12:1–7). His gifts should be made in proportion to what he has (Tob 4:8), lest he also fall into poverty (Sir 29:14–20). There are, however, examples of extreme sacrifices (Tob 1:16–20 [on burying the dead]; cf. Sir 7:32–35; 38:16–18).

It seems to me that the story would well have resonated for all Jewish auditors in the context of the late Jewish ideal of a righteous man, of which the Torah injunctions of love for the neighbor and sojourner were only a part.[95] In the story of the Samaritan the first two travelers by not extending themselves to care for the wounded man failed to act "righteously." Even if they thought the man was dead, they had an affirmative obligation as an act of charity to see to his burial (cf. Deut 21:1–9 and 1 Kgs 13:29; Isa 58:6–8; Sir 7:32–35),[96] but, on the other hand, if they knew him to be merely injured they also had an obligation to care for him (Deut 24:10–13; Job 31:19; Sir 38:16–18). That they did nothing— not even determining if the man were dead or alive—in a situation that clearly called for human compassion and affirmative action—graphically demonstrates their complete failure to live up to the ideal. The third man, on the other hand, goes beyond the expected ideal and acts in a remarkably radical, "irresponsible" way, i.e., even to the extent of placing his own life and possessions at risk.[97]

Hence the story would have been heard over against the concept of what it meant to be a righteous man in late Judaism. The story appears as a parody of that ideal. The behavior of the first two travelers is burlesque. The situation in which each finds himself calls for some kind

---

[94] CD 15; Vermes, *Scrolls*, p. 116.

[95] It clearly resonated in this way for Luke as Luke's context (10:25–28) shows.

[96] See Scott, *Hear Then the Parable*, 195–97.

[97] See Matt 19:21; Luke 18:22; Mark 10:21; cf. Matt 5:14 and Luke 6:30.

of humane response on the basis of Israel's ideal of a righteous man, but these two travelers are so insensitive that they do nothing. The behavior of the third man, on the other hand, would have been taken as satire. It is an exaggeration of the ideal, and hence the Samaritan appears to be a caricature of what it means to be a righteous man: a righteous man risks his life and living for the nobodies of the world.

7 ✤

The Treasure Parables in Matthew and Thomas

THERE EXIST IN EARLY CHRISTIAN LITERATURE TWO QUITE DIFFERENT narratives about Hid Treasure, both of which are attributed to Jesus of Nazareth. Hence readers of these narratives are initially faced with issues of originality and relationship, if any, between them. I begin with both narratives, considering their literary settings, reviewing how interpreters have read them, and making formal comparison of their structures. Then follow arguments for Matthew's revision of the tradition and Thomas's preservation of a traditional story. The elements of Thomas's story are then analyzed as first-century narrative fiction. Finally I propose another reading of the story.

THE SETTING OF THE STORIES:
EARLY CHRISTIAN READINGS

The *Gospel of Thomas*

The gospels of Thomas and Matthew each preserve two rather different narratives about treasure hidden in fields. Both attribute their story to Jesus of Nazareth. The story in Thomas (log. 109 = II,2:51,31–52,3), as with virtually all of Thomas's sayings, lacks a narrative context, such as setting and interpretation, that clues the reader into Thomas's reading of the story. The literary frame for the entire gospel (log. 1 = II,2:32,12–14), however, prompts the sequential reader[1] of the sayings to regard them all as having a particular secret meaning: "whoever discovers the interpretation of these sayings will not taste death." There is no obvious clue inside the narrative world of the Hid

---

[1] Readers of the Coptic *Gospel of Thomas*—with its codex format—would not have been encouraged to read the sayings seriatim, however.

Treasure in Thomas, however, that deliberately points the reader toward a particular secret meaning.

The immediate context of Thomas's treasure story capitalizes on the motif of "finding." Logion 107 is Thomas's version of the Lost Sheep: a large sheep *goes astray,* and the shepherd searches till he *finds* it (51,24–26); log. 108, without parallel in the canonical tradition,[2] ends: "and the *hidden* things shall be *revealed* to him" (51,30); log. 110 begins: "whoever has *found* the world and become rich" (52,4–5); log. 111 concludes with a saying about "*finding* oneself" (52,9–10); and log. 113 concludes with the unseen kingdom being "spread over the earth" (52,16–18).

One might argue that log. 110 is an interpretation of the Hid Treasure by virtue of its position following the treasure story: "Jesus said: 'whoever has found the world [i.e., the treasure] and become rich, let him deny the world.' " If that is the case, the compiler of this particular segment takes the finding of the treasure, and the finder's subsequent change of occupation to banker, to be a negative decision.[3] Hence in context Thomas's story may warn the reader that true riches consist in something other than material possessions.

This short collection of seven sayings (107–113) begins with the kingdom as a valuable "commodity" that must be searched for (107). It can be discovered through union with Jesus (108). The kingdom should not be confused with material prosperity (109–110). Materiality and the world are ephemeral (111–112); the one who recognizes that true wealth lies within, no longer belongs to the world (111). The "kingdom," therefore, is not a future possibility but a present reality (113). Hence the segment concludes with a tacit encouragement to seek the kingdom that is "already spread upon the earth."

The Gospel of Matthew

In Matthew's gospel the Hid Treasure appears in a section deliberately arranged by Matthew as a series of brief stories and their interpretations (13:1–53) spoken by Jesus to crowds (13:1–3, 34) and to his disciples (13:10, 36). The section 13:1–53 is organized with literary introduction (13:1–3) that breaks with the previous unit (11:1–12:50), which appears to be an early Christian homily on the theme: "The Son of David has Come." It is provided in 13:53 with a typical Matthean conclusion for

---

[2]Related sayings in the canonical tradition have been cited as John 4:7–15 and 7:37–39.

[3]Compare the conclusion to the parable of the Dinner Party in log. 64. It concludes with a narrator's comment "tradesmen and merchants shall not enter the places of my father" (44,34–35). And log. 95 in Thomas specifically forbids lending money for interest gained.

the discourses (cf. Matt 7:28; 11:1; 19:1a; 26:1). Hence Matthew structures 13:1–53 as a cohesive and integrated unit.

Matthew takes "parables" to be allegories that deliberately conceal Jesus' teaching on the kingdom from the crowds (13:3, 34).[4] Parables are not transparent, but cryptic stories and hence require explanation. The explanations (13:18–23, 37–43, 49–50) to these "allegories" are given only to the disciples (13:10–11, 16–17, 36, 51–52) because the crowds have deliberately hardened their hearts and closed their ears, just as the prophet had predicted they would (13:14–15).

According to Matthew these allegorical interpretations are "secrets (plural) of the kingdom" (13:11; cf. Mark's [singular] secret, 4:11). The plural "secrets" fits Matthew's allegorical method better; a study of the interpretations reveals that Matthew finds them to be full of multiple secrets. The revealing of the secrets to the disciples in what Matthew takes to be allegorical stories is unique revelation that comes just to them; not even the idealized worthies of the past (i.e., prophets and righteous men) knew it (13:16–17). Indeed, these secrets revealed in the "allegories" have been hidden since the foundation of the world (13:25). That explains why a Sower and other stories need explanation; it is because they are the heretofore hidden "word of the kingdom" (13:19; cf. Mark's "word," and Luke's "word of God"). Matthew's collection of stories in chapter 13 concerns for Matthew nothing less than the unlocking of the secrets of the kingdom of Heaven (13:24, 31, 33, 38, 41, 43, 44, 45, 47, 52). Hence Matthew has selected for this discourse stories about "fields" into which seed is sown (i.e., "concealed"; 13:3–4, 19–20, 24, 31, 36–37, 44), about things "hidden" (13:33), and about things that must be sought (13:45, 47–48).[5]

In the context of Matthew 13 what the man in the Hid Treasure finds in his field is heavenly treasure, specifically the "secrets of the kingdom of Heaven" (13:11). And a disciple willing to "invest all" (i.e., sell everything) for that treasure (cf. 6:19–21) becomes like the "householder," a scribe schooled in the arcane lore of the "secrets" of the kingdom (13:52). Such a scribe is, like Jesus (and one must also assume, like Matthew), able to bring out of his "store of treasure" (12:35; cf. 24:45) the new (i.e., Christian) and previously hidden secrets of the kingdom of

---

[4]Note that Matthew does not have Mark's more positive statement (at Mark 4:33) that implies the crowds could understand the parables.

[5]Matthew's reorganization of Mark 4 includes adding more stories that fit this concealment/discovery theme. Matthew also shortens the Markan discourse to accommodate the additions. A Sprouting Seed (Mark 4:26–29) is eliminated, though it would have fit Matthew's thematic concerns in the chapter. Matthew uses Mark 4:21 (= Matt 5:15), Mark 4:22 (Matt 10:26) and 4:24(= Matt 7:2) elsewhere, but Mark 4:25 Matthew uses immediately following Matt 13:11 in order to reinforce the theory that the secrets of the kingdom are for the disciples only. In no way is this information available to the crowds (Matt 13:13–15).

Heaven in terms of the "old" (i.e., Judaism) in ordinary stories about farming, baking, and fishing (13:52).[6] In some ways the Hid Treasure story provides the programmatic theme for the chapter.

There is nothing new in Matthew's portrayal of treasure as knowledge, wisdom, or lore. In the Hebrew scriptures wisdom is a hidden treasure that must be sought (Prov 2:1–5; cf. Isa 33:6). Since wisdom is hidden from the eyes of the living (Job 28:21; cf. Job 28:12–28), only God knows where and how to find it (Job 28:23). Wisdom's value exceeds riches (Prov 3:13); indeed it surpasses all value systems (Job 28:15–19). Happy is the one who finds wisdom (Prov 3:13); for whoever finds wisdom finds life (Prov 8:35).

MODERN INTERPRETATIONS

Virtually all modern interpreters understand the kingdom of God to be the real substance of Matthew's Hid Treasure parable.[7] For most, the story turns (i.e., from hidden treasure to kingdom of God) on the high cost the finder pays for the field: it cost the man everything to acquire the field. Hence commentators conclude the kingdom is of such extreme value that those who would acquire it must be willing to sacrifice everything.[8] Others assert the story turns on the treasure-finder's *risk* of everything.[9]

---

[6] See Argyle, *Matthew*, 108; Klostermann-Gressmann, *Matthäus*, 259; Holtzmann, *Synoptiker*, 251. This "reading" of the story fits Matthew's method elsewhere in the gospel. Matthew usually "blends" the new and the old. For example, in the formula quotations Matthew shows the new by means of and in concert with the old. And in the Sermon on the Mount Matthew portrays Jesus as setting himself over against the law (viz., "you have heard it said . . . but I say unto you"), but on the other hand, the law does have abiding value (5:17–20).

[7] Derrett (*Law*, 15–16) has an odd interpretation of the story: He notes that the idea that the substance of the story is about the kingdom of God (i.e., that it "explained what it should be like when an individual discovers . . . the kingdom of heaven and makes it his own") is "not in any sense untrue," but in a "topsy-turvy" way it explains something else that Matthew had "in mind": "In short, just as a man treasures a chance find or something else he is looking for for years, so God will treasure his servants. If an ordinary man will take such pains over a find of bullion . . . how much the more will God gloat . . . over those who have served him faithfully."

[8] Allen, *Matthew*, 154; Smith, *Parables*, 145; Oesterley, *Gospel Parables*, 83; Montefiore, *Synoptic Gospels* 2.213; Boucher, *Parables*, 112–13; Manson, *Sayings*, 196–97; Albright-Mann, *Matthew*, 170; Stein, *Introduction*, 104; Kingsbury, *Matthew 13*, 116; Holtzmann, *Synoptiker*, 250; Klostermann-Gressmann, *Matthäus*, 257; Weiss, *Schriften*, 336; Bugge, *Haupt-Parabeln*, 196–97; Jülicher, *Gleichnisreden Jesu*, 2.583, 585; Jeremias, *Parables*, 201; Sabourin, "Parables," 154–56; Dupont, "Paraboles du Trésor et de la Perle," 415–16.

[9] Dodd, *Parables*, 85–86; Linnemann, *Parables*, 101–3; Linnemann (p. 100) specifically rejects the notion that the man makes a sacrifice.

Two interpreters find that the parable turns on the scandal of the finder's immorality. Crossan for example, argues:

> The parabolic protagonist abandons, explicitly, his *goods*, and, implicitly, his *morals* to obtain the treasure. The parabolic challenge of the Kingdom then operates outward in three concentric circles. The innermost . . . circle has the Kingdom demand all our *goods*. . . . [It] then . . . threatens to consume our *morals*. . . . Finally . . . comes a third . . . circle. . . . The Kingdom demands our "all," demands the abandonment not only of our *goods* and of our *morals* but, finally, of our *parables* as well. The . . . demand of the Kingdom is for the abandonment of abandonment itself.[10]

Scott finds that the coming of the kingdom of God brings with it potential corruption:

> In the *Thomas* parable the treasure tempts the man to gain more treasure, and in the Matthean parable his joy at discovery so overtakes him that he brashly sells all and buys the field. His joy has led him astray. So now the man has sold all, is impoverished, yet possesses a treasure he dare not dig up unless he wants to face the rather embarrassing question of whence it came. This corrupting aspect of the kingdom is part of the scandalous, hidden aspect of the kingdom that Jesus' parables reveal. . . . The kingdom, according to the parable Treasure, comes before our deeds. And that is not only grace but potential corruption.[11]

Few modern interpreters trouble themselves with Thomas's Coptic version of the Hid Treasure story. Thomas was first published in 1959;[12] hence scholars who published before 1959 would not have had access to the text. The few who know and allude to Thomas's parable in their analysis disregard it either as a corruption of Matthew's more original story or as a different "gnostic story."[13] Virtually everyone else ignores Thomas's story.[14]

In 1982 Robert Gundry argued that Matthew himself created the Hid Treasure story.[15] Several years later (1986) I argued that Thomas's version of the Hid Treasure fitted the ministry and teaching of Jesus quite well and hence had a high claim to having originated with Jesus himself. I also argued, independently of Gundry but for similar reasons, that

---

[10] Crossan, *First Act*, 93.

[11] Scott, *Hear Then the Parable*, 402–3.

[12] Guillaumont, *Thomas*.

[13] Stein, *Introduction*, 99; Jeremias, *Parables*, 198; Dehandschutter, "Parabole du Trésor Caché," 214, 218; Dupont, "Paraboles du Trésor et de la Perle," 408; Crossan, *First Act*, 105–6; Sabourin, "Parables," 154.

[14] Albright-Mann, *Matthew*, 170; Linnemann, *Parables*, 70, n. 9; Kingsbury, *Matthew 13*, 162, n. 89; Derrett, *Law*, 1–15; Gundry, *Matthew*, 275–78; Boucher, *Parables*, 112–13; Jüngel, *Paulus und Jesus*, 142–45.

[15] Gundry, *Matthew*, 275–77. Gundry makes no reference to Thomas's version of the Hid Treasure story.

Matthew's version represented Matthew's radical revision of a traditional story.[16] Scott, dismissing both my arguments and those of Gundry,[17] takes both the parables of Thomas and Matthew to be different performances[18] of one "originating structure." Hence both stories, according to Scott, are "original" parables of Jesus in the sense that both derive from one originating structure.[19] In his discussion, however, Scott treats only the plot of the Matthean parable, and never addresses which of the two parables more accurately represents the originating structure.[20]

The most extensive treatment of the two Hid Treasure stories is by far that of Crossan. On the basis of a structural analysis, he argues that Thomas's version is a gnostic adaptation of a traditional Jewish parable.[21] Crossan's study is of immediate interest since he regards the *Gospel of Thomas* as reflecting a tradition independent of the Synoptic Gospels[22] and prefers two parables from Thomas to their Matthean versions as structural paradigms for studying all the parables of Jesus. His third paradigmatic parable is Matthew's version of the Hid Treasure.[23] Hence, in the light of his positive treatment of the Thomas tradition in other instances,[24] his rejection of Thomas's version of the Hid Treasure must be carefully considered.

COMPARATIVE STRUCTURAL ANALYSIS

Rabbinic Story[25]	Gospel of Thomas[26]	Matthew
It	The kingdom	The kingdom of Heaven
is like	is like	is like
a man	a man who had a [hidden] treasure	
		treasure hidden
	in his field	in the field,

---

[16] Hedrick, "Treasure Parable," 41–56.

[17] Scott, *Hear Then the Parable*, 392, n. 13; 393.

[18] See Crossan, *In Fragments*, 37–66.

[19] Scott, *Hear Then the Parable*, 395.

[20] His position is not that different from my own. I argued that Matthew had "radically revised a traditional parable" (Hedrick, "Treasure Parable," 49); I noted that "the Matthean parable may ultimately derive from Jesus" (55). In my judgment, however, there has been less manipulation in the Thomas version of the story.

[21] Crossan, "Hidden Treasure Parables," 360, 374; id., *First Act*, 106; id., *In Parables*, 33.

[22] Crossan, "Hermeneutical Jesus," 237–49; esp. pp. 238–39.

[23] Crossan, "Hidden Treasure Parables," 360, 374; id., *In Parables*, 33–36.

[24] Most recently see Crossan's comments: *Historical Jesus*, 282.

[25] Freedman-Simon, *Midrash Rabbah*, 219–20.

[26] Layton, *NHC II*, 1.90–93.

	without knowing it. And [after] he died, he left it to his [son]. The son [did] not know (about the treasure).	
who inherited a piece of ground used as a dunghill. Being an indolent man he went	He inherited the field	
and sold it for a trifling sum.	and sold [it].	
The purchaser	And the one who bought it went	which a man
began working and digging it up and he found a treasure	plowing and [found] the treasure.	finding
		concealed and from his joy he goes and sells all he has and buys that field.
	He began to lend money at interest to whomever he wished.	
out of which he built himself a fine palace. He began going about in public followed by a retinue of servants, all out of the treasure he found in it. When the seller saw it, he was ready to choke and exclaimed, "Alas what I have thrown away."		

All three stories have basically the same narrative structure, if a reader focuses on the treasure. In all three stories a fabulous "treasure"[27] has been deliberately concealed on an individual's property.[28] The

[27] One may project its "fabulous" character from the facts that in the rabbinic story the man builds a palace and acquires a retinue; in the Thomas story the man opens his own bank. In Matthew the fabulous character of the treasure is evident in that the man invested everything he had to secure it.

[28] Such is made completely clear in the case of Thomas/Matthew by the expression "hidden." In the case of the rabbinic story it would appear to be the case. Since it was valuable enough for the finder to build himself a "fine palace," it is unlikely that it was only a small but valuable object that someone had chanced to *lose* while working on the dunghill. Hence it was most probably concealed.

owner(s) is/are unaware of its existence. Its discovery is a fortuitous, random event that brings about significant change in the life of each of the finders.[29] The differences are, perhaps, greater than the similarities, but many of these are, to some extent, merely cosmetic, since the basic plot of all three stories is the same: i.e., the chance finding of a valuable treasure produces significant change in the finder's life.

The Thomas story stresses that the multiple owners do not know about the treasure: the treasure was in the field without the original owner "knowing it." The son who inherited the field "did not know about it." And he sold it. The man who bought it from the heir was likewise ignorant of its existence; he only happened to find it "while he was plowing."

The motifs of ignorance, inheriting, selling, buying, and finding are likewise present in the rabbinic parable. The rabbinic parable, however, stresses the motif of "industriousness," rather than ignorance. The land inherited by an "indolent" man was sold to another for a trifling sum. The purchaser, when he began to "work" the land, "digging it up," happened to find the treasure.[30] The feature of ignorance is implied in that the first owner would not have sold the land had he known about it, and the purchaser does not become aware of the treasure until after he begins to dig up the dunghill.

Matthew's story contains no feature of "inheriting," but has the motifs of selling, buying, and finding, although in a different order: finding, selling, and buying.[31] The motif of ignorance is implied; if the owner had known of the treasure, he would not have sold the land. Hence the owner was ignorant of the existence of the treasure. Matthew's parable introduces two new elements not present in the other two versions: The finder conceals the treasure immediately after its discovery and then is "overjoyed" at the discovery.

All three stories differ on the issue of the cost of the land: In the rabbinic story the price paid for the land is a "trifling amount"; in Thomas the cost of the land is apparently not germane to the narrative since it is not specified. But in Matthew's story the finder was moved by his joy at finding the treasure to liquidate everything he had in order to purchase the land. The reader does not know how much the land is worth, but it was certainly expensive, since the purchaser invested everything he had.

---

[29] See n. 27 above.

[30] One could find the motif of industriousness in the Thomas story as well, since it was not until the man started working (i.e., plowing the land) that he found the treasure. The motif is not emphasized in Thomas as it is in the rabbinic story, however.

[31] See Crossan, *In Parables*, 34.

Another difference among all three is that Thomas (he becomes a banker) and the rabbinic parable (he builds a fine palace; goes about in public, followed by a retinue of servants) specify what the man does with his newly acquired wealth. In Matthew, on the other hand, nothing is said about what he did with the treasure once he had acquired the field: Matthew's story ends with the man's acquisition of the field. Hence one must conclude that Matthew's story is constructed to work without an account of what the man did with the treasure[32] just as Thomas's apparently works without specifying how much the property cost. In the rabbinic story the "trifling cost" of the land is set in clear contrast to the finder's subsequent abundant wealth that the discovery provided him (builds fine palace, etc.)

Finally, only the rabbinic story describes the reaction of the previous owner at the new owner's good fortune: about to choke he exclaims "Alas! What I have thrown away!" It is interesting, however, that this expression of bitter regret assumes that the old owner had no claim on the buried treasure, once he had sold the land. It was just his loss.

One can conclude that the rabbinic story and the version in Thomas have more similarity to one another than to Matthew's story. None of the stories agree in their specifics, and yet they all three have the same basic plot, although with significant variations and twists.

AN ARGUMENT FOR MATTHEW'S REVISION OF THE TRADITION[33]

Even without a detailed comparison of the three stories, the similarities between the rabbinic story and the Thomas story are striking. The structural sequence is: treasure hidden,[34] property inherited, property sold, property worked, treasure found, options exercised. The structural sequence of Matthew's story, while similar, is nevertheless different: treasure hidden, treasure found, treasure rehidden, property sold, field purchased. Oddly, Crossan does not regard the reconcealing of the treasure as a significant structural element in Matthew's story,[35] even though it is not paralleled in the other two stories.

---

[32] For this reason Scott's conclusion (*Hear Then the Parable*, 402) that the man has impoverished himself for a treasure he cannot use is simply not cogent. Scott is writing his own story. Matthew's story concludes with the man's purchase of the land. There is no indication as to what happened next. That would be another story.

[33] See Hedrick, "Treasure Parable," 43–49.

[34] The rabbinic story does not mention that the treasure was hidden, but it is logically to be assumed that the treasure had been "concealed" prior to its discovery at the conclusion of the story.

[35] In all fairness to Crossan, however, Crossan does regard the rehiding of the treasure as the significant point on which Matthew's story turns (Crossan, *First Act*,

Further it is not clear, as Crossan argues, that the Thomas story is a *gnostic* version of the rabbinic story.[36] True, Thomas emphasizes the ignorance of the son who inherited the property, but all three stories, in order to work, mandate the owner's ignorance of the treasure hidden in his field, otherwise the owner would not have sold the field! Hence the Thomas version is only verbalizing what is clearly essential to the other two stories as well.[37] It is not even clear that the Thomas story is a different version of the rabbinic story (although their similarity does argue for the traditional character of Thomas's story). They are not identical, and the Thomas story does have at least two similarities to the version in Matthew that are not shared by the rabbinic story: they both begin in the same way (The kingdom . . . is like . . . treasure hidden in . . . field), and they both specifically mention the "hiding" of the treasure.

Arguably Matthew could have radically revised a traditional story (i.e., perhaps something like Thomas's performance). That being the case, he retained the traditional opening (the kingdom . . . is like . . . treasure hidden in . . . field), eliminated the multiple owners so as to focus on the discovery of the treasure, and then wrote a new conclusion. Two items suggest that this may well be the case. One instance is provided by Matthew's version of a Net Thrown into the Sea (Matt 13:47–50). Matthew's story has two very close parallels, one in the *Gospel of Thomas* log. 8 and another in Aesop's Fables.[38] Some scholars regard Thomas's version of a Net Thrown into the Sea as a completely new story, while others argue that Matthew and Thomas reflect different performances of the same story.[39] Scott argues that all three stories derive, apparently independently of one another, from a traditional "proverbial insight."[40] It seems more likely, however, that both Matthew and Thomas inherited a traditional story about a Net Thrown into the Sea (Aesop) which they performed in different ways.[41] But whoever is

---

90–93; 104–6). This makes it all the more striking that he does not regard it as a significant structural element to the story; that would thus produce a four-point structure: Finding, hiding, selling, buying.

[36] Crossan, "Hidden Treasure Parables," 360, 374; *First Act*, 106; *In Parables*, 33.

[37] If the motif of "ignorance" is gnostic, one wonders why the "discovery" of the treasure, or the coming to knowledge of its existence, should not also be regarded as a "gnostic" motif. Would this then render all three stories "gnosticized" versions?

[38] Perry, *Babrius and Phaedrus*, 8–11.

[39] See Hedrick, "Treasure Parable," 44, n. 10.

[40] Scott, *Hear Then the Parable*, 313–16. Scott argues that Matthew has inherited a saying about a net, which he has then conformed to the format of the parables in Matthew 13.

[41] "A fisherman drew in the net that he had cast a short time before and, as luck would have it, it was full of all kinds of delectable fish. But the little one [Perry = little ones] fled to the bottom of the net and slipped out through its many meshes, whereas the big one [Perry = big ones] was caught and lay stretched out in the boat"; Perry, *Babrius and Phaedrus*, 8–11.

correct in tracking the tradition history of the story, the result is the same: Matthew has revised (or created—Scott) the story (13:47-48) to fit personal theological interests, and accordingly Matthew provides it with an appropriate conclusion (13:49-50).[42]

The story of a Merchant in Search of Pearls in both Matthew and Thomas, however, is the second and most convincing demonstration of Matthew's tendency to revise the parables tradition. The structures of a Merchant in Search of Pearls in Matthew and Thomas (Matt 13:45 = *Gos. Thom.* log. 76) are virtually identical:

Matthew	Gospel of Thomas
The kingdom	The kingdom
of Heaven	
	of the Father
is like	is like
a man	a man
a merchant	a merchant
	who had
	merchandise.
searching for	
fine pearls,	
and when he found one	When he found a pearl,
pearl of great value,	
	that merchant was wise:
he went and sold	he sold
	the merchandise
all that he had	
and bought	and bought
it	the special pearl
	for himself

And likewise the Hid Treasure and a Merchant in Search of Pearls in Matthew have not only an identical structure but even verbal parallels as well:

The Treasure	The Pearl
ὁμοία ἐστὶν	ὁμοία ἐστὶν
ἡ βασιλεία τῶν οὐρανῶν	ἡ βασιλεία τῶν οὐρανῶν
θησαυρῷ	
κεκρυμμένῳ ἐν τῷ ἀγρῷ,	
	ἀνθρώπῳ ἐμπόρῳ
	ζητοῦντι καλοὺς μαργαρίτας;
ὃν εὑρὼν	εὑρὼν δὲ
ἄνθρωπος ἔκρυψεν,	

---

[42] See Scott, *Hear Then the Parable*, 313–14, who argues: Matthew inherited a saying (13:47) he expands into a parable (13:48) and added his own conclusion (13:49–50). Compare Gundry, *Matthew*, 279, who argues that this story is Matthew's construction "on the model of the parable of the tares and its explanation."

καὶ ἀπὸ τῆς χαρᾶς αὐτοῦ

ἕνα πολύτιμον μαργαρίτην

ὑπάγει καὶ πολεῖ ·   ἀπελθὼν πέπρακεν
πάντα ὅσα ἔχει   πάντα ὅσα εἶχεν
καὶ ἀγοράζει   καὶ ἠγόρασεν
τὸν ἀγρὸν ἐκεῖνον.   αὐτόν.

The Hid Treasure	*a Merchant in Search of Pearls*
The kingdom of heaven	The kingdom of heaven
is like	is like
treasure	
hidden in the field,	
which a man	a man,
	a merchant,
	searching for fine pearls
finding	and when he found
concealed.	
And from his joy	
	one pearl of great value,
he goes and sells	he went and sold
all he has	all that he had
and buys that field.	and bought it.

Only three substantive differences exist between these two stories. First, the Hid Treasure's motif of concealing is only implied in a Merchant in Search of Pearls (i.e., the pearl must be sought by the merchant). Second, the Hid Treasure emphasizes the joy of finding, but that does not appear in a Merchant in Search of Pearls. Third, the Hid Treasure begins with the object sought, while a Merchant in Search of Pearls begins with the one who seeks. Actually either could easily have been made to resemble the other in this latter respect, for example:

The kingdom of heaven is like	ὁμοία ἐστὶν ἡ βασιλεία τῶν οὐρανῶν
a valuable pearl,	τῷ πολυτίμῳ μαργαρίτῃ
which a man, a merchant, finding,	ὃν εὑρὼν ἄνθρωπος ἐμπόρας
went and sold	ἀπῆλθεν καὶ πέπρακας
all that he had	πάντα ὅσα εἶχεν
and bought	καὶ ἠγόρασεν
that pearl.	τὸν μαργαρίτην ἐκεῖνον.

Matthew and Thomas have in common all the stories in Matthew 13,[43] and a comparison of the structures of Matthew's stories to their parallels in Thomas reveals that only the Hid Treasure's structure in Thomas differs radically from the version in Matthew. In the light of the

---

[43] While they share all the stories in Matthew 13, the stories do not appear in the same sequence: Matt 13:3–9 = *Gos. Thom.* 9; Matt 13:24–30 = *Gos. Thom.* 57; Matt 13:31–32 = *Gos. Thom.* 20; Matt 13:33 = *Gos. Thom.* 96; Matt 13:44 = *Gos. Thom.* 109; Matt 13:45-46 = *Gos. Thom.* 76; Matt 13:47–50 = *Gos. Thom.* 8.

correspondence between a Merchant in Search of Pearls in Matthew and Thomas and the striking, even verbatim, agreement between Matthew's versions of the Hid Treasure and a Merchant in Search of Pearls, it appears that Matthew has revised a traditional Hid Treasure story to match a Merchant in Search of Pearls,[44] and it is therefore more likely Thomas that preserves a traditional story.[45]

While the motif of "joy" (Matt 13:44) is generally understood as an original feature of Jesus' parables,[46] it should, nevertheless, be remembered that early Christianity as well emphasized joy.[47] In the interpretation of a Sower, long considered as having been derived from early Christian preaching,[48] the word is received with joy (Mark 4:16 par.; cf. 1 Cor 1:6; Luke 19:6; Luke 15:7–10 par.). The angels' announcement of the birth of Jesus was "good news of great joy" (Luke 2:12). Early Christians participated in their community meal celebrations with "glad and generous hearts" (Acts 2:46).[49] Paul says that the kingdom of God is characterized by peace and joy (Rom 14:7), and he also includes joy as a product of the Spirit (Gal 5:22). In Matthew's special material, joy appears as a particular interest (2:10; 13:44; 25:21, 23; 28:8), as it is also in Luke (1:14, 44; 6:23; 10:17; 24:41, 52).

While the motif of joy in the Hid Treasure may ultimately derive from Jesus, it should at least be suspected that its appearance in the Matthean parable is due to its importance for early Christianity (and for Matthew in particular) as a symbol for the messianic banquet that the church would celebrate with Jesus at the end time.[50] The motif does not

---

[44]Therefore, "finding" as the first act (Crossan) is Matthew's own theological necessity: "Seek first the kingdom and his righteousness . . . " (to Matt 6:33 cf. Luke 12:31).

[45]Gundry (*Matthew*, 278–79) argues that Matthew composed a Merchant in Search of Pearls and that Thomas does not reflect a traditional story. What Gundry's position requires me to assume seems implausible, however: i.e., that Thomas used Matthew as a source for parables, took them out of Matthew's literary context and scattered them indiscriminately throughout the text; revised a Net Thrown into the Sea; radically revised the story of the Hid Treasure, although he/she used its twin, the Pearl story, virtually as it was, and finally eliminated all three of Matthew's allegorical interpretations to the parables (13:18–23; 13:37–43; 13:49–50).

[46]See, e.g., Jeremias, *Parables*, 200–202. Jeremias even "reads" the motif of joy into the parables of a Merchant in Search of Pearls and a Net Thrown into the Sea, where it does not appear.

[47]For references see Conzelmann, "χαίρω," *TDNT* 9.359–72.

[48]See Jeremias, *Parables*, 77–78.

[49]See Kuhn, "Lord's Supper," 77, 87. Kuhn concludes that the earliest communal meal was an eschatological banquet in anticipation of the coming kingdom of God and was a meal characterized by great joy. See also Koester, *Introduction*, 2.87–88.

[50]See Jeremias, *Parables*, 58–63, who acknowledges that this is an allegorical feature. See also Kingsbury, *Matthew 13*, 18. In the Isaiah Apocalypse (Isa 24–27) one finds a model for this banquet: "On this mountain the Lord of Hosts will make for all peoples a feast of fat things" (Isa 25:6).

appear in Matthew's versions of a Merchant in Search of Pearls and a Net Thrown into the Sea (although many commentators read it into them) or in the *Gospel of Thomas* version of the Hid Treasure. This feature suggests rather strongly that Matthew's version of the Hid Treasure is really an allegory. It is not a hid treasure that has been discovered, but the "secrets of the kingdom of God." See pp. 118–20 above where a redactional analysis of Matt 13:1-52 demonstrates Matthew's manipulation of his traditions in line with particular concerns about the kingdom of God. There is no clear redactional theme evident in Thomas's use of the traditions it shares with Matthew. It appears likely that Matthew radically revised or rewrote a traditional parable, constructing a uniquely Matthean parable of the Hid Treasure out of Jewish wisdom speculation by modeling it after a Merchant in Search of Pearls specifically for this literary context.[51]

Matthew's version of the Hid Treasure exhibits a certain universal quality from which virtually all specific social details have been stripped.[52] This universal quality has motivated interpreters to "complete" the story by providing details in order to make "better" sense of it. Hence the man finding the treasure becomes "a day laborer,"[53] and the treasure is "buried" "out in an open field" "almost certainly in an earthenware jar."[54] The "day laborer does not remove it from its position,"[55] however, but "reburies" it.[56] And thus by "defrauding" the owner of the property of what was rightfully his, he commits, if not an "illegal" act, certainly an "immoral" act.[57] And in acquiring the land fraudulently, the day laborer has come into a treasure that he cannot use.[58]

But the story itself furnishes none of these details; moreover, it is possible to propose other equally plausible details that slant the story in other directions, were one so inclined to "write" one's own story.[59] We must, however, grant Crossan's assessment—at least partially: the finder

---

[51] See, however, Scott (*Hear Then the Parable*, 392, n. 13), who dismisses this conclusion as "without foundation." For a more balanced evaluation of the argument see Perkins, *Gnosticism and the New Testament*, 62–64.

[52] This might be due simply to the brevity of the narrative, but compare the Leaven (the shortest of the parables) in which leaven "is concealed" in "three measures of flour," and even a Merchant in Search of Pearls, a story having a similar universal quality, describes a "merchant" finding "one" pearl.

[53] Scott, *Hear Then the Parable*, 398; Derrett, *Law*, 9–13; Jeremias, *Parables*, 198.

[54] Derrett, *Law*, 7; Linnemann, *Parables*, 98.

[55] Derrett, *Law*, 13.

[56] Jeremias, *Parables*, 199; Jülicher, *Gleichnisreden Jesu*, 2.581; Gundry, *Matthew*, 276–77.

[57] Crossan, *First Act*, 91–93, and Scott, *Hear Then the Parable*, 399–401.

[58] Scott, *Hear Then the Parable*, 402.

[59] See Hedrick, "Treasure Parable," 49–52.

of the treasure did not own the land, and the owner did not know about the treasure.[60] But whether the treasure finder's actions should be labeled illegal or immoral turns on whether or not full disclosure is required in business transactions. Would projecting different circumstances for the finder affect how one judges the finder's actions?[61]

Actually what is interesting about the story is the problem facing the finder. Crossan is probably correct that the finder had no formal, legal claim to the treasure until he owned the land.[62] We do not have enough information, however, to know whether or not he may have had a "moral" claim; under certain circumstances, he may have. Nor do we have enough information to judge whether or not his action was immoral. As the story is performed, logically the finder had four options if he wanted to remain a part of the community: (1) reconceal and forget about the treasure; (2) take the treasure to the owner and hope for a reward; (3) tell the owner about the treasure, and ask the owner to sell the property to him anyway; (4) reconceal the treasure, buy the property, and possess the treasure. If the finder selected options (1)–(3) he would subsequently have been labeled a fool (cf. for example, the bitter regret of the former owner in the conclusion to the rabbinic parable). Option (4) was the finder's only real choice. But in taking it he leaves himself open to criticism—but only from the audience hearing the story! No one else in his fictional world would have known about the facts of the situation. Scott's assessment that the finder could not use the treasure once he owned the land is specifically contradicted by the rabbinic parable, where the former owner has no counter claims on the treasure. A reader is led to believe that a resourceful man, like the finder of the treasure in the Matthean story, would not have been so blatant about the later "rediscovery" of the treasure so as to compromise his good fortune. We have no way of knowing that, however, and Scott's invented "conclusion" is as possible as that provided by any other reader.

The story has a "non-ending" ending. It concludes with the discoverer buying the field! A reader is prompted to ask: "And . . . ?" In this abrupt ending the treasure that had been the focus of the story and had motivated the finder's action is simply ignored. A curious reader would want to know—"so, what happened next?" The reader is not even told that the finder received the treasure, but only that he acquired the land. By its very design Matthew's story throws attention on the finder's decision and action; and because the "ending" fails to resolve the

---

[60] Crossan, *First Act*, 91.

[61] See the discussion of this point in Hedrick, "Treasure Parable," 51–52.

[62] Crossan, *First Act*, 91. However, I am not willing to grant his conclusion that what is illegal is *de facto* immoral. I (as can every reader) can imagine situations in which it would be immoral to act according to the letter of the law. It is a matter of perspective and the morality of the law.

situation with the treasure, the story invites the reader to judge the treasure finder's actions: was it smart to sell *everything?* Was it a moral act to keep information about the treasure from the owner? Interpreters have not hesitated to pass judgment on his actions. Matthew regarded him as a "wise" man; Scott sees him as a foolish man who sold everything to possess a treasure he could not use; to Crossan he is an immoral shyster; Derrett regards him as a shrewd man who obeyed the letter of the law, and I have described him as a resourceful, decisive man. One must attribute the multiplicity of interpretations to the universal and nonspecific making of the story. Its imprecision creates a "polyvalence" that leaves it open to many possible readings, none of which in the final analysis exhausts the story.

AN ARGUMENT FOR THOMAS'S PRESERVATION OF THE TRADITION

The fact that interpreters can give Thomas's Hid Treasure story a gnostic reading[63] no more makes it gnostic than reading the parable of the Lost Sheep in a gnostic way makes it gnostic.[64] Indeed, if one does not approach the Thomas story predisposed to read the text "gnostically" simply because it appears in Thomas, one discovers that it is easily incorporated into the context of first-century Judaism (or early Jewish Christianity). Its general similarity to the rabbinic parable alone demonstrates this point. Further the story has parallels to other parables attributed to Jesus that emphasize transversion, or reversal of values.[65] In the Thomas story, the man who finds the treasure suddenly abandons his life as peasant farmer and becomes money lender. By making this reversal of roles its climax, the story seems to commend the resourcefulness of the individual who found the treasure—i.e., it commends his loaning of money for interest (ⲚϮ ⲢⲞⲘⲦ' ⲈⲦⲘⲎⲤⲈ). And this motif is yet another indicator of the traditional character of the Thomas story, since in *Gospel of Thomas* log. 95 it is specifically forbidden to loan money for interest.[66]

The issue of loaning money at interest is a focus of Torah (Exod 22:25–27; Deut 23:19–20; Lev 25:36–37; Ezra 18:8, 13, 17; 22:12; Neh 5:6–13) and reflects a rabbinic concern (*m. B. Meṣiʿa* 5.1–11; *ʿArak.* 9.3),

---

[63] See Gärtner, *Theology,* 237–38; Ménard, *Thomas,* 207–8.

[64] *Gos. Truth* I,3:31,35–32,17.

[65] See Hedrick, "Treasure Parable," 52. This is the point that convinced Scott that the story is to be taken seriously as having an origin in the life of Jesus of Nazareth: *Hear Then the Parable,* 392–93.

[66] See the discussion above; log. 110 may provide a negative interpretation to the Thomas Hid Treasure story.

where it is specifically forbidden to loan money at interest to a fellow Israelite—though one may loan money at interest to a Gentile (*m. B. Meṣi'a* 5.6). In that sense the man's decision to loan money at interest to "whomever he chose" would have resonated with impiety for Torah-observing Jews. With first-century pious Jewish audiences the motif would have been offensive, since it recommends loaning at interest with no restrictions whatever.

A similar "recommendation" occurs in another story attributed to Jesus of Nazareth. In the Entrusted Money (Matt 25:14–30) the master of the house chides the one-talent servant for failing to "invest" the talent with bankers, so that when the master returned he would have received back the one talent "with interest" (Matt 25:27). The "master" in this story likewise places no qualifications on loaning money at interest.

This reversal of worlds/values with which the Thomas story ends—a peasant farmer becomes a money lender and discards traditional Jewish beliefs—is paralleled by similar twists in other stories told by Jesus: The Samaritan, Pharisee and Toll Collector, Wage of the Workman, Date Palm Shoot, and the Ear of Grain.[67]

The Thomas story challenges traditional Jewish religious values by contradicting Jewish piety at a specific point of Torah interpretation (i.e., indiscriminate loaning of money for interest). This gives the story a certain secular character that contrasts sharply with the religious world view of Torah and rabbinic Judaism, a character also reflected in other sayings that quite likely derive from Jesus of Nazareth.[68] At the very least this feature pushes the story's concern back into the debates between Palestinian Christianity and Judaism, if not into the ministry of Jesus himself. The story in Thomas is simply not the late product of Christian gnosticism.

Crossan stresses that in Matthew the motif of "finding" is the "first act" in the story,[69] whereas in Thomas the motif of "finding" is the turning point. A number of parables in the Jesus tradition also have the same stress, i.e., the motif of finding as the climax to the story. It is probably to these that Thomas's Hid Treasure story is to be compared. For example, in the Leaven the woman "hides" the leaven in the meal, and only after the dough rises is a "discovery" made. The Prodigal Son/Elder Brother underscores the sudden return of the prodigal. The Lost Coin stresses the finding of the coin. The Lamps of the Maidens turns on the unexpected appearance of the bridegroom. In the Lost Sheep, the sheep is "found" after being "lost." In the "planting" type parables (a Sprouting Seed, a Mustard Seed, and Good Seed and Weeds) the first motif

---

[67] See Hedrick, "Kingdom Sayings," 1–24.
[68] For example, Mark 2:27; 7:15; Matt 23:5–7.
[69] Crossan, *In Parables*, 34–36.

is the concealing (or the "hiding") of the seed that is followed by the later "discovery" at the budding or harvest. In the Empty Jar the woman does not find her jar empty until her trip is concluded. All of these parables present "finding" as the last act. Thomas's Hid Treasure story seems to be such a story of reversal, like other such stories, it ends with the major accent on the sudden finding of the treasure. Of such stories one probably ought to say that finding is the only significant act and that they emphasize the twist at the end.

The Hid Treasure in Thomas clearly reflects a Jewish environment in its similarity to the rabbinic parable. It is not identical with that parable, however, and does not reflect any characteristic emphasis of Palestinian Judaism. Neither does it reflect any characteristic concern of early Christianity. On the contrary, if Matthew did reject the version represented by Thomas, then it may be said for that reason to reflect a tradition that Matthean Christianity found objectionable, and in that sense it stands in tension with early Christianity. On the other hand, the Thomas version of the Hid Treasure is entirely in harmony with some parables in the synoptic tradition and therefore has a strong claim to "originality"; certainly it has a claim to belonging to a tradition level earlier than Matthew's Hid Treasure story. While the Matthean parable may ultimately derive from Jesus, in the light of Matthew's careful construction of chapter 13 and the role played by the Hid Treasure story in that context it unquestionably reflects Matthew's own theology. Further, it is not only possible that its form is due to Matthew but it seems the more probable conclusion. Assuming that both versions are related, it seems clear that the Thomas parable is earlier than Matthew's parable. The only question is whether it is a traditional Jewish or Jewish Christian parable, or a parable spoken by Jesus of Nazareth. On balance, the Hid Treasure in Thomas has a slightly higher claim to originality than does Matthew's shorter parable.

THOMAS'S HID TREASURE STORY

The Text

50,31　ΠΕΧΕ ΙC ΧΕ ΤΜΝΤΕΡΟ ΕCΤΝΤωΝ ΕΥΡω

　32　ΜΕ ΕΥΝΤΑϥ ΜΜΑΥ ʽϨΝ ΤΕϥCωϣΕ ΝΝΟΥ

　33　ΕϨΟ ΕϥϨΗ[Π Ε]ϥΟ ΝΑΤCΟΟΥΝˈ ΕΡΟϥ ΑΥ

　34　ω Μ[ΠΑΤϥΜΟΥ Π]ΡΕϥΜΟΥ ΑϥΚΑΑϥ ΜΠΕϥˋ

　35　[ϣΗΡΕ ΜΠΕ]ΠϣΗΡΕ CΟΟΥΝ ΑΝˈ Αϥϥιˈ

51,1　ΤCωϣΕ ΕΤΜΜΑϥ ΑϥΤΑΑC [ΕΒΟ]λ ΑΥω ΠΕ[Ν]

2   ⲧⲁⲣⲧⲟⲟⲩⲥ ⲁϥⲉⲓ ⲉϥⲥⲕⲁⲉ̣ⲓ̣ ⲁ[ϥϩ]ⲉ ⲁⲡⲉϩⲟ ⲁϥ

3   ⲁⲣⲭⲉⲓ ⲛ̅ϯ ϩⲟⲙⲧ' ⲉⲧⲙⲏⲥⲉ ⲛ̅[ⲛⲉ]ⲧϥⲟⲩⲟϣⲟⲩ[70]

50,32   M̄MⲀⲨ: Layton M̄MⲀⲨ; `ϩ'Ⲛ: ϩ written above the line by scribe.

50,34   M̄[ⲡⲀⲧϥⲘⲞⲨ ⲡ]ⲣⲉϥⲘⲞⲨ: Layton M̄[ⲘⲚⲚⳞⲀ ⲧ]ⲣⲉϥⲘⲞⲨ. Layton's restoration (*NHC II*) is one or two letters too short for the lacuna.

Translation

50,31   Jesus said: the kingdom is like a man
32   Who has, there in his field, a
33   [hidden] treasure—[although] he does not know about
        it. And
34   [before he died, the] deceased (man) left it to his
35   [son.] The son [did not] know (about the treasure)
        either, and he took
51,1   that field (i.e., the one having the treasure) and sold
        it. And he
2   that bought it went and plowed, and [found] the
        treasure. He
3   began to lend at interest to whomever he wanted.

The Story

A man has, there in his field, a [hidden] treasure. The reader learns nothing about the man, except that he owns property. The text does not clarify whether or not the field is or ever has been under cultivation. Perhaps it is simply an untilled field or meadow. The Coptic word ⲤⲰϢⲈ allows both translations.

Although he does not know about it (i.e., the treasure). In Coptic normally the third feminine singular is used to express the neuter.[71] I have therefore taken ⲚⲀⲧⳞⲞⲞⲨⲚ' ⲈⲢⲞϥ (3d masc. sing.—50, 33) to be a direct reference to the treasure, since the Coptic word ϩⲞ is masculine; that is to say, the man was unaware of the treasure. Other translations take ⲈⲢⲞϥ to be neuter and the direct object of ⳞⲞⲞⲨⲚ:[72] the man did

---

[70] The transcription of the text of this story was made on 5 January 1986 when I collated log. 109 under ultraviolet light in the Coptic museum in Cairo.

[71] See Till, *Dialektgrammatik*, par. 113.

[72] Ⲉ', ⲈⲢⲞ⸵ seems to be used sparingly with ⳞⲞⲞⲨⲚ. Normally the direct object with the absolute infinitive is indicated with Ⲛ', M̄MⲞ⸵. In my translation I have tried to reflect the intransitive character of ⳞⲞⲞⲨⲚ (cf. Crum, 570a). Compare the translations of Kasser, *Thomas*, 117: "etant ignorant ‹de la chose›" and his Greek retroversion: ἀγνῶν (τοῦτον).

not know "it," i.e., he did not know the abstract idea that he had a treasure hidden in his field.

And [before he died,] the deceased (man) left it to his [son]. The usual restoration of the lacuna M̄[MNNCA T]PEЧMOY,[73] generally translated "after he died," creates the logical problem of how he could bequeath to his son following his death. In order for that to make good sense one must provide the story with an extra structural element, i.e., that the deceased before he died made out a will that named his son as heir. The Meyer translation seems to recognize this awkwardness of the restoration and translates M̄MNNCA as "at death."[74] This translation solves the awkwardness of the (too short) Coptic restoration by having the father name his son as heir "on the occasion" of his death. Hence it is unnecessary for one to provide another structural element in the story to make sense out of the text. Meyer's translation, however, does not do justice to M̄MNNCA, which carries the idea of "after."[75] The present restoration fits the lacuna and makes sense of the sequence of the narrative.

Another problem that has gone largely unnoticed is AЧKAAЧ (50,34). What is it that the deceased father bequeathed to his son? None of the translations specify the antecedent of the masculine suffix pronoun. All translations leave it indefinite,[76] giving the impression that the son inherits the field. This, however, seems to be excluded by the gender of the Coptic word for field (CⲰⲰE, feminine). The nearest antecedent of the correct gender is the masculine ⲢO (50,34), but this creates the problem of the father's bequeathing to the son something he did not know that he had, i.e., the treasure. It is possible the text has in view something like the man's "property," or "land," (i.e., ⲡϬⲰM; Crum, 817b), although it is not specified in the text. Such an assumption seems to make the best sense of the text. Coptic is not known for its precision.

Layton's restoration at the beginning of 50,35 appears to be at least one letter short for the lacuna. Restoring the Negative Perfect rather than the Imperfect better accommodates the size of the lacuna.

The son did not know (about the treasure) either, and he took that field and sold it. The expression "took that field and sold it" is odd.[77] If the field had been previously left to him in his father's will, why does he need to

---

[73] See Layton, *NHC II*, 1.90; Guillaumont, *Thomas*, 54 (M̄[NNCA); Kasser, *Thomas*, 117; Meyer in *Q-Thomas Reader*, 153.

[74] See also the translation in Miller, *Complete Gospels*, 321: "when he died."

[75] See Till, *Koptische Grammatik*, par. 324, 339, and Crum, 314a–315b.

[76] See n. 71 above: to regard "it" as indefinite seems to be excluded by Coptic usage.

[77] Compare Layton's translation of AЧЧI, as "he inherited," a concept that seems to be contained in the earlier statement that the Father "left" or bequeathed property to the son (*NHC II*, 1.91). Meyer (*Q-Thomas Reader*, 153) also has trouble with AЧЧI, which he translates as "took over" the field. Kasser (*Thomas*, 117) translates

"take" it. The statement that he "took" the field is clearly not meant literally, since he could not transport it someplace. And even if one assumes that the "taking" is figurative language and that it refers to the son "receiving" the field as a part of his inheritance, the act of "taking" at this point is really unnecessary. The son had already "received" it when his father left it to him. The idea of receiving would have been better expressed with the Coptic expression ϫι: (Crum, 747b).

The expression "took and sold" is best understood as a semiticism. The expression "take X and do Y with X" is a common idiom in the Hebrew scriptures, and one finds it in the New Testament as well (for example: Gen 2:15; Exod 7:9; Lev 8:10; Num 16:17; Deut 22:15; Josh 2:4; Judg 9:43; Ruth 4:16; 1 Sam 6:8; 2 Sam 8:7; 1 Kgs 17:23; 2 Kgs 8:15; 1 Chron 19:4; Matt 13:33; Mark 9:36; John 12:3; Acts 9:25).[78]

The son, like the father, is also ignorant of the presence of the treasure in "that" (ⲉⲧⲙ̄ⲙⲁⲩ) field; that is to say, the field having the treasure. The expression suggests that there were more "fields" in the property (ϭⲱⲙ) that the son inherited from the father, although it is always possible that the son simply decided to "sell the family farm." There is no hint of this in the story, however. And such a radical act as disposing of the family's source of income should have been mentioned.

And he that bought it went and plowed, and [found] the treasure. The statement "went and plowed" in Coptic is expressed by the perfect ⲁϥⲉⲓ plus the Circumstantial ⲉϥⲥⲕⲁⲉⲓ. I have translated the circumstantial as a separate act.[79] Scholars differ on how the text is to be regarded. Layton's translation[80] (followed by Meyer[81]) that the purchaser "went plowing" appears to treat the expression as a virtual periphrastic construction, although such usage is only typical of ϣⲱⲡⲉ.[82] Occasionally ⲉⲓ is used with the Circumstantial of the Future to form a periphrastic construction,[83] which is not the case in the present text. The Guillaumont and Ménard translations take the circumstantial as a dependent

---

as *"a pris"* but says that the Coptic word "literally" means *ôter*, i.e., to take away or remove. The Guillaumont edition (*Thomas*, 55) translates as "he accepted."

[78] These references to the idiomatic expression are not intended to be exhaustive: Gen 8:9; 16:3; 17:23; 18:8; 20:14; 21:14, 17; 22:6; 28:11, 18; 29:23; 30:9, 37; 31:45; 32:23; 37:24; 38:28; 39:20; Exod 16:33; 17:12; 24:7–8; 33:7; Lev 8:29–30; 9:2; Num 19:18; 22:41; 25:4; 27:22; Deut 15:17; 22:18; 31:26; Josh 4:2–3; 7:24; 8:12; 24:26; 1 Sam 6:10; 7:9, 12; 8:11; 9:22; 10:1; 11:7; 14:32; 16:13, 20; 17:54, 57; 25:18; 31:13; 2 Sam 17:19; 18:14, 17; 20:3; 21:10; 24:22; 1 Kgs 18:4, 26; 19:21; 2 Kgs 9:3, 13, 17; 10:7; 12:9; 25:20; Matt 16:22; 21:35; Mark 8:32; John 19:23, 40; Acts 16:3.

[79] See Till, *Koptische Grammatik*, par. 331.

[80] Layton, *NHC II*, 1.91.

[81] *Q-Thomas Reader*, 153.

[82] Till, *Koptische Grammatik*, par. 332; id., *Dialektgrammatik*, par. 276.

[83] Till, *Koptische Grammatik*, par. 333; id., *Dialiktgrammatik*, par. 277.

clause that is construed as a circumstance associated with finding the treasure: "he went, while he was plowing he found the treasure."[84]

The translation, as I have rendered it, takes the expression "went and plowed" as a semitic idiom reflected in the Hebrew scriptures and the New Testament. The verb "to go" in the idiomatic expression is not required logically to complete what appears to be conceived as a single action. The addition of "go" actually appears to be logically unessential; the logic of the activity envisioned in the text is adequately expressed without the attendant description of "going" to do a certain thing. Logically the attendant activity means nothing in terms of the narrative. It derives from the proclivity of Hebrew to express actions concretely (Gen 21:16; 35:22; Deut 31:1; Josh 5:13; Judg 1:16; 3:13; 9:6; 15:4; Ruth 2:3; 2 Sam 6:12; 11:22; 21:12; 1 Kgs 2:40; 9:6; 17:5; 2 Kgs 3:7; Job 1:4; Jer 29:12; Dan 2:24; Matt 13:46; 18:30; 25:25; Luke 15:15).[85]

In this story the narrator describes how the man found the treasure, i.e., by plowing, and thereby it also suggests where he found the treasure. Since in plowing one turns over the soil, this treasure was buried in a field. The narrator remains silent about the nature of the treasure. We may construe, however, that we are not talking about a "few" coins, since the narrator calls it "treasure," and since the finder was able to finance a new career as money lender.

He began to lend at interest to whomever he wanted. This is a most interesting "punch line" to the story. The man who bought the field did so for the purpose of actually farming it, unlike the previous owner, whom one must understand left it to lie fallow. But with the discovery of the treasure, he suddenly abandons a respectable farming career for a quite common, albeit disreputable, career as a private "money lender."[86] The

---

[84] Guillaumont, *Thomas*, 55. This is also true of Kasser's translation to judge from his Greek retroversion: ὁ ἀγοράζων αὐτὸν ἦλθεν, καὶ ἀροτριῶν ηὗρεν τὸν θησαυρόν. His French translation is not as clear: "il est allé, labourant, il a trouvé le trésor": *Thomas*, 117; but cf. *Evangile Thomas*, 74, for a different translation.

[85] Compare also: 2 Chron 7:19; Gen 21:19(?); 22:13; 38:11(?); Deut 28:26; Judg 4:6; 9:7, 21; 21:23; 1 Sam 15:3, 6, 18; 17:32; 20:40; 23:2; 1 Kgs 1:50(?); 17:31; 2 Kgs 4:7, 25; 8:25; Jer 3:8. A special form of the idiom is the inclusion of an imperative "go" before the operative imperative that specifies what one is to do: Exod 8:1; Deut 26:3; Isa 38:5; Jer 3:12; 17:9; 28:13; 34:2; 35:13; 39:16; Ruth 1:8; 1 Sam 23:22; 26:19; 2 Sam 7:5; 1 Kgs 14:17; 17:13; Amos 7:12, 15. In some cases the formula "went and *x*" is a direct response to the formulaic command "Go and *x*": Gen 27:14; Exod 2:8; 4:18, 27; 1 Sam 3:9; 1 Kgs 17:15; Job 42:9; Jer 13:5; New Testament: Matt 27:5, 16; Mark 6:27; Luke 9:59; 22:8.

[86] Cato rated farming as the most respectable life style and that of money lender as worse than a thief: Tenney, *Economic Survey* 1.161, 207–8; 5.28; See also Coleman-Norton, *Studies*, 44. A monetary crises arose in Rome in 33 CE due to a government "crack-down" on money lenders who were charging excessive interest rates (usury) for loans: Tenney, *Economic Survey*, 5.32–35.

narrator's statement that the finder began to lend at interest "to whomever he wanted" seems innocent enough, but in reality it provides a real twist to the conclusion. In the banking system of the Hellenistic world money could generally be loaned to anyone. Limits were imposed on the amount of interest that could be charged[87] and on the items that could be taken as collateral.[88] But money lenders loaned to anyone they wanted.[89] Hence the statement, "at interest to whomever he wanted," makes sense only in a context in which loaning is restricted, as it was in Judaism.[90] Moreover, the conclusion to this narrative involves the finder of the treasure in a calculated act to subvert a specific teaching of Torah. In short, the statement reflects a basic change in the man's outlook on life and in his lifestyle. He becomes an "outsider," a sinner, at least in the eyes of those who would judge his actions by Torah.

ANOTHER READING OF THE STORY

In some ways the story seems to work against itself. The only reason to have the previous owners in the story (i.e., the father and the son) is to emphasize that the land had not been worked. Had the father and the son plowed the land, one of them would have found the treasure—since the treasure finder found the treasure by doing what farmers do, i.e., plowing. To this point in the story the thrust seems to be that there are treasures out there for the finding, if one only applies oneself conscientiously and industriously, just as the man in the rabbinic story who found the treasure due to the negligence of the previous owner. One might therefore draw the following conclusion: farming is an honorable profession; you will be rewarded by applying yourself.

But the discovery of the treasure in this story is really a false conclusion, since the story ends not with the discovery but with the finder's change of life from reputable farmer to disreputable money lender. The failure of the father and son to plow is not required to make this point. The story would work just as well with the father and son segment eliminated. In the light of the conclusion the presence of the father and son functions only to explain why the treasure had not been found previously. If the owner had always owned and worked the land, why had he not already found the treasure? So the narrator creates the father/son segment to explain why the treasure had not been found earlier.

---

[87] Tenney, *Economic Survey*, 1.352; 2.450–59.
[88] Tenney, *Economic Survey*, 2.716.
[89] Tenney, *Economic Survey*, 3.310–14 (Roman Sicily).
[90] See above, pages 132–33.

In a similar way the rabbinic story explains why the treasure had not been found before: it was concealed in a piece of land used as a dung heap, and rather than work that piece of land (which would have been quite fertile!) the owner sold it. In the Matthean parable it is not necessary to create farm failures to explain why the treasure remained hidden; its location is left obscure, and the circumstances of the finding do not indicate how it was concealed.

The finder's decision in the Thomas story to become a money lender focuses a reader's attention on the nature of the business he chose to enter. Innately there is nothing wrong with being a "banker" who loans money at interest. Even in Greco-Roman antiquity, where money lending was regarded as a disreputable occupation, money lenders were regulated, tolerated, and even patronized. In modern society bankers (who loan money at interest) are highly respected and powerful members of the community. Banking is a credible choice as a career field in the modern world and can be highly rewarding both in terms of community standing and personal finances.

So what is a reader/auditor to make of this story? Was the life of the treasure finder enhanced or subverted? Is it a success story or the story of a good man's tragic fall into corruption? But the narrator pronounces no judgment on the man's actions. The judgment is left to auditors and readers.

A reader may well dismiss the actions of the father and son with a wisdom saying: "The sluggard does not plough in the autumn; he will seek at harvest and have nothing" (Prov 20:4, RSV; cf. Prov 24:30–34); that is to say, "the conscientious farmer is rewarded for his work," or some other similar moralism. But what about the actions of the treasure finder? Two possibilities exist: "wealth corrupts," or "wealth liberates."

A pious Torah-observing first-century Jew might judge that the man's new wealth had so corrupted him that it led him to violate a specific prohibition of Torah (i.e., loaning money at interest, even to a fellow Jew) and to defy community values by associating with the group of sinners as such money lenders were thought to be. By this reading the farmer becomes the worst kind of person: he cares neither for God's law nor for community standards. He deliberately chooses to be impious and socially deviant.

One could, however, put another "spin" on the man's actions. The man's new wealth has brought him a freedom of choice that was not open to him before the discovery. He is no longer bound to the land or by poverty to the community and its standards, ideals, and values. Because of his new-found wealth, he can choose any career he wants, and can act in almost any way he chooses.

Because of ancient Israelite and rabbinic identification of God's will with social custom and value, and because the narrator of this story gives no guidance as to how one should understand the conclusion, it would appear that the story puts on trial both the actions of the treasure finder and the standards that one uses to judge the treasure finder. In short, this story has no morals; it puts the reader and the reader's reading on trial.

Because the story does not criticize the man for choosing to become a money lender, it calls into question the judgment that all money-lenders are disreputable, and more specifically, it questions the idea that money lenders who do not discriminate among those to whom they lend money are impious and socially deviant. By silence the narrator seems open to the proposition that the disrepute into which an occupation has fallen does not necessarily taint the individual who chooses the occupation. In other words, some money lenders could be ethical, honorable, and pious people. Hence the standard is relativized, and the story forces the hearer to look beyond the rule to the individual. In so doing the story calls both first-century Jewish religious values and the absolute rule of Torah into question—it relativizes them.

On the other hand, the story places no limits on the treasure finder. He apparently can ignore the most treasured rules of his community with impunity. The story raises the specter of an absolute freedom from all community restraints and all religious obligations. The story's vision of an unhindered future for the treasure finder is both breathtaking and frightening. It calls forth a world where people are free to be what they want with no interference from social custom or religious dogma. It evokes an unqualified freedom–the complete disregard of all social conventions, the casting off of all encumbrances; in short it evokes a freedom without constraints. And for people of religious faith such a vision raises the disturbing question: should traditional social values and cherished religious beliefs be identified as the will of God? But the narrator is silent, and the reader is left with the image of a treasure finder become banker loaning money at interest to whomever he wants.

8 🌿

The Rich Man in Thomas; the Rich Fool in Luke

IN THIS CHAPTER A READER IS FACED WITH TWO DIFFERENT NARRATIVES about a rich man, both of which are attributed to Jesus. Hence the relationship between the two narratives, if any, must be resolved and the question of originality addressed. I first discuss the literary contexts of both narratives and analyze how they were read in early Christianity and then discuss their modern interpretations. A comparative analysis of the structures of the two narratives and their stories reveals their similarities and differences. It appears that they are derived from a common core that Luke's narrative, without Luke's revisions, best represents. The reconstructed core is examined to see what its poetics implies for a reading of the narrative and then it is analyzed as a first-century fiction. I discuss how the story may have worked in the first century and offer another reading. Finally the chapter closes with a consideration of how the story might have been heard in the context of first-century Judaism.

THE SETTING OF THE STORIES: EARLY CHRISTIAN READINGS

The *Gospel of Thomas* (log. 63 = II,2:44,2–10) and Luke (12:16b–20) have each preserved two different versions of a story commonly known as the "Rich Fool," whose title derives from Luke's version. The Thomas version has no narrative setting, other than the usual introductory formula, "Jesus said."[1] Thomas concludes with a floating saying that invites the reader to hear more in the story than actually appears there: "whoever has ears to hear, let that one hear."[2] In Thomas the story is neither presented as a parable nor interpreted as an example.

---

[1] See above, pp. 23–24.
[2] See above, p. 24.

There is no evident connection with the logia that immediately precede the story in Thomas.[3] Two other stories immediately follow log. 63, however: log. 64, the Feast, and log. 65, a Vineyard. As is the case with log. 63, the stories are not described by literary genre (i.e., parable, story, example, etc.), but their narrative character is clear. Hence, an ancient scribal grouping on the basis of form seems more plausible than a grouping on the basis of specific content or theological proclivity of the collector.

In Luke, however, the story of the "Rich Fool" does appear in a rather complex narrative setting. In 12:13 Jesus is approached by a man requesting that he settle an inheritance dispute with his brother. Jesus refuses (12:14) and censures the man for his covetousness, warning him that life is more than an "abundance of possessions" (12:15). The example of the "Rich Fool" (12:16–20) then follows to illustrate the logion in 12:15. Luke's interpretation of the "example story" appears in 12:21.[4] It is not a part of the story proper, but is rather Luke's moralizing application. Luke concludes that the fate of the fool in the example will also befall whoever is more concerned with "laying up treasures for himself" and "is not rich toward God."

Luke continues the theme of "spiritual riches" versus the transitoriness of material possessions in 12:22–34. Hence the story of the Rich Fool (12:16–20) serves Luke as an example of a farmer who hordes his abundance, but neglects to seek the kingdom of God (12:31). It is a warning about the dangers of material prosperity and greed. Luke seems to be saying that the community of faith need not worry about its physical needs, for all that the disciple needs comes with the discovery of God's kingdom.

Luke's occasion for the story, the debate over the inheritance (12:13–15), is an independent incident in Thomas log. 72 (46,1–6). This dialog and the story of the Rich Man in Thomas have no connection as they do in Luke, showing that they were once completely separate traditions until Luke united them for the homily on material possessions in chapter 12 (see Appendix A). The parallel between Luke and Thomas in the debate over the inheritance is extremely close:

Luke	*Thomas*
One of the multitude	[A man]
said to him	said to him
"Teacher,	
tell my brother	"Tell my brothers
to divide	to divide

---

[3] There may, however, be a "catch word" connection with log. 61 in the use of the word "fill" (ΜΟΥϨ, 43,32–34), a word that also appears in log. 63 (44,6).

[4] Luke 12:21 is lacking in the fifth-century codex D and the Old Latin manuscripts a, b, d (fourth to fifth century).

the inheritance	my father's possessions
with me."	with me."
But he said to him,	He said to him,
"Fellow, who made me	"O man who made me
a judge or	
divider	a divider?"
over you?"	
	He turned to his disciples;
	he said to them,
	"I am not a divider am I?"

On closer examination it appears that Luke's version has been refined to some degree, while the Thomas version has a certain naive quality about it. Luke uses quite properly "inheritance" (κληρονομίαν, 12:13), while Thomas reads "my (not our) father's possessions" (ⲠⲚⲀⲀⲨ). In Luke, Jesus' response to his interlocutor may have been influenced by Septuagint language: to Luke 12:14 (κριτὴν ἢ μεριστὴν ἐφ᾽ ὑμᾶς)[5] compare Luke's use of Exod 2:14 LXX in Acts 7:27, 35 (ἄρχοντα καὶ δικαστὴν ἐφ᾽ ἡμῶν).

In Thomas, on the other hand, the rhetorical questions that Jesus asks his disciples make him appear uncertain or indecisive, suggesting a tradition that antedates the development of a high Christology. In the early church Jesus was, of course, regarded as both judge and "divider" (2 Tim 4:1, 8; Matt 25:31–46; but cf. John 3:17; 8:15). The dispute over the inheritance is an independent tradition—as shown by the fact that it was transmitted in Thomas independently of the story of the Rich Fool. Luke used the dispute to provide the story of the Rich Fool with an appropriate (for Luke) literary setting.

MODERN INTERPRETATIONS

Under the influence of Luke's literary setting, the story has routinely been taken as an example of the ultimate fate of a greedy man. Cadoux: "It is the *reductio ad absurdum* of selfishness by showing it at work systematically and unencumbered. . . . Systematic self-love is thus characteristically occupied with laying up things for its own safety, comfort, indulgence and glory."[6] Oesterley: "We have here selfishness and self-indulgence . . . the roots from which covetousness grows."[7] Plummer: "The parable . . . illustrates both . . . that the life that is worth living does not depend upon wealth . . . and that even mere existence

---

[5] A number of manuscripts read δικαστήν rather than κριτήν, suggesting that certain ancient scribes may have heard the same Septuagintism in the expression.

[6] Cadoux, *Parables*, 205.

[7] Oesterley, *Gospel Parables*, 171.

cannot be secured by wealth."[8] Talbert: "The parable of the rich fool . . . functions as an exposition of what covetousness is and why such an attitude is folly."[9]

Others, however, take the story to be an eschatological parable. Jeremias: "Jesus is not thinking of the inevitable death of the individual as the impending danger, but of the approaching eschatological catastrophe, and the coming Judgment."[10] Boucher: "The exemplary story is not, as we might think, a lesson against greed. Neither is it teaching about the suddenness of death. Jesus here points to the last judgment."[11]

Scott reads the parable against the background of Jesus' preaching of the kingdom of God in the Synoptic Gospels:

> The parable's dramatic tension results from the relation of the narrative to the metaphorical structure that represents the kingdom as a village. The part of the village system that governs the use of wealth and bounty for the community's good is the implied metaphor for the kingdom. . . . The man takes the fruit of the harvest for his own benefit and attempts thereby to ward off the threat of death. . . . His idolatry, his usurpation of story and harvest, and his crowding out all around him can only be remedied by God's intervention. . . . The parable's metaphor for the kingdom is not simply the harvest but the good life it is intended to produce for the community.[12]

A COMPARATIVE ANALYSIS OF THOMAS AND LUKE

Luke	*Thomas*
1. The land	
2.	There was
3. of a certain rich (πλουσίου)	a rich (πλούσιος)
man	man
4.	who had much money.
5. brought forth well.	
6. And he deliberated with himself	
7. "What shall I do	
8. for I have nowhere	
9. to gather my crops (καρπούς)?"	
10. And he said	He said,
11.	"I will use my money
12.	that I may sow and reap, and plant,
13. "I will do this,	
14. I will pull down my barns	
15. and build larger ones;	

---

[8] Plummer, *Luke*, 323.
[9] Talbert, *Reading Luke*, 141; see also Bailey, *Poet and Peasant*, 2.70.
[10] Jeremias, *Parables*, 165.
[11] Boucher, *Parables*, 134.
[12] Scott, *Hear Then the Parable*, 139.

16. and there I will gather	and fill my storehouses
17. all the grain and my goods.	with fruit (καρπός)
18. And I will say to myself,	
19. 'Self you have many good things	
20. laid up for many years;	
21. take your ease;	
22. eat, drink; enjoy yourself.' "	
23.	so that I lack nothing" (cf. lines 19–22).
24.	These things
25.	he thought in his heart (cf. lines 6 and 18 above),
26. But God said to him,	
27. "Fool, this night	and that night
28. your 'self' is demanded back from you	
29. and the things you have prepared,	
30. whose will they be?"	
31.	he died.

Luke's Story

While the two narratives have features in common, their substantial differences impact the story in dramatic ways. Luke's story is about a wealthy farmer whose fields unexpectedly produced an abundant crop. Thinking he did not have enough room to store the large crop, he decided to tear down his old "barns" and build larger ones. As he contemplated his good fortune, thinking that this unusual harvest would provide for him many years in the future, God addresses him—in an aside intended for the audience only—announcing his demise that very evening and ironically noting the uselessness of the man's possessions.[13]

The basic story concerns a man who wisely tries to accommodate an unusually large crop. The only indications that the man's action may be improper are found in Luke's narrative setting (12:13–15, 21), which programs the reader to see the man as self-centered and greedy, and God's judgment on the farmer as "fool" (12:20). But neither of these is a part of the action in the story. One precedes/follows the story and the

---

[13] Aristotle allows the use of a god outside the dramatic presentation to explain to the audience what lies outside the drama, either what happened earlier or what happens later. But the unraveling of the plot, the denouement, according to Aristotle, should be a result of action inside the plot. In this case Luke has apparently dropped the "unraveling" of the plot and resolved the "complication" by the outside voice. The net result of this is to close off the story: who would argue with God's authoritative pronouncement? It may be "good theology" on Luke's part, but clearly according to Aristotle it is "bad poetics."

other is an aside to the reader/auditor. The only inconsistency in the action of the story proper is that the farmer pulls down his old storage facilities to build larger ones. This is really not a question of the man's morality, however, but rather an action that threatens the realism of the story. Why didn't the farmer simply build additional storage facilities to supplement what he already had? How would a first-century audience have reacted to this decision of the farmer? In order to answer this, one must know something about farming practices in the first century.

Farmsteading in the Roman period in Italy comprised rather tightly constructed compounds that included storage facilities for all the produce of the farm.[14] Columella discusses the villa[15] with its storage facilities[16] that include

> rooms for oil, for presses, for wine, for the boiling down of must, lofts for hay and chaff, storerooms, and granaries that such of them as are on the ground floor may take care of liquid products for the market, such as oil and wine; while dry products such as grain, hay, leaves, chaff, and other fodder, should be stored in lofts. But the granaries . . . should be reached by ladders and should receive ventilation through small openings on the north side. . . . [17]

The reason for storing the grain in lofts is to keep it from spoiling. He acknowledged that some stored their grain in specially prepared rooms with vaulted ceilings,[18] or in drier climates, under the ground.[19]

It is not immediately clear why the farmer in Luke's story decided to tear down his ἀποθήκη to build larger ones rather than simply adding storage space. Vitruvius advised that villas should be built to suit the amount of land and crops;[20] that is to say, one should not overbuild one's land. If the steading were too large there would be less land in cultivation, and hence the fields would produce less. And while Vitruvius also advised that "barns, stores for hay and meal, and bakehouses should be outside the farmhouse,"[21] they were still built within a secure complex, because of the danger of theft. According to White, "every effort was made, at least until well into the first century CE, to keep all personnel, livestock, and equipment, as far as possible, under one roof. The important exceptions to this rule . . . were made either for reasons of health, or because of fire hazard."[22] The same tight compounds can be seen at

---

[14] See White, *Roman Farming*, 415–41.
[15] Columella, *Res Rustica* 1.6.1–24.
[16] Columella, *Res Rustica* 1.6.9–17.
[17] Columella, *Res Rustica* 1.6.9 (Ash, *Columella*, 1.69, 71).
[18] Columella, *Res Rustica* 1.6.12–15.
[19] Columella, *Res Rustica* 1.6.15–16.
[20] Vitruvius, *De Architecture* 1.6.2; see also Columella, *Res Rustica* 1.4.8.
[21] Vitruvius, *De Architecture* 1.6.5.
[22] White, *Roman Farming*, 431.

Masada[23] and Qumran.[24] While these complexes are not "farms" in a narrow sense, they do reflect a similar construction and rationale. I know of no Hellenistic period farms that have been excavated in Palestine.[25]

Hence there are at least three practical reasons why a farmer might decide to rebuild rather than simply adding storage facilities in a new location: (1) building additional ἀποθήκαι in a different location would take land out of cultivation; (2) off by itself outside the complex an ἀποθήκη would become an easy target for thieves; (3) to protect the integrity of the compound. If the owner decided to increase storage space he may well have opted to tear down and rebuild; simply tacking onto the present compound might have exposed the new "addition" to increased possibility of theft.

Such an analysis suggests that the farmer's actions in Luke's story in tearing down and rebuilding do not necessarily in themselves threaten the first-century realism of the story. It is at least a plausible action given the advice of "farm planners" in the first and early second centuries CE. Whether his timing was appropriate, however, is a different question.

A Comparison of the Stories in Luke and Thomas

The feature of "rebuilding" is not part of Thomas's story, as it was in Luke. Indeed, the Thomas story is quite different. Thomas's story is about a "rich man" who decided to *become* a farmer, so that he might "lack nothing." Hence, the abundant crop that comes upon Luke's farmer by chance is the deliberate goal of Thomas's entrepreneur, who has decided to invest his wealth in a farm. The wealthy man in the Thomas story is motivated by a desire for big profits, while Luke's hero was simply trying to capitalize on an unexpected bonus. In Luke the abundant productivity of the fields that prompted thoughts of future security and ease was totally unexpected, while Thomas's entrepreneur hoped for extensive profits. Like Luke's farmer, Thomas's entrepreneur was self-reflective about his future (*Gos. Thom.* II,2:44,7–8), but unlike Luke's farmer this man actually died the very evening the story takes place (*Gos. Thom.* II,2:44,8–9). He never has the opportunity to invest as he had planned to do. Luke's farmer, on the other hand, was highly successful, and is still alive at the end of the story.

The apparent irregular sequence of the agricultural season in Thomas (44,5–6: sow and reap, and plant) probably refers to two separate farming activities, viz., sowing and reaping wheat (or some other cereal crop) and planting grape vines or fruit trees.[26]

---

[23] See Yadin, *Masada*, 87–106.
[24] See Betz, "Dead Sea Scrolls," *IDB* 1.790–802.
[25] See Avigad, *Discovering Jerusalem*, 64–203.
[26] So Drury, *Parables*, 136–37.

Close parallels to Luke's story exist in Jewish literature precisely in the material not paralleled by the Thomas story. To Luke 12:18–20 compare Sir 11:18–19 LXX:

> Some are wealthy by diligence and greed. And this is his allotted reward: When he says, "I have found rest, and now I may consume some of my goods." And does not know that a certain time shall pass and he will leave those things to others and die.[27]

The phrase "eat, drink, enjoy yourself" (Luke 12:19) as a statement reflecting temporary ease, comfort, and security (without negative overtones) is known also from Tob 7:9–11 and Ecclesiastes (2:24; 3:12–13; 8:15; cf. 3:22).[28]

The two stories in Luke and Thomas appear to be different performances of a common original core.[29] The essentials of Luke's story are as follows: a wealthy farmer unexpectedly had an abundant crop; he debates with himself how to handle the situation; he decides to store up his crops for future use; but the very evening of this decision, the reader is told the farmer will die. The essentials of the Thomas story are strikingly similar: A wealthy entrepreneur ponders what to do with his wealth; he decides to invest in a farm for profit so that he will have no lack in the future; but the very evening this decision is made, he dies. The similarities are obvious: wealthy man, ponders situation, decides, produce of the fields to be stored to accommodate future needs, dies the very night of his decision, neither gets to act on his plan.

Of course, the performances of the story obviously differ. Luke's story has been crafted in the light of Luke's homiletical interests, reflected in 12:15 and 21. The only structural element of Luke's narrative, however, that appears to be due to Luke is the intrusion of the voice of God, a feature lacking in Thomas's performance.[30] The condemning voice, pronouncing judgment on the farmer, clarifies for readers the true character of the farmer. According to Luke's reading, the farmer is a fool who has attempted to secure his life with material possessions. Apparently the farmer hears nothing.[31] God's voice closes off the story, takes the judgment out of the hands of the reader, and tells the reader how to understand the farmer. "God" finds him (12:20) to be a "covetous" man (12:15) who has "laid up treasure for himself" (12:21). And the reader is now programmed to view the farmer's plan to pull down barns and build

---

[27] Compare also 1 Enoch 97:8–10.

[28] For other parallels see also Smith, *Parables*, 142–43 and Fitzmyer, *Luke*, 2.973.

[29] See Scott, *Hear Then the Parable*, 130–31.

[30] Naturally since it is Luke writing the story, one finds characteristic Lukan features in the way the story is narrated; see Scott, *Hear Then the Parable*, 129–30.

[31] But see Fitzmyer (*Luke*, 2.973), who transforms the statement into a dream vision of the man.

larger ones (12:18) as the act of a greedy man who had a great opportunity to share with the needy but did not. Rather he selfishly plans to keep everything.

God's judgment in 12:20 also prompts the reader to place the worst possible interpretation on the farmer's statement about "eating, drinking, and enjoyment." In the light of Luke's setting for the story the statement suggests to most readers a "carefree, luxurious, even dissipated living."[32] In Luke's performance he is depicted as a rich man catering to his every excessive whim (while the poor starve). Of course, the farmer's statement in 12:19 does not carry that connotation in itself. It is Luke's setting and editing that lead the reader to hear it that way. The parallels in Tob 7:9–11 and Ecclesiastes scarcely carry such negative connotations. In Eccl 2:24; 3:12–13; 8:15, the statements of Koheleth reflect the pleasures that God gives to those whose lives are generally characterized by toil and death. Hence in that setting, at least, these activities must be understood in some sense as gifts of God, divine blessings that compensate for a life of toil. The Tobit parallel reflects only the transitory pleasures of the moment (as do the Ecclesiastes parallels), but one senses nothing in Tobit of the grotesque self-indulgence and dissipation that has come to characterize the Rich Farmer under the influence of Luke's reading of the story.

Luke's reading has quite probably been influenced by Sir 11:18–19, though the sayings are not the same at all. Luke's story and Sirach share the feature of the rich man saving up for his future ease, perhaps old age (Luke 12:19–20 = Sir 11:19); they also share some verbal correspondences: Luke, "take your ease" (ἀναπαύου); Sirach, I have found rest (ἀνάπαυσιν). Luke, "goods (ἀγαθά) laid up"; Sirach, "eat of my goods (ἀγαθῶν)." Luke "eat (φάγε), drink, enjoy yourself"; Sirach, "eat (φάγωμαι) of my goods." Luke, "things you have prepared, whose will they be"; Sirach, "leave those things to others." None of these features exists in the Thomas version.

The differences between Luke and Sirach are equally striking. The individual in Sirach secures his wealth by frugality and miserliness, while the farmer in Luke is a wealthy man whose good fortune comes by chance. In Luke the death of the farmer follows immediately his good fortune, while in Sirach the uncertain time of the individual's death continues to haunt him.

By contrast Thomas turns the hero of the story into a wealthy entrepreneur who decides to invest in a farm for the specific purpose of preparing for a comfortable future, but he dies the very evening he makes this decision and never even gets to make the investment. It is possible that the conversion of the farmer into a "businessman" is part of

---

[32] This is exactly the way Fitzmyer takes it: *Luke*, 2.973.

Thomas's prejudice against such persons (cf. *Gos. Thom.* II,2:44,34–35: "Tradesmen and merchants shall not enter the places of my father"). Or such a feature may be why Thomas selected this version of the story. In any case, what Luke's narrative casts as a de facto event (i.e., the fields have already produced an abundant crop), the *Gospel of Thomas* casts as only anticipated (i.e., abundant harvest was the goal of the entrepreneur).

The originating core[33] likely looked much like Luke's version, minus the intrusion of the divine voice, which appears to be due to Luke. It is more likely Luke that supplied this hermeneutically correct (for Luke) conclusion to replace a simpler conclusion "and that night he died," as it is preserved in the Thomas version and implied in Luke 12:20 (i.e., "this night your 'self' is required of you").[34]

The core of the story (as reflected in Luke) closely resembles Sir 11:18–19: each story is about wealthy people who conserve for the future, but neither of whom have an unlimited time to enjoy what each saved up/intended to save up. The differences are, however, far greater: In Sirach the wealthy man saved up for the future by frugality; in the core the surplus comes by chance. In Sirach the time the man has to enjoy his savings is indefinite; in the core of the Jesus story the man dies that very night. Hence I do not see Sirach and Luke as stories derived from a common core.

A POETIC ANALYSIS OF THE RECONSTRUCTED CORE

As was done in chapter 3, this section will consider what an analysis of the poetics of the narrative implies for reading the story. Assuming that Luke's version more closely approximates the core, the narrative consists of five periods of various clauses.

PERIOD I		ἀνθρώπου τινὸς πλουσίου εὐφόρησεν ἡ χώρα.
PERIOD II	1	καὶ διελογίζετο ἐν ἑαυτῷ λέγων,
	2	τί ποιήσω, ὅτι οὐκ ἔχω ποῦ συνάξω τοὺς καρπούς μου;
PERIOD III	1	καὶ εἶπεν, τοῦτο ποιήσω, καθελῶ μου τὰς ἀποθήκας
	2	καὶ μείζονας οἰκοδομήσω
	3	καὶ συνάξω ἐκεῖ πάντα τὸν σῖτον καὶ τὰ ἀγαθά μου

---

[33] See Crossan, *In Fragments*, 37–66, and for a recent example of this approach to the sayings traditions see Hedrick, "On Moving Mountains."

[34] Scott (*Hear Then the Parable*, 131) also regards the Lukan version as better reflecting the original structure.

PERIOD IV   1   καὶ ἐρῶ τῇ ψυχῇ μου,
             2   ψυχή, ἔχεις πολλὰ ἀγαθὰ κείμενα εἰς ἔτη πολλά·
             3   ἀναπαύου, φάγε, πίε, εὐφραίνου.

PERIOD V   [ταύτῃ δὲ τῇ νυκτὶ ἀπέθανεν][35]

I list below by period all examples of assonance or consonance, four
or more in a given period.

PERIOD II
Assonance   ε = 6   ω = 5   ου = 5
                  ο = 4   ι = 4

Consonance   τ = 5   σ (+ζ, ξ) = 6

PERIOD III
Assonance   ο = 7   α = 11
                  ω = 4   αι = 4

Consonance   κ = 8   τ = 7   μ = 4
                  π = 4   σ (ζ,ξ) = 9   ν = 6

PERIOD IV
Assonance   ε = 6   η = 4   α = 9

The story reflects little prosodic quality. The periods and clauses
exhibit only slight verbal similarity and structural balance. In form and
content the narrative appears quite prosaic.[36] It divides into five periods
of various clauses each. Period I is a short statement that sets up the
situation to which the rich farmer reacts in a soliloquy in clauses two
through four. Hence the weight of the story is thrown on the soliloquy.
Period V presents a brief denouement.

---

[35] Based on the Thomas version this is likely the conclusion of the originating
core.

[36] Scott (*Hear Then the Parable*, 131–32) finds a series of four chiasms in the
soliloquy:
A.   12:17, συηάξω τοὺς καρπούς μου
      12:18, καθελῶ μου τὰς ἀποθήκας
      (He also notes the ironic contrast between "gathering fruit" and
      "tearing down" the storehouses.)
B.   12:17, οὐκ ἔχω ποῦ συνάξω
      12:18,   συνάξω ἐκεῖ
C.   12:18, καθελῶ μου τὰς ἀποθήκας
             μείζονας οἰκοδομήσω
D.   12:19, ἔχεις πολλὰ ἀγαθά
             κείμενα εἰς ἔτη πολλά
Bailey (*Poet and Peasant*, 2.66–67) finds word play in
      εὐφορέω (12:16, εὐφόρησεν) and εὐφραίνω (12:19,
      εὐφραίνου).

The narrative's structure focuses attention on the reaction and introspection of the rich farmer in response to the crisis produced by his good yield; that is to say, on his soliloquy. Period II sets out his basic problem: a lack of storage space. Period III presents his resolution of the problem: tear down his old storage facilities and build larger ones. Period IV offers his basis for this decision: to provide for his future comfort. Therefore any interpretation of the story that turns on the issue of the man's wealth is questionable, since the story focuses on the man and his response to the crisis produced by his good fortune.[37]

In terms of Aristotle's *Poetica*,[38] the story represents an action that has beginning, middle, and end. Its magnitude, as to length, may not correspond to Aristotle's dictum that longer is better, but the plot has sufficient magnitude to identify its beginning (wealthy farmer has better than usual crop), middle (farmer ponders his options and decides to store up the crop), and end (farmer dies before he can carry out his plans). The length is, then, sufficient to allow for a change in fortune from good to bad.

The hero appears initially to be cast in the high mimetic mode (i.e., superior to other men by virtue of his wealth), but as will be seen the story is actually ironic. The man is wealthy and hence successful. He resolves to secure his unexpected good fortune so as to provide for his future comfort. But the very evening of his decision, he suddenly dies. This is a dramatic reversal of the movement of the plot. Up to this point it seems to be moving upward toward well being and a happy ending, but that movement is suddenly reversed when calamity strikes (Aristot. *Poet.* 9.11–12); the man dies. Hence because of the reversal the plot is complex.

It is at this point that the hero's character becomes clear. As a rich man he could undoubtedly resonate negatively in the social context of first-century Palestinian Judaism; yet the man does not appear to be deliberately cast as "wealthy" so as to play off against the Jewish popular wisdom tradition. Nothing is ever made of his wealth in the story. The farmer's personal reflections and intended action in both performances of the story are consistent with his character as a wealthy man, and the representation of the action is consistent with Hellenistic antiquity. Hengel, for example describes the Hellenistic period in Palestine as a period involving active business ventures: "The type of the restless businessman who is so fascinated by the hunt for money that he has no possibility of enjoying it is a typical manifestation of the early Hellenistic period. . . ."[39]

On the one hand, the denouement of the Thomas story occurs as a natural, though unexpected, event. Luke, on the other hand, has

---

[37] Against Scott, *Hear Then the Parable*, 132.
[38] See the discussion above, pp. 46–50.
[39] Hengel, *Judaism and Hellenism*, I.51.

unraveled the complication by other than natural means: the man's demise will be accomplished through an act of God.

THE CORE STORY

The estate of a certain rich man bore well. The auditor/reader knows little about this "rich man," except that he owned a lot of land that was under cultivation. Hence, for the purposes of the story he might be described as an "upper class" farmer. Luke uses χώρα for larger areas of land that would have included extensive steading as well as cultivated land. Ἀγρός, in contrast, generally denotes smaller plots of cultivated land, i.e., fields.[40] This rich man is no small country farmer; rather he is master of a large country estate[41] (or perhaps, estates).[42]

One harvest season his estate produced in abundance (εὐφόρησεν); he had a bumper crop (καρπούς, 12:17) that year. The fields produced so abundantly that he was faced with storage problems for his wheat crop in particular (σῖτον, 12:18). The Roman farming manuals advised a farmer to build storage facilities appropriate to the yield of the land. This was apparently generally followed for a potential buyer of land would judge the amount of the farm's potential yield based on the storage facilities available for the crops.[43] Because they were expensive[44] and used land that could have been cultivated,[45] storage facilities should not be overbuilt.[46] Hence if a reader assumes that the

---

[40] Ἀγρός as "field": Luke 12:28; 14:18; 15:25; 17:7, 31; Acts 4:37. Ἀγρός as "countryside" (i.e., "fields"): Luke 8:34; 9:12; 23:26. Χώρα as "region": Luke 2:8; 3:1; 8:26; 15:13, 14; 19:12; 21:21 ("countryside"); Acts 8:1; 10:39; 12:20; 13:49; 16:6; 18:23; 26:20; 27:27 ("land"). The difference between the two words, for Luke, seems clear from their contrast in Luke 15:15. Scott (*Hear Then the Parable*, 132) notes the differences between the two words.

[41] White (*Roman Farming*, 385–88) breaks down Roman farm units into the following sizes: the small holding (10–80 iugera); the medium-sized estate (80–500 iugera); the large estate (over 500 iugera). One iugerum = about two-thirds of an English acre (one iugerum = 28,800 square feet; English acre = 43,560 square feet). The estate of the man in the story would appear to be at least the size of a large estate, approximately one square mile plus.

[42] Compare the use of χώρα in Xenoph. *Oec.* 4.8. Here the individual in charge of a χώρα is referred to as a governor (ἄρχων): "To those governors who are able to show him (the king) that their country (χώρα) is densely populated and that the land (γῆ) is in cultivation and well stocked with the trees of the district (χώρα) and with the crops (καρπούς), he assigns more territory and gives presents and rewards them with seats of honor": Marchant, *Xenophon*, 392–95. It is possible that the rich man in the story is more than simply a farmer.

[43] Cato, *On Agriculture* 1.4–5.
[44] Columella, *Res Rustica* 1.4.6–7.
[45] Plin. *Hist. Nat.* 18.7.32.
[46] Varro, *On Agriculture* 1.8.5.

master of this estate knew his business, his need to expand storage facilities was due to the unusual nature of this harvest, rather than to his poor management.[47]

And he thought to himself: "What shall I do, for I have nowhere to gather in my crops?" The reader is told that he has not yet gathered in his crop; hence the entire incident occurs at the precise moment the farmer realizes that he has a bumper crop and that he is unprepared to store it. One difficulty with the verisimilitude of the story is that an experienced farmer would have known several weeks before harvest how large a crop was going to be. This farmer, however, does not recognize that he had a bumper crop until time to harvest (12:16, εὐφόρησεν, aorist).[48] If he had known ahead of time, the verb in 12:16 likely would have been imperfect or perhaps would have been used with μέλλω (cf., e.g., Luke 7:1; 9:31; 10:1; 19:4; Acts 16:27; 27:33) to indicate that the crop had not yet come to fruition. The narrator does seem to use verb tenses with deliberation. The farmer's pondering of his problem is cast in the imperfect (διελο-γίζετο), probably to show that he deliberated at some length. For some reason the solution did not come easily. That the farmer "spoke," when he finally decided to act is cast in the aorist (εἶπεν). His contemplated action is all cast in the future (12:17b, 18b, 19a).

What is the reader to make of this apparent irregularity in the realism of the story, i.e., the fact that the farmer fails to recognize his bumper crop some weeks prior to its fruition? In the irregularity Luke has either been careless in the use of the aorist in 12:16 (εὐφόρησεν) or the farmer is being deliberately cast in the ironic mode.

The "crops" that produced so abundantly could be either "dry," such as grain, hay and/or fodder, or "moist," such as grapes or olives.[49] In 12:18, however, he appears to be primarily concerned about extra storage space only for the grain (σῖτον), as opposed to his "moist" produce.

And he said, "I will do this; I will pull down my storage facilities and build greater.[50] The Roman farming guides attest to several kinds of granaries, including a shed called a *nubilarium*, which was large enough to hold the entire grain yield of the farm. It is built next to the threshing

---

[47] This is not an unusual assumption, since the farmer would not have attained and kept his wealth without being an experienced farmer. Were one to reason that he had just purchased the estate, it would still lead to the judgment that it was a bumper crop.

[48] This is clear from his comments in 12:17 (οὐκ ἔχω ποῦ συνάξω τοὺς καρπούς μου) and 12:18 (συνάξω ἐκεῖ πάντα τὸν σῖτον).

[49] Roman farmers distinguished between moist (i.e., fruits) and dry (i.e., grains) produce; so, for example, Columella, *Res Rustica* 1.6.9. Note the same distinction in Xenoph. *Oec.* 5.20: ὑγρῶν καὶ ξηρῶν καρπῶν.

[50] Cato (*On Agriculture* 3.1) advises an owner to think a long time before building.

floor so that when inclement weather threatens, the farmer may quickly restore the grain to the shed.[51] Other facilities include: a storage building with lofts,[52] a tiled facility with a vaulted ceiling[53] or a concrete floor,[54] and caves or pits dug in the ground.[55]

The term ἀποθήκη by itself indicates simply a place of storage with no reference at all to a particular commodity or type of storage facility. For example, in the Septuagint, with one exception (1 Chron 28:13), it has numerous functions and does not house a specific commodity (Exod 16:23, 32; Deut 28:5; 1 Esd 1:54; 1 Chron 28:11–12; 29:8). In the synoptic tradition ἀποθήκη refers almost exclusively to a granary (σῖτον: Matt 3:12 = Luke 3:17; Matt 6:26 = Luke 12:24; Matt 13:30). On the issue of "tearing down" and rebuilding, rather than adding new facilities, see the discussion above.[56]

And there I will gather all my grain and my goods. Under the rubric "goods" (ἀγαθά) is included far more than just the season's produce. The farmer plans to build facilities that will ensure his future comfort and well-being.[57]

And I will say to myself, "Self you have many good things laid up for many years." The farmer is literally "talking to himself." Ψυχή, of course, is the entire person, the "self" and not some discrete inner spiritual reality inhabiting the body.[58] In the light of the farmer's death that very evening, there is sharp irony in his expectation of being able to enjoy these goods "for many years."

He plans to store his produce as any good businessman might. The Roman scholar Varro described the farming process as being complete in six stages: preparing, planting, cultivating, harvesting, storing, marketing.[59] In fact, Varro specifically mentions the storage of crops as one of the major tasks in farming.[60] This farmer decided to store his grain, which according to Varro might keep fifty to one hundred years,[61] against the profits of future markets. If he were to

---

[51] Varro, *On Agriculture* 1.13.5. In Palestine such a shed would have scarcely been necessary.

[52] Columella, *Res Rustica* 1.6.9–10.

[53] Columella, *Res Rustica* 1.6.12–15; see also Plin. *Hist. Nat.* 18.72.301–3.

[54] Vitruvius, *De Architecture* 6.6.4.

[55] Columella, *Res Rustica* 1.6.15–16; Varro, *On Agriculture* 1.57.1–3.

[56] Compare also the design and reconstruction of Roman villas in Britain: Scullard, *Roman Britain*, 113–23; Collingwood, *Roman Britain*, 113–26.

[57] *TDNT* ἀγαθός, 1.11; see, e.g., the letter of Sitalces to Oenopion in Alciphron (Benner and Forbes, *Letters*, 102–3).

[58] See Scott, *Hear Then the Parable*, 135 and Fitzmyer, *Luke*, 2.973.

[59] Varro, *On Agriculture* 1.37.4.

[60] Varro, *On Agriculture* 1.17.3.

[61] Varro, *On Agriculture* 1.57.2–3.

market his produce at the right time in the future, he just might double his profits.[62] Hence in the context of these farming manuals, this farmer would appear to have been a shrewd businessman, rather than a "covetous hoarder."[63]

Take it easy; eat, drink, enjoy yourself. This is not an inappropriate response for someone who has just resolved two problems with one decision: what to do with an unexpectedly abundant crop and how to provide for his future welfare. The words, "take it easy; eat, drink, enjoy yourself," do not in themselves reflect the behavior of an uncaring and miserly person (see the discussion above). Cicero, for example, in summing up the character of a farmer's life said:

> No life can be happier than that of the farmer, not merely from the standpoint of the duty performed, which benefits the entire human race, but also because of its charm . . . and the plenty and abundance it gives of everything that tends to the nurture of man and even to the worship of the gods. . . . For the provident and industrious proprietor always has his store-room and cellars well filled with oil and wine and provisions; his entire farmhouse has an air of plenty and abounds with pork, goat's meat, lamb, poultry, milk, cheese, and honey. . . . Hawking and hunting, too, in leisure times, furnish the sauce for these dainties.[64]

The farmer in the story likely saw himself much like Cicero saw the successful farmer. His occupation has benefited humankind by providing for the necessities of life for the community, but it also benefits the farmer himself with a comfortable living. That this particular farmer in Jesus' story does not act in what some might consider an appropriate religious way is a criticism that might be leveled against all the heroes in the stories of Jesus. To criticize this farmer for not "sharing" his harvest by giving it to the poor is a particular reader reaction to the story and has virtually nothing to do with the story itself.

[And that night he died]. But the farmer died that very evening and never had opportunity to act on his decision.

---

[62] Varro, *On Agriculture* 1.69.1. Varro further advised that wine, if made from the proper variety of grape, should be stored for one year (*On Agriculture* 1.65), but the sooner one uses up walnuts, dates, and figs the better it is (*On Agriculture* 1.67). See also Josephus (*Bell.* 7.295–98) who describes the durability of produce in Herod's stores at Masada as lasting around one hundred years. Cato advised that the farmer should "have a well-built barn and storage room and plenty of vats for oil and wine, so that he may hold his products for good prices; it will redound to his wealth, his self-respect, and his reputation" (*On Agriculture* 3.2; Hooper-Ash, *Cato*, 10–11).

[63] As Talbert (*Reading Luke*, 141) and Scott (*Hear Then the Parable*, 136) would have it.

[64] Cic. *Sen.* 16.56 (Falconer, *Cicero*, 69).

HOW DOES THE STORY WORK?

The story in its pre-Lukan form is thoroughly secular, as are virtually all these stories attributed to Jesus.[65] It describes a successful and powerful man who ironically on the eve of his sudden and unanticipated death optimistically plans to capitalize on still further success. His wealth and his holdings (12:16) distinguish him from the small family farmer.

How does one explain the fact that he failed to foresee the need for additional storage space some weeks prior to the harvest, as an experienced farmer would surely have done? His wealth and holdings suggest that he is both an experienced farmer and a successful businessman. Possibly he is a "gentleman" farmer who leaves the day-to-day operations of his estate(s) to hired overseers and calls only periodically to check on his investments.[66] On the other hand, it could simply be a burlesque feature that makes the farmer, for all his wealth, property, and consequent community standing, appear ridiculous and so inept and incapable that he could not even recognize what was happening in his own fields. If the story is burlesque, how seriously should one take it? Is the caricature of the farmer significant for the working of the story, or is the narrator simply having a little fun with the audience at the farmer's expense?

The yield of the farmer's fields that proved to be too much for his storage facilities is unusual but not unrealistic (see above). What is more surprising is the farmer's decision to tear down and rebuild his existing storage facilities rather than expanding or erecting temporary facilities. While it is plausible that a farmer might need to tear down existing storage facilities and build larger ones, it is virtually inconceivable that he would do so with his ready-to-be-harvested crop sitting in the fields.[67] Hence it is likely that the narrator has caricatured the farmer with this feature.

Such a reading of the text is supported by the Roman farming manuals. The virtually uniform advice of the manuals is that the farmer should not overbuild the productivity of the land. This farmer, however, intends to rebuild his storage facilities to accommodate a greater-than-

---

[65] Cf. pp. 39–43 above.

[66] See the advice on farm management Cato (*On Agriculture* 2.1–7; Hooper-Ash, *Cato*, 6–7) gives the absentee proprietor "Let him call in his overseer . . . and inquire . . . what was the yield of wine, grain, and all other products" (cf. Luke 16:1–7). This was clearly not the case for the active "hands on" farmer; see Cic. *Sen.* 7.24.

[67] See Yadin, *Masada*, 88. Such walls as were found in Herod's storage rooms at Masada would have been a major project not to have been undertaken in harvest season.

normal yield. Hence, he would "overbuild" to accommodate more than the land normally produces.

The farmer's intention to store his crop, once gathered, rather than selling it on the current market, is not the act of a miser, but rather the act of a man who understands commodities markets.[68] Since it was an unusually good year, it is likely that the market would be flooded and prices would be low. He decides to wait for leaner years and better prices.[69] He expects this particular crop and the other "goods" he intends to store in his new storage facilities to provide for more than the foreseeable future.

If the narrator had stopped at this point, the farmer's final statement (12:19) would have led the story to a comic ending. It at least prepares the reader to expect a happy ending. The final line of the story, announcing the farmer's unexpected death, however, reverses the direction of the plot; the farmer's soliloquy becomes instead a final irony in a tragedy: "many good things . . . for many years . . . enjoy yourself."[70] Many commentaries make a great deal of the repetitive use of the first-person possessive in the soliloquy as an indication of the man's egotism and selfishness.[71] But the language is quite natural in the context of a soliloquy.[72]

ANOTHER READING OF THE STORY

The story parodies the rich farmer—not as wealthy but as a farmer, a human being. His wealth is not the target of the narrator's ridicule. It is a feature, however, that makes the burlesque more effective. The entire story takes place at harvest time in the brief moments when the farmer suddenly realizes that he has misjudged the extent of his crop. He has a bumper crop needing to be gathered in immediately, and he has insufficient storage space. Weighing his various options (which the narrator does not share with the reader), the farmer comes up with a laughably inappropriate action, given the fact that the crop is standing in the field and ready for harvest: He plans to tear down(!) his existing storage

---

[68] Oesterley (*Gospel Parables*, 170) likewise sees the act of storing the crops as appropriate.

[69] The idea of "retirement" as cessation from all revenue producing activities, and living on a fixed income, is a modern concept; see Cic. *Sen.* 7.23–24; 15.51–18.60.

[70] Compare Cic. *Sen.* 7.24: "no one is so old as to think that he cannot live one more year" (Falconer, *Cicero*, 32–33).

[71] Compare, e.g., Oesterley, *Gospel Parables*, 170; Jones, *Teaching*, 132; Bailey, *Poet and Peasant*, 1.65.

[72] Compare, e.g., the response of Cyrus to Lysander in Cic. *Sen.* 17.59: "It was I who planned it all; mine are the rows and mine the arrangement, and many of those trees I set out with my own hands" (Falconer, *Cicero*, 70–71).

facilities and commence a building program to erect larger facilities. He
reasons that this particular crop, plus other provisions, will provide him
a comfortable life for many years to come. In his soliloquy he appears to
bask in the warm glow of his good fortune, whimsically fantasizing his
future life of comfort and pleasure—with the crop still in the field!

The farmer's great wealth initially makes a reader think that he
must surely be a shrewd and capable man. The bumper crop also initially
suggests that he is a good farmer. A reader is simply not prepared for
what follows. The fellow is, in fact, in spite of his wealth and massive
land holdings, a laughable fool. He commits a series of ludicrous blunders
that even a non-farmer would find humorous.

He inexplicably misjudged the extent of his harvest. He apparently
initially mistook what turned out to be an unusually good yield to be
merely average—not a mistake that an experienced farmer should have
made.[73] He misjudged the appropriate course of action to take—with a
bumper crop in the field. With his crop needing to be harvested, he
decided first to begin tearing down his existing storage facilities.[74] Under
the circumstances, the most appropriate action would have been to begin
gathering and storing the crop in the existing facilities, with crews
simultaneously expanding (if possible) existing facilities, or building
additional temporary facilities. It is clearly not good management to
dismantle his present storage space with the crop needing to be harvested
and stored. He has misjudged his need for future storage. In short, he is
now planning to build permanent storage facilities to accommodate an
unusual harvest, and he is running the risk that in future harvest
seasons he will have expensive and unnecessary storage facilities standing idle.[75]

All these misjudgments the farmer makes, while potentially quite
disastrous, may actually be quite harmless for this particular farmer. He
is after all a "wealthy" farmer and perhaps he can afford the extra cost
of carrying on two major activities at once (construction and reap-
ing/storage), although it does appear that the activities would even then
conflict with one another. In the final analysis they do make him appear
inept and foolish, and hence, because of his position, humorous.

---

[73] The yield of the wheat crop in antiquity was evaluated on the basis of its
density. Harvesting was relatively easy with a "thin" crop, but difficult with a "thick"
one (Columella, *Res Rustica* 2.20.3). The "density" of the crop refers both to the
number of stalks with spikes of wheat (Plin. *Hist. Nat.* 17.21) and to the number and
weight of individual grains in the spike (Theophrastus, *Enquiry into Plants* 8.4.3). This
is still the way a cereal crop yield is evaluated; see Stoskopf, *Cereal Grain Crops*, 75;
and 261–62, 386–402.

[74] See Columella, *Res Rustica* 2.20.1–2: "But when the grain is ripe it should be
quickly harvested. . . . Delay is costly" (Ash, *Columella*, 1.214–15).

[75] Compare Columella, *Res Rustica* 1.4.6–8.

His final miscalculation, however, is far more serious. He misjudges how much time he has left to his life. He assumes that he will live several years, at least till he has enjoyed some of the benefits of this harvest season. Neither he nor the reader at this point, however, realize that his brief fantasy (12:19) is all that he will enjoy of the harvest. Then the narrator comes to the shocking conclusion: That very evening he died! He never had opportunity to act on any of his plans. He dies, his fields overflowing with abundance and his storage facilities yet unmodified.

The story raises in a dramatic way the question of life's meaning—and more specifically what is the significance of "my" life—but it offers no leads to answering these questions, except to affirm the sheer absurdity of amassing commodities to secure one's future. While economic abundance can improve one's physical comfort and enhance one's lifestyle, the story affirms that there are no "hedges" that in the final analysis either guarantee the longevity of life or ensure its value. "Things" will, inevitably, be surrendered to others, and one never knows when that will happen. What then brings meaning to life, and what quantifies its precise value? Do my "three score and ten" years constitute all there is to human life? Will I actually have that much time? If I do, is that life I know all there is to my reality, to my existence? But the narrator is silent.

The story has ceased to be funny. I was amused at the ridiculous behavior of the wealthy farmer, since I too, like he, am capable of miscalculation. It appears to be endemic to the human condition to err and respond inappropriately at times. Abruptly, however, the narrator reverses the story, and turns burlesque into tragedy. The ending of the story hardly satisfies readers with eternity on their minds. As a reader I find myself searching for something in the farmer's story (in which I suddenly find my own "self") that endures, some value, whether humanistic or religious, that affirms in other ways that life is fraught with eternal significance. The story has effectively scuttled any thought of the enduring validity of a life that consists in economic prosperity.

The purpose of tragedy, according to Aristotle (*Poet.* 6.2; 9.11–12; 11.4–7; 13.2; 14.2–5), is to produce pity and/or fear, or better, to effect the release of these emotions through an action that produces pity and/or fear. The story of the rich farmer achieves this objective in an admirable fashion. The compact plot provides a brief dramatic glimpse into the yawning abyss of nothingness, nonexistence. The shocking denouement "and that night he died," at first does not even register. But on reflection one finds oneself confronted by the sheer absurdity of life in the face of this ending. The story's dark vision of reality is ultimately nihilistic, causing the mind to recoil in fear—even horror. One finds in the story no hope, only despair; no future, only death; no meaning, only absurdity; no theology, only *mimesis*; no affirmation, only denial; no comfort, only fear.

That understanding of the story, or something similar, is probably what led Luke to recast the story as a warning to the "covetous man"

(12:15) that death (i.e., annihilation) is the ultimate end of life for one who is "not rich toward God" (12:21). In this way Luke combines the horror of the dark vision with hope, and selectively applies the despair to one group: the covetous, those who are not rich toward God.

Against the background of farming practices in antiquity, the story has more subtlety and depth than Luke was able to appreciate. Luke's heavy moralistic and judgmental reading of the story obscures its subtle nuances, realism, and the playful humor of the narrator. By turning it into an example story that condemns the farmer as a greedy miser, Luke ensures that no reader will be able to identify with the character. Hence Luke's reading lessens both the appeal of the story and its effectiveness.

HOW MIGHT THE STORY HAVE BEEN HEARD IN THE CONTEXT OF ISRAEL'S FICTIONS ABOUT ITSELF

Casting the hero as a wealthy man (*Gos. Thom.* II,2:44,3–4: a "rich man who had much money"; Luke 12:16: a rich man) suggests that the story may well have been heard in the context of Jewish wisdom literature. There was, according to Martin Hengel, a clear social contrast between rich and poor in Palestine in the Hellenistic period that played off the wisdom tradition.[76] The prosperity of the rich and the contrasting condition of the poor were both seen in the literature as due to the providence of God (Prov 10:22; 22:2; Eccl 5:19; 6:2; Job 34:19; 1 Sam 2:7; 1 Chron 29:28; 2 Chron 1:11–12; Sir 11:14; 44:6; Tob 4:21; 1 Macc 4:23–25). Hence in themselves prosperity and wealth were good (Sir 13:24–25) and desirable (Wis 8:5; Sir 19:1; Prov 10:4), for they brought comfort and honor (Sir 10:30–31; Prov 14:20).

Nevertheless, wealth and the wealthy were viewed negatively as well; due, no doubt, to the acute distance in station between the rich and the poor with virtually no middle class to mitigate the attitudes of the poor. The "rich" and the "poor" are regularly cast as two contrasting groups (Wis 8:5; Sir 13:15–23; 30:14; 1 Esd 3:19; Job 34:19), with the rich generally cast as the exploiters of the poor (Sir 13:2–7; 2 Sam 12:1–6). The rich are seen as wicked (Ps 73:12), perverse, and haughty (Prov 28:6, 11).

To the pious, wisdom is held out as the "true riches" (Wis 7:8–14; 8:5, 18; 10:11; Prov 3:16), since material wealth and riches cannot bring happiness (Sir 14:3–5; 28:2; 30:15–16; 31:1–2; 40:25–27; Eccl 5:12). Even the rich have as their only boast "the fear of the Lord" (Sir 10:22), for they cannot count on their riches to protect them from misfortune (Sir

---

[76] Hengel, *Judaism and Hellenism*, 1.50. See also pages 136–38 for another contrast between rich and poor. See also the discussion in Heinish-Heidt, *Theology*, 199–200, 327.

5:1, 8; 18:25; 21:4; 40:13; Prov 22:16), death (Sir 11:18–19), or judgment (Prov 11:4; Job 27:19). Therefore it is futile and foolhardy to make the quest for riches the primary focus of life (Prov 11:28; 13:7; 23:4; 27:24; 28:20; Eccl 6:1–2), since wealth can corrupt one's life (Sir 31:5–11). The image of a rich man toiling to amass a fortune and then relaxing to enjoy the pleasures of his prosperity was paralleled in the popular wisdom tradition with the image of a poor man's working to the bitter end and then relaxing in lack and deprivation (Sir 31:3–4).

Against such a religio-social construct, this story could resonate as an anti-upperclass story. Thus the hero would have been cast as a rich man precisely because of the negative perception of the wealthy in society. Both his intended investment of wealth to amass more wealth (*Gospel of Thomas*) and his intent to enjoy the pleasures of his amassed fortune (Luke) would fit the poor's stereotypical view of the rich: i.e., the pursuit of still more wealth to create security and comfort for oneself (Sir 31:1–4). But that very evening the man in the story dies. Hence the story reaffirms the inability of wealth to protect the wealthy from misfortune, death, and judgment. By implication and contrast the story could be understood to promote the pursuit of true riches: wisdom and Torah.

On the other hand, the story could have easily been heard in the context of the skeptical tradition of Ecclesiastes, where it does seem to be most at home. At least Koheleth seems to have stood at the very point that my reading of the story has taken me (Eccl 1:2–3; 2:4–6, 11; 9:11–12).

Koheleth,[77] of course, finds meaning and comforts himself in some of the simple pleasures of life (Work: 3:22; social involvement: 2:24; 3:12–13; 5:18; 9:7; friendship: 4:9–12; marriage: 9:9; physical delights: 2:24; 3:12–13, 22; 8:15; 9:7). Having persevered in his religious faith (3:10–11; 5:18–19; 12:1–7), he finds meaning in religious obligations (5:1, 4). Nonetheless, Koheleth hardly champions the meaningfulness of life.

Those who did not take themselves out of the story by hearing it as an anti-upper class story[78] may have seen the farmer as someone not unlike themselves. Hence they laugh at him, not because he is rich, but because he made laughable mistakes. It is such an auditor/reader who may have been faced at the end of the story with the uncertainty of life and its apparent meaninglessness. Luke, for one, apparently read the story this way and hence recast the farmer as one whose primary focus of life consisted in the "abundance of possessions" rather than God.

---

[77] See the brief analysis by Kuntz, *Ancient Israel*, 462–65. The idea of life ending suddenly, hopelessly, but not as the result of God's judgment on humankind for wickedness, rather as a more or less natural event, is found elsewhere in the wisdom tradition (Job 7:6; 9:25–26; 10:20–22; 14:1–2, 7–12; Sir 11:18–19; 17:2).

[78] Upper class folk who heard the story in this way would likely have taken the story as political satire and opted out; the poor who criticized the rich for their wealth, would not have been able to identify with the farmer in the story, except negatively.

9 🌿

A Sower

STORIES OF JESUS, LIKE THE SOWER, THAT FOCUS ON THE NATURAL PROC-
esses, are much more difficult for readers to relate to religious values. As
a result the Sower has inspired a wide range of interpretations. I will first
address the settings of the stories in early Christian literature, their
earliest extant readings, before surveying how modern interpreters have
made sense of the story as a "parable." A comparison of their structures
and poetical designs reveals few variations that are significant for reading the story. Initially the narratives appear to do little more than present
accurate pictures of farming practices in first-century Palestine, but
when placed in the context of a Hebrew faith that relied completely upon
God for even the produce of the field, the story resonates with a distinctive secularity.

THE EARLY CHRISTIAN READING OF THE STORY

This parable is one of only three stories attested in all three of the
Synoptic Gospels and the *Gospel of Thomas*.[1] Throughout the history of
parables interpretation the Sower has enjoyed a variety of explanations,
beginning with Mark's allegorical reading, an interpretation followed by
Matthew and Luke.[2] Mark takes the story to be an allegory about
evangelism in the first-century church;[3] for Mark it is not specifically
about the kingdom of God, but describes the vicissitudes of Christian
evangelism and the inevitable success of the church's preaching.

---

[1] See Appendix B.
[2] Mark 4:13–20 = Matt 13:18–23 = Luke 8:11–15.
[3] This understanding of Mark's interpretation may be regarded as a consensus
of scholarship; see Jeremias, *Parables*, 77–79, and Scott, *Hear Then the Parable*, 343–45.

What the "sower" sows in the Synoptic Gospels is not seed but "the word." This "word" that is "sown" should probably be associated with the "gospel" proclaimed by Mark's church and assumed by it to be synonymous with Jesus' preaching.[4] Hence it was the "gospel of God," announcing the immediacy of the kingdom and the fulfillment of "the time" and calling for repentance and faith (Mark 1:14–15). According to this interpretation the sower is not a farmer but a preacher—any preacher in Mark's community. Locations where the seed is sown are explained as different kinds of hearers. The path is the hard-hearted hearer on whom the word cannot make any impression. The birds are Satan, who "takes away" from hearers the word that has been proclaimed to them. The rocky ground constitutes the apostates, who make a good beginning in faith, but eventually renounce it because of the rigorous persecution associated with confession. The ground overgrown with thorns denotes materialistic auditors, who hear the word, but take greater delight in material wealth and goods; hence the proclamation of the word does not lead them to true faith.[5] The good soil equals persistent converts whose productiveness in faith witnesses to their status as true believers. Matthew and Luke simply modify stylistically Mark's explanation to the story.[6]

MODERN INTERPRETATIONS

Modern interpreters differ widely in their understanding of the story. Accordingly the meaning of the story: (1) focuses on responses to the preaching of Jesus (Cadoux,[7] Smith,[8] Jones,[9] Perkins[10]); (2) is about the kingdom of God (Dodd,[11] Taylor,[12] Crossan,[13] Lane,[14] Carlston,[15] Mann[16]); (3) is lost (Linnemann[17]); (4) is about the eventual success of

---

[4]Matthew does interpret the "word" as the "word of the kingdom" (cf. Mark = "the word" and Luke = "the word of God"). I understand Matthew to mean by this that "the word" is Jesus' preaching about the kingdom of God. Mark and Luke make no association of the story with the "kingdom."

[5]The interpretation reasonably demanded by the story at this point (4:7) should associate this kind of hearer with "unproductive" Christians, rather than "failed" Christians, as the allegorical interpretation has it (4:19).

[6]See the discussion below.

[7]*Parables*, 155.

[8]*Parables*, 126.

[9]*Art and Truth*, 101–2.

[10]*Parables*, 80–81.

[11]*Parables*, 134.

[12]*Mark*, 251.

[13]*In Parables*, 50–51.

[14]*Mark*, 163.

[15]*Triple Tradition*, 146.

[16]For four main types of interpretation for the parable see Mann, *Mark*, 261.

[17]*Parables*, 117.

Jesus' preaching (Jeremias[18]); (5) has an authority of its own and witnesses to Jesus "in its own way" (Wilder[19]); (6) is substantially preserved in Mark's interpretation (Michaels[20]); (7) presents God's ruling activity under the most unfamiliar guises (Scott[21]).[22]

Most interpretations (with the exception of Wilder and Scott) turn on assumptions about the nature of the ministry of Jesus or the primary focus of his preaching. These assumptions, however, are extraneous to the story proper and provide a hypothetical matrix for the story under whose influence the story takes on a particular significance. This hypothetical matrix controls the story and inevitably forces elements of the story into an allegorical-like interpretation having little or nothing to do with the story. In short, the story is swallowed by the assumptions and hence loses its autonomy.

The truth is, the story does not concern itself with preaching, the characteristics of hearers, the success of the kingdom of God, or the ministry of Jesus. In its present form(s), it is a story about farming:

> What is the parable about? (1) It is about the sower. (2) It is about the seed. (3) It is about the different types of ground on which the seed falls. (4) It is about the different things that prevent the seed from bearing fruit. And (5) it is about the wonderful yield of the seed when it falls on good ground. The story is about any one or all of these themes.[23]

Everything else has been brought to the story by its various interpreters. And as was discovered regarding the interpretations of the synoptic evangelists, a successful interpretation seems to hinge upon the creative ability of the interpreter to make sense of the story in the context of the ministry of Jesus rather than upon a specific innate feature within the story itself.[24] It is, however, easier to determine relevance for the stories that deal with human activity or for stories dealing with society and individual human activity than for the mythical or nature stories.[25] This is probably because readers are interested more in their contemporary religious significance for modern life than in the stories. Stories that deal with human activity seem to lend themselves more readily to our making sense of them in terms of proper, or ideal, human behavior.[26]

---

[18] *Parables*, 150–51.

[19] *War of Myths*, 98–99.

[20] *Servant and Son*, 90.

[21] *Hear Then the Parable*, 361–62.

[22] For another brief survey of the ways the story has been understood see Bultmann, "Interpretation von MK 4, 3–9."

[23] Breech, *Silence of Jesus*, 82.

[24] See above, chapter 2, pp. 25–28.

[25] Scott (*Hear Then the Parable*, 345) is of a similar opinion.

[26] At least this seems to be true judging from Via's existential interpretation of the "parables." Via did not treat any of the nature "parables."

A COMPARATIVE AND STRUCTURAL ANALYSIS

MATTHEW	MARK	LUKE	THOMAS (#9)
	Listen!		
Behold,	Behold,	Behold,	Behold,
the sower went forth	the sower went forth	the sower went forth	the sower went forth;
to sow.	to sow.	to sow his seed (sg.);	
And as he sowed,	And as he sowed,	and as he sowed,	he filled his hand,
			he threw.
some (pl.) fell beside the path.	one (sg.) fell beside the path,	it (sg.) fell beside the path,	Some (pl.) fell upon the path;
		and it was trampled under foot,	
And the birds,	and the birds	and the birds of the air	the birds
having come,	came and		came
devoured them (pl.).	devoured it (sg.).	devoured it (sg.).	and gathered them (pl.).
And others fell on	And another (sg.) fell on	And another (sg.) fell on	Others (pl.) fell on
the rocky places,	the rocky area (sg.),	the rock;	the rock;
where they did not have much soil,	where it did not have much soil,		
and immediately they sprang up	and immediately it sprang up	and after it had sprouted,	
since they did not have depth of soil.	since it did not have depth of soil.		
And after the sun rose they were scorched;	And when the sun rose it was scorched;		
and since they did not have root,	and since it did not have root,		they did not strike root
they were withered.	it was withered.	it was withered,	
		since it did not have moisture.	
			into the earth
			and did not send up ears toward the sky.
And others fell	And another (sg.) fell	And another fell	And others fell
on	into	in the midst of	upon
the thorns.	the thorns.	the thorns.	the thorns;
And the thorns grew up	And the thorns grew up	And the thorns grew together	they
and stifled them (pl.).	and throttled it (sg.),	and choked it (sg.).	choked the seed (sg.),
	and it yielded no fruit.		
			and the worm ate them.
But others (pl.) fell	And others (pl.) fell	And another fell	And others (pl.) fell
upon	into	into	upon
the good soil	the good soil	the good soil;	the good soil;
		and after it sprouted	
and produced	and produced	it produced	it produced
			good
fruit,	fruit	fruit	fruit
	rising and increasing and each bore:		
	one, thirty		
	and one, sixty		sixty per measure
some, a hundred	and one, a hundred.	one hundred times as much.	
some, sixty			
some, thirty.			
			and one hundred twenty per measure.

Though the four versions closely resemble one another, each is distinctive. The story describes a farmer sowing a field; it continues with the vicissitudes that befall the seed once it is sown, its early misfortunes, and the eventual success of the harvest. Only the versions of Luke (σπόρος) and Thomas (ϬΡΟϬ) use the word "seed." Matthew and Mark assume that the auditor/reader understands that the sower sows "seed." The kind of seed is unspecified.

Mark seems to conceive of what is sown in a generic or collective sense; that is, with one exception (4:8) Mark uses the singular when referring to the seed. I am taking it as a collective singular.[27] After all, sowers in antiquity do not "sow" only one seed at a time (that would be "planting"); nor does a group of birds eat the same singular seed. As Thomas indicates "he *fills his hand* [i.e., with seeds] and throws." Mark's use of the plural in 4:8 seems to substantiate the collective sense of the other references to seed. Luke, on the other hand, is careful to use the singular throughout (but again probably a collective use of the word seed). Matthew, however, clarifies the collective nature of the seed by using the more clearly understood plural. Thomas, like Mark, shifts between singular and plural. Only once in Thomas does seed appear in a singular form (34,10). In Thomas 34,12, however, what produced the good fruit is probably the good soil (34,11), rather than the good seed (34,10); see the plural at 34,11 (ϨⲚⲔⲞⲞⲨⲈ).

The basic structure of the story in all four versions is the same. Variations occur only in features scattered through the various performances of the story.[28] All versions begin with an introductory "behold."[29] Thomas's description of the act of sowing ("he filled his hand, he threw") graphically portrays the actions of the farmer. Matthew, Mark, and Luke leave the readers to create their own mental image. The story continues describing seed sown in four general areas (of a field?—it is not so specified, but an auditor/reader would normally, and naturally, assume this to be the case): on/along a path, on a rocky area/rock, on/into/in the thorns, upon/into the good soil.

The Seed Along the Path

Seeds sown along a path face three different hazards. All versions agree that these seeds are taken by the birds[30] who devour/gather

---

[27] For the collective see Winer-Lünemann, *Grammar*, 174–75.

[28] For discussions of the differences see Scott, *Hear Then the Parable*, 350–55, and Crossan, "Seed Parables," 244–51.

[29] Mark has two introductory words: "listen" and "behold." "Listen" is probably Mark's introduction that fits with the Markan emphasis elsewhere in the section: 4:9, 12, 23, 33.

[30] Luke adds that these are "birds of the air." It is probably an idiomatic expression (cf. Mark 4:32), but the expression clearly delineates between wild fowl

them.[31] Thomas's use of the word "gather" could be a metaphorical expression for "eating," but "gathering" does create a visual image of the birds "harvesting" a crop. Birds do "gather" food to feed their young; hence the use of the word "gather" could indicate a "taking off the path." It is interesting that the sower in Matthew, Mark, and Luke appears to have carefully avoided getting seeds *on* the path—thus protecting or preserving the seed from being destroyed by the villagers using the path through/bordering[32] the field; it suggests that the sower in the Synoptic Gospels never intended to plow the path area and hence did not want to waste more seed by casting it *on* the path. He could not, however, avoid seed falling *along* the path, and it was that seed that was lost due to birds and the traffic of the villagers (wherever the path was located). In Thomas, however, the sower does cast seed *on* the path, suggesting that this sower did intend to plow, and hence the "path" also would probably have been tilled (though none of the versions record a plowing of any sort).

The Seed on the Rocky Ground

The seed that falls on the rocky area faces three different threats.[33] Matthew and Luke agree that it quickly sprouts then withers away.[34] The sparse soil of the rocky area is enough apparently for the seed to germinate, but not enough to support its root system for any period of time. As a consequence, the sun burns the sprout. It then withers and presumably dies. In Luke and Thomas the seed has no soil at all but rests

---

and domesticated fowl. These are not farm animals, like "chickens," but wild birds. Presumably the farmer would have guarded against farm animals taking the seed. Hence, if this is the case, the expression is a novelistic feature that intensifies the realism of the story. The loss of the seed to the birds is an ordinary hazard of farming.

[31] Luke also adds that the seed is "trampled on," but since Luke had described the seed as falling "beside" (παρά) the path rather than "on" the path, it seems likely that this is Luke's intensification of the hazards faced by the seed, prompted by the allegorical interpretation he appropriated from Mark: i.e., the gospel (word) is rejected by the audience who hears it. This added feature would have been more appropriate in Thomas's version, however, where the seeds fall "on" the path.

[32] See Jeremias, *Parables*, 12, who seems to envision the path running through the field, although this is not an inevitable interpretation.

[33] The rock is clearly not a christological feature here. The "rocky area" is different from "the rock," it seems to me. The suggestion is that a rocky area can be plowed and the seed turned over and under the rocky soil. If it is an actual rock (stray large rock? flat area? threshing floor?), it could not be plowed, but would have to be removed or bypassed.

[34] If the word "immediately" is taken seriously, then one should probably regard this feature as an allegorical element that Mark introduces under the influence of his inherited interpretation, since seeds do not germinate "immediately." If one takes it to mean "quickly," then it is reasonable that seed sown in shallow soil will sprout sooner than those sown in deeper soil.

on a rock. In Luke in spite of the lack of soil it sprouts anyway (is a reader to think of soil caught in the crevice of the rock?), but withers because it has no moisture (drought?). In Thomas the seed does not "strike root" and hence produces no fruit; its fate is not described.

The Seed Among the Thorns

The seed that falls on/into/in the midst of the thorns likewise perishes because the thorns choke or stifle its germination. The image is the same in all versions except that Luke's is more graphic. The seed in Luke perishes because the thorns grow together to form a dense over-growth: it can receive neither sun nor moisture. Thomas also adds a hazard not found in the Synoptic Gospels: a worm eats the seed. Mark adds that the seed falling among the thorns yielded no fruit, a circum-stance less clear in the other three versions. This suggests that the seed in Mark germinated and produced a shoot. Hence the story at this point, at least as far as Mark is concerned, appears to be describing *plants* among the thorns and not seeds that fail to germinate.

The Seed in the Good Soil

Only that seed falling on the good soil yields any fruit at all; the rest perish without germinating, except for the seed sown on the rock in Thomas and the seed sown among the thorns in Mark. In these latter two instances the seed apparently germinates, but it produces no fruit.

Mark describes the fruit of the seed sown in good soil as "rising and increasing"; probably the language is designed to portray the maturation of the spikes of grain as full of kernels. In Matthew and Mark the yield varies between thirty, sixty, and one hundredfold (Matthew lists the same yield only in reverse order). Luke says the seed bore one hundred times as much fruit as the seed that was sown. In Thomas the seed produces "good fruit" at the rate of sixty ECOTE and one hundred twenty ECOTE.[35]

---

[35] The term ECOTE is uncertain in Coptic. Crum (362a) lists its translation as "a measure (?)." Hence the translation of the passage would then be "sixty per measure and one hundred twenty per measure" (so Ménard, *Thomas* [par mesure], Guillaumont, *Thomas* and Lambdin, "Thomas"); that is to say: sixty to a measure (of seed sown) and one hundred twenty to a measure (of seed sown). Other translations are Grant, Freedman, Schoedel, *Secret Sayings*, 125: "at times it came as sixty and at times as one hundred twenty"; Davies, *Gospel of Thomas*, 150: "it bore sixty measures and one hundred-twenty measures." One could take the expression as a Bohairicism (Crum, 361b) for "thing cast," or "seed" and translate: sixty to (a) thing cast and one hundred twenty to (a) thing cast. This is similar to Luke: One hundred times as much (sc. as the seed that was sown).

Exactly what kind of image is projected by the descriptions of the yield? White[36] has correctly pointed out that the amount of yield is reported in relation to individual seeds sown, rather than to bushels per field, as is usually done in modern agriculture.[37] This seems clear from the way Mark and Luke report the yield. Mark reports that "others" (4:8) fell into the good soil. The rest of Mark's story suggests that the narrative envisions multiple individual seeds producing yields rather than one act of sowing per field, viz.,

one fell beside the path (4:4)
birds devoured it (4:4)
another (one) fell on the rocky area (4:5)
it did not have soil (4:5)
it sprang up (4:5)
it did not have depth of soil (4:5)
it was scorched (4:6)
it withered (4:6)
another (one) fell into the thorns (4:7)
thorns throttled it (4:7)
it yielded no fruit (4:7)
others (individual seeds) (4:8) fell into the good soil
it (each) bore: one, thirty; one, sixty; one, a hundred (4:8).

The size of the yield makes sense if it relates to the produce of single seeds. Luke eliminates potential confusion by changing Mark's "others" (ἄλλα, Mark 4:8) to "another" (ἕτερον, Luke 8:8) and by reporting that the "other" seed that fell into the good soil produced one hundred times as much fruit (as the [individual] seed that was sown).[38]

THE "BOUNTIFUL HARVEST" AND THE FAILURE TO PLOW

Two incongruities mark all four versions of the story. (1) The seed sown on the good soil faces no hazards at all and at harvest produces a yield apparently inevitably and naturally with no help from the farmer. Indeed (2) the farmer apparently never plows the land, either before or after the sowing—so far as one can determine from the story. Would not

---

[36] See White, "Parable of the Sower," 301–3.

[37] This is exactly the way that the version in 1 Clem 24:5 reports the yield: "and from one (grain) more grow and bring forth fruit."

[38] White, "Parable of the Sower," 302. White cites a text from Pliny (*Hist. Nat.* 17.94–95) that reports nearly four hundred shoots from a single grain. White thinks that Pliny substituted *germina* (shoots) for *grana* (grains), but that emendation is not necessary to make his point. Pliny still reported the yield in terms of the individual seed sown.

seed sown on good soil also have faced precisely the same hazards as that sown elsewhere? And in a story that reflects the conditions of Mediterranean agriculture with such realism, why is there no mention of plowing? That feature is lacking at the beginning of the story as well as sometime prior to the report of the yield, where one would have expected it to appear in all versions of the story. The absence of these two features (no dangers to the seed in the good soil, and the failure to mention plowing) is an incongruity that becomes crucial for understanding the narrative; unless the interpreter presumes these features were accidentally omitted, then something must be made of them. While the story may work without them, their absence threatens the realism of the story.

The Bountiful Harvest

Some commentators argue unconvincingly that the "bountiful harvest" is the point of the story.[39] What these commentators cite as unusual productivity in this story, however, is actually just an expected outcome of Mediterranean agriculture. Similar language is elsewhere used of anticipated harvests.[40]

Theophrastus:

And, if the ground is ill-cultivated, it produces fifty fold, if it is carefully cultivated, a hundred fold.[41]

Pliny:

It [i.e., secale] grows in any sort of soil with a hundred-fold yield. . . . [42]

Even so the exceptional fertility of the soil returns crops with a fifty-fold increase, and to more industrious farmers even with a hundred-fold.[43]

[In Egypt, the soil's] fertility is so great that a second crop grows of its own accord in the following year from the seeds trodden in by the reapers.[44]

Nothing is more prolific than wheat—Nature having given it this attribute because it used to be her principal means of nourishing man—inasmuch as a peck of wheat, given suitable soil like that of the Byzacium plain in Africa, produces a yield of 150 pecks. The deputy governor of that region sent to his late Majesty Augustus—almost incredible as it seems—a parcel of very nearly 400 shoots obtained from a single grain as seed, and there

---

[39] Cf., e.g., Jeremias, *Parables*, 150–51, Taylor, *Mark*, 251, and Crossan, *In Parables*, 50–51.

[40] See the brief study by White, "Parable of the Sower," and the reply by Jeremias, "Gleichnis vom Säemann."

[41] Theophrastus, *Enquiry into Plants*, 8.7.4; Hort, *Theophrastus*, 2.187.

[42] Plin. *Hist. Nat.* 18.40.141; Rackham, *Pliny*, 5.279.

[43] Plin. *Hist. Nat.* 18.40.162; Rackham, *Pliny*, 5.291.

[44] Plin. *Hist. Nat.* 18.40.162; Rackham, *Pliny*, 5.291.

are still in existence dispatches relating to the matter. He likewise sent to Nero also 360 stalks obtained from one grain. At all events the plains of Lentini and other districts in Sicily, and the whole of Andalusia, and particularly Egypt reproduce at the rate of a hundredfold. The most prolific kinds of wheat are branched wheat and what they call hundred-grain wheat. Also a single beanstalk has before now been found laden with a hundred beans.[45]

Hence, a yield of 30, 60, 100, or even 120 is not really surprising in the sense of "miraculous" or exceptional; rather, under certain conditions the soil did produce in such quantities as a matter of course.

It could be argued that in the story of a Sower the yield is surprising in view of the dangers or hazards facing this particular farmer in this particular field. But as it turns out there is also nothing unusual in these threats. The same ancient authors consider many of the hazards mentioned in the New Testament story as the same hazards or dangers faced by the fields of any farmer: plants are "trodden down" (Theophrastus, *Enquiry into Plants* 7.7.5), plants are "strangled" (ἀποπνίγει—Theophrastus, *Enquiry into Plants* 8.8.4), plants are eaten by bugs and worms (Aristot. *Hist. An.* 9.39.1; Theophrastus, *Enquiry into Plants* 8.10.1 and 4–5; 8.11.2–3; Plin. *Hist. Nat.* 18.45.152 and 154), sun chars the roots of plants (Varro, *On Agriculture* 1.9.3), different qualities of soil are noted (Varro, *On Agriculture* 1.9.3–6; Plin. *Hist. Nat.* 18.55.198–99; Columella, *Res Rustica* 2.9.3–6 and 14–15 and 17–18), and specifically "thin" soil is noted (Plin. *Hist. Nat.* 18.46.165 and 65.243; Varro, *On Agriculture* 1.9.6); one finds weeds, and sun scorching the seed (Plin. *Hist. Nat.* 18.42.145–46).

Hence the threats to the seed in the story of a Sower are in no way unusual. Nevertheless, in spite of these same kinds of hazards it was customary in antiquity for there to be a productive harvest (i.e., fiftyfold and one hundredfold).

What I do find striking is the realism of the story. The hazards of farming in antiquity are accurately and realistically portrayed in all versions of the story. Realism breaks down, however, when it asserts that only the "good" soil produces a yield. The term "good" (ἀγαθός in Luke but καλός in Matthew and Mark), along with terms like "rich" and "fat," ordinarily refers in antiquity to the richest and most productive kind of soil (Theophrastus, *Enquiry into Plants* 8.6.2; 8.6.4; 8.11.9). To assert that only the "good" soil produces a crop, however, is not realistic. Different kinds of plants require different kinds of soil, and in some cases the "thinner" soil is more appropriate for a more vigorous plant. For example, lupine thrives in lean, gravely, dry, and even sandy soil. When its seed falls on soil that is overgrown with briars, it penetrates and even

---

[45] Plin. *Hist. Nat.* 18.21.94–95; Rackham, *Pliny*, 5.249.

gets its roots into the ground (Plin. *Hist. Nat.* 18.36.134–35; Columella, *Res Rustica* 2.1–4). Hence, under certain conditions the seed sown on the shallow ground, and even that falling among the thorns, would have produced a crop. And in like manner the seed falling on the good soil would have been subject to eating by worms, birds, and other small creatures, and to scorching by the sun, drought, etc. Hence, for the story to be realistic, there should have been some loss experienced by the farmer among the seeds sown on the good soil. Some of the hazards faced by the farmer had nothing to do with the character of the soil; for example, why didn't the birds eat seed sown on the good soil? The farmer, according to the story, never plowed it under, hence the seed on the good soil was also subject to this threat.

It is probably more reasonable, however, to see in the story a stylizing of the kinds of hazards facing any seed that a farmer sows in any field. If this is correct, the point is that some seed falling in the right place under the right conditions produces a yield, but other seed falling on "poor" ground, or on "good" ground under the wrong conditions (and hence it is still "poor" soil) is threatened by the farmer's natural enemies—birds, thorns, worms, sun, lack of moisture, etc. If that is the case, the hazards described in the story are not intended to describe exhaustively what can destroy the farmer's crops; rather they only represent the kinds of hazards the farmer faces. Hence, the "good soil" in this story becomes any soil that produces a crop rather than the story having a particular kind or quality of soil in view.

The elements of the story bear this out. For example, in Mark the soil beside the path may have been "good" soil in the sense of the most fertile soil, but we will never really know since the birds ate the seed before it germinated. Again the soil in which the thorns were growing may also have been "good" soil (in the sense of fertile), but we will never really know since the thorns throttled the seed. Good soil can fail to produce because of birds, thorns, worms, lack of moisture, etc. The point is, Mark was not describing productive and unproductive soils, but rather different kinds of hazards facing the seeds that the farmer sows. Hence, the story seems to affirm the following: get the seed in the right place under the right conditions and the seed will germinate and produce a yield.

The Failure to Plow

The second incongruity is that so far as can be determined from the story, the farmer has not plowed his land in connection with this act of sowing. As a matter of fact, the farmer gives no care at all to the land! If a reader regards the elements of the story seriously, this circumstance seems rather clear. Had the farmer plowed the land in preparation for sowing there would have been no "path" of impacted earth running through the field,[46] and the thorns would have been plowed under.[47] As can be seen from the comparative structural analysis of the story (see above), the farmer does not even plow the seed under after sowing, as would normally be expected in Mediterranean agriculture.[48] The farmer should have plowed at the conclusion of the sowing (i.e., following the seed falling on the "good" soil—Mark 4:8a) or sometime before the harvest scene (Mark 4:8b) reported at the end of the story.

The realism of the story of a Sower suffers at this point, since harvest does not immediately follow sowing. Compare a Sprouting Seed (the farmer scatters seed, sleeps night and day, and the seed sprouts) and the Good Seed and Weeds (a man sows seed, an enemy sows weeds, plants came up and bear, wheat and weeds are allowed to grow together *until* the harvest), where a required time interval between sowing and harvest becomes clear, even though there is not even here any mention of plowing.

Plowing of fields is regarded as an extremely important act in Mediterranean agriculture.[49]

> Give ear, and hear my voice;
> hearken and hear my speech.
> Does he who plows for sowing plow continually?
> does he continually open and harrow his ground?
> When he has leveled its surface,
> does he not scatter dill, sow cummin,
> and put in wheat in rows and barley in its
> proper place, and spelt as the border?
> For he is instructed aright;
> his God teaches him (Isa 28:23–26 RSV; see also Sir 6:19; 20:28; 38:24–26;
> 1 Esd 4:6; 2 Esd 16:24).

Here it is clearly represented that the Israelite farmer plows and levels the ground *before* sowing. And such is the case in Jer 4:3 and Thomas log. 20.[50]

---

[46] Of course there may not have been a path through the field at all. It may have simply bordered the field. See the note by White, "Parable of the Sower," 306.

[47] Indeed, the fact that the farmer is careful to sow the seed "beside" (παρά) the path (Matthew, Mark, Luke) suggests that the farmer never intended to sow the impacted earth that would have comprised the "path."

[48] For the literature see in particular Jeremias, *Parables*, 11 n. 3, and "Gleichnis vom Säemann," 48–53. There is a discussion in Mishnah in this regard concerning diverse kinds of seed. If a farmer sows his field with wheat and then he determines to sow it with barley, he must wait until the seed sprouts, then plow his land *before* he sows with barley (*m. Zer.* 2.3–4). This suggests that in certain select cases, even if Jeremias were correct, the sowing-before-plowing practice was not always followed. For a thorough discussion of the questions see Payne, "Order," 123–29.

[49] On the issue of plowing in Palestinian agriculture see Hopkins, *Highlands of Canaan*, 192–95, 214–17; Borowski, "Agriculture," 79–87.

[50] See in particular Borowski, "Agriculture," 84–85.

Among the Greeks and Romans,[51] plowing the land ensured a productive harvest, and only rarely under very special circumstances did the farmer purposely not plow.

> What is good cultivation? Good ploughing. What next? Ploughing. What third? Manuring.[52]

Varro distinguishes between three kinds of plowing: (1) "breaking up"—probably the fallow ground is meant, since he describes ground as being turned up in large clumps in this procedure; (2) "breaking down"—i.e., breaking the large clods prior to broadcasting the seed; (3) "ridging"—plowing the field with mould boards attached to the plow in order both to cover the broadcast seed in ridges and at the same time to cut ditches of furrows to let the water drain off.[53] Generally farmers plowed before sowing,[54] followed by hoeing.[55] In some cases, however, a farmer might sow before any plowing at all, particularly with respect to lupine (Columella, *Res Rustica* 2.10.1–4; Theophrastus, *Enquiry into Plants* 8.11.8–9) and beans (Plin. *Hist. Nat.* 18.49.181 [beans and vetch]; Columella, *Res Rustica* 2.10.5–6). Vetch may be sown on untilled land but does better if the land is tilled (Columella, *Res Rustica* 2.10.29 and 33). Pliny goes so far as to say that lupine is the only seed that is sown without the ground having first been plowed (*Hist. Nat.* 18.36.133–36); nevertheless, even then it is covered with a light furrow (*Hist. Nat.* 18.36.135). Flax may be sown in sandy soil with a single plowing (Plin. *Hist. Nat.* 19.2.7), and silicia or fenugreek is sown after a scratching of the ground in a four-inch deep furrow.[56]

In actual practice the agricultural methods of antiquity were far more sophisticated than simply scattering and covering seed, even in Palestine. It is not the case that Palestinian farmers plowed only after sowing. Hence the farmer in the story of a Sower might have tilled his land after the first rain, sown the seed, and then covered it by plowing.

---

[51] See White, *Roman Farming*, 174–81.

[52] Cato, *On Agriculture*, 61 and quoted by Plin. *Hist. Nat.* 18.49.174; Hooper-Ash, *Cato*, 73.

[53] Varro, *On Agriculture*, 1.29.2–3. After the "ridging" or "furrowing," the field is apparently "harrowed" (Columella, *Res Rustica* 2.10.5–6). Pliny is of the opinion that a field needing harrowing after the seed is sown is badly plowed (*Hist. Nat.* 18.49.179).

[54] Varro, *On Agriculture*, 1.32, 43; Columella, *Res Rustica* 2.10.24–27, 31–32; 11.2.54–55; Plin. *Hist. Nat.* 18.35.131–32, 36.137, 43.144–46, 48.173, 62.258.

[55] Columella, *Res Rustica* 2.11.1–3, 6–7. But in countries like Africa or Egypt the farmer does not need to tend a crop from the time of sowing to reaping because the lack of rain and the quality of the soil is such that only the crops that were sown will come up. Hence one does not need to hoe (Columella, *Res Rustica* 2.11.3; cf. Plin. *Hist. Nat.* 18.1.186). In Egypt, on the other hand, because of the flooding of the Nile, the seed is sown into the mud and then plowed in (Plin. *Hist. Nat.* 18.47.168–69).

[56] Plin. *Hist. Nat.* 18.39.140.

In this case the field would have been plowed twice. On other occasions seed might be sown on untilled land, but that was clearly the exception rather than the rule. The rule was to work the land. But in the gospel story of a Sower the farmer never plows or gives any attention at all to the land.

It is the absence of that feature at the end of the story before the reported yield of the "good" soil that requires explanation. Plowing or furrowing the soil after sowing would surely have added to the realism of the story of a Sower. Of course, even though the feature of plowing does appear in two of the stories of Jesus (the Hid Treasure in Thomas; a Mustard Seed in Thomas), there are two other stories (Good Seed and Weeds; a Sprouting Seed) where, as in the story of a Sower, plowing is not mentioned. Hence, it could be argued that its absence in a Sower is not that unusual. Nevertheless, its absence is particularly striking in a Sower where such realistic features of Mediterranean agriculture are portrayed. Further, the lack of verisimilitude in time sequence between the seed's falling on the good soil and the subsequent harvest suggests a lapse of time in which one would have expected the farmer to plow and otherwise tend his land.

The farmer's lack of care for the land in the story of a Sower forces the reader's attention to the natural processes in the story. The soil produces a yield inevitably and naturally without any effort by the farmer or even intervention by God. Hence the story is a completely secular story of the natural processes. The gist of the story is, get the seed on the right spot under the right conditions and the land will produce without help from any one.

FARMING AND FAITH

In its secularity the story tends to subvert a religious view of the natural processes, a view that looks to God as the source of the blessings and the curses of nature, a view that sacramentalizes the cosmos. And therefore this story subverts both an ancient Roman and Hebrew view of reality, where it is affirmed that God rewards the pious with material prosperity and brings drought, pestilence, and blight to the fields of the farmer who fails to fulfill his pious obligations to God.

Roman thought, like Hebrew and Jewish thought, associated the productivity of the fields and all natural prosperity ultimately with the proper and appropriate exercise of piety. Cato, for example, described the offering and eating of a sacred feast before beginning spring plowing (*On Agriculture* 50.2); and Pliny advises the sower to offer a prayer before sowing the seed with the words: "I sow for myself and my neighbors" (*Hist. Nat.* 18.35.132; Rackham, *Pliny,* 272–73). In order to protect the crops during particular seasons of the year the Romans instituted three festivals: Robigala, Floralia, and Vinilia (Plin. *Hist. Nat.* 18.69.284–85). Cato (*On Agriculture* 134.1–4) describes in detail the required prayers for the sacrifice of a sow before harvesting spelt, wheat, barley, beans, and rape seed. Pliny describes an odd custom of sowing basil "with curses and imprecations to make it come up more abundantly" and also says that people sowing cummin pray for it not to come up (*Hist. Nat.* 19.36.120–21; Rackham, *Pliny*, 498–99). Pliny, however, thinks that success from sowing for some farmers ultimately derives from simple luck rather than careful method (*Hist. Nat.* 18.54.197), but this is an exception.

And in the Greek tradition (*Op.* 465–471) Hesiod says:

> Pray to Zeus of the Earth and to
> pure Demeter to make Demeter's holy
> grain sound and heavy,
> when first you begin ploughing . . .
> (Evelyn-White, *Hesiod*, 36–37).

Hebrew literature likewise emphasizes that farmers are to observe proper religious acts if they expect to be successful at the harvest. Torah is specific:

> If you walk in my statues and observe my commandments and do them, then will I give you your rains in their season, and the land shall yield its increase and the trees of the field shall yield their fruit. And your threshing shall last to the time of vintage, and the vintage shall last till the time for sowing, and you shall eat your bread to the full and dwell in your land securely (Lev 26:3–5 RSV; see also Lev 26:9–10; 25:1–7, 18–24; Deut 11:13–15; 26:5–10; 28:1–6, 11–12; Gen 27:28).

And if one fails to observe all the commandments of God, the fields shall be cursed:

> But if you will not obey the voice of the Lord . . . cursed shall you be in the field. Cursed shall be your basket and your kneading-trough. Cursed shall be the fruit of your body and the fruit of your ground, the increase of your cattle and the young of your flock (Deut 28:15–18 RSV; see also Deut 11:13–21; Lev 26:16, 19–20, 32; cf. *Jub.* 50:12–13).

The Hebrew scriptures (the Writings) clearly affirm that God controls nature and is directly responsible for the productivity of the field (Ps 107:35–38; 105:40–42; cf. *Jub.* 20:9). Moreover, it is God who curses the land because of the wickedness of its inhabitants and their refusal to heed God's word (Ps 107:35–38; 105:16, 28–36). But a faithful man who tills his land will have plenty of bread (Prov 28:19–20; cf. 12:11). Indeed the cursing of the land can be reversed, when the people repent and return in obedience to God (2 Chron 7:13–14).

And likewise the prophets associate the productivity of the land with the obedience of the people to God.

A new heart I will give you, and a new spirit I will put within you. . . . and I will summon the grain and make it abundant and lay no famine upon you. I will make the fruit of the tree and the increase of the field abundant, that you may never again suffer the disgrace of famine among the nations. Then you will remember your evil ways, and your deeds that were not good; and you will loathe yourselves for your iniquities and your abominable deeds (Ezek 36:26–31 RSV; see also Jer 44:22; Isa 5:4–6, 10; 7:17, 23–25; 32:9–15; Amos 4:7–9; Joel 1:11–14; 2:21–26).

And the Mishnah similarly associates the discharge of religious obligations with the productivity of the field (*Ber.* 6.1–2; *Bik.* 1.1).

AN ANALYSIS OF THE POETICS

I begin with the assumption that Matthew and Luke depend upon Mark,[57] and I regard the version in Thomas as an independent tradition, unless it can be shown to be dependent on one or more of the canonical gospels.[58] However, in a poetic analysis it is really immaterial which is earlier, since in view are the distinctive poetics of each version, i.e., how each independently is constructed. While Matthew and Luke may have taken the story from Mark, their performance of it is their own. A comparative analysis of the poetics of each will reveal the various designs of the narratives.

Mark

PERIOD I	1	ἀκούετε.
	2	ἰδοὺ ἐξῆλθεν ὁ σπείρων σπεῖραι.

PERIOD II	1	καὶ ἐγένετο ἐν τῷ σπείρειν
	2	ὃ μὲν ἔπεσεν παρὰ τὴν ὁδόν,
	3	καὶ ἦλθεν τὰ πετεινὰ
	4	καὶ κατέφαγεν αὐτό.

PERIOD III	1	καὶ ἄλλο ἔπεσεν ἐπὶ τὸ πετρῶδες
	2	ὅπου οὐκ εἶχεν γῆν πολλήν,
	3	καὶ εὐθὺς ἐξανέτειλεν διὰ τὸ μὴ ἔχειν βάθος γῆς·
	4	καὶ ὅτε ἀνέτειλεν ὁ ἥλιος ἐκαυματίσθη
	5	καὶ διὰ τὸ μὴ ἔχειν ῥίζαν ἐξηράνθη.

---

[57] This is a general assessment of scholarship; however, the assessment has been challenged. See, e.g., Corley, *Colloquy*, Part II: "Seminar on the Synoptic Problem," 29–194. See also Scott (*Hear Then the Parable*, 350–52) who identifies an "originating structure" independently reflected in Mark, Luke, and Thomas.

[58] See Appendix A.

PERIOD IV   1   καὶ ἄλλο ἔπεσεν εἰς τὰς ἀκάνθας,
            2   καὶ ἀνέβησαν αἱ ἄκανθαι
            3   καὶ συνέπνιξαν αὐτό,
            4   καὶ καρπὸν οὐκ ἔδωκεν.

PERIOD V   1   καὶ ἄλλα ἔπεσεν εἰς τὴν γῆν τὴν καλὴν
            2   καὶ ἐδίδου καρπὸν ἀναβαίνοντα καὶ αὐξανόμενα
            3   καὶ ἔφερεν ἓν τριάκοντα
            4   καὶ ἓν ἑξήκοντα
            5   καὶ ἓν ἑκατόν.[59]

Mark's version breaks down into five periods of various clauses: 2-4-5-4-5. The most striking feature of Mark's performance is the recurring paratactic style (using καί 17 times) and the casting of the main verb near the beginning of each sentence. In fact, only in periods III,4 (ἐκαυματίσθη), III,5 (ἐξηράνθη), and IV,4 (ἔδωκεν) does the main verb appear at the end of the sentence. In every other instance (15 times) the main verbs appear in the second position (9 times), or the third position (6 times).[60]

On each occasion that the seed is described as falling at a particular location the incident is introduced with a similar phrase:

            ὃ μὲν   ἔπεσεν παρὰ   (II,2)
    καὶ ἄλλο   ἔπεσεν ἐπὶ   (III,1)
    καὶ ἄλλο   ἔπεσεν εἰς   (IV,1)
    καὶ ἄλλα   ἔπεσεν εἰς   (V,1)
[cf. καὶ ἔφερεν ἐν   (V,3)]

There is some repetition of similar phrases in and among the periods:

---

[59] I see little difference between Matthew's poetics and Mark's. The changes seem innocuous enough. What Matthew eliminates from the story, however, is a different matter. It appears to be a mild attack on Mark's paratactic style and "excessive" use of καί.

1.   Matt 13:4: the independent verb ἐγένετο (Mark 4:4) is omitted. The independent verb ἦλθεν (Mark 4:4) becomes a dependent participle (ἐλθόντα) and the paratactic καί is omitted.
2.   Matt 13:5: καί (Mark 4:5) becomes δέ.
3.   Matt 13:6: καί (Mark 4:6) becomes δέ.
4.   Matt 13:7: καί (Mark 4:7) becomes δέ.
5.   Matt 13:7: καὶ καρπὸν οὐκ ἔδωκεν (Mark 4:7) is omitted.
6.   Matt 13:8: καί (Mark 4:8) becomes δέ. Ἀναβαίνοντα καὶ αὐξανόμενα καὶ ἔφερεν (Mark 4:8) is omitted. Καί . . . καί (Mark 4:8) becomes μέν . . . δέ.

It should be noted in this connection that Thomas agrees with Mark in its paratactic style.

[60] In III,4 the main verb of the dependent clause (ἀνέτειλεν) is not counted in this connection.

(I,2) σπείρων σπεῖραι   /(II,1) σπείρειν
(I,2) ἐξῆλθεν   /(II,3) ἦλθεν
(III,2) εἶχεν   /(III,3) ἔχειν   /(III,5) ἔχειν
(III,3) διὰ τὸ μῆ ἔχειν   /(III,5) διὰ τὸ μῆ ἔχειν
(III,3) ἐξανέτειλεν   /(III,4) ἀνέτειλεν
(IV,1) ἀκάνθας   /(IV,2) ἄκανθαι
(IV,4) καρπὸν   /(V,2) καρπὸν

Period III contains the following concluding vowel pattern:

line 2 ήν
line 3 ῆς
line 4 η
line 5 η

And period V exhibits the recurring vowel pattern:

line 2 καρπὸν . . . νοντα
line 3 κοντα
line 4 κοντα
line 5 εκατόν

Assonance and consonance reveal a clustering of similar vowel and consonantal sounds.[61] If one assumes that four instances of similar sounds in a period might simply be accidental, and therefore raises the number of instances to seven or more required in order to establish a stronger case for a nonaccidental pattern, the following recurring sound patterns emerge:

PERIOD II
1 καὶ ἐγένετο ἐν τῷ σπείρειν
2 ὃ μὲν ἔπεσεν παρὰ τὴν ὁδόν
3 καὶ ἦλθεν τὰ πετεινὰ
4 καὶ κατέφαγεν αὐτό[62]

PERIOD III
1 καὶ ἄλλο ἔπεσεν ἐπὶ τὸ πετρῶδες
2 ὅπου οὐκ εἶχεν γῆν πολλήν
3 καὶ εὐθὺς ἐξανέτειλεν διὰ τὸ μὴ ἔχειν βάθος γῆς
4 καὶ ὅτε ἀνέτειλεν ὁ ἥλιος ἐκαυματίσθη
5 καὶ διὰ τὸ μὴ ἔχειν ῥίζαν ἐξηράνθη[63]

PERIOD IV
1 καὶ ἄλλο ἔπεσεν εἰς τὰς ἀκάνθας
2 καὶ ἀνέβησαν αἱ ἄκανθαι
3 καὶ συνέπνιξαν αὐτό
4 καὶ καρπὸν οὐκ ἔδωκεν

[61] The reader is referred to chapter 4 above for the method followed in identifying assonance and consonance.
[62] If I lowered the number of occurrences to 6 then α would be included.
[63] If I lowered the number of occurrences to 6 then κ and ι would be included.

PERIOD V   1   <u>καὶ ἄλλα ἔπεσεν</u> εἰς <u>τὴν γῆν τὴν καλὴν</u>
             2   <u>καὶ ἐδίδου καρπὸν</u> ἀναβαίνοντα <u>καὶ</u> αὐξανόμενα
             3   <u>καὶ ἔφερεν ἓν τριάκοντα</u>
             4   <u>καὶ ἓν ἑξήκοντα</u>
             5   <u>καὶ ἓν ἑκατόν</u>[64]

Luke

In Luke's version the structure and poetics are rather different:

PERIOD I   1   ἐξῆλθεν ὁ σπείρων τοῦ σπεῖραι τὸν σπόρον αὐτοῦ.

PERIOD II   1   καὶ ἐν τῷ σπείρειν αὐτὸν
            2   ὃ μὲν ἔπεσεν παρὰ τὴν ὁδὸν
            3   καὶ κατεπατήθη,
            4   καὶ τὰ πετεινὰ τοῦ οὐρανοῦ κατέφαγεν αὐτό.

PERIOD III   1   καὶ ἕτερον κατέπεσεν ἐπὶ τὴν πέτραν,
            2   καὶ φυὲν ἐξηράνθη διὰ τὸ μὴ ἔχειν ἰκμάδα.

PERIOD IV   1   καὶ ἕτερον ἔπεσεν ἐν μέσῳ τῶν ἀκανθῶν,
            2   καὶ συμφυεῖσαι αἱ ἄκανθαι ἀπέπνιξαν αὐτό.

PERIOD V   1   καὶ ἕτερον ἔπεσεν εἰς τὴν γῆν τὴν ἀγαθὴν
            2   καὶ φυὲν ἐποίησεν καρπὸν ἑκατονταπλασίονα.

Luke breaks down into five periods of various clauses each as follows: 1-4-2-2-2. Hence, it is clear that Luke's version is much shorter than Matthew and Mark. Luke eliminates many of the paratactic elements (καί used only 9 times), but does retain Mark's style of casting the main verb near the beginning of the sentence. κατέφαγεν (II,4) and ἀπέπνιξαν (IV,2) fall at the end of their sentences, but other main verbs, as was the case in Mark, fall in first (ἐξῆλθεν, I,1) position, second (κατεπατήθη, II,3) position and third position (seven times).

Each description of the seed at a particular location is similarly introduced:

II,2   ὃ μὲν   ἔπεσεν   παρὰ
III,1   καὶ ἕτερον   κατέπεσεν   ἐπὶ
IV,1   καὶ ἕτερον   ἔπεσεν ἐν   μέσῳ
V,1   καὶ ἕτερον   ἔπεσεν   εἰς

When compared to Matthew and Mark, Luke's beginning of the story is much more alliterative:

ὁ σπείρων τοῦ σπεῖραι τὸν σπόρον αὐτοῦ

---

[64]If I lowered the number of occurrences to 6 then o would be included.

And there is some similarity of sound among the following:

II,3 κατεπατήθη
II,4 τὰ πετεινὰ
III,1 κατέπεσεν

Note the following recurring pattern:

II,3 καὶ . . . κατε—
II,4 καὶ . . . κατέ—
III,1 καὶ . . . κατέ—

There is also repetition of similar words and phrases in and among the periods; only one instance of which was noted in Mark (ἀκανθῶν [IV,1]/ ἄκανθαι [IV,2]; cf. Mark IV,1 and IV,2):

I,1 σπείρων τοῦ σπεῖραι τὸν σπόρον αὐτοῦ / II,1 . . . τῷ σπείρειν αυτὸν
IV,1 ἀκανθῶν /IV,2 ἄκανθαι
III,2 φυὲν /IV,2 συμφυεῖσαι /V,2 φυὲν

An examination of assonance and consonance reveals, as in Mark, a clustering of sounds. Retaining the same criterion that was used for Mark, I assume that a multiple repetition of similar sounds is part of the author's conscious/unconscious design. But assuming that four similar sounds in a period could be understood as accidental, I raise the number of occurrences required to establish a pattern to seven or more. The following recurring sound patterns emerge:[65]

PERIOD II   καὶ ἐν τῷ σπείρειν αὐτὸν
               ὃ μὲν ἔπεσεν παρὰ τὴν ὁδὸν
               καὶ κατεπατήθη
               καὶ τὰ πετεινὰ τοῦ οὐρανοῦ κατέφαγεν αὐτό

PERIOD III   καὶ ἕτερον κατέπεσεν ἐπὶ τὴν πέτραν
               καὶ φυὲν ἐξηράνθη διὰ τὸ μὴ ἔχειν ἰκμάδα

PERIOD IV   καὶ ἕτερον ἔπεσεν ἐν μέσῳ τῶν ἀκανθῶν
               καὶ συμφυεῖσαι αἱ ἄκανθαι ἀπέπνιξαν αὐτό

PERIOD V   καὶ ἕτερον ἔπεσεν εἰς τὴν γῆν τὴν ἀγαθὴν
               καὶ φυὲν ἐποίησεν καρπὸν ἑκατονταπλασίονα

---

[65] The rationale for retaining the same requirement is that Luke saw Mark and opted not to use what Mark had developed, or was unaware that Mark had a specific style.

The story in all its versions represents a complete action with beginning (the sower goes forth and sows), middle (hazards and failures of the seed), and end (the success of the seed). The story realistically portrays ancient farming practices and conditions from first-century Mediterranean life. The differences among the various versions really do not substantially affect the story in any appreciable way and are best seen as individual "performancial" variants, i.e., variants in a basic story structure that can occur with each performance in an oral culture, and for that matter in a literate culture where stories are also "told."[66] The basic structure of the story remains intact. Everything up to the end of the story is the complication, and the "end" is the unraveling (denouement).

In one sense the story is about individual human action. It is after all a sower who sows the seed and expects a positive result. But all the action focuses on the seed and the difficulties that it encounters in its various chance locations. The plot, therefore, moves steadily downward toward catastrophe as each seed fails to achieve its hoped-for end, until the sudden reversal of this trend at the end of the story (Mark 4:8, par.), when one (some) seed by chance happens to land in the right place. Hence the plot would be both complex and comic.

ANOTHER READING OF THE STORY

In the context of an agrarian culture that understood its well-being and prosperity to be dependent on how faithfully the commandments of God were followed, the secularity of this story sounds a particularly discordant note. The story affirms that the productivity of the seed sown by the farmer depends on the kind of soil in which the seed chances to fall, and on the absence of natural threats to the survival of the seed. If the farmer gets it at the right place and the conditions are sympathetic, the seed will produce. If the seed falls at the wrong location under less than favorable conditions, the seed will likely not produce.

The silence of the story on certain matters helps to illuminate the character of this particular story. Its silence on matters important for Israel's piety reflects the clear difference between the story and a first-century Jewish vision of reality. The sower in the story is just any farmer. Nothing indicates that he is a faithful and pious observer of Torah. The hazards faced by the seed are just that: chance hazards, as any Palestinian farmer might expect to meet. Nothing in the story suggests that the birds, the excessive heat of the sun in Thomas, the lack of moisture in Luke, etc. are due to the actions of God who was displeased with the

---

[66] The term is derived from Crossan, *In Fragments*, 40–66.

failure of the farmer faithfully to discharge his pietistic obligations under Torah. Not even Mark's interpretation understood the story this way. Nor is there any indication that the yield of the seed sown on the good soil is due to any kindness or generosity on the part of God. The story does not conclude with an expected harvest festival in which the farmer expresses his gratitude to God for the harvest. Proper religious obligations or the activity of God are not matters with which the story is even obliquely concerned. Such ideas are patently excluded by the story.

Apart from its probable origin in the mind of Jesus it is a fairly uninteresting story describing the hazards and the gamble of a farmer in the ancient Mediterranean culture who, through negligence or intentionally, does not cover his seed after it is sown. The farmer is eventually successful but not because he is a particularly good farmer. He is successful because he accidentally happened to get the right natural elements together. He might be considered "lucky."

But, on the other hand, in the context of first-century Jewish faith and piety, the story does become interesting. Because of its secularity and its tacit failure to acknowledge God's sovereignty over nature and to insist on the fulfillment of an individual's holy obligations to God in order to ensure the harvest, the story resonates with impiety. Hence the story subverts the faith of Israel by challenging its fictive view of reality. In fact, the story frontally assaults the first-century Jewish notion of what it means to be a pious, and hence whole, human being. All of the nature stories will likely resonate with this same secularity and impiety.

In its secularity the story specifically subverts the second section of the Shema (Deut 11:13–21) whose recitation was required of every pious Jewish male at the beginning and close of the day:[67]

> And if you will obey my commandments which I command you this day, to love the Lord your God, and to serve him with all your heart and with all your soul, he will give the rain for your land in its season, the early rain and the later rain, that you may gather in your grain and your wine and your oil. And he will give grass in your fields for your cattle, and you shall eat and be full. Take heed lest your heart be deceived, and you turn aside and serve other gods and worship them, and the anger of the Lord be kindled against you, and he shut up the heavens, so that there be no rain, and the land yield no fruit, and you perish quickly off the good land which the Lord gives you (Deut 11:13–17 RSV).

Note in particular verses 11:14–15, 17, where the produce of the field or the barrenness of the field is directly attributable to the work of God, which is contingent on the proper pious response of the people. Hence the Shema reinforces Jewish piety by reminding the people of the cove-

---

[67] See *m. Ber.* 2.1–2 and Wharton, "Shema," *IDB* 4.321–22; see also Deut 6:7 and *m. Ber.* 1.1–4.

nant who they are and exactly what their obligation is to God and what God's obligation is to them. The story of a Sower, on the other hand, ignores the religious dimension of life and affirms risks, losses, and gains as natural and areligious occurrences. In short, the story secularizes life rather than sacramentalizing it.

This way of reading the story does not focus on the intention of Jesus in telling the story, if indeed it was invented by Jesus of Nazareth.[68] Nor does it focus on how the story might have been heard by an anonymous group of hypothetical auditors. To achieve both of these ends requires that the reader supply a subjective framework in the context of which the story is read. Rather the focus in this study is on how the story resonates in the context of Israel's "story" as represented in the literary constructs of Israel's faith.

---

[68] The story is generally recognized as originating with Jesus of Nazareth. See, e.g., Perrin, *Rediscovering*, 156: "There is no good reason to doubt the authenticity of the parable." The National Jesus Seminar, sponsored by the Westar Institute, after discussion of the story, concluded with a two-thirds vote of the participants present that the story should be included in a data base for determining who Jesus was: Funk, "Poll on the Parables," 54–80. Compare, however, Carlston's hesitation to attribute it firmly to Jesus of Nazareth: *Triple Tradition*, 146, 148. Because of its basic subversion of, and difference from, Judaism and because it likewise reflects no characteristic concerns of early Christianity, I regard it as most probably deriving from Jesus of Nazareth. Indeed early Christianity rapidly became a religion of the cities and the trades rather than remaining a religion of the countryside and the farm. Little interest is shown in early Christian literature in human dependence on the seasons of nature and concern with God's blessing of the fields.

10 🌿

The Unjust Judge

THE JUDGE IN THIS STORY IS A TRAGIC FIGURE, A THOROUGHLY HONEST MAN who permits himself to be corrupted for his personal convenience. That is not, of course, the way Luke sees him. For Luke he is a disreputable and impious man. Most interpreters, following Luke, find few redeeming qualities in the judge's character. An analysis of the poetics of the story is instructive. The story is designed to focus on the judge rather than the widow, where modern interpreters tend to focus. The story is burlesque, reversing the stereotype of judge and widow. It is most readily understood in the context of those "deeds of righteousness" required of devout first-century Jews.

THE SETTING OF THE STORY:
AN EARLY CHRISTIAN READING

According to Luke, Jesus told the story of the Unjust Judge (18:1–5) toward the end of his trip from Galilee to Jerusalem (9:51–19:27) prior to his crucifixion. In its more immediate context it follows Jesus' brief response (17:20b–37) to the Pharisees' question concerning when the kingdom of God was to come (17:20a). In that context the story becomes for Luke an allegory of the social situation of the church in his own day, and it provides Luke an opportunity to encourage Christians to hold on to their faith until the Lord's return. This interpretation is borne out by Luke's literary introduction (18:1):[1] "And he told them a parable so that they should always pray and not lose heart." This statement directly concerns the nonappearance of the parousia,[2] and any question that this

---

[1] See Freed, "Judge and Widow," 39–40.

[2] The delay of the parousia is, of course, one of Luke's favorite themes; see Conzelman, *Theology of St. Luke*, 95–136, and the excellent brief analysis of the context of this story by Talbert, *Reading Luke*, 169.

is the case is answered by Luke's interpretation of the story: "Hear what the unrighteous judge is saying: will God not exact vengeance in behalf of his elect who are crying to him day and night? Will he delay long over them? I say to you that he will exact vengeance quickly on their behalf. However, when the Son of Man comes, will he find faith on the earth?" (18:6–8).[3]

Luke's application derives from the judge's statement in 18:5: "Because this widow wearies me, I will avenge her that she might not 'give me a black eye'[4] by her continual coming." Luke understands this to mean that the church should be persistent in its prayers to God and not become discouraged, for as the story says, persistence is rewarded in the end.

Luke's designation of the judge as "unrighteous" (ἀδικίας, 18:6) refers not to the quality of the judge's legal decisions, but rather to the character of the judge; that is, it plays off of the statement that he did not "fear God" (18:2, 4). But it is likewise possible that this is simply an early Christian title for the story. Even in that case, however, the designation of the judge as "unrighteous" still derives from the same locus in the story. And the future action of the Son of Man in Luke's interpretation is likewise taken directly from the widow's request of the judge to avenge her (ἐδίκησόν με, 18:3; used also by the judge in 18:5). Luke's image of God's elect as "crying day and night" (18:7) further derives from the story's description of the widow's persistent appeals to the judge (ἤρχετο πρὸς αὐτόν, 18:3). But aside from these convenient literary hooks, the interpretation bears no resemblance to the story and actually stands in some tension with it, were one to press a full allegorical alignment of the elements of the story with the interpretation. By such a reading the widow represents God's elect and the unrighteous judge represents God—a most unfortunate parallel. The latter may explain why

---

[3]Jeremias (*Parables*, 153–57) argues that 18:6-8 have Aramaizing features that show verses 6–8 to be pre-Lukan and Palestinian on linguistic grounds (cf. Bultmann, *Synoptic Tradition*, 175 for a different opinion), and hence he concludes that the story derived from Jesus of Nazareth. Aramaizing features, however, do not prove origin with Jesus, but only suggest an origin in a pre-Lukan Palestinian setting. Scott is of the same mind (*Hear Then the Parable*, 177). Jeremias' second argument for the conclusion (so also Kümmel, *Promise and Fulfillment*, 59) that verses 6–8 are original with Jesus (i.e. "Jesus' choice of the brutal judge to illustrate God's helpfulness must have shocked his audience to a degree which simply made an interpretation indispensable," 156) is a problem only if one assumes that the story is crafted to project that kind of image, and that the judge is a negative figure in the story (see below). See Scott's discussion of the issue (*Hear Then the Parable*, 176–77) and that by Fitzmyer (*Luke*, 2.1176). It appears to me that Luke's interpretation of the story in 18:6-8 has been developed under the influence of Sir 35:15–19. The interpretation may well be earlier than Luke.

[4]See the discussion below, p. 200.

Luke did not press the story to a full allegorical reading, as was allowed in the story of a Sower (Luke 8:11–15).

MODERN INTERPRETATIONS

Many modern interpreters of the story accept Luke's conclusion to the narrative (18:6–8) to be the original interpretation of Jesus himself, and hence they simply agree with Luke's explanation. For example, Bailey: "In the gathering gloom of intensified opposition we need not fear. God has put his anger far away and He hears us. We must trust and be steadfast in prayer. We do not appeal to a disgruntled judge but to a loving Father who will vindicate His elect and do so quickly."[5]

While Linnemann does not believe the story to have originated with Jesus, she takes it to "mean one of two things. Either it would be a general exhortation to persistence in prayer when it is not granted. . . . Or it is an exhortation to persistent prayer for the coming of the kingdom of God. . . . "[6] Fitzmyer: "If a dishonest judge would yield to the persistence and prayer of a widow, how much more would the upright God and Father of all! If the helpless widow's persistent prayer accomplishes so much with a dishonest judge how much more will the prayer of Christian disciples."[7] For Boucher the "point is either the faithfulness and justice of God or persistence in prayer."[8] And for Smith "the parable was intended to teach its hearers that 'they ought always to pray and not faint.' "[9] Bultmann also takes the story to be an "exhortation to prayer."[10]

On the other hand, both Donahue and Scott explain the story specifically with reference to the kingdom of God. Donahue suggests "that the parable be seen under the aegis of the proclamation of the kingdom with its reversal of human expectations. . . . The hearers are confronted with a new vision of reality, inaugurated by God's reign, where victims claim their rights and seek justice—often in an unsettling manner."[11] And Scott says, "the parable bypasses the implied metaphor of God as just judge in favor of the widow's action, her continued wearing down of him, as a more viable metaphor for the kingdom. The kingdom

---

[5] Bailey, *Poet and Peasant*, 2.141; See also Cadoux, *Parables*, 182–83, and Oesterley, *Gospel Parables*, 223; Jeremias, *Parables*, 156–57.

[6] Linnemann, *Parables*, 188; cf. also 121.

[7] Fitzmyer, *Luke*, 2.1177.

[8] Boucher, *Parables*, 121.

[9] Smith, *Parables*, 151.

[10] Bultman, *Synoptic Tradition*, 199.

[11] Donahue, *Gospel in Parable*, 184.

keeps coming, keeps battering down regardless of honor or justice. It may even come under the guise of shamefulness (lack of honor)."[12]

As to the story's being an exhortation to prayer, even Jeremias himself recognizes that the story has nothing to do with prayer.[13] Hence any interpretation that finds the original story to encourage persistence in prayer has simply been misled by Luke's literary setting. As to an interpretation that identifies the judge with God, one only need ask what is the justification for such an allegorizing of the story from the givens of the story itself? Likewise, a reading of the story as a parable of the kingdom of God derives from the assumption that such is the original thrust of the parables; neither the story nor Luke uses the term "kingdom." Of course if one *assumes* the story is about the kingdom of God, then it is easy enough to make it say something about the kingdom. But if one met the story in a non-Christian environment, there is nothing about it that would inevitably lead to such a reading. Scott and Donahue begin with the assumption that Jesus preached the kingdom of God and conclude that his stories must have had something to do with the kingdom, and hence their interpretation is based on their assumption. It does not arise from the story itself.

THE POETICS OF THE STORY

Luke's is the only extant version.[14] The narrative is designed so as to focus on the judge's monologue. It consists of three periods of various clauses, the longest period being the judge's monologue.

PERIOD I	1	κριτής τις ἦν ἔν τινι πόλει
	2	τὸν θεὸν μὴ φοβούμενος
	3	καὶ ἄνθρωπον μὴ ἐντρεπόμενος.
PERIOD II	1	χήρα δὲ ἦν ἐν τῇ πόλει ἐκείνῃ
	2	καὶ ἤρχετο πρὸς αὐτὸν λέγουσα,
	3	ἐκδίκησόν με ἀπὸ τοῦ ἀντιδίκου μου.
PERIOD III	1	καὶ οὐκ ἤθελεν ἐπὶ χρόνον.
	2	μετὰ δὲ ταῦτα εἶπεν ἐν ἑαυτῷ·

---

[12] Scott, *Hear Then the Parable*, 187.

[13] Jeremias, *Parables*, 156.

[14] It is pointed out by some interpreters that Luke 11:5–8 (the Friend at Midnight) is a "parallel" to the Unjust Judge. It is, however, obviously not a parallel in the narrow sense that it is a second version of the Unjust Judge. What is meant is that these interpreters take the "meaning" of the stories to be similar. They both deal with "persistence in petitions." In this sense they may be misled by Luke's interpretation in each instance (11:8–10 and 18:6–8). See Bultmann, *Synoptic Tradition*, 175; Jeremias, *Parables*, 157, 159.

3   εἰ καὶ τὸν θεὸν οὐ φοβοῦμαι
4   οὐδὲ ἄνθρωπον ἐντρέπομαι,
5   διά γε τὸ παρέχειν μοι κόπον τὴν χήραν ταύτην
6   ἐκδικήσω αὐτήν,
7   ἵνα μὴ εἰς τέλος ἐρχομένη ὑπωπιάζῃ με.

One finds verbal and structural similarity between the initial clauses of periods I and II as follows:

I,1   κριτής τις ἦν ἔν τινι πόλει
II,1 χήρα δὲ   ἦν ἐν τῇ πόλει ἐκείνῃ

And there are similar structural and verbal parallels between periods I and III as follows:

I,2   τὸν θεὸν μὴ φοβούμενος
III,3 εἰ καὶ τὸν θεὸν οὐ φοβοῦμαι

——————

I,3   καὶ ἄνθρωπον μὴ ἐντρεπόμενος
III,4 οὐδὲ ἄνθρωπον   ἐντρέπομαι

Part of the widow's request in period II,3, is picked up in the judge's monologue in period III,6, as follows:

II,3   ἐκδίκησόν με
III,6 ἐκδικήσω αὐτὴν

To examine the assonance and consonance of the story I list here all occurrences of four or more in a given period.

PERIOD I
Assonance	ε = 6	ο = 8	η = 4
	ι = 4		
Consonance	ν = 10	μ = 4	σ = 4
	τ = 5		

An interesting feature of period I is that the two largest incidents of assonance and consonance, ε and ν, coalesce four times:

κριτής τις ἦν <u>ἔν</u> τινι πόλει
τὸν θεὸν μή φοβού<u>μενος</u>
καὶ ἄνθρωπος μὴ <u>ἐντρεπόμενος</u>

PERIOD II
Assonance	α = 4	ο = 6	ου = 4
	ε = 7	η = 6	
Consonance	κ,χ = 6	ν = 5	τ = 5

Period III is considerably longer than either period I or II. One might expect more instances of both assonance and consonance, and so there are, but not nearly as many as might be expected. The more numerous instances are limited to certain select letters and sounds.

PERIOD III

Assonance	α = 8	αι = 4	ι = 5
	ε = 19	ου = 4	ει = 4
	ο = 12	αυ = 4	ω = 4
	η = 9		
Consonance	κ,χ,γ = 11	μ = 7	π = 8
	τ = 12	ρ = 6	δ = 4
	ν = 18		

Several patterns emerge from period III. The combination εν occurs five times and the combination ον six times. But what is most striking about period III is that in clauses 5, 6, 7 there is an intensive clustering of the following: κ/χ/γ, ν, π, τ, μ, σ/ζ, ο, α, ε, η.

5   διά γε τὸ παρέχειν μοι κόπον τὴν χήραν ταύτην
6   ἐκδικήσω αὐτήν
7   ἵνα μὴ εἰς τέλος ἐρχομένη ὑπωπιάζῃ με

Hence in these three clauses the following pattern emerges with regard to consonants and vowels:

	usage in Period III as a whole	usage in clauses 5, 6, 7 only
α	8	5 †
ε	19	7
ο	12	5
η	9	8 *
κ,χ,γ	11	7 †
ν	18	8
π	8	4 ‡
τ	12	6 †
μ	7	4 †
σ,ζ	4	4 *

* = significant majority
† = simple majority
‡ = as many uses in three clauses as were earlier used
      in four.

The clustering of these consonants and vowels in the last three clauses does give the unit a certain euphony. However, these features are not able to overcome the basic prosaic character of the narrative. There does not appear to be a deliberate use of either assonance/consonance and balanced stylized structuring.

The basic structure of the narrative draws attention to the reaction and reflections of the judge (seven clauses), rather than to his description by the narrator (three clauses) or the widow's demands (three clauses).

The introspection of the judge constitutes more than half the narrative. Hence the narrator's description of him (period I) and the widow's persistent demands (period II) are merely the context and background for the judge's monologue. The judge is the "hero," i.e., the main character in the story. Therefore, any interpretation that turns on the actions of the widow is rendered suspect, since it focuses on an aspect of the story not emphasized by the structure of the narrative.[15]

THE STORY

There was a certain judge in a certain city. The reader (auditor) knows nothing about this figure or about the city in which he administers justice. He is simply a "certain judge" (κριτής τις). What must a reader think about this figure to make his role in the story sensible? It is probably not a Roman court setting, since the judge is apparently not removed from plaintiffs and defendants but is readily and regularly accessible. It thus appears to be a small village setting in which the judge cannot be isolated so readily from his clientele.[16]

Little is known of the administration of justice in Palestine during the time of Jesus. Generally the Romans did not interfere in the internal administration of province and vassal states but allowed them to conduct their own affairs with the least possible intervention.[17] But precisely how the small Palestinian villages administered justice is far from clear.

Derrett describes two different "judicial" systems in Palestine: what he calls "customary" law courts (i.e., religious courts in which pious Jews bring a complaint before pious judges) and "administrative" courts (i.e., courts of the ethnarch/tetrarch and governor that assisted in the maintenance of law and order, applying the ordinances that came from the political authorities and overseeing the collection of revenues). In other words, there were the "synagogues" with their "rulers," on the one hand (customary), and the "authorities," with their "kings" and "governors," on the other (administrative; cf. Luke 12:11 and 21:12).[18] Most of Derrett's primary evidence comes from the Ptolemaic-Seleucid period in Egypt and elsewhere,[19] but it is clear, as Derrett points out, that the royal adminis-

---

[15] Against Fitzmyer, *Luke*, 2.1176.

[16] Cf. e.g., Isa 7:3; the accessibility of Ahaz to the Prophet suggests a certain "small-town" character and informality to Ahaz's kingship. That seems to be the case with the judge in Luke 18:2–5.

[17] Stevenson, "Provinces and their Government," 461–68; id., "Imperial Administration," 182–217; id., *Roman Provincial Administration*, 83; Duckworth, "Roman Provincial System," 171–217; Stevenson and Momigliano, "Rebellion within the Empire," 840–65; Smallwood, *Jews under Roman Rule*, 149; Jos. *Bell*. 3.54–55.

[18] Derrett, "Unjust Judge," 180–86.

[19] Derrett, "Unjust Judge," 181–86.

tration of Herod the Great proceeded on the basis of "administrative" divisions in the country, down even to the level of the villages.[20] And the Romans later had divided the province of Judea into eleven administrative toparchies.[21] Each toparchy collected revenue through a system of indirect and direct taxation that would have required administrative representatives besides the *publicani*.[22] Even Josephus, when he became the military governor of Galilee prior to the war with the Romans in 66–73 C.E., appointed administrative judges throughout the villages of Galilee.[23] Thus it must be assumed that during the time of Jesus, Herod Antipas and Herod Philip governed by means of their representatives throughout their respective tetrarchies; and Roman administration of the imperial province of Judea would likewise have used government administrators throughout the province. Derrett's conclusion that the widow in the story had taken her case before a civil hearing officer is, therefore, at the very least possible and at best probable.[24] Indeed, characterizing the judge this way better fits such a situation than assuming that he was a religious leader administering the "customary" law.[25]

Who neither feared God nor respected (any) man. Quite obviously the expression is important since it is applied to the judge in the story not once but twice, once by the narrator (18:2) and once by the judge himself in a soliloquy (18:4). Most commentators take the expression as a negative description. For example, Marshall describes the judge as "corrupt,"[26] and Scott[27] says, "for the judge neither to fear God nor to have respect for men makes him without honor, shameless. In a dyadic society this is a severe description, for in essence it describes a person outside the bounds of

---

[20] Safrai and Stern, *The Jewish People in the First Century*, 1.250–51.

[21] Jos. *Bell.* 3.54–55. Pliny also reports (Plin. *Hist. Nat.* 15.70) there were ten local government areas.

[22] Stevenson, "Imperial Administration," 190–92.

[23] Jos. *Bell.* 2.569–72. It is my contention that these were administrative appointments and should not be identified with the popular and customary judicial system that would have continued in the synagogues.

[24] Derrett, "Unjust Judge," 180. Plummer (*Luke*, 411) describes the judge as a Gentile official.

[25] See below. This is true particularly in the light of the fact that he is a single hearing officer. Normally Jewish religious practice was that each case involving property be heard by three judges (*m. Sanh.* 1.1), but in the Babylonian Talmud it is noted that if a judge were recognized as an expert by the community he could hear the case by himself (Neusner, *Talmud of Babylonia*, 50: VII. A–H; cf. also p. 42: II. A–B, where one judge on the basis of Lev 19:15 may hear cases involving loans. In Matt 5:25 the individuals go before a single hearing officer, and there is one hearing officer reflected in 1 Cor 6:5 and Luke 12:13–14. Hence the hearing officer could have been either "administrative" or "customary," but on balance it is more plausible that he is a civil hearing official. But see Herzog, *Subversive Speech*, 220–23.

[26] Marshall, *Luke*, 672.

[27] Scott, *Hear Then the Parable*, 180.

society, who is determined by no significant other, whether God or man. He is an outlaw judge." Both derive this rather severe view of the judge from a series of Hellenistic parallels collected by Wettstein.[28] All but two[29] of these are derived from the Greek and Roman traditions, and are quite similar, though not identical, to the expression in Luke's story. For example, in light of the two Hellenistic Palestinian parallels, both similarity and difference are obvious. Josephus describes people who "abandoned the customs of their fathers for a life of depravity. They no longer rendered to God his due honors (μήτε τὰς νενομισμένας τιμὰς ἔτι τῷ θεῷ παρέχοντες) nor took account of justice towards men (μήτε τοῦ πρὸς ἀνθρώπους δικαίου ποιούμενοι λόγον)" (*Ant.* 1.72). Josephus also describes "Joakeimos" as "unjust and wicked by nature; he was neither reverent toward God (μήτε πρὸς θεὸν ὅσιος) nor kind to man (μήτε πρὸς ἀνθρώπους ἐπιεικής)" (*Ant.* 10.83).[30]

The expressions that Wettstein lists, as Scott notes, do have a "formulaic" character in that they seem to be a standard way of discrediting someone; such people have no redeeming value with either God or men. And all the examples are clear enough with this meaning in the context. But they do not use Luke's language, nor is Luke's instance distinctly negative. With the exception of Josephus (who does not use the language of Luke), none of Wettstein's examples comes from a Jewish setting, and other examples in Jewish texts are elusive.

The expression "fear of the Lord" is a technical expression in Jewish literature (and in Luke probably because of the LXX); it would have been heard in a pious Jewish context as meaning the judge was an impious or irreligious man who made no pretense of following the Torah.[31] That is somewhat different from "corrupt" or "shameless." Nor should one automatically assume that it is the equivalent of "immoral." Further, Luke's use of the term elsewhere suggests that Luke understands its use here as meaning this judge gave no evidence of traditional religious piety. A man who "feared the Lord" would have expressed that piety in concrete ways as did Cornelius (Acts 10:2, 22, 35; cf. 13:16, 26).[32] But this judge was not "religious" in the sense of traditional Jewish piety.[33]

---

[28] Wettstein, *Novum Testamentum Graecum*, 1.778–79.

[29] Jos. *Ant.* 1.72 and 10.83.

[30] See also the example quoted by Scott where a Tribune refers to the plans of certain conspirators as devised "without either fearing the anger of the gods or heeding the indignation of men [οὔτε θεῖον φοβηθέντες χόλον οὔτε ἀνθρωπίνην ἐντραπέντες νέμεσιν]." Dion. Hal. *Ant. Roma.* 10.10.7; Cary, *Dionysius*, 6.196–97.

[31] See *TDNT* 9.201–3; especially 203: "As legal piety invades the wisdom of Israel in the post-exilic period the idea of fear of God undergoes a shift in meaning. The man who fears God is now the man who keeps the law."

[32] Cf. also 1 Pet 2:17 where the expression seems to mean one who fulfilled one's religious obligations.

[33] Cf. the following passage in the LXX where "fearing the Lord" has the

As for the judge's "not respecting man," in itself this is not a negative comment. The statement probably means that this judge refused to be intimidated by anyone. It functions this way in Wis 6:7, where it is used of God: "For the Lord of all will not stand in awe of anyone, nor show deference to greatness (RSV; LXX = οὐδὲ ἐντραπήσεται μέγεθος)." Indeed Sirach (4:22) specifically admonishes against partiality: "Do not show partiality, to your own harm, or deference (LXX = καὶ μὴ ἐντραπῇς) to your downfall" (RSV). Elihu in his address to Job (32:21 LXX) declares that he will speak: "For I am not awed because of man, nor indeed do I show deference to (any) mortal (ἀλλὰ μὴν οὐδὲ βροτὸν οὐ μὴ ἐντραπῶ)." Any deference to others might have limited his openness and honesty.[34]

And it is precisely to this kind of independence from community influence that Moses called the judges he appointed: "you shall not have respect to persons in judgment" (lit. not regard the face—οὐκ ἐπιγνώσῃ πρόσωπον ἐν κρίσει: Deut 1:17 LXX; cf. Sir 32:12). The judge in this story is therefore a man bound by neither traditional piety nor community obligations that could have influenced his judgment. In short, he is free to render judgments based solely on testimony in his court; thus he is a thoroughly *honest* judge bound neither by the limitations of religion nor by customary law, nor by "under the table" ties to anyone in the community, and hence he is something of an anomaly in the east.[35]

Wettstein's collection of parallels appears to be instances of standard invective; it is a rhetorical device used to discredit thoroughly an opponent and is not a "proverb."[36] Apparently Wettstein collected instances of the *negative* use of the expression, under the assumption that the judge in the story was a negative figure.

If the description in 18:4 is intended to cast the judge as immoral and thoroughly lacking in any redeeming moral consciousness, it is indeed strange. Even the most virtueless character would hesitate to make such an admission to himself.[37] Further, if it is an admission that he is absolutely without morals, then verse 5 makes no sense at all. An absolutely immoral man would scarcely have to be "continually" bothered in order to bring himself to make a decision in the widow's behalf so as to make things easy on himself. Acting in character he would have rid himself of her immediately by whatever means necessary. Nor would an absolutely immoral man have worried about "getting a black eye." A

---

connotation of traditional Jewish praxis: 4 Kgs 17:24–41.

[34] See also for positive uses of ἐντρέπω: Isa 45:16–17 LXX, and Isa 50:7 LXX; see also Haslam, *Oxyrhynchus Papyri*, s.v. ἐντρέπεσθαι 3720, line 72.

[35] See Derrett, "Unjust Judge," 191.

[36] See for example; Quint. *Inst. Orat.* 3.7.19–22 (called "denunciation" vituperatio): Aristot. *Rhet.* 1.9 (called "invective," ὄνειδος). See Scott (*Hear Then the Parable*, 179–80) who calls it formulaic or proverbial.

[37] Bruce (*Parabolic Teaching*, 159) is of the same opinion.

thoroughly immoral man would do whatever he needed to make himself comfortable. Luke 18:5 makes sense only if the judge is thoroughly impartial (cf. Deut 1:16–17) but willing finally to be compromised for the sake of his own comfort.

There are two levels on which one must consider the plausibility of the expression as a rhetorical device. Taking "not fearing the Lord" as standard invective (which is demanded by Wettstein's examples) does not seem to make much sense in the context of the preaching of Jesus. In first-century Palestinian Judaism the expression "the fear of the Lord" would have resonated as an idiom for being "religious" or "pious" in a traditional sense to persons familiar with Torah, rather than having been heard as standard rhetorical invective. That being the case, one is then forced to consider the latter half of the expression independently of Wettstein's examples.

Possibly the expression is Lukan redaction. In that case the odds are increased that Luke is employing a standard rhetorical device to discredit the judge. Others have pointed to Luke's editing of the story in other ways.[38] But this seems improbable since it is specifically Luke who, under the influence of the LXX, uses the idiom the "fear of the Lord" in a traditional sense.[39] Hence I find the expression to be a way of telling the reader that the judge is a thoroughly honest man, one who is not influenced in his judgment by traditional religious piety or other community obligations.[40]

And there was a widow in that city. In the Hebrew scriptures and ancient Judaism widows were accorded a privileged status by the devout Israelite and Jew.[41] The pious Israelite saw God as the protector of widows (Exod 22:22–24; Deut 10:18; Mal 3:5; Ps 67:5; 146:9; Prov 15:25; Sir 35:14–15; Ep Jer 6:38). Hence, it was clear to the pious Jew that the God who protected widows expected that his people would, following his example, also give them preferential treatment (Deut 24:17–22; 26:12–13; 2 Macc 3:10; 8:28; 2 Esd 2:20). In ancient Israel widows were regarded as a special protected class and were treated differently from other women. The "widow's vow" (and that of a divorced woman) was allowed to stand with no modification (Num 30:9), but the vows of married women were subject to their husband's approval (Num 30:1–15). They even wore a special garment marking out their widow's status (Gen 38:14; Jdt 8:5). Indeed Jdth 9:9 subtly implies that widows expected special treatment by

---

[38] Fitzmyer, *Luke*, 2.1178–9.

[39] *TDNT* 9.212–13.

[40] Compare the similar statement made of Jesus in Matt 22:16: "We know that you are true and teach the way of God truthfully, and care for no man" (καὶ οὐ μέλει σοι περὶ οὐδενός).

[41] See *TDNT* χήρα, 9.444–48.

God. The popular view held that widows indeed received special consideration in the courts (2 Sam 14:1–5). For example, a widow's garment could not be taken in pledge (Deut 24:17). In fact, one way of validating personal piety was by appealing to one's positive treatment of widows (Job 31:16; Isa 1:17 LXX). Likewise the classic description of the ungodly is that they are unconcerned with the "widow's plight" (Job 22:8–9; Ps 94:6; Isa 1:23; Jer 5:28 LXX, 7:6); such people oppress and take advantage of widows (Job 24:3; Isa 10:2; Jer 22:3; Ezek 22:7; Zech 7:8–10; Wis 2:10). Hence the pious Jew regarded those who pervert justice for widows as cursed (Deut 27:19), but on the other hand, those who give right judgment to widows are blessed (2 Enoch 42:9).

and she kept on coming to him. The imperfect tense of ἤρχετο stresses that this was not a single request; rather, she had made numerous requests; she "kept on" coming to him with her petition. The image of the widow's continual requests created by the imperfect tense is reinforced in Luke 18:4 with the judge's equally persistent rejection of her plea (ἤθελεν ἐπὶ χρόνον). Whether the incident in Luke occurred in a formal judicial setting, as Tristram suggests based on a scene he personally observed in Nisbis in Mesopotamia,[42] is simply not known.[43] Luke's story is silent on the context(s) in which these repeated pleas were made.

saying, "Avenge me on my adversary!"[44] The widow demands that the judge "avenge" her by bringing vengeance on her antagonist. She is not asking for justice or vindication with respect to her antagonist;[45] rather, she is asking the judge to advocate her cause[46] and punish her adversary.

In the LXX ἐκδικέω usually means to "take vengeance on" someone.[47] That appears also to be its use in this context. The widow's

---

[42]Tristram, *Eastern Customs*, 228–29.

[43]Smith (*Parables*, 150), however, seems to imply that Luke's story did occur in a formal judicial setting.

[44]Even in English the idiom is unclear. What seems to be at issue is the exacting of retribution; inflicting comparable pain on someone for harm done to oneself. But it could be: avenge me "against my adversary." The usual preposition used with ἐκδικέω in the LXX is ἐκ but Luke uses ἀπό. It is probably due to Luke's preference for ἀπό over ἐκ (Cadbury, *Method of Luke*, 202).

[45]As Fitzmyer would have it (*Luke*, 2.1175, 1179).

[46]Following Derrett, "Unjust Judge," 187; see also Smith, *Parables*, 151.

[47]Gen 4:15, 24; Num 31:2; Deut 18:19; 32:43; Ezek 23:45; 24:3; 25:12; 1 Macc 2:67; 6:22; 9:26, 42; 13:6; 4 Macc 17:10; Rom 12:19; 2 Cor 10:6; Rev 16:10; 19:2. In particular the following make it clear that trial and judgment *precede* the taking of vengeance, i.e., the act of ἐκδικήσεις: 1 Macc 6:22; Rev 6:10; 19:2. In the Septuagint and elsewhere in antiquity the establishment of justice is usually expressed through δικαιόω: Schrenk, *TDNT* δικαιόω, 2.211–14. Hence had the widow wanted to be declared "right" or "just" in court she should have used δικαιοῦν (as Luke does at Luke 10:29 and 16:15).

demand of the judge is not for a "fair" hearing before an impartial hearing officer. Rather she wants her opponent to suffer.[48] This fits the strident demanding tone of the woman, particularly in her omitting the usual title of respect in approaching the judge.[49]

Virtually nothing is known of her antagonist, except that he is a male[50] and the defendant (ἐχθρός); he is further identified by the widow as adversary (ἀντίδικος).[51] Nor does the reader know anything about the substance of the widow's complaint against him. The situation, however, reflected in the story plays off the proverbial status of widows in Jewish society as disadvantaged women in a male-dominated world who "had no means of financial support and thus needed special protection."[52] Hence the reader is set up to think the worst of the widow's adversary and then, conditioned by the widow's favored status in pious Jewish society, to sympathize with her.

And for a while he was unwilling. The judge is simply unwilling to heed the widow's strident demands to act against the man. Matching her persistence, he resists (the imperfect οὐκ ἤθελεν answers to the imperfect in verse 3: ἤρχετο), at least for a while. How long he holds out is unclear, but in the last analysis that is not really important, since he eventually gives in. Why he initially holds out is equally unclear, but his renewed insistence on his integrity ("though I neither fear God, nor show deference to man") before he gives in, suggests that it is at least possible that his resistance may have been for conscience' sake.

But after these (exchanges) he said to himself. The transitional phrase μετὰ ταῦτα signals a major shift in the narrative's action.[53] It focuses the reader's attention on the judge's soliloquy—as a transition to a separate

---

[48] In the papyri the verb ἐκδικέω can have the idea of adjudicating a case (Moulton and Milligan, *Vocabulary of the Greek Testament*, s.v. ἐκδικέω, pp. 192–93) and thus Luke 18:3 would carry the idea of "doing right" and "protecting" the widow (followed by Plummer, *Luke*, 412). Derrett ("Unjust Judge," 186, n.1) finds in the widow's demand both "the typical cry of the injured petitioner" and the call for vengeance. Scott (*Hear Then the Parable*, 182) argues that the usage in the story follows the papyri, but "the LXX notion of avenging should not be discounted." It should not be overlooked that in the papyri the word also carries the stronger idea of vengeance, as for example, in the Jewish prayer for vengeance for a murdered girl where God is implored to "avenge" innocent blood (Moulton and Milligan, *Vocabulary of the Greek Testament*, s.v. ἐκδικέω, p. 193).

[49] As noted by Scott, *Hear Then the Parable*, 183.

[50] It does not appear to me to be a generic use of the masculine but an intentional use in order to contrast ironically the fragile vulnerability of the widow disadvantaged in a male world. In this situation as represented by Luke, however, the widow is anything but vulnerable.

[51] She does not call him her enemy (ἐχθρός), however, but rather uses the language of litigation: adversary (ἀντίδικος): see Schrenk, *TDNT* 1.373–75 and Moulton and Milligan, *Vocabulary of the Greek Testament*, 47.

[52] Scott, *Hear Then the Parable*, 180.

and distinct element of the narrative. Hence the judge's soliloquy takes place apart from the nagging demands of the widow. Not only is he alone in his thoughts in this moment, he is away from the irritation that drove him to ponder his situation. Thus he can weigh the merits of any action with relative objectivity. Hence the narrative casts his decision as a deliberate, dispassionate, and calculated act.

Although I neither fear God nor respect (any) man, yet because this widow wearies me, I will avenge her. The translation "bother"[54] for παρέχειν . . . κόπον fails to do justice to the sense of physical debilitation conveyed by the expression. The woman's constant badgering was actually "wearing him down" physically. She was (by this expression) considerably more than a "bother" or minor annoyance; her persistence had begun to drain his energies. Hence she was not a minor irritation.

The fact that he endured significant stress (by his own admission) before yielding to her constant demands makes him appear somewhat less petulant and his decision less capricious. In short, in his own thoughts (to which the reader is privy) he reasoned that he had endured a significant amount of harassment before he took the drastic step of compromising his integrity. The soliloquy justifies his plans to grant the woman's demands.

So that she may not come in the end and give me a black eye.[55] What the judge really fears is that the woman will finally (εἰς τέλος) run out of patience with his irresolution, and physically assault him (ὑπωπιάζῃ). The expression ὑπωπιάζῃ με suggests that the widow's violence (i.e., the emotional stress) against the judge has been escalated. It contrasts well as an escalation with παρέχειν μοι κόπον, and hence I take ὑπωπιάζω to be actual physical violence. The translation "give me a black eye" best preserves the ambiguity of the word: actual black and blue injury beneath the eye/humiliation in the community.[56]

---

[53] See Fitzmyer, *Luke*, 2.845. Fitzmyer calls it a "stereotyped Lukan transitional phrase," but it also is used 8 times in John and 11 times elsewhere in the New Testament; see Hawkins, *Horae Synopticae*, 20, 43–44. See also its extensive use in the Septuagint. The typical use of the device is to mark a major transitional break in a narrative.

[54] RSV, Goodspeed, Berkeley; Weymouth = annoy.

[55] Compare the New American Bible: "Or she will end by doing me violence." εἰς τέλος ἐρχομένη is a circumstantial use of the participle expressing an attendant circumstance that is best translated in verbal rather than participial construction: see Goodwin, *Greek Grammar*, 366 (§1563, 7); Dana and Mantey, *Manual Grammar*, 228–29; Blass-Debrunner-Funk, *Greek Grammar*, 216 (§419, [2]).

For my translation see Klostermann-Gressmann, *Lukasevangelium*, 541; Weiss, *Schriften*, 1.495; but compare Blass-Debrunner-Funk, *Greek Grammar*, 112 (§207, [3]).

[56] See the study by Weiss in *TDNT* ὑπωπιάζω, 8.590. But see also Bruce (*Parabolic Teaching*, 160–61), who recognizes the physical violence connoted by the word.

The story concludes in an unfinished state. The reader never really learns the outcome. The judge only *resolves* to grant the widow's demands. Does he follow through with what he resolved? The reader is never told. Perhaps he never had the opportunity to render a decision and the widow assaulted him before he could follow through. In that case he would have been somewhat like the prodigal son who practiced a speech he intended to tell his father (Luke 15:18–19), but never delivered (Luke 15:20–22). In short the story ends without achieving resolution, and the audience is left to ponder how it may have concluded, though a conclusion is not really necessary for most readers, as they tend to assume the worst of the judge.

HOW DOES THE STORY WORK?

The structure of the narrative focuses the attention of the reader on the introspection of the judge, due to the Lukan break at 18:4b (μετὰ ταῦτα), and due to the fact that virtually two-thirds of the story concerns the judge, whether it is his reputation (18:2) as communicated in an aside to the reader, his irresolution in rendering a decision (18:4a), or his own soliloquy (18:4b–5). Hence any reading of the narrative that reduces it to the persistence of the widow, as Luke's reading has done (18:7–8), ignores that the judge is actually the structural focus of the story. The widow's persistence is required only to make sense of the judge's fear that she may eventually physically assault him. It is of course not required that the judge's antagonist be a widow. The antagonist could have been anyone, but a widow in that role introduces additional features into the narrative. In the Israelite tradition widows are the ultimate symbol of vulnerability, and the championing of a widow would have been regarded in Israelite tradition as the ultimate act of charity and piety. When the judge is initially unmoved by her persistence, it would to a pious Jew reflect negatively on his traditional piety. And such disregard for the widow also reinforces what both the narrator and the judge himself have had to say about his character: he does not make decisions based on what the Torah teaches. Hence for the pious Jew, he is an impious man. And thus his character as an administrative judge is reinforced: it is difficult to conceive of this judge rendering decisions in a religious court when he has such a reputation for being irreligious.

Of course, the widow does not fit the stereotype of vulnerability that led to her protected status in Israel and Judaism.[57] Her persistent harassment of the judge does not portray her as a sympathetic character.

---

[57] Cf., *m. Ketub.* 4.12; 11.1–4; 12.3; *m. Giṭ.* 5.3.

Neither her demands for vengeance nor her total disregard for justice in the matter (ἐκδικέω rather than δικαιόω) win her sympathy. She evidences no respect for the court in either her address to the judge or her petition of the court. Her demand for vengeance itself violates Torah (Lev 19:18; Deut 32:35, 43), and therefore in a certain sense she rejects her status as the protected of the Lord (Exod 22:22–24; Deut 10:18). She is demeaned in the story, making it difficult for a knowledgeable reader to identify with her.

And the judge likewise is sharply ridiculed. The narrator (and the judge himself) describe him as an honest man who renders just decisions irrespective of the demands of religious law or influential community leaders. Thus both the widow and her unidentified adversary were equal in his court. The widow pressed him hard for preferential treatment: "Avenge me!" she demands. But the judge was unwilling to take such an action.[58] Why he would not have simply done what she wanted so as to avoid all the pressure she put on him is unclear. What is clear is that had the judge been thoroughly disreputable, as he is usually regarded, he would not have subjected himself to such treatment without good reason. No reasons are given, however; the judge is merely portrayed as irresolute. A thoroughly disreputable man would have either made it easy on himself by favoring the widow with her petition early in the narrative, thus sparing himself the personal discomfort, or would have found some other way to get rid of her. This judge, however, holds out to the point of physical exhaustion, and finally decides to do what the widow wants only when he begins to fear she will do him bodily harm. Thus the judge scarcely measures up as a powerful community leader who arbitrates disputes and administers justice. Nor does he quite fit the stereotype of a corrupt judge who for personal aggrandizement lines his own pockets at the expense of the poor and uninfluential.

A reader is genuinely surprised that the judge fears violence from the widow.[59] The widow is stereotyped in the Hebrew scriptures as a vulnerable woman who has no man to care for her needs in a male society, and a judge is stereotyped as a powerful community figure who holds in his hands the fate of those who appear in his court. But in this story their characterization is reversed. Instead the impotent is cast in the role of self-centered power broker, while the power broker suddenly senses his vulnerability. In fact, the judge's reason for compromising his

---

[58] It was not a refusal of her request—which would have been then ἠρνεῖτο (imperfect of ἀρνέομαι: cf. Acts 7:35). The judge for some reason was irresolute. He couldn't make up his mind. That he was unwilling suggests that he at least considered the widow's demand as one possible alternative.

[59] This may be the reason that most translators weaken their translation of ὑπωπιάζῃ: it does not seem reasonable that a "powerful" judge would fear violence from a "weak" widow.

integrity makes him seem to be something of a "wimp," afraid of a black eye from a widow!

It is entirely conceivable that a small village bureaucrat, as this judge seems to have been, would be readily accessible to the vagaries of his clientele in the village.[60] But irrespective of that, it is clear that the story is burlesque and that the typical characters of both the widow and the judge are ironically reversed. The sharp humor in the story, however, is at the judge's expense, since it is he who is made to look ridiculous or absurd; and the widow, on the other hand, is demeaned.

ANOTHER READING OF THE STORY

This humorous, sarcastic, and rather complex story contains a series of unexpected reversals. The judge is a hopelessly ridiculous figure. He is initially cast as a thoroughly honest man who renders impartial judgments with no deference paid either to "God or man." What this means in the story is that he does not rule based on the mandates of religious laws, i.e., Torah (for example, in his court widows will not be shown any special preference, as they would have been under religious law). Nor is it possible for any person in the community to gain an advantage in his court by influencing his decisions. He is an impartial judge that, in short, "calls them as he sees them." Hence the story initially casts him as a strongly principled man of incorruptible character (18:2–3). The fact that the plaintiff in the story is a widow to whom he is unwilling to show deference in spite of her persistent demands illustrates his independence of the religious law (18:4). But unexpectedly (18:5) the judge turns out to be a "wimp" when he is confronted by an aggressive widow. And he resolves to compromise his principles, when he feels threatened with what he appears to regard as certain physical harm (a black eye!). And he does in fact resolve to show deference to a plaintiff, and thus to pervert the system of impartial justice he had affirmed so strongly. In a sense, like Esau he proposes selling his birthright for a bowl of beans (Gen 25:29–34); he resolves to compromise high principles, his integrity, and an impartial judicial system to make himself more comfortable and to secure himself against a perceived (actually minor) physical threat. A figure that began heroically ends tragically. So one may be amused at the ridiculous contrast between what he claimed about himself and what he eventually turns out to be. But upon reflection, there is a cutting edge to the humor that tends to take a reader out of the story: there is nothing at all funny about the

---

[60]There are stories in the gospels that suggest the accessibility of village officials to the public. For example, Luke 19:1–10; Matt 8:5–13; 9:9–10.

tragic fall of a principled man or about the perversion of an impartial system of justice.

The story has condemned the judge to eternal ridicule, and at the same time forces a reader's judgment on his or her own similar compromising behavior. For every time one laughs at the ridiculousness of the judge—then sharing the judgment of the story—one passes the story's judgment over on to one's own lapses of integrity.

Ironically, the judge's final resolution (Luke 18:5), in spite of his protestations to the contrary (18:4), will cause him to follow the religious law after all, when he executes due "justice" for the widow (Deut 10:18; Isa 1:17), although that is really not his intention (Luke 18:5). But that is actually immaterial, because in performing this "deed of righteousness,"[61] he is due the blessing of God (2 Enoch 42:7–9). Widowhood symbolized in Israel the ultimate extremity of life, the ultimate state of vulnerability, need, and deprivation (Ruth 1:13, 20–21; Isa 49:7; Lam 1:1; Rev 18:7). But the widow was also the special ward of God whose people were expected to exercise special care for her (Deut 24:17–22). James, for example, regards care for widows (and orphans) as the first of two indicators of true religion (1:27)! Thus the judge in the story intends to perform the ultimate act of charity and religious devotion (in Israel), but for the wrong reason. And hence the story raises the whole issue of motivation for religious behavior and charitable deeds.

It is very difficult to give the judge any credit for his intended action, since I know that he really could not care any less about the widow. Were it not for his soliloquy, however, and were Luke 18:4a followed by a statement that he had avenged the widow,[62] I would probably have regarded him as the ideal of an honest judge (in contrast to all those disreputable judges who took advantage of widows: Isa 1:23; 10:2), who had followed Torah and avenged a widow on a man who had tried to exploit her (cf. 2 Sam 14:4–11). And so he might have appeared to anyone who had not overheard his soliloquy. But a reader knows his motives and knows he is not really motivated by concern for the widow. His "charitable deed" is really an attempt to make his own life more comfortable. The narrator of this story would only chuckle at the prospect of this judge receiving any community acclaim or recognition for his deed.

The story is kinder than I would be, however; the only judgment it pronounces on the magistrate is to have a little fun at his expense. And I can laugh too at the irony, but when I think about it, I am forced to wonder about the value of my own acts of religious piety and charity. Is it really true that acts of piety, charity, and deeds of righteousness are ludicrous if they are performed for the wrong reasons? I know that

---

[61] See the discussion above on the Samaritan, pp. 114–15.

[62] I.e., "For a while he was unwilling, but then he avenged her."

individuals on the receiving end of the charitable deed will benefit and could not care less why the deed was done, but what about the doer of the charitable deed; what is the benefit to the doer if the motivation is wrong? But the narrator of this story would only chuckle, since even my raising of that question in that way assumes that I, like the judge in the story, should benefit in some way from doing charitable deeds.

Because this story is ironic, it ridicules and condemns the narrative's world view; at the same time it affirms its opposite. Hence to understand the story the reader must consider a world where judges act with impartiality and integrity, where justice is not perverted for personal gain, where religious obligations do not have to be mandated and charitable acts are liberally done with no thought of personal benefit. That ideal concept by comparison condemns my world and my participation in it.

HOW MIGHT THE STORY HAVE BEEN HEARD IN THE CONTEXT OF ISRAEL'S FICTIONS ABOUT ITSELF

Undoubtedly the story could have been heard in a number of ways, since the storyteller does not completely control the audience's reaction. The variety of modern interpretations suggests its innate polyvalence; and the situation would have been no different in Jesus' own day, assuming that it was originally told to a first-century audience by Jesus of Nazareth, as I think it was.

If members of an audience missed the ironic characterization of widow and judge, they probably heard it as a story about a thoroughly disreputable man (as Luke and others take it). For them the judge in the story epitomizes what it means to be an unrighteous man.[63] He boasts of his impiety and his disregard for the welfare of any member of the community. He is unmoved by the plight of the widow, any widow. In the story, his irresolution suggests that he has conspired with the widow's opponent to exploit her. And even though he cares nothing for anyone, least of all the poor widow, he will nevertheless rule in her favor because it is convenient.

Such a hearing of the story would have taken it to be a criticism of the judicial system, and as such it would have won instant affirmation from a poor audience who would have reasoned: everyone knows that poor people do not stand a chance in the court; the wealthy have all the advantages; the judges line their pockets at our expense and thus pervert justice, etc. Or in the words of Isaiah:[64]

---

[63] The early Christian title for the story, "the Unrighteous (ἀδικίας) Judge" verifies this as an early reading of the story.

[64] Cf. Mic 3:9, 11; 7:3; Jer 5:28; Ezek 22:6–12; Prov 17:15, 26; 18:5; 24:23–24; Sir 7:6.

> The Lord enters into judgment
>> with the elders and princes of his people:
> It is you who have devoured the vineyard,
> the spoil of the poor is in your houses.
> What do you mean by crushing my people,
> by grinding the face of the poor?" says the Lord of Hosts
>> (Isa 3:14–15 RSV).

> Woe to those who decree
>> iniquitous decrees
> and the writers who keep writing oppression,
> to turn aside the needy from justice
>> and to rob the poor of my people
>> of their right,
> that widows may be their spoil,
>> and that they make the fatherless their prey
>> (Isa 10:1–2 RSV).

Such a reading of the Unjust Judge might be called "prophetic" in that the story from this standpoint (like the Hebrew prophets) is concerned with justice and the plight of the poor.

But if the audience had caught the irony of this particular judge granting "justice" to this particular widow and thus thereby qualifying himself as a "righteous man," the story might have been heard differently. Auditors might have been led to question the "theology" that said God rewards his people for simple obedience to his laws[65] and for simply performing deeds of righteousness,[66] particularly those that ensured justice for the widow.[67]

The story of Tobit is a classic statement of the theology that God rewards the person who performs righteous deeds. The book opens with Tobit performing acts of charity for which he suffers loss of property (1:16–20) and loss of his eyesight (2:1–10). In his distress at his calamity, like Job, he asks God to let him die (3:6). Nevertheless he still counsels his son to practice charity (4:7–11, 16) and at the end of the book his sight is restored (11:7–15). The book blatantly promotes "deeds of righteousness" for the benefits that accrue to the righteous:

> Prayer is good when accompanied by fasting, almsgiving, and righteousness. A little with righteousness is better than much with wrongdoing. It is better to give alms than to treasure up gold. For almsgiving delivers from death, and it will purge away every sin. Those who perform deeds of charity and of righteousness will have fulness of life; but those who commit sin are the enemies of their own lives (Tob 12:8–10 RSV).

---

[65] Exod 23:22–33; Lev 26; Deut 7:12–16; 28.
[66] Prov 11:18.
[67] 2 Enoch 42:9; Jer 22:1–4, 15–16.

See, my son, what Nadab did to Ahikar who had reared him, how he brought him from light into darkness, and with what he repaid him. But Ahikar was saved, and the other received repayment as he himself went down into the darkness. Ahikar gave alms and escaped the deathtrap which Nadab had set for him; but Nadab fell into the trap and perished (Tob 14:10–11 RSV).

In such a literary context, Luke's story raises the issue of the motivation for religious behavior. Only by the most far-fetched string of ridiculous logic could Luke's judge be regarded as a righteous man because of his vindication of the widow. And yet that is precisely the way his decision would have been seen by those in the story world not privy to his inner thoughts. Hence Luke's story challenges Jewish theology that taught God rewarded righteous behavior completely apart from any consideration of motivation.

Such an emphasis on motivation for behavior was not even recognized by Israel's ethical prophets. They criticized a perfunctory or routine worship of God that failed to associate worship with ethical behavior. They were the social conscience of Israel, and they cried for justice and moral behavior in the social order. They also called for ethical social behavior to match proper ritual behavior.[68] But not once did they raise the issue of *motivation* for religious or "righteous" behavior. In a sense their view of righteous behavior was simplistic. If you "lived righteously" (i.e., according to Torah), God rewarded you. If you did not "live righteously," you fell under the judgment of God.[69]

Luke's story, however, raises the issue of altruistic behavior and disinterested piety. The difference can be seen in a saying attributed to a pre-Christian rabbi, Antigonus of Soko: "Be not like slaves that minister to the master for the sake of receiving a bounty, but be like slaves that minister to the master not for the sake of receiving a bounty."[70] The prophetic tradition likewise contrasts with the early Christian tradition that portrayed Jesus of Nazareth as stressing motivation for human behavior. For example, "You have heard that it was said 'You shall not commit adultery.' But I say to you that everyone who looks at a woman lustfully has already committed adultery with her in his heart" (Matt 5:27–28 RSV). "The eye is the lamp of the body. So, if your eye is sound, your whole body will be full of light; but if your eye is not sound, your whole body will be full of darkness" (Matt 6:22–23 RSV).[71]

---

[68] Cf., e.g., Amos 5:21–24; Mic 6:6–8.
[69] Cf., e.g., Jer 7.
[70] *m. 'Abot* 1.3; Danby, *Mishnah*, 446.
[71] On this saying see Bultmann, *Theology*, 1.11–15.

11

The Pharisee and the Toll Collector

MOST INTERPRETERS, FOLLOWING LUKE'S READING, TAKE THE STORY OF THE Pharisee and the Toll Collector as a simple example story that contrasts a self-righteous Pharisee and a contrite toll collector. It appears, however, to be more complex than Luke and others allow. The story is prosaically narrated and is designed to focus on the soliloquy of the Pharisee. It is one of a very few in the parable corpus that lacks a resolution, and the narrator gives no hint as to how the story concludes. The reader is left with the conundrum: whose prayer does God accept?

THE SETTING OF THE STORY: AN EARLY CHRISTIAN READING

This story, attributed to Jesus, immediately follows the story of the Unjust Judge, joined to it almost as an afterthought by an intensive καί (i.e., "also," 18:9). The story itself (18:10–13) and Luke's immediate interpretive context (18:9, 14),[1] however, actually have little to do with the preceding context (17:20b–37; 18:1–8; see the discussion in chapter 10 above). This story serves Luke as a graphic illustration of what Jesus meant by two cryptic sayings following the story: Luke 18:16–17. For Luke, receiving the kingdom of God "like a child" (18:17) means doing precisely what the toll collector[2] in the story did: he became "like a child" in that he "humbled" himself, i.e., did not make a pretense of himself before God (Luke 18:9, 13–14; cf. Matt 18:1–5). It is only to people of such childlike, humble, and trusting attitudes that Luke believes the kingdom of God belongs (18:16).

---

[1] See Linnemann, *Parables*, 146, n. 12 and 13; see below for 18:14a.
[2] For the translation "toll collector," see the discussion below.

The idea of humility as an essential Christian trait is not unique to Luke, but rather is a widespread motif in early Christian texts. Matthew, for example, specifically links both humility and the child in Matt 18:4: "Whoever humbles himself like this child is greatest in the kingdom of Heaven" (see also Jas 4:10; 1 Pet 5:6; cf. Jas 1:10–11). Luke's concluding interpretation to the story (18:14b) makes use of a traditional early Christian saying attributed to Jesus (Luke 18:14 = Luke 14:11 = Matt 23:12) that sets forth a reversal theme extolling humility and condemning pride,[3] a motif well-known in the Hebrew scriptures.

Elsewhere Luke picks up on the theme of humility (i.e., an attitude that is unassuming, self-deprecatory, unpretentious, etc.). In 9:46–48 Luke adds the following to material used from Mark (9:33–37) against those who claimed greatness: "For the one who is least among you all is the one who is great" (Luke 9:48c). And twice Luke condemns those who make a pretense of themselves (i.e., seek to justify themselves) before God (Luke 10:29–37; 16:14–15).

Luke reads the two men in this story (18:10–13) as examples of improper and proper attitudes before God. The Pharisee has a haughty, arrogant attitude in that he looks down on others and presumes himself to be righteous (i.e., justified before God). The toll collector, in contrast, is properly humble and unassuming before God. In Luke's reading, therefore, God justifies the contrite toll collector rather than the self-righteous Pharisee (18:14a).[4]

The story proper consists of only Luke 18:10–13. What is meant by "story proper" is the self-contained narrative unit that *shows* the actions of Pharisee and toll collector in the temple (18:10–13). Luke 18:9 is clearly not a part of that fictional "world." It belongs to the agenda and world of Luke's Jesus, and as such is part of a literary frame telling the reader how Luke wants the story to be read.

Luke 18:14b is also not a part of the fictional world of the story. Rather it is a traditional saying that Luke uses as a moralistic interpretation of the story. By means of this introduction and conclusion Luke

---

[3] Hence the saying was not considered in its present form as a saying of Jesus of Nazareth by the Jesus Seminar. See the voting records of the Seminar: *Forum* 6.1 (March, 1990), 3-55. It is likely a saying of an early Christian prophet that derives from Ezek 21:26 (cf. Ezek 33:13), the repeated emphasis in the Hebrew tradition that God will honor the humble (Job 22:29; Prov 16:19; 29:23; Sir 2:17; Isa 2:11–12, 17; 10:33; 2 Chron 7:14; 12:6–7; 32:26; 33:12–13; 34:27; 36:12; Mic 6:8), and the equally strong warnings against pride (Prov 16:5, 18; Sir 10:12; Isa 2:12; 3:11, 16–17; 10:12–19).

[4] Clearly Luke could have been more precise in 18:14a, though what is intended can scarcely be misunderstood. Οὗτος, "this one," refers to the toll collector who had just been mentioned in Luke 18:13, while ἐκεῖνον, "that one," refers to the previously mentioned Pharisee; see Goodwin, *Greek Grammar*, 216, par. 1004. It is curious that Luke did not specify "Pharisee," "toll collector" in 18:14a, rather than using the oblique "this" and "that."

places the story in the context of a later rabbinic debate as to which type of person should be ranked over the other: the nominally righteous or the penitent.[5] Luke's sympathy is decidedly with the penitent in this regard (Luke 18:14a).

The status of Luke 18:14a (i.e., is it part of the fictional story or part of Luke's conclusion?) is problematic. Most commentators never address the issue directly, but simply assume that 18:14a is the original conclusion of the historical Jesus.[6] Others take Luke 18:14a as part of Luke's conclusion and hence do not regard it as a saying of the historical Jesus.[7]

There are two issues raised with Luke 18:14a. The first-person (λέγω ὑμῖν) narrative voice takes the reader out of the fictional world of the story where two people are praying in the temple. The statement is not formally a part of that world; that is to say, it is not made by a third actor at the temple. It may possibly be the voice of a self-aware narrator who pauses to address directly the reader/auditor, thus closing off the conclusion to the story with interpretive commentary. But even then it is a narrator's "aside" and still not part of the fictional world of the characters in the story. It is part of the world of the narrator/auditor/reader.

There are two options for the identity of the narrator: (1) the voice of the narrator is the voice of the historical Jesus, in which case 18:14a is the original conclusion to the story; (2) the voice of the narrator is the voice of Luke's Jesus, in which case 18:14a is Luke's ending. If the voice of the narrator is an original part of the fictional story it would be the only instance in the parables corpus in which the narrator is self-aware. In every other instance of first-person address at the conclusion of stories, the voice at the end is the voice of the evangelists' Jesus addressing the evangelists' literary audience.[8] *The narrative voice of the parables is simply not a self-aware narrator.*

Hence it appears that in this instance, as well, Luke 18:14a should be regarded as the voice of Luke's Jesus addressing some of the Pharisees (Luke 17:20; 18:1) who thought they were righteous and who despised others (18:9). It may very well be the earliest interpretation to the story, and as such it may antedate Luke, who constructed the literary sequence

---

[5] See *TNDT*, 2.186, s.v. "δίκαιος": Strack-Billerbeck, 1:603. Luke uses δίκαιος ten times (1:6, 17; 2:25; 5:32; 12:57; 14:14; 15:7; 20:20; 23:47; 23:50); Mark, twice; John, three times; Matthew, seventeen.

[6] Cadoux, *Parables*, 216; Jones, *Art and Truth*, 44; Manson, *Sayings*, 312; Donahue, *Gospel in Parable*, 187; Oesterley, *Gospel Parables*, 230; Bultmann, *Synoptic Tradition*, 178; Linnemann, *Parables*, 64; Fitzmyer, *Luke*, 2.1183; Bailey, *Poet and Peasant*, 2. 154–55; Boucher, *Parables*, 100; Talbert, *Reading Luke*, 170; Smith, *Parables*, 179.

[7] Crossan, *Dark Interval*, 82; Scott, *Hear Then the Parable*, 97; Jones, *Teaching*, 196; Bugge, *Haupt-Parabeln*, 478; Jülicher, *Gleichnisreden Jesu*, 2.605. Jeremias (*Parables*, 144, n. 62) is undecided.

[8] Compare Luke 14:24; 15:7, 10; 16:9 (as is all of 16:8–13); 18:8; Matt 18:14, 35; 21:42–43.

in chapters 17 and 18 around it. But it is not a part of the fictional world of Luke 18:10–13 in any case. The only question is, does it derive from Jesus of Nazareth? In my judgment it does not, for reasons set out in chapter 2 above. Hence one is left with an original story (18:10–13) that has beginning (18:10), middle (18:11–13), but no conclusion. The story stops abruptly with the two men still in the temple. The complication remains unresolved.

MODERN INTERPRETATIONS

Virtually all interpreters regard this narrative as an example story[9] rather than a story having specific metaphorical qualities. Following Luke, most critics regard the story as the simple condemnation of a self-righteous and arrogant Pharisee and the affirmation of a contrite sin-conscious toll collector. For such critics the story illustrates the type of religious attitudes that God rejects and accepts.

In order for the story to work as an example, interpreters generally take the prayer of the Pharisee as hypocritical—as an altogether insincere prayer. Linnemann, however, finds nothing in the prayer of the Pharisee that mandates understanding it as insincere, but rather, pointing to parallels of similar rabbinic prayers in the Talmud, she argues that the Pharisee's prayer is a genuine prayer of gratitude.[10] From this perspective she can read the parable as an attack on traditional Jewish piety: i.e., the law is no longer the standard for measuring an individual's righteousness before God. The Pharisee represented the ideal type of those people who trusted in Torah.[11] In Linnemann's reading, the story holds forth two ways of achieving righteousness: through the Law (Pharisee) and by God's grace (the toll collector).

There are two interpreters who take the story to have metaphorical qualities that specifically evoke the kingdom of God. For these readers the coming of the kingdom of God subverts and overturns the usual and accepted conventions of human society, creating a new order of reality.[12] Neither of these interpreters regard the Pharisee's prayer as insincere or self-righteous.[13]

---

[9] Curiously there are few journal articles that make this story the subject of a special study. See also Downing, "Ambiguity," 96–97.

[10] Linnemann, *Parables*, 59–60.

[11] Linnemann, *Parables*, 61, 63. See also Manson, *Sayings*, 310, 312. While Manson regards the prayer of the Pharisee as a sincere prayer, in Manson's judgment he still reflects a self-righteous attitude (312).

[12] Scott, *Hear Then the Parable*, 97; see also Donahue, *Gospel in Parable*, 190.

[13] Scott, *Hear Then the Parable*, 95–96; Donahue, *Gospel in Parable*, 188–89.

How one understands the character of the Pharisee's prayer is essential to reading the story. For example, in order for the story to function as a clear example of proper and improper attitude before God, the prayer of the Pharisee must be insincere and hypocritical[14]—if the toll collector's prayer is going to represent a proper attitude. This must be the case if there is to be a sharp contrast. On the other hand, for the story to be cast as an attack on the Torah, the Pharisee must become an example "of complete devotion to the law as the supreme standard of Jewish faith and morals,"[15] i.e., the Pharisee must be a man who is not subject to criticism in the discharge of his religious obligations under Torah.

In order to regard the story as a "parable" that evokes the coming of a kingdom that overturns the old order, readers must assume that the Pharisee is the ideal model of a pious man, a representative of the best the old order had to offer. Otherwise the adherents of the old order could object that the Pharisee in the story was an unfair, inferior caricature.

THE POETICS

Luke's version is the only extant copy of the story; there exist no other ancient versions for comparison. In this instance the design of the narrative appears to emphasize the soliloquy of the Pharisee.

PERIOD I	1	Ἄνθρωποι δύο ἀνέβησαν
	2	εἰς τὸ ἱερὸν προσεύξασθαι,
	3	ὁ εἷς φαρισαῖος
	4	καὶ ὁ ἕτερος τελώνης.
PERIOD II	1	ὁ φαρισαῖος σταθεὶς
	2	πρὸς ἑαυτὸν ταῦτα[16] προσηύχετο,
	3	ὁ θεός,

---

[14] For this reason Manson's reading of the character of the Pharisee's prayer should have led him to Linnemann's interpretation of the story, i.e., that the story was an attack on Jewish law, rather than to Manson's much weaker reading that the story contrasts two attitudes before God (*Sayings*, 312).

[15] Manson, *Sayings*, 310.

[16] The reading ταῦτα πρὸς ἑαυτόν has the strongest attestation, but the more difficult reading is preferred (πρὸς ἑαυτὸν ταῦτα: A W 063 f[13] M Sy[h]) because the more difficult reading creates the possibility that πρὸς ἑαυτόν can be read with σταθείς. This conclusion provides a plausible explanation of the variant readings: some texts corrected to ταῦτα πρὸς ἑαυτόν (P[75] א[2] B [L αὐτόν] T Θ Ψ f[1] 892 Origen) to distance πρὸς ἑαυτόν from σταθείς; others omitted πρὸς ἑαυτόν (א* it sa); others omitted ταῦτα to bring πρὸς ἑαυτόν in closer connection to the main verb (Sy[s]); others changed πρὸς ἑαυτόν to read καθ' ἑαυτόν (= "by himself," D it[d] geo[2]). It appears that a reading of the text construing πρὸς ἑαυτόν with σταθείς was a problem for the earliest scribes (see Metzger, *Textual Commentary*, 168).

(PERIOD II) 4 εὐχαριστῶ σοι
5 ὅτι οὐκ εἰμὶ ὥσπερ οἱ λοιποὶ τῶν ἀνθρώπων,
6 ἅρπαγες, ἄδικοι, μοιχοί,
7 ἢ καὶ ὡς οὗτος ὁ τελώνης·
8 νηστεύω δὶς τοῦ σαββάτου,
9 ἀποδεκατῶ πάντα
10 ὅσα κτῶμαι.

PERIOD III 1 ὁ δὲ τελώνης μακρόθεν ἑστὼς
2 οὐκ ἤθελεν
3 οὐδὲ τοὺς ὀφθαλμοὺς ἐπᾶραι εἰς τὸν οὐρανόν,
4 ἀλλ' ἔτυπτεν τὸ στῆθος αὐτοῦ λέγων·
5 ὁ θεός,
6 ἱλάσθητί μοι τῷ ἁμαρτωλῷ.

In period I the fact that the identity of the two men as Pharisee and toll collector is introduced following the main verb and is placed in apposition to the subject (ἄνθρωποι δύο), appears to be a deliberate rhetorical feature to create a little suspense. It would have been easy enough for the narrator to have begun: Φαρισαῖος τις καὶ τελώνης ἀνεβήσαν, as Luke begins at Luke 10:30; 14:2; 15:11; 16:1, 19; 19:12. Luke's usual practice makes for a shorter text and is more direct, but also it is more prosaic.

Beyond this feature there appears to be no attempt by the narrator to introduce euphony through assonance, consonance, and the stylized balancing of phrases. The strongest use of assonance and consonance occurs in period I. Omicron is used 11% of the time (8 occurrences in 14 words/71 letters), and sigma is used 13% of the time (9 occurrences in 14 words/71 letters); but there appears to be no deliberate clustering of these sounds within the period.[17] Neither does there appear to be deliberate clustering of sounds within the other two periods.[18] The story is prosaically narrated.

Its construction is designed to focus attention on the soliloquy of the Pharisee (Period II,3–10). The toll collector is allowed only a brief statement (Period III,5–6), although the narrator does use more text describing the toll collector (I,4; II,7; III,1–4) than the Pharisee (I,3;

---

[17] For example, I,1: o = 1; σ = 1
I,2: o = 3; σ = 3
I,3: o = 2; σ = 3
I,4: o = 2; σ = 2

[18] The most frequently used consonants and vowels in periods II and III are as follows: *Period II* α = 9% (15 occurrences in 36 words/175 letters); τ = 9% (16 occurrences in 36 words/175 letters); σ = 10% (18 occurrences in 36 words/175 letters). *Period III* ε = 9% (11 occurrences in 26 words/122 letters); τ = 10% (12 occurrences in 26 words/122 letters); σ = 8% (10 occurrences in 26 words/122 letters).

II,1–2). It appears that both figures are fairly evenly balanced in terms of the narrator's interest.

I find no obvious metaphorical language in the narrative.

THE STORY: LUKE 19:10–13

Two men went up into the temple to pray. At first the reader knows nothing of the identity of these two men. They could have been anyone, a farmer and a merchant, for example—it is an innocuous enough beginning. "Going up" into the temple is, however, a clear allusion to the temple mount in Jerusalem,[19] and hence the reader is provided a particular historical location as the setting for this fictional story. Whether the allusion reflects the historical roots of the story—that is to say, that it was originally narrated when the temple was still standing (i.e., before 70 CE), or whether the setting was created ad hoc by the imagination of an author out of the ruins of the temple (i.e., post 70 CE) is not possible to say. The only other story, attributed to Jesus, that has a specific historical location is the story about the Samaritan on the road to Jericho (see above).

Some commentators[20] have suggested that these two men are probably to be thought of as going to the temple at one of the regular hours of public prayer.[21] But the story does not specify time of day, day of week, or even if the two men went up at the same time; the story works without that information. People were in the temple praying and performing sacrifices at times other than those times prescribed for formal public worship.[22] Providing a time for their worship in the temple is unnecessary speculation; it is information that the narrator omits.

The one a Pharisee and the other a toll collector. The narrator identifies the two men by their social group: a Pharisee and a toll collector. Little is known of the origins of the Pharisees,[23] but during the New

---

[19] The site of the various temples (Solomon's, Zerubbabel's, Herod's) through the years was originally an elevated area used as a threshing floor (cf. 2 Sam 24:16–25). David was directed by his seer, Gad, to build an altar to the Lord. So David "went up" (2 Sam 24:18–19) to inquire of Araunah, the Jebusite, about the purchase of the property, and Araunah "looked down" (2 Sam 24:20) and saw David coming. See Jos. *Ant.* 15.380–425 and *Bell.* 5.184–287. The literature speaks of "going up" to the temple, e.g., Acts 3:1; Ps 122:1; 1 Sam 1:7; 37:14; 38:22; 2 Kgs 20:5, 8.

[20] Plummer, *Luke*, 416; Jülicher, *Gleichnisreden Jesu*, 2.600; Fitzmyer, *Luke*, 2.1186; Smith, *Parables*, 176; Jeremias, *Parables*, 140; Bailey, *Poet and Peasant*, 2.144–47; Jones, *Teaching*, 191; Scott, *Hear Then the Parable*, 94.

[21] See the discussion below.

[22] See Bailey, *Poet and Peasant*, 2.147; Manson, *Sayings*, 310; Safrai and Stern, *Jewish People in the First Century*, 2.885–90 (889); cf. also 1 Sam 1:9–18; 2 Sam 12:20.

[23] See Rivkin, "Pharisees," *IDBS* 657–63.

Testament period they were popularly regarded as the chief interpreters of the law (Jos. *Bell.* 2.162–66), and were held in high regard by the masses (Jos. *Ant.* 13.293–98; 15.400–404; 18.11–15). They differed from the Sadducees in that the Sadducees accepted only Torah as authoritative, while the Pharisees used the Law, Prophets, Writings, and a developed corpus of oral interpretation (Jos. *Ant.* 13.293–98; Mark 7:3, 5, 8–9; Matt 15:2–3, 6). This body of interpretive tradition functioned as a "fence around the law" (*m. 'Abot,* 1.1), a hedge around the law as it were, to help pious Jews better observe Torah so as to avoid inadvertently breaking it.

While the Pharisees, as the opponents of Jesus (Mark 3:6; Matt 19:3; 23:13; Luke 5:30; John 6:7; 7:32; 11:47–57; 15:2), have been caricatured in the New Testament as blind (Matt 23:26), hypocritical (Matt 23:13–39; Luke 11:37–44), negligent of justice and love of God (Luke 11:42), egotistical (Luke 11:43), and covetous (Luke 16:14), their goal in everything, according to Josephus, was to please God (Jos. *Ant.* 13.288–92). In the New Testament they are depicted as the guardians and chief interpreters of Torah; and hence they rebuke Jesus for allowing his disciples to "work" on the Sabbath (to pluck ears of corn: Mark 2:23–27); they criticize Jesus for allowing his disciples to violate the "tradition" (Matt 15:1–9); they challenge his teaching on divorce (Matt 19:1–9) and his "political" opinions (paying tribute to Caesar: Matt 22:15–22). Yet Jesus is portrayed explicitly confirming their popular authority as the chief interpreters of the Law in Matt 23:2–3: "The Pharisees sit on Moses' Seat."[24] He dined with them (Luke 7:36; 11:37; 14:1), extolled their righteousness (Matt 5:20), and engaged in friendly discourse with them (John 3:1). The Pharisees are even portrayed as warning Jesus about Herod (Luke 13:31).

Hence the Pharisees—as a group—were not self-righteous, sanctimonious hypocrites, in spite of their frequent caricature in the New Testament; rather, they were recognized as devout observers of Torah and as its authoritative interpreters. One would naturally expect to see men of such piety "going up" to the temple to pray.

With the τελώνης (Latin: *publicanus,* "toll collector"), however, it is an entirely different matter. A τελώνης was a private contractor who purchased a "tax" franchise from the civil authorities. Under the Romans in first-century Palestine (and throughout the history of tax farming in general) there were two types of taxes: direct taxes, paid by those who occupied lands or owned businesses, and indirect taxes, such as tolls or customs. The latter were collected by the authorities for the purpose of raising specific amounts of revenue for the state, rather than for regulating

---

[24] See *m. 'Abot,* 1.1: "Moses received the Law from Sinai and committed it to Joshua, and Joshua to the elders, and the elders to the prophets, and the prophets committed it to the men of the Great Synagogue" (Danby, *Mishnah,* 446). Hence for the Pharisees the "tradition of the elders" has an authority equal to Torah.

or controlling the population.[25] The civil authority sold the power to collect these indirect taxes to individuals or corporations (τελώνης = τέλος "toll," or indirect tax, plus the verb ὠνέομαι = I buy). This franchise owner assured the civil government of a certain monetary yield from his "farming" of taxes in a given year, and then the franchise holder had to make good on that commitment. Hence, customs, duty, import taxes, and an additional amount for profit were set by the franchise holder, the τελώνης. If the τελώνης failed to meet his obligations to the government, he paid it with his personal private funds or with monies from his partners, if he had any. The τελώνης seems not to have had the authority to force collection, but the toll collector could report any noncompliance to the civil authorities, who would then compel the violator to pay the tax, imprison the violator, or confiscate the property.

At the time of Jesus, in Judea (an imperial province whose taxes were paid into the Roman treasury) the τελώνης would have dealt with Roman officials, while in Galilee he would have dealt with Herod Antipas. It was not necessary to hold Roman citizenship in order to purchase a franchise to collect indirect taxes, but under the Romans, natives could hold the franchise. Toll collection stations are known to have existed in: Gaza, Ascalon, Joppa, Caesarea (Maritima), Jerusalem, Jericho, Capernaum, and probably Caesarea Philippi, the capital of Philip's tetrarchy. Because the area was divided into customs districts, travelers might have to pay more than once as they journeyed through the various districts. Such multiple taxation would not have contributed to a positive image of toll collectors in Palestine.

Toll collectors, while powerful, did not have a good reputation in the ancient world. They were feared, disliked, and generally regarded as extortionists. In Judaism, because of their contacts with Gentiles, they were regarded as "unclean." In rabbinic Judaism they were placed on a level with gamblers, usurers, thieves, robbers, and men of violence. They were looked upon as people who not only disregarded the Torah, but also transgressed the commandments of God.[26]

In the New Testament toll collectors are regularly linked as an inseparable part of those groups that the Pharisees excluded from the Jewish community of faith, i.e., toll collectors, sinners,[27] and prostitutes

---

[25] Tax farming was practiced throughout the ancient world from the time of classical Greece; the discussion that follows is indebted to Michel, *TDNT* τελώνης, 8.88–105, and Ferguson, *Backgrounds*, 72.

[26] There were exceptions, of course; see Michel, *TDNT* 8.103.

[27] "Sinners," ἁμαρτωλοί, are those individuals who did not follow the pharisaic interpretations of Torah (Rengstorf, *TDNT* ἁμαρτωλός, 1.328) and hence, in the pharisaic mind, they are automatically violators of Torah and guilty of immorality. They are also linked by the Pharisees with the '*Am Ha-aretz*, the people of the land, whom the Pharisees regard as not knowing the Torah (John 7:49). Hence a sinner might simply be one who followed a non-pharisaic understanding of Torah, or one who made no pretense of following Torah. There is no such group in John.

(Matt 9:10–11 [= Mark 2:15–16 = Luke 5:29–30]; 11:19 [= Luke 7:34]; 21:31–32). They were placed on a level with Gentiles (Matt 18:17) and regarded as having low moral and ethical standards (Matt 5:46).

While it is somewhat surprising to see such a man going up to the temple to pray, one must suppose that even toll collectors could have crises of conscience. That some of them had an interest in religious matters is shown by their association with Jesus. And at least one toll collector became a follower of Jesus.[28] Apparently their widespread lack of popularity did not exclude them from entering the temple, and some enjoyed an excellent reputation.[29]

The Pharisee, having stood, began to pray these things to himself. Between the activities of 18:10 and 18:11 there is a gap in the narrative. In 18:10 the two men are depicted as "going up" to the temple. In 18:11 they are at the temple and already in position for prayer. The narrator does not show them arriving at the temple; nor are they shown finding a place for prayer. It is left to the imagination of an auditor/reader to fill in this gap.

One issue in 18:11 is: does one construe πρὸς ἑαυτόν with the dependent participle σταθείς (having stood to himself, i.e., apart from other worshipers),[30] or does one take it with the main verb προσηύχετο (i.e., praying to/with reference to himself)?[31] In the Septuagint πρός is used with ἵστημι several times. Twice (Judg 9:35; 4 Kgs 23:3) it is used with the apparent intended meaning "with respect to" or "at." Four times (1 Macc 10:54; 12:1; 14:18, 24) ἵστημι is used with an object and πρός to give the idea of establish a friendship/league "with reference to. . . . " Once (Lev 18:23) it is used with the idea of present herself (middle voice) "with reference to . . . ," and once (Tob 7:11) it is used in an odd, apparently idiomatic, expression: "until you have established, and have been established with reference to me."

It seems, however, that it is better to take πρὸς ἑαυτόν with προσηύχετο, and to regard σταθείς as used independently, as it occurs, for example, in Luke 18:40, 19:8, and Acts 25:18. In Acts 2:14, 17:22, and 27:21 the prepositional phrase could be taken with either the participle or the main verb, but on balance it seems better to construe it with the main verb.

---

[28] Matt 9:9; 10:3; Luke 5:27–29.

[29] See Michel, *TDNT* τελώνης, 8.103.

[30] Jeremias, *Parables*, 140; Bailey, *Poet and Peasant*, 2.147; Scott, *Hear Then the Parable*, 94; Klostermann-Gressmann, *Das Lukasevangelium*, 543; Manson, *Sayings*, 310.

[31] Linnemann, *Parables*, 143, n. 2; Donahue, *Gospel in Parable*, 188; Smith, *Parables*, 177; Fitzmyer, *Luke*, 2.1186; Jülicher, *Gleichnisreden Jesu*, 2.601; Bugge, *Haupt-Parablen*, 476.

Translations of Luke 18:11 that construe the prepositional phrase as meaning "by himself" (i.e., standing apart) are excluded, since such meaning is expressed by καθ' ἑαυτόν (as later scribes change Luke 18:11 to read; see also Jas 2:17), κατ' ἰδίαν (Mark 4:34), or κατὰ μόνας (Mark 4:10; Luke 9:18). In taking the phrase with προσηύχετο one should probably translate prayed "to himself" (cf. Goodspeed). This should not be taken as meaning that he directed his prayer to himself, but rather it describes the quietness with which he prayed, as it is taken by Linnemann.[32] The prayer was uttered in an undertone inaudible to those standing around him (*m. Ber.* 2.3: Danby). Hence he prayed like Hannah (1 Sam 1:13–15), who quietly poured out her heart to God. But only her lips moved; her voice was not heard (cf. 2 Macc 11:13).

Some commentators have argued that these two men went up to the temple at one of the usual times for public worship: at 9 A.M. (third hour) or 3 P.M. (ninth hour).[33] These times roughly correspond to the morning and afternoon daily whole offering in the second temple.[34] The assumption that they went up at these times derives from an attempt to explain the Pharisee standing πρὸς ἑαυτόν (i.e., by himself), and the toll collector standing μακρόθεν (i.e., far away). In both instances, the phrases are generally understood as evoking an image of the two men standing apart from the rest of the worshipers in the temple, each for his own reason.

The fact that the two men were there at the same time, however, does not mean that they had gone up "at the same time," at the hour of formal worship surrounding one of the two daily whole offerings. During the time between these two customary sacrifices, worshipers presented their individual offerings and private prayers.[35] Hence it is equally possible that their presence in the temple was not directly related to the daily whole offering.[36]

While their prayers may not have been associated with the daily whole offering, it is unlikely that they would have been the only two

---

[32] *Parables*, 143, n. 2; see also Bruce, *Parabolic Teaching*, 315.

[33] Bailey (*Poet and Peasant*, 2.146) has the most extensive argument for this position. See also Scott, *Hear Then the Parable*, 94; Jeremias, *Parables*, 140; Donahue, *Gospel in Parable*, 189; Oesterley, *Gospel Parables*, 228; Jones, *Teaching*, 191; Jülicher, *Gleichnisreden Jesu*, 2.600. See Safrai and Stern, "The Temple," *Jewish People in the First Century*, 2.885.

[34] See Safrai and Stern, "The Temple," *Jewish People in the First Century*, 2.885. The ancient evidence usually cited for these specific times is Dan 6:10; Luke 1:10; Acts 2:15, *Prot. Jas.* II.3 (James, *Apocryphal New Testament*, 39); and *m. Tamid* (Danby, 582–89).

[35] See Safrai and Stern, "The Temple," *Jewish People in the First Century*, 2.876, 885, 889, and Manson, *Sayings*, 310.

[36] I find Bailey's argument that "the tax collector specifically mentions the *atonement* in his prayer" to be unconvincing (*Poet and Peasant*, 2.145 and 154).

people worshiping at that particular moment.[37] But the narrator does not bother to clarify this issue. Nor does the narrator specify where in the temple they were praying. If they went up to the temple at one of the times of the daily whole offering, they may have been conceived as praying in the court of the Israelites immediately before the sanctuary.[38] It seems more likely, however, that they are praying not during the time of the whole offering but during the more individualized worship surrounding the later incense offerings or the time when individual sacrifices were offered. People prayed both in and outside the temple on these occasions.[39]

Assuming that the toll collector was a Jew and not a Gentile "God fearer,"[40] he could have been in the court of the Israelites, had he rendered himself ritually clean; facilities for ritual cleansing were located in the temple area.[41] Hence, while it may be surprising to find a toll collector in the temple,[42] it does not violate the realism of the story. Exactly where he stood, however, the narrator does not tell the reader, except that it was "far away," a location corresponding to his sense of religious estrangement from God (18:13).

It has also been argued that the physical positioning of the body from which position the prayers of these two men are addressed to God (i.e., standing) was the usual attitude for formal prayer in Judaism.[43] But this does not seem to be the case; there were various body positions from which prayer was made: kneeling (1 Kgs 8:54; 18:42; 2 Chron 6:12–13; Ps 95:6; Dan 6:10; 10:9–11; Eph 3:14), stooping/bowing down (Gen 24:48; Exod 4:31; 1 Chron 29:20; Mic 6:6; 2 Chron 7:3; 29:29–30; Neh 8:6), standing (1 Sam 1:26; Neh 9:2; 12:40; Ps 135:2; Jer 28:5; Mark 11:25; Matt 6:5; *b. Ber.* 31a), and prostrating oneself (2 Sam 12:16–17, 20; Sir 50:16–19; *m. Tamid* 7.3). It would appear that the body attitude for public worship (and one would assume prayer) included some standing (Neh 9:2; 12:40; 1 Kgs 8:14, 22; Ps 135:2; Jer 28:5), some kneeling (1 Kgs 8:54), some bowing (1 Chron 29:20; Mic 6:6; 2 Chron 7:3; 29:29–30; Neh 8:6), and some

---

[37] See Safrai and Stern, "The Temple," *Jewish People in the First Century*, 2.885-90.

[38] See Safrai and Stern, "The Temple," *Jewish People in the First Century*, 2.867, 888; Sir 50:1–21.

[39] See Safrai and Stern, "The Temple," *Jewish People in the First Century*, 2.888–889. This is the situation in Luke 1:10, 21. Luke represents people praying *outside* the temple.

[40] Were he a "God fearer" he would have prayed in the court of the Gentiles; see Safrai and Stern, "The Temple," *Jewish People in the First Century*, 2.866.

[41] Safrai and Stern, "The Temple," *Jewish People in the First Century*, 2.876–78.

[42] See Michel, *TDNT* τελώνης, 8.101–3.

[43] Oesterley, *Gospel Parables*, 229 (but he notes there are other body attitudes: lying prostrate, kneeling, sitting); Donahue, *Gospel in Parable*, 188; Scott, *Hear Then the Parable*, 94; Plummer, *Luke*, 416; Bugge, *Haupt-Parabeln*, 476.

prostration (Sir 50:16–19; *m. Tamid*, 7.3). If the situation reflected in the story were in the context of formal public worship, the body stance of Pharisee and toll collector tells a reader very little about the stance of other worshipers (if such there were). Likewise if these are private prayers, a reader still learns nothing about the body attitude of other imagined worshipers, since the narrator does not mention them to the reader.

"Oh God I thank you that[44] *I am not as the rest of men."* How is one to understand his reference to the "rest of humanity"? Smith argues that "this does not mean that he believes the faithful to be so minished from among the children of men that there is not one Godly man left save himself, but he sees himself, as one of the small class of practicing Jews standing out against the dark background of the rest of mankind. . . . "[45] The expression λοιποί . . . ἀνθρώπων also appears in Rev 9:20 as an expression encompassing all human beings not belonging to the people of God who had survived the plagues. In this story of Pharisee and toll collector, at the very least, it appears to be a way of sorting out humankind into two classes: the Pharisees (or perhaps just this Pharisee?) and everyone else.

"robbers, reprobates, adulterers—or even as this toll collector." The first word the Pharisee uses to characterize "the rest of humanity" is ἅρπαγες, a word that communicates a sense of violence in the "violation" of community property laws. To some extent it is a violation of one's person rather than just the theft of an item or property.[46] Hence it might be translated "extortioners" (RSV).[47] Paul uses the term in two separate lists characterizing groups of people, classified by types of behavior, with whom Christians should not associate (1 Cor 5:9–13), and with whom they will not share the kingdom of God (1 Cor 6:9–11).[48] The parallels are quite appropriate since Paul, exactly like the Pharisee in Luke's story, is sorting out "true Christians" from the "rest of humanity." Paul's assumption, again like the Pharisee's, appears to be that the true believer is not characterized by these immoral acts that he lists. If such reflects their character, they are not really part of the community of faith (1 Cor 5:12–13; 6:11).

---

[44]Bailey (*Poet and Peasant*, 2.150) and Jones, (*Teaching*, 191) translate ὅτι as "because." Such a translation is specifically rejected by Jülicher, *Gleichnisreden Jesu*, 2.599.

[45]Smith, *Parables*, 177 and Holtzmann, *Synoptiker*, 397.

[46]See *TDNT* ἁρπάζω, 1.472; cf. Matt 7:15 RSV: "ravenous wolves."

[47]Goodspeed (greedy); TEV (greedy); NIV (robbers); CEV (greedy); Williams (robbers); NEB (greedy); NAB (grasping); Weymouth (thief).

[48]In the lists one can see that "greedy" is not really an adequate translation for ἅρπαγες since Paul also includes πλεονέκτης "greedy" (1 Cor 5:10; 6:10) as another similar negative character item. All of the items in the lists have to do with immoral behavior or idolatry.

For the second term (ἄδικοι) one must consider two different levels of meaning: Luke's Christian level and the level of the Jewish actor in the tale, the Pharisee. In early Christianity ἄδικος serves as a general classification for all those who do not belong to the community of faith (Matt 5:45; Acts 24:15; 1 Cor 6:1, 9; 1 Pet 3:18; 2 Pet 2:9).[49] But for the Pharisee in the story it would have had a different and very specific meaning. A person characterized as ἄδικος is described that way because he or she does not follow the teachings of Torah;[50] hence such a person is a "sinner," in the sense that he or she transgresses the Law (cf. Mark 2:15–17, contrasting Pharisees and toll collectors).

The third term, μοιχοί, describes persons who have violated a basic commandment and, therefore, the norm of the Jewish community: "You shall not commit adultery" (Exod 20:14; Deut 5:18).[51] It was a serious sin in both Judaism and early Christianity. Torah prescribed stoning as the usual punishment for those found to be guilty of adultery.[52] In early Christianity Paul says that adulterers (along with reprobates [ἄδικος] and robbers [ἄρπαγες]) will not inherit the kingdom of God (1 Cor 6:9–10).

The three terms appear to form an extreme caricature of every category of sin under Torah: robbery—violent theft of property; reprobate—impious as to religious obligations; adultery—sins of the flesh, i.e., immorality. The Decalogue can be broken down into religious obligations (Exod 20:3–11) and community obligations (Exod 20:12–17). The narrator of this story lists both of these basic types: religious (reprobate) and community (robbery, adultery), but apparently distinguishes between property violations and immorality.

It is not clear how the narrator intends the toll collector to be understood in connection to this list.[53] On the one hand, the toll collector may be offered in the Pharisee's prayer as an epitome of the religious/community sins that precede his mention; the toll collector, therefore, epitomizes for the Pharisee the condition of the rest of humanity. If this is the case, the Pharisee has probably interrupted what might have

---

[49] In Rom 3:5 and Heb 6:10 ἄδικος is not a trait of God. In Luke 16:10 it is contrasted with πιστός; and in Luke 16:11 it is contrasted with ἀληθινόν.

[50] For the man declared δίκαιος see Schrenk, *TDNT* 2.183–84 (Josephus); 185–86 (LXX); 186–87 (the righteous in the synagogue). See also Ps 118:121–128 (LXX); Ezek 33:15; in particular see Ezek 18:5-9. The term ἄδικος in the Septuagint is made more clear by other terms with which it is contested: dissolution (Wis 12:23); sinners (Job 31:3); the evil man (Ps 139:1); lawlessness (Job 5:22); ungodly (Job 16:12); the wicked (1 Esd 4:39); iniquity (Sir 5:8); the crafty (Ps 17:48); transgressors (Ezek 21:4–5 LXX). See also the discussion above on the Pharisee.

[51] Hauck, *TDNT* 4.730–32.

[52] Hauck, *TDNT* 4.730.

[53] Linnemann (*Parables*, 59) takes the statement "or even as this toll collector," as a narrator's aside used to link 18:10–12 and 13 together. Hence in her judgment it is not part of the Pharisee's prayer.

been a much longer "litany" of the sins of the "rest of humanity," and the list is probably to be thought not as exhaustive but rather as exemplary. On the other hand, the Pharisee may be contrasting the toll collector with the "rest of humanity," i.e., I am not like either this (robbers, reprobates, adulterers) or (ἤ) that (i.e., toll collectors). In this latter instance, the toll collector is probably to be thought of as either somewhat better[54] or considerably worse[55] than the "rest of human-kind."[56] If it is the former, the toll collector is intended to epitomize what the Pharisee considers the "rest of humanity" to be; if it is the latter, the toll collector is cast as a little better or worse than the worst.

Bailey has an extensive argument for the former: the toll collector is an example of what it means to be robber, reprobate, adulterer.[57] His argument turns on the fact that ἤ can join either contrasting or similar elements in a sentence. But perhaps it makes no difference after all and the narrator is simply obscure at this point. On the other hand, if the list of "sins" may itself be thought as representative of, and intended to evoke, the Decalogue, then it is possible that a contrast is intended, and hence the tax collector is to be thought of as the lowest of the low. This literary allusion, if such it is, threatens the realism of the story.

I fast twice each week;[58] *I tithe all things—as much as I acquire.* In the Hebrew scriptures the custom of fasting played a significant role in the religious life of ancient Israel. Fasting was a custom whereby one deprived oneself of food (Ps 109:24; 2 Sam 12:15–23; Esth 4:16) for a limited period of time,[59] humbled oneself, repented, prayed, and hoped that God would be moved by this display of repentance, self-humiliation, and physical self-deprivation so as to act differently toward the individual/nation.[60] According to Torah, only one fast day a year was required:

---

[54] Smith, *Parables,* 177: The toll collector may be guilty of being a robber and reprobate, but he "is nevertheless a Jew, and, as his presence in the temple shows, to some extent, observant of his religious duties." See also Manson, *Sayings,* 311.

[55] Robertson (*Word Pictures,* 2.233) includes the toll collector in the list as its "climax."

[56] Bailey (*Poet and Peasant,* 2.150–51) sees the problem and understands the toll collector to be included in the categories of robbers, reprobates, and adulterers as an example of what it means to be those things.

[57] Bailey, *Poet and Peasant,* 2.150–51.

[58] For σαββάτου as week, see Mark 16:9 (cf. 16:1) and 1 Cor 16:2; cf. Luke 17:4; Did. 8:1. See Safrai and Stern, *Jewish People in the First Century,* 2.816: Mondays and Thursdays were the preferred days for fasts. The Didache (8:1) urges that fasting be done (for Christians) on Wednesdays and Fridays, so Christians are not fasting when the "hypocrites" (Pharisees) fast.

[59] One-day fasts: Judg 20:26; 1 Sam 7:6; 2 Sam 1:12; Jer 36:6; Neh 9:1–3; Dan 6:18; three-day: Esth 4:16; seven-day: 1 Sam 31:13; 2 Sam 12:15–23.

[60] Isa 58:3–9; Judg 20:19–28; 1 Kgs 21:21–29; Ezra 8:21–23; Jer 14:12; Ps 69:10; Joel 2:12–14; Dan 9:3–20.

the Day of Atonement.[61] But other special days of fasting were observed through the years.[62] There is some evidence that during the New Testament period Monday and Thursday were preferred days for fasting. Some Pharisees fasted twice a week, on both days.[63] If that is the case, then the Pharisee in this story, while doing considerably more than Torah required, may not be unusual, since his piety was matched by others. In the New Testament the Pharisees are noted for their frequent fasts, but then, so also were John's disciples.[64] Later even early Christians adopted the practice of fasting twice a week.[65]

According to Torah, a tithe, or a tenth, of the produce of one's fields, seed, grain, wine, oil, and the firstborn of herds and flocks was required (Deut 14:22–23). If the distance was too great for an individual to bring in the tithe in commodities, then the produce/animals could be sold and the money brought to the harvest festival (Deut 14:24–26).[66] Torah did not require tithing on garden herbs, however.[67] The Pharisees in Jesus' day apparently, however, tithed even herbs (Matt 23:23), though it was not required for all herbs.[68] Later the general rule evolved that one must tithe "whatsoever is used for food, and is kept watch over and grows from the soil. . . . "[69]

One of the issues that arose on tithing was prompted by pious Jews acquiring items from the *'am ha-aretz*. Because these "people of the land" could not be trusted dutifully to pay their tithes, rules developed as to conditions when tithes must be paid, or not paid, on items procured from them or sold to them (see *m. Demai*).[70] Anyone wishing to be scrupulous in tithing "must give tithes from what he eats, and from what he sells and from what he buys [to sell again]" (*m. Demai*, 2.2; Sarason).

---

[61] Lev 16:29, 31; 23:27–29, 32; Num 29:7; cf. Acts 27:9. The language of Leviticus is not really clear. The Israelites were commanded to "afflict" (ענה) themselves. Apparently one is to understand "afflict" in the sense of "afflict themselves with fasting" (Ps 35:13; 69:10). Fasting was usually accompanied by sackcloth, ashes, and self-humiliation, weeping, mourning, ripping of garments, earth upon the head (Isa 58:5; Joel 1:13; 2:12–13; Jonah 3:5, 8; Zech 7:5; 2 Sam 1:11–12; 1 Kgs 21:27; Neh 9:1; Esth 4:1–3; Dan 9:3). See *m. Yoma* 8.1–6 and the note in Noth, *Leviticus*, 173–74.

[62] See Safrai and Stern, *Jewish People in the First Century*, 2.814–16. There was regularity for some of the fast days; cf., e.g., Zech 7:5; 8:19; Esth 10:29–32). See Strack-Billerbeck, 2.241–43.

[63] Safrai and Stern, *Jewish People in the First Century*, 2.816.

[64] Matt 9:14 = Mark 2:12 = Luke 5:33.

[65] Did. 8:1.

[66] Cf. also Deut 12:6–9; Lev 27:30–33; Neh 10:35–39; 2 Chron 31:3–12. See the extensive discussion in Oppenheimer, *'Am Ha-aretz*, 23–51 and 69–79.

[67] See the discussion in Fitzmyer, *Luke*, 2.948, 1187–88.

[68] Certain herbs were not subject to the tithe: *m. Šeb.* 9.1 (Danby).

[69] *m. Ma'aś.* 1.1 (Danby); see the discussion throughout *m. Ma'aśerot* and *m. Ma'aśer Šeni*.

[70] Sarason, *Law of Agriculture*, see esp. pp. 1–21.

Under certain conditions items procured in dealings with the '*am ha-aretz* were not subject to the tithe.[71] For example, certain figs and fruits may be exempted from the tithe on *Demai* produce (*m. Demai* 1.1); if one bought *Demai* produce "for sowing or for [feeding] cattle, or if it was meal for [preparing] hides or oil for the lamp, or oil for greasing utensils, it is exempt from the rules of *Demai* produce" (*m. Demai* 1.3; Sarason).[72]

The Pharisee in the story apparently does not concern himself with these exceptions and specifically claims that he pays tithes on *everything* he acquires (κτῶμαι)—with no exceptions. The deliberate choice of words used by the Pharisee in the story ("on all I acquire"), however, raises the question: was he intentionally excluding items he *sold* to the '*am ha-aretz*? There were rules on what items sold to the '*am ha-aretz* were to be tithed and what could be exempt from tithing.[73]

There were three tithes that had to be paid at different periods: first tithe, second tithe, poor man's tithe and offerings (cf. Tob 1:6–8), so it was usually 20% plus of one's produce in a given year[74] that was required to be contributed. The Pharisee apparently practiced a standard not unlike that later required of Christians by Did. 13.

Some have criticized the Pharisee's prayer (Luke 18:11b–12) as being self-righteous (in line with Luke's introduction to the story) and note that his prayer betrays his "arrogant comparison of himself with the toll collector."[75] Others, however, take the Pharisee's prayer to be a genuine prayer of gratitude.[76] One of the reasons for not regarding the Pharisee as an impious caricature is that close parallels in language and attitudes occur in other rabbinic prayers.[77]

I give thanks to Thee, O Lord my God, that thou has set my portion with those who sit in the Beth ha-Midrash [the house of study] and Thou hast not set my portion with those who sit in [street] corners; for I rise early and

---

[71] See *m. Demai*. See also Neusner, *Philosophical Mishnah*, 121–29.

[72] See *m. Ma'aśerot*; Sarason, *Law of Agriculture*, 11–12.

[73] See Sarason, *Law of Agriculture*, 13–14.

[74] See Safrai and Stern, *Jewish People in the First Century*, 2.818–28. The Pharisee in the story does not mention offerings, but one may assume that he was circumspect in that regard as well. See *m. Ned.* 3.4 (Danby): even toll collectors respected the wave offering. See also the brief discussion in Sarason, *Law of Agriculture*, 3–8.

[75] Fitzmyer, *Luke*, 2.1186, referring to Luke's overall description; see also Plummer, *Luke*, 417–18; Jeremias, *Parables*, 144; Oesterley, *Gospel Parables*, 229; Jones, *Teaching*, 194; Talbert, *Reading Luke*, 171; Bailey, *Poet and Peasant*, 2.143, 148, 149, 150.

[76] Linnemann, *Parables*, 50–60; Scott, *Hear Then the Parable*, 96, 97; Donahue, *Gospel in Parable*, 188–89; Manson, *Sayings*, 310; Smith, *Parables*, 177; Bruce, *Parabolic Teaching*, 315.

[77] Linnemann, *Parables*, 59; Jeremias, *Parables*, 144; Scott, *Hear Then the Parable*, 95; Donahue, *Gospel in Parable*, 188–89; Manson, *Sayings*, 311; Smith, *Parables*, 179; Klostermann-Gressmann, *Lukasevangelium*, 543; Bugge, *Haupt-Parabeln*, 477.

they rise early, but I rise early for words of Torah and they rise early for frivolous talk; I labour and they labour, but I labour and receive a reward and they labour and do not receive a reward; I run and they run, but I run to the life of the future world and they run to the pit of destruction.[78]

R. Judah (c. 150) said: one must utter three praises every day: Praised (be the Lord), that he did not make me a heathen; for "all the heathen are as nothing before him" (Isa 40:17); praised be he, that he did not make me a woman, for woman is not under obligation to fulfill the law; praised be he that he did not make me . . . an uneducated man; for the uneducated man is not cautious to avoid sins.[79]

One also finds similar language in a statement by Paul: Phil 3:4–6.

As a result of these parallels, the Pharisee appears to some less as a caricature of a self-righteous Pharisee, and hence his prayer is more easily seen as a genuine prayer of gratitude. The representation of the Pharisee is at least realistic *mimesis*, whether his attitude be judged self-righteous or not. But in principle, thanking God for the blessings of "salvation" is not automatically to be conceived as "self-righteousness," regardless of Luke's reading of the story. The Pharisee is cast as a man confident that his relationship to God is assured, for, like Paul, he has met the demands of Torah, going even beyond what was required.

And the toll collector, standing far away, would not even lift his eyes to heaven, but kept beating his breast. The narrator is also imprecise as to the location of the toll collector: he stands "far away." But is he "far away" from the Pharisee?[80] From others praying in the general vicinity?[81] From the altar? From the temple itself?[82] The fact is, it is unclear what the narrator is using as a point of reference for the measurement of distance.

It is unlikely, however, that the toll collector is standing "far away" from the Pharisee and other worshipers (if any). Μακρόθεν "far away" carries the idea of considerable distance. For example, after infiltrating Saul's encampment and taking his spear and water jug, David stood "far away" (μακρόθεν; 1 Sam 26:13 LXX) on the top of a nearby mountain, close enough to be heard but too far to be recognized (1 Sam 26:13–17). Yet in this story the toll collector is near enough for the Pharisee to recognize him as a toll collector and to refer to him as "this" (οὗτος) toll collector

---

[78] *b. Ber.* 28b; translation from Scott, *Hear Then the Parable*, 95.

[79] *t. Ber.* 7:18; as translated in Linnemann, *Parables*, 59.

[80] Plummer, *Luke*, 418; Robertson, *Word Pictures*, 233.

[81] Oesterley, *Gospel Parables*, 230; Donahue, *Gospel in Parable*, 189; Jones, *Teaching*, 194; Bailey, *Poet and Peasant*, 2.152–53; Jülicher, *Gleichnisreden Jesu*, 2.603; Bugge, *Haupt-Parabeln*, 478.

[82] Linnemann (*Parables*, 60), like the narrator in the story, is also imprecise: he stood in the most remote corner. Fitzmyer (*Luke*, 2.1188) says he stood within the court of Israel in the temple.

(i.e., over here, near) rather than "that" (ἐκεῖνος) toll collector (over there, i.e., afar). Compare Luke's conclusion to the story (18:14) for a similar use of "this" and "that."

Perhaps in the last analysis μακρόθεν is not only an obscure spatial reference, but it is as well the narrator's attempt at an existential reference in order to describe the toll collector's distance from God. In this word the narrator describes the toll collector as taking a position, as Linnemann says, in the most remote corner of the worship area, wherever that is. Hence μακρόθεν describes his religious situation (i.e., his relationship with God), as much as his physical location (i.e., position in the worship area).

The toll collector did not even lift up his eyes when he prayed, so consumed was he with the shame of his sins.[83] In the Hebrew tradition when one had properly fulfilled the obligations of Torah and humbled oneself, one worshiped by lifting one's face/head (Job 22:21–30; John 6:5; 11:41; 17:1; Luke 16:23; 12:28), hands (Lam 2:19; Ps 119:48; 134:2), and eyes (Ezek 18:6, 12, 15; Deut 4:19; Ps 123:1) to that One, or thing, worshiped. The lifting of countenance/eyes was not done haughtily (2 Kgs 19:22; Isa 37:23) but humbly. Hence the sinful person could not "face" the lord in worship (Job 11:13–15), because of shame and guilt (Ezra 9:5–6; 1 Enoch 13:5). For the "sinner" was aware that he did not have clean hands and that his heart was not pure (Ps 24:4–6). Hence the toll collector would have stood out from other worshipers in terms of physical location and stance. He is cast as a man who knew himself to stand condemned before God because his life did not meet the requirements of Torah. Distraught with his guilt and grieved over his situation, he kept on beating his breast, a physical expression of deep grief (Luke 23:48; *Joseph and Aseneth* 10; Jos. *Ant.* 7.252; Arr. *Anab.* 7.24.3).[84]

While saying, "Have mercy on me, sinner that I am."[85] The toll collector was so distraught with guilt and shame that he kept on repeating "have mercy on me,"[86] i.e., because of my sin—it is a petition for mercy and forgiveness. Yet the narrator does not show the toll collector as repenting, or even offering to make restitution, as was required by Torah. The toll collector Zacchaeus, for example, resolved that he would give half of his goods to the poor and compensate anyone he defrauded four times the defrauded amount (Luke 19:8), as Torah re-

---

[83] See Fitzmyer, *Luke*, 2.1188.

[84] Jeremias, *Parables*, 143, 161; Fitzmyer, *Luke*, 2.1188, and Scott, *Hear Then the Parable*, 96, n. 86.

[85] Translation following Miller, *Complete Gospels*, 158.

[86] See Fitzmyer, *Luke*, 2.1188; Hermann and Buchsel, *TDNT* ἱλάσκομαι, 3.301–18, esp. 314; and Robertson, *Word Pictures*, 2.233. The word is also used in inscriptions.

quired.[87] But not so this toll collector; apparently he wanted mercy without repentance or restitution.

HOW DOES THE STORY WORK?

The absence of a narrative resolution[88] makes it impossible to describe precisely how the story finally works out. One can describe, however, how what is left of the story is constructed. Period I is programmatic; there the narrator sets up the "plot" as a contrast between representatives of two social classes in first-century Judaism: a Pharisee and a toll collector. Periods II and III elaborate the contrast in terms of certain details the narrator finds significant: the fact that both are in the temple, the character of their prayers (gratitude for the Pharisee; petition for the toll collector), the character of their piety as regards Torah (the Pharisee exceeding Torah; the toll collector failing in Torah observance). Both men, however, come before the Lord, one thanking God for what he has already received; the other asking God for what seems impossible (under prevailing attitudes) as an admitted "sinner."[89]

The complication the narrator sets up by a deliberate choice of language in the contrast (viz., 18:11: σταθείς; 18:13: ἐστώς) is: which one of these two men is really able to "stand before the Lord"? The expression "stand before the Lord" is idiomatic in the Hebrew scriptures for that one the Lord finds "acceptable."[90] The classic expression is Psalm 24:3–6:

> Who shall ascend the hill of the Lord? And who shall stand in his holy place? He who has clean hands and a pure heart, who does not lift up his soul to what is false, and does not swear deceitfully. He will receive blessing from the Lord, and vindication from the God of his salvation. Such is the generation of those who seek him, who seek the face of the God of Jacob (RSV).

The Hebrew tradition taught that it was only the righteous man, i.e., the one who faithfully discharged the obligations of Torah, who would be able to "stand" before the Lord.[91] It was assumed that the murderer, adulterer (LXX: μοιχᾶσθε), thief (LXX: κλέπτετε), the one who swears falsely (LXX: ὀμνύετε ἐπ' ἀδίκῳ) and goes after other gods (Jer 7:8–11) would not be able to "stand" before God's perfect holiness.

---

[87] See Fitzmyer, *Luke*, 2.1225. The amount of restitution in Torah varied from simply replacing the item plus one-fifth of its value (Lev 6:1–5) to as much as five times its value (Exod 21:37; English 22:1).

[88] See the discussion above, and Downing, "Ambiguity," 98–99.

[89] It is not clear from the story that he is repentant, however.

[90] Hence those who "stand before the Lord" are those whom the Lord "accepts"; cf., e.g., Ps 5:5; 76:7; Gen 18:22; 19:27; Exod 3:5; Lev 9:5; Deut 4:10; 10:8; 18:5; 19:17; 1 Kgs 3:15; 17:1; 18:15; 2 Kgs 3:14; 5:16; 2 Chron 20:13; 29:11; Jer 15:19.

[91] Ps 1:1–6; Ezek 9:15; Neh 9:1–3.

Hence the complication set up for the reader in this story concerns whose prayer is heard. Who will in the last analysis be able to "stand" before the Lord in his holy temple—i.e., who will be found "acceptable" in the sight of God?

HOW MIGHT THE STORY HAVE BEEN HEARD IN THE CONTEXT OF ISRAEL'S FICTIONS ABOUT ITSELF?

In one sense the narrator has "set up" the reader for a particular judgment by how the complication has been cast.[92] The uniform witness of the Hebrew tradition is that Torah is God's gracious gift to human-kind.[93] God's approval and blessing can come only from faithfully observing Torah.[94] There is no criticism of Torah in the Hebrew tradition. Even prophetic criticism was brought against only those who imperfectly observed Torah and hence failed to live up to its spirit. They never criticized Torah as such, rather they agree that the Law is good.[95]

Hence there is only one evident way the Pharisee could have been viewed by the masses—he was the hero of the story. He had to be. Pharisees were, after all, the chief interpreters of Torah,[96] and this Pharisee describes himself not only as meeting, but as exceeding, its requirements. How could one even consider the toll collector in the same class as the Pharisee?[97] By the definition of the Hebrew scriptures the Pharisee is the man zealous for Torah and hence the man who wins the favor of God. The toll collector, however, must be rejected, for he has failed to observe the Torah. Such men God will not accept, rather they fall under God's judgment.[98] In the popular mentality of the day, therefore, to put a Pharisee and toll collector side by side in the temple "standing before the Lord" in prayer and then to ask which one does the

---

[92] Christian readers tend to hear the story differently. In the light of a post-Pauline situation the Torah is part of the problem rather than the solution; cf. e.g., Galatians 3 and 4.

[93] See Ps 1:1–2; 19:7–10; 119:9–16, 33–35, 44–48, 54–56, 92–93, 97–99, 103–5, 162–68; Deut 30:11–14; *m. 'Abot* 1.2; See Heinisch-Heidt, *Theology*, 16–17.

[94] Heinisch-Heidt, *Theology*, 17–18.

[95] Isa 1:10–17: Isaiah criticizes the cultus; he calls for social justice and even describes his call as the "teaching (i.e., Torah) of our God" (1:10): 2:3; 5:24; 24:5; 30:9; 42:4; 51:4–7; Jer 2:8; 8:8; 6:19; 9:13; 16:11; 18:18; 26:4; 31:34; 32:23; 44:10; 44:23; Lam 2:9; Ezek 7:26; 22:26; 43:11–12; 44:5, 24; Dan 9:10–13; Hos 4:6; 8:1, 12; Amos 2:4; Mic 4:2; Hab 1:4; Zeph 3:4; Hag 2:11; Zech 7:12; Mal 2:1–9; 4:4. Cf. also Gutbrod, *TDNT* νόμος, 4.1039–40: not even Paul criticized Torah as such; see pp. 1071–78. In the Hebrew tradition there is even an intensification of Torah, in the sense that it should become an existential reality within the consciousness of God's people: Ps 37:31; 40:8; 78:8; 119:2, 7, 11; Isa 51:7; Jer 31:31–34.

[96] See above; Linnemann (*Parables*, 58–60) is of the same opinion.

[97] See the discussion above.

[98] Lev 26; Deut 28; *m. 'Abot* 2.6: "The *'am ha-aretz* cannot be pious."

Lord hear would have been humorous.[99] The answer is the Pharisee—of course! Surely such a man must have the ear of the Lord! The toll collector, on the other hand, stands already condemned.[100] Given a general attitude toward the Pharisees as the chief interpreters of the Law, and the general attitude toward the Law as God's gracious gift to Israel, there could have been no other conclusion. Heard in this way the story affirms Torah and the Pharisee's understanding of what it means to be a religious man.

But were one so inclined, it is possible to read selected passages in the Hebrew scriptures in a more radical way, one that does not see God's mercy as conditioned upon the fulfilling of the requirements of Torah. One first-century Pharisee that did in fact read the Scriptures this way was Saul/Paul who argued in his letters to the Galatians and Romans that Abraham was declared righteous by God on the basis of his faith (Gal 3:6–7; Rom 4:1–25; Gen 15:1–6; 17:1–10; 22:17–18), rather than on the basis of his Torah observance, for the Law had not yet been given (Gal 3:10–18; Deut 27:26; Hab 2:4; Lev 18:15). He further understood Ps 32:1–2 (Rom 4:6–8), and Isa 28:16 (Rom 9:32–33; 10:11) as promising forgiveness to "sinners" apart from judicial observance of Torah.[101]

Once one begins to read texts in the way that Paul did, there are other passages in the Hebrew scriptures where one so inclined might "discover" this same sense of the unmerited favor of God toward sinners. For example:[102]

> If his children forsake my law
>> and do not walk according to my ordinances,
> if they violate my statutes
>> and do not keep my commandments,
> then I will punish their transgression with the rod
> and their iniquity with scourges;
> but I will not remove from him my steadfast love,
>> or be false to my faithfulness.
> I will not violate my covenant,
> or alter the word that went forth from my lips
>> (Ps 89:30–34 RSV; see also Ps. 51:1–4, 9, 17; 130:1–8).

---

[99] Cf. Ps 52:1–7. On the prayer of the "wicked" man being accepted see also Ps 109:7; Prov 21:27; 28:9.

[100] See, e.g., Ps 37:28; 145:20; 146:8–9; Prov 15:8–9.

[101] See also, e.g., Rom 9:14–18 (Exod 9:16; 33:19); Matt 9:10–13 (Hos 6:6). Compare also Luke's combination of Isa 61:1–2 (cf. Ps 146:7–9), God's blessing on the widow of Zarephath (as non-Jew; 1 Kgs 17:1, 8–16), and God's healing of the Syrian general Naaman (2 Kgs 5:1–14) in Luke 4:16–30.

[102] Compare also: Ps 9:10; 25:16–18; 66:13–20; 78:35–39; 85:1–7; 86:15–17; 94:18; 103:6–14; 106:40–46; 109:21–25; 123; 145:8–9; Hos 2:19–3:1; 14:1–4; Isa 55:6–7; Jer 3:12–14; Jonah 4:1–2 (of the Ninevites); Ezek 20:44; Gen 18:22–26 (the Lord is willing to spare the wicked for the sake for the righteous).

Passages such as these complicate the solution to the narrator's comparison in the story. From this perspective the toll collector apparently has some basis "in scripture" for his unqualified petition to God. Under the influence of such passages, thoughtful readers face a dilemma: is there more merit in humility and appealing to God for mercy (toll collector), or in formal obedience and thankfulness to Yahweh (the Pharisee)? In fact, later rabbis debated this precise issue: does the penitent rank over the average righteous person—the average righteous person being one who had an equal balance of Torah observance and violation, and the penitent being ungodly, but at least penitent.[103]

From just such a perspective hearers of this story in the first century might have sensed that the story was more complex than it seemed on the surface. From this perspective the story ultimately raises the twin questions: "What does it mean to be religious, and how is the character of God to be understood?" In any case, from such a perspective this comparison of two men praying in the temple provokes readers to question the norm of what it means to be religious, and hence the story challenges the absolute rule of Torah in Jewish life. The story, however, in its abbreviated form offers no obvious leads as to the unraveling of what would have been a very provocative first-century complication.

ANOTHER READING OF THE STORY

The story compares two men, each flawed in different ways. The Pharisee is neither so perfect nor so flawed as his interpreters have cast him.[104] In the first place he claims to exceed Torah's fasting requirements, and so he does, but he is actually doing no more than many (or most?) other first-century Pharisees did in that regard.[105] So while he clearly surpasses the *'am ha-aretz* as to fasting, he is not really unique as a first-century Pharisee. So one may regard him, at the very least, as representative of first-century Pharisaism as to the issue of fasting.

With regard to his tithing, however, he may well have exceeded the norm, if we may take his confession seriously. He claims that he is careful to tithe *everything* he gets—even to the extent of tithing items that were apparently exempt from tithing rules. In this sense he may well surpass other Pharisees, since the rabbis did not require tithing of every garden herb; and some *Demai* items under certain conditions were likewise exempt from tithing when disposed of.[106] But this Pharisee pays tithes

---

[103]See Schrenk, *TDNT* δίκαιος, 2.186; *b. Ber.* 34b: Strack-Billerbeck, 1.603.

[104]Downing ("Ambiguity," 98–99) is of the same opinion.

[105]Paul, for example, claimed to have achieved totally acceptable righteousness under the law (Phil 2:6).

[106]See the discussion above, and Sarason, *Law of Agriculture*, 11–14.

on *everything* he *acquires*, and presumably that includes items normally excluded, as well as any items secured from the *'am ha-aretz* that were excluded from tithing as *Demai* produce. Hence this Pharisee would have been recognized at the least as a typical representative of the Pharisaism of his day as to tithing, and perhaps as a bit more zealous.

His self-congratulation for not being a violator of Torah (robber, reprobate, adulterer) should be read as genuine gratitude to God that he has been true to Torah, and hence he is a fit subject for God's approval. Being thereby excluded from God's judgment, he is a "righteous" man. This attitude is not unusual, as other similar prayers in the rabbinic tradition show. One could easily find similar prayers in the Christian tradition. Critics usually overlook the fact that his gratitude ("I thank you that . . . ") is directed to God; hence in the Pharisee's mind, gratitude is directed to God who has provided Torah and created the condition whereby he could be saved from a sinner's life and ultimate fate. In short, he gives God the credit for what he has become ("I thank you that I am not . . . "). His litany of personal religious practices (18:12), while not formally controlled by ὅτι in 18:11, is best understood as comparison with the toll collector (i.e., this toll collector does not observe Torah's requirements for fasting and tithing, but I do), and therefore the reference to the toll collector should also be heard as gratitude, rather than "self-righteous" congratulations.

The reference to the toll collector (18:11) is generally read as a snide deprecating statement, and in a sense it is. The toll collector (at least according to the Pharisee)[107] is a robber, reprobate, adulterer (or worse).[108] While he may comply with Torah obligations to some degree,[109] his activities have little merit; his positive behavior in no way corresponds to the Pharisee's zealous observation of Torah. Yet the Pharisee is more reserved in his criticism of the toll collector than he might have been. For example, in Ps 119:53 "hot indignation" seizes the psalmist when he "thinks of the wicked"; and again (Ps 119:158) the psalmist "looks at the wicked with disgust." Another psalm (Ps 109:2–19) dramatically prays for the cursing of the wicked, and Jeremiah (18:23) even prayed that God not forgive the sin of the wicked! The Pharisee in this story is not so extreme as all this. For the Pharisee the toll collector represents all the Pharisee is grateful to God that he is not.

---

[107]The reader must remember that this is only the Pharisee's opinion. Is his opinion based on certain knowledge of this particular toll collector's behavior, or is it the narrator's stereotyping based on the ways that Pharisees generally understood all toll collectors? It is clearly the latter.

[108]See the discussion above.

[109]It is possible that the toll collector was observant of Torah in some respects. Even the rabbis acknowledged that the *'am ha-aretz* observed some Torah practice, and hence were to some extent pious; see Sarason, *Law of Agriculture*, 1–2.

The real ethical problem with the Pharisee is his universal condemnation of the "rest of humanity" (18:11), whom he characterizes as "robbers, reprobates, adulterers," i.e., the worst kind of sinners. It is not that they simply failed in certain ritual acts, but that they are apparently guilty of the worst kinds of deliberate sins. In short, people who do not observe Torah, according to this Pharisee, are involved in immorality, violent criminal acts, and total impiety. This condemning and intolerant attitude of *everyone* unlike himself reflects a lack of compassion for others, a lack of personal insight into his own failures, and a lack of discernment as to what real wickedness means. In his judgment anyone that was not as observant of Torah as he, was totally corrupt. The criterion he applied was: "observe the Torah like me or you are robber, reprobate, adulterer." There was no middle ground. This meant to the Pharisee that all non-Pharisees fell under the condemnation of God as the worst imaginable sinners, because they were not Torah observant. He overlooks the possibility that someone might have lived a "decent" life, although that person may not have been ritually correct.

He felt that Torah observance alone brought him God's approval and total absolution. Everyone else stood under God's judgment as the worst kind of sinner. His view of God was quite simplistic: God rewarded those who observed Torah and completely rejected those who did not.

He failed to consider that God may have been somewhat more complex, and he did not see that even Torah, which he so scrupulously observed, allowed a dimension to God's character that he had apparently missed in its study: i.e., God's love and mercy.[110] Completely apart from Torah observance, God had forgiven the Ninevites on the basis of their repentance (i.e., they believed Jonah's preaching: Jonah 3:1–4:2; cf. Luke 11:30–32 = Matt 12:29–41). God showed mercy even to the Canaanites (Wis 12:3–11; Exod 23:29–30). God extended blessing to the Phoenician widow of Zarephath (1 Kgs 17:8–16), even though there were many starving widows in Israel (Luke 4:25–26); God granted healing to a leprous Syrian General (2 Kgs 5:1–14), though there were many lepers in Israel (Luke 4:27). God's mercy was, in short, regarded as inexhaustible (Lam 3:22; Ps 100:5; cf. Ps 57:10). While his judgment was extended on the sinner's descendants to the third and fourth generation, his love was extended to the thousandth (Exod 20:5–6; cf. Wis 11:24; Sir 18:13). God valued even those who were deliberately wicked (Isa 44:6–8).

The Pharisee's lack of tolerance and his judgmental attitude do not make his character particularly sympathetic. But the Pharisee's biggest mistake was thinking that his view of God accurately reflected God's character. For the Pharisee in the story, God was completely predictable, and the Pharisee had him "boxed in": God had to regard the Pharisee as

---

[110] See the discussion above, and Heinisch-Heidt, *Theology*, 91–101.

righteous, since the Pharisee had done everything that Torah required. But along the way the Pharisee had overlooked another facet of God's character, his mercy, his love (Mic 6:6–8). The Pharisee was a "righteous" man (i.e., meticulously religious), but not a particularly "good" man (i.e., compassionate) (Rom 5:7).[111] He had simply overlooked the dry observation of Koheleth: "Surely there is not a righteous man on earth who does good and never sins" (Eccl. 7:20).[112]

But then neither is the toll collector an ideal hero. Because of the nature of the contrast, it would seem that the narrator is trafficking in the stereotypical poor reputation of the toll collector. He is described as a humble penitent seeking God's mercy, one must imagine, on account of his sins (18:13) and, by virtue of his comparison with the Pharisee, because of his failure to observe Torah (Luke 18:11–12). So he throws himself on God's mercy, hoping, the reader must assume, that God will, in accordance with his bounteous and benevolent mercy, blot out his transgressions, forgive his sins (Ps 5:1–2), and no longer remember these transgressions against him (Ps 25:6–7).

Surprisingly[113] the toll collector does not confess any sins at all (Ps 32:3–5; Prov 28:13) as required by Torah (Num 5:7; Exod 26:40–42); he does not repent (i.e., express any regret for his sins: Ps 38:18; Job 34:32), offer to make restitution as Torah required (Exod 22:1; Lev 6:4–7; Num 5:5–7; cf. Luke 19:8–9), or resolve to observe Torah in the future (Prov 28:13; Ps 51:10–13; 119:76–78). In short, he apparently simply casts himself on God's mercy with no stated intention of changing his profession or his life. This view of God seems to assume that God will forgive him with nothing further required on his part. The toll collector's prayer for mercy seems to assume that one may rely solely on the mercy of God for forgiveness. He seems to think that God did not require that he live morally or religiously (in the sense of observing Torah); in short, the toll collector does not seem to assume that his profession as toll collector has

---

[111] See Lightfoot, *Notes on the Epistles*, 286–87. According to the examples collected by Lightfoot, the distinction between one "who is scrupulously just" (righteous) and one "who is prepared to make allowances" (good) was widely recognized in the ancient world.

[112] It would appear that in the Hebrew scriptures righteous persons are also expected to reflect goodness, kindness, and generosity as a part of their characters: Ps 112:5; 125:3–5; Prov 12:2; 13:22; Eccl 9:1–2.

[113] I say "surprisingly" because the narrator has already used the Pharisee to caricature the toll collector as a deliberate sinner, guilty of terrible crimes and sins. In the light of this characterization one simply expects the toll collector to confess his sins and repent—particularly in a prayer asking for God's mercy. The fact that there is no repentance by the toll collector raises questions about the Pharisee's thoroughly negative perception of him (a reader is not, after all, told how he knows all this information), and about the extent of the toll collector's honesty and sincerity, as well.

any bearing on whether or not God will forgive him. So it appears that
the toll collector, like the Pharisee, has God "boxed in." He expects God
to act graciously toward him on the basis of his contrite attitude
alone—since God is a God of mercy.

So a dilemma faces a reader: which of these two flawed heroes is,
in the final analysis, acceptable to God? Whom will God accept? Who in
the final analysis will "stand before the Lord"? Will it be a man who
comes to God on his own merits, having fulfilled the Law perfectly, but
lacking a sense of grace, tolerance, or awareness of the imperfections of
his own humanity—the Pharisee? Or will it be a man who all too clearly
knows the imperfections of his own humanity, and who by his own
admission has not fulfilled (nor apparently does he intend to meet) his
obligations to God and community to live morally and religiously by
conventional community standards—the toll collector?

The question is not a modern imposition on the story. It is as old
as the Hebrew tradition itself. For example, the Deuteronomist argues
that the way to win God's approval is by the minute ritual observance
of Torah (Deut 28:1, 15; cf. Gal 3:10), while the prophets stressed ethical
social action and "internalization" of the Torah (Jer 31:33). Job is totally
perplexed over what God expected of him, since so far as he knew he had
lived a "blameless" life (Job 27:1–12; cf. 1:12). And Koheleth (aside from
the pious postscript 12:13–14) regarded everything as "emptiness," even
the distinction between the righteous and the wicked (9:1–6).

In the New Testament Paul argues that God wants faith and that
human beings can do nothing on their own merit to affect God's
judgment (Rom 4:1–25), but James takes a different approach and argues
that God's acceptance is conditional on certain righteous behaviors (Jas
2:8–26). Both positions are argued from the same passages(!) in Torah
(Gen 22:1–14; Gen 15:6). Jesus is depicted in the New Testament as
violating ritual purity laws in associating and eating with toll collectors
and sinners without even requiring that they first repent (Mark 2:15–16
= Matt 9:10–11 = Luke 5:29–30; Matt 11:19 = Luke 7:34; Matt 21:31; Luke
15:1–2), while Peter on the other hand is depicted as refusing to associate
with other Christians because they were not Torah observant (Gal
2:11–14). The question is also, however, a modern one that divides
Christians and Jews; Christians and Christians, Jews and Jews; not to
mention Christianity and Judaism from other world religions.

For people with a religious "bent," the question, "what does God
expect of me?"/"whom does God accept?" may not be just a modern
question, but rather it may be *the* modern existential question, since it
has the potential of affecting every area of human life.[114] How do I, as a

---

[114]I recognize that people "without a religious bent" may read the story
differently.

modern human being, a reader with a religious "bent," relate to the story? Do I, like the Pharisee, divide humanity into two groups; those like me, "the good guys," and everybody else, "them"? Do I make negative value judgments on "them," simply because "they" are not like me? And ultimately do I decide that God can accept "them" only if they become like me? Taken to its logical conclusion such an approach leads inevitably to intolerance and persecution of minority religious views.

Or at the other end of the spectrum, do I assume that all God requires is a contrite heart and remorseful spirit? Are confession, repentance, and restitution really necessary for me to win God's favor? Of course, this raises the question: if forgiveness is there merely for the asking, why do we need religion, and why should any religious person live morally and observe any ritual act at all?

As one modern reader, I find myself in the middle. I can relate completely neither to the Pharisee nor to the toll collector. I see some value in each of them, and I can recognize what I judge to be the potential danger in each of them, should either one be given free reign to shape the world according to his own views. One results in a world dominated by a religious attitude intolerant of diversity (Pharisee); the other in a world without religion (toll collector).

The narrator, however, never answers the question, "whom does God accept?" The reader is instead left with a frightening glimpse into two possible alternatives, neither of which the narrator affirms or criticizes, and neither of which is completely satisfying. And I leave the story wondering where I should situate myself on the spectrum between these two men. The only guidance the story gives are the two extremes, and I am left to resolve the tension as best I can. The narrator is silent, and I am left to ponder what I am coming to suspect may be a humorous burlesque, a caricature of two men (a caricature representing two extreme views in first-century Judaism), each presuming to know how God responds. And on the basis of the caricature I know they are both wrong and that neither man really has God "boxed in," though they may think so. So the narrator pokes fun at the "righteousness" of the Pharisee and the "nonrepentance" and lack of restitution of the toll collector, but it is not harmless fun. The humor has an edge to it, as readers may well find bits of the Pharisee and the toll collector in their own religious experience.

Who is it that this narrator *might* affirm as that one able to "stand before the Lord"—who is that one whom God accepts? Perhaps it is, in the final analysis, anyone who is able to recognize the absurdity in their own cherished religious convictions that presume on the divine prerogative. This is something that neither the Pharisee nor the toll collector in the story was able to do.

Appendix A
Thomas and the Synoptics: Aiming at a Consensus[1]

THE VALUE OF THE *GOSPEL OF THOMAS* AS A WITNESS TO THE JESUS tradition is perhaps the most serious issue currently facing New Testament scholarship. If Thomas is not dependent upon the Synoptic Gospels, it will, at least in part, provide access to a stage in the development of the Jesus traditions prior to the standardization of the tradition by the synoptic kerygma. In this appendix, I assess the evidence for Thomas's independence of the Synoptic Gospels.

OPTIONS FOR EXPLAINING THE RELATIONSHIP BETWEEN THOMAS AND THE SYNOPTICS

While the exact nature of the relationship between the *Gospel of Thomas* and the Synoptic Gospels has not been satisfactorily resolved for all, there does seem to be a consensus that much more than a superficial relationship exists among them. Rather, the extensive parallels demonstrate that a substantive relationship exists between Thomas and the Synoptic Gospels. Previous discussions of the close parallels have assumed two possible explanations:[2] (1) Thomas used the Synoptic Gospels as written sources;[3] (2) Thomas drew upon parallel sources independent of the Synoptics.[4] Both of these options assume that Thomas and the

---

[1] An earlier version of this chapter originally appeared in *Second Century* 7 (1, 1989–90) 39–56.

[2] Montefiore and Turner, *Thomas and the Evangelists*, 40–42. See the excellent survey of the literature by Fallon and Cameron, "The Gospel of Thomas," 4213–24.

[3] Cf. Koester for scholars who hold this position: "GNOMAI DIAPHOROI," 130, n. 45. To this list should be added Schoedel, "Parables." See also n. 4 below.

[4] Koester, "GNOMAI DIAPHOROI," n. 50, and Dehandschutter, "La Parabole du Trésor caché," 201, n. 7. Note, however, that Perrin (*Rediscovering*, 254) cites

Synoptic Gospels share, at least in their parallel material, a common tradition but disagree as to the way they are related.

To a certain extent resolution of the issue has centered on the question, which came first, Thomas or the Synoptics? However, a third, and a more fruitful, approach to Thomas has emerged; it proceeds on the assumption that Thomas, *at least in part*, contains early Christian tradition transmitted by Thomas independently of the Synoptic Gospels. Indeed, it has long been recognized by some that Thomas does reflect, at least in part, tradition independent of the Synoptic Gospels.[5] Such an approach to Thomas does not polarize itself on the issue of date or priority/dependency in discussing Thomas and the synoptics.

For example, Koester's study of the canonical and rejected gospel literature argues that the rejected literature, including Thomas, should be brought into "their rightful place in the history of [the gospel] genre."[6] And Robinson's study of the genre of Q, bringing Thomas into the discussion of the trajectory of early Christian literature, does precisely that.[7] Perkins's study of the pronouncement stories and kingdom sayings in the *Gospel of Thomas* shows how Thomas may be brought into the form-critical discussion of the gospels.[8] Jeremias[9] and Perrin[10] long ago recognized the value of Thomas in reconstructing the history of the Jesus tradition and found Thomas to contain original sayings of Jesus not present in the canonical tradition. Crossan, suspending for the purposes of his study a genealogical (i.e., historical-chronological) approach to the study of the parables, prefers the *Gospel of Thomas* form of the parable of the Great Fish to its parallel in Matthew because it (along with the

---

Gärtner, Schrage, and Turner as regarding Thomas in part dependent on and in part independent of the Synoptic Gospels. The independence of Thomas from the canonical gospels has been argued by Cameron ("Parable and Interpretation") and assumed by King ("Kingdom in the Gospel of Thomas"), Stroker ("Extracanonical Parables"), and Davies ("Christology and Protology"). See also the recent book by Patterson, *Gospel of Thomas*. Patterson argues that Thomas is independent of the Synoptics.

[5] See Grant, Freedman, Schoedel, *Secret Sayings*, 89; Gärtner, *Theology of the Gospel of Thomas*, 55–65; Montefiore and Turner, *Thomas and the Evangelists*, 31, 39. Davies, *Gospel of Thomas*, treats the text as an early Christian document (mid-first century CE) that is completely independent of the Synoptic Gospels (p. 145). Robinson has shown that the late date usually given to *Thomas* is an "unexamined assumption," and that Thomas, potentially at least, reflects a tradition independent of the synoptics ("Bridging the Gulf").

[6] Koester, "Apocryphal and Canonical Gospels," 130; "Extracanonical Sayings of the Lord."

[7] Robinson, "LOGOI SOPHON." See Koester's positive assessment of Robinson's use of Thomas as representing a "basic shift" in the discussion: "One Jesus and Four Primitive Gospels," 166. See also Robinson, "Bridging the Gulf," and his paper, "Study of the Historical Jesus."

[8] Perkins, "Pronouncement Stories"; "Kingdom Sayings."

[9] Jeremias, *Unknown Sayings*.

[10] Perrin, *Rediscovering*, 44, 89–90, 126–27.

parables of the Pearl and the Hid Treasure in Matthew) exhibits a structural paradigm for all the parables of Jesus.[11] The treatment of the *Gospel of Thomas* reflected in these studies brings Thomas into the discussion of early Christian literature in a more creative and responsible way than the polarizing approach offered initially by Montefiore and Turner in 1962.

In principle, of course, there is no compelling reason why all, or even any, sayings of Jesus reported in noncanonical literature having close—or even verbal—parallels with sayings in the synoptic tradition must derive from the Synoptic Gospels. The oral tradition remained a competitor to the written gospels well into the second century CE,[12] and such oral reports would have been equally accessible to the author of Thomas, even assuming a mid-second-century CE date for Thomas. And if one accepts, as I do, the priority of Mark in the synoptic relationship, then at least one other written source (i.e., Q) existed closely parallel to the Synoptic Gospels. And the sayings with synoptic parallels in Thomas could have been derived from this (hypothetical) text as well.[13] It seems almost self-evident that the canonical gospels were not the only sources for synopticlike sayings available to late first- and early second-century writers. If so, then whence do the special Matthean and Lukan materials originate? It is also clear that Q and Mark overlap at least in the John-the-Baptist traditions. Thus, whereas Matthew and Luke usually used Mark and supplemented with the Q sayings tradition, they occasionally used Q material instead of Mark. For example, they used the fuller form of the Q temptation narrative (Matt 4:1–11 = Luke 4:1–13) rather than Mark's shorter version (Mark 1:12–13). This may also be true of Thomas and the synoptics; Thomas may use the synoptic tradition for some sayings, but elsewhere draw upon other similar, yet independent, sources for other sayings.

THOMAS DRAWS ON NONSYNOPTIC "CHRISTIAN" LOGIA

If, however, one is convinced that all the synoptic parallels in Thomas derive from the Synoptic Gospels because Thomas is *de facto* a second-century CE text, it must still be allowed that Thomas used at least one additional source, for this is the only way to explain sayings

---

[11] Crossan, *In Parables*, 33–36. But see n. 18 below.
[12] See, e.g., Grant, Freedman, Schoedel, *Secret Sayings* 22–29. As important a churchman as Papias, bishop of Hierapolis (ca. 130 CE), collected sayings of Jesus from the oral tradition as late as the middle of the second century CE; see Lake, *Eusebius*, 1.291–99 (Eusebius, *Hist. Eccl.* 3.39, 1–17).
[13] Koester, "One Jesus and Four Primitive Gospels," 186; cf. 166–87.

attributed to Jesus plainly not derived from the Synoptic Gospels. Higgins provided such a list of nongnostic ("Christian") sayings in 1960, including logia 28, 39, 77b (Coptic page 46,26–28), 82, 97, 98, 102.[14] He regards these sayings as having a probable claim to being original sayings of Jesus. His evaluation of the character of Thomas is balanced and reasonable and deserves repeating:

> There is no inherent improbability in the view that they [i.e., the sayings listed above] are remnants of a very early tradition, for there is no doubt that the Gospel of Thomas is made up of a variety of elements of varying age and provenance. Considerable caution, however, must accompany the fascinating and not unimportant quest for possible remnants of reliable tradition of the words of Jesus in the Gospel of Thomas. On the other hand, excessive scepticism is hardly justified. Further study may perhaps lead to a more positive estimate of other sayings in this curious document.[15]

Since it is unlikely that Thomas created everything but the sayings paralleled in the canonical gospels, the use of (an)other source(s) by Thomas must be allowed. And if Thomas did use the Synoptic Gospels for some sayings, then that very use of multiple sources (i.e., Matthew, Mark, and Luke) sets the precedent and increases the probability that Thomas used other early Christian sources as well.

During the years since the article by Higgins, further study has indeed led to a more positive estimate of certain sayings in Thomas. For example, different scholars have argued independently that four of Thomas's synopticlike sayings are not derived from the canonical gospels but are original sayings of Jesus: the parable of the Killer (log. 98:49, 15–20);[16] the parable of the Empty Jar (log. 97:49,7–15);[17] the parable of a Net Thrown into the Sea (log. 8:33,28–34,3),[18] and the saying on the Fire (log. 82:47,17–19).[19] The criteria used to validate such sayings in noncanonical literature as traditional sayings of Jesus are the same as those applied to sayings in the canonical literature. They are attributed

---

[14] Higgins, "Non-Gnostic Sayings," 301–6.

[15] Higgins, "Non-Gnostic Sayings," 306.

[16] Hunzinger, "Unbekannte Gleichnisse Jesu"; Perrin, *Rediscovering*, 126 and Jeremias, *Unknown Sayings*, 13. But compare the mixed judgment of the Jesus Seminar: Funk, Scott, Butts, *Parables of Jesus*, 23.

[17] See the positive judgment of the Jesus Seminar: Funk, Scott, and Butts, *Parables of Jesus*, 21.

[18] Hunzinger, "Unbekannte Gleichnisse Jesu," 217–19; Perrin, *Rediscovering*, 89 and Jeremias, *Unknown Sayings*, 88–89. I regard both Matthew's Net Thrown into the Sea (Matt 13:47–48) and Thomas's Great Fish parable as versions of the traditional story in Aesop's Fables: "the Fishermen and the Fish." See Perry, *Babrius and Phaedrus*, 8–11. See also the discussion in Cameron, "Parable and Interpretation," 24–30. For a different concept of the origin of the parable see Scott, *Hear Then the Parable*, 313–16.

[19] Jeremias, *Unknown Sayings*, 66–73 and Perrin, *Rediscovering*, 44–45.

to Jesus, hence they deserve to be taken as seriously as those attributed
to Jesus in the canonical literature. They reflect a semitic environment
and lack characteristic early Christian ecclesiastical or characteristic
first-century Palestinian Jewish emphasis. And, most importantly, they
contain emphases typical of Jesus' sayings from the canonical literature
that have on similar grounds previously been determined to originate
with Jesus. A strong case has been made for the traditional character of
these sayings and for their possible origin with Jesus. The burden of proof
now shifts to those who deny their traditional character and the probable
origin of the sayings with Jesus. If these synopticlike sayings are traditional and likely original sayings of Jesus, as they appear to be, then they
clearly are not the creations of Thomas but have been appropriated from
(a) separate traditional source(s), since they are not found in the canonical New Testament.

One also finds in Thomas a proverbial saying that was apparently
well known in the second century CE, namely, the Dog in the Manger
(log. 102:50,2–5). This saying simply does not originate with the *Gospel
of Thomas* or with the canonical New Testament; rather, it probably stems
from Aesop's Fables. It is significant for the tradition history of Thomas
in that it proves beyond any doubt that Thomas did not create all of
his nonsynoptic material but in at least one completely unambiguous
and verifiable instance drew on another traditional source. And since
Thomas did draw from sources other than the Synoptics, then it follows
that Thomas's sayings with synoptic parallels might also have derived
from another source.[20]

Some additional support for the nonsynoptic origin, and traditional
character, of the saying on the Fire (log. 82:47,17–19: "Jesus said: the one
near to me is near to the fire, and the one far from me is far from the
Kingdom") occurs in the writings of Origen (3d cent. CE). Origen quotes
the saying, with some misgivings, as a genuine saying of Jesus.[21] He
does not, however, specify where he got the saying. Indeed, he states
that he does not know its source, even though he clearly knows the
Gospel of Thomas, which he rejects as apocryphal.[22] Grant, Freedman,
and Schoedel find an easy solution for this interesting contradiction, i.e.,

---

[20] Grant, Freedman, Schoedel, *Secret Sayings*, 184 and Higgins, "Non-Gnostic
Sayings," 306. It has even been suggested that the logion could have been used by
Jesus and would have therefore become a logion of Jesus when he "appropriated" it:
Bauer, "Echte Jesusworte," 76–77. See fable 228 in the edition by C. Halm, *fabulae
Aesopicae collectae*, 111. Contrary to Grant, Freedman, Schoedel (*Secret Sayings*, 188),
the parable of the Hid Treasure in Thomas does not appear to be a variant form of a
fable known from Aesop (Halm, *fabulae Aesopicae collectae*, 49[98a and b]).

[21] Origen, *hom. in Jer.* 20,3 (Migne, *PG*, 13, 531D–32A). Patterson (*Gospel of
Thomas*, 89) is convinced by Bauer's argument ("Echte Jesusworte," 122–24) that the
saying is a version of a Hellenistic proverb.

[22] Origen, *hom. in Luc*, 1 on Luke 2. (Rauer, *Origenes Werke*, 5).

the fact that Origen knows Thomas but does not cite it as the source
for the saying:

> Origen's hesitation can be readily explained. In a homily on Luke he
> vigorously condemned the Gospel of Thomas as apocryphal; he could hardly
> say in another homily that he was relying on what he had read in it.[23]

Hence, they conclude that Origen used the *Gospel of Thomas* as a source
for the saying!

This line of reasoning, however, leaves many questions unan-
swered. Since Origen rejects the *Gospel of Thomas* as apocryphal, why
would he feel constrained to validate as genuine one saying from a
document that he rejects? And if for some reason he did feel so constrained, why would he pick just that particular saying from Thomas,
unless, of course, he had some strong reason for doing so? Why would
he even have affirmed as genuine any saying at all from Thomas,
considering how he felt about the document, unless he knew that the
saying he was quoting was independent of Thomas? And, in fact, this
appears to be his evaluation, since he cites it as a traditional saying!
These kinds of questions push one to conclude that Origen likely knew
Thomas log. 82 from a source other than Thomas. He would scarcely
have cited Thomas as the source for the saying, even though he knew
Thomas also reported it (assuming, of course, the saying was found in
the version of Thomas that he knew). Such an act would have validated
a book that he rejected as apocryphal.

More probably—or plausibly—Origen knew log. 82 from a source
other than the *Gospel of Thomas*. The independent circulation of this
saying apart from Thomas further strengthens the probability that the
"author" of Thomas did not create the saying. It is simply an instance of
a rejected gospel preserving traditional sayings of Jesus just as canonical
texts other than the gospels preserve sayings attributed to Jesus that are
unknown to the canonical gospels, such as Acts 20:35 and 1 Cor 9:14.

Logion 17 (36,5–9: "Jesus said: I will give you what eye has not seen,
nor ear heard, nor hand touched, nor entered into the heart of man") is
quite clearly a verifiable instance of Thomas preserving traditional
material drawn from a source independent of the canonical gospels. Paul
quotes the logion in 1 Cor 2:9 with the introductory formula associated
with quotations from the Hebrew scriptures, i.e., "it is written," γέ-
γραπται. The difficulty is that Paul is not quoting from the Hebrew
scriptures.[24] Indeed, Paul's quotation of the logion is its earliest extant

---

[23] Grant, Freedman, Schoedel, *Secret Sayings*, 88 and 174–75; cf. Higgins,
"Non-Gnostic Sayings," 303.

[24] Some do take 1 Cor 2:9 as a combination of Isa 64:4; 65:16–17; but there is
no evidence that it is Paul who originally made the combination, if indeed 1 Cor 2:9
is such a combination.

attestation.[25] Origen (3d cent. CE), who knew the *Gospel of Thomas*, asserted that the saying was not known in any apocryphal writing except in the (lost) *Apocryphon of Elijah*.[26] The saying, however, does also appear in a number of ancient texts: for example, in a Coptic (Bohairic) version of the *Testament of Jacob*;[27] in Pseudo-Philo's *Liber antiquitatum biblicarum* (26,13), a late first-century CE Jewish writing, as a statement made by God;[28] in the second-century CE *Martyrdom of Peter* 10 (= *Acts of Peter* 39); in the *Pseudo-Titus Epistle* as a saying on the lips of Jesus;[29] in the second/third-century CE *Acts of Thomas* 36 as a saying of the apostle Thomas; in the Nag Hammadi Tractate, *Prayer of the Apostle Paul*, 1,A,26–29; and in the fourth-century CE *Apostolic Constitutions* 7.32.[30] It even appears in a fragment of a Manichaean text.[31] Thomas could have known the saying either in a non-Christian form (i.e., Paul's source—represented by the *Apocryphon of Elijah*, Pseudo-Philo, or the non-Christianized[?] version of the *Testament of Jacob*) or from a Christian version (represented by 1 Corinthians, *Prayer of the Apostle Paul*, *Acts of Thomas*, *Martyrdom of Peter* = *Acts of Peter*).

Thomas may have derived the saying from 1 Corinthians and then simply transferred it to the lips of Jesus. This seems highly unlikely, however, since Thomas reflects no clear awareness of 1 Corinthians, and it is not convincing to argue that Thomas selected only this one saying out of Paul's letters. It is equally conceivable that Thomas knew the logion in its non-Christian form and made it into a saying of Jesus. What is more plausible, however, is that Thomas drew from a Christian tradition that had already identified the logion as a saying originating with Jesus. The widespread and diverse use of the logion in antiquity confirms its traditional character and shows that the saying most probably did not originate with the *Gospel of Thomas*. It is a traditional saying that Thomas has appropriated from sources other than the canonical New Testament.

---

[25] Conzelmann, *1 Corinthians*, 63, n. 70.

[26] Origen, *comm. in Matt.* 5,29 on Matt 27:9. The *Apocryphon of Elijah* is not to be equated with the *Apocalypse of Elijah*: Charlesworth, *Pseudepigrapha*, 96. The saying does, however, appear in Latin and Slavonic versions of the *Ascension of Isaiah*; see Charles, *Ascension of Isaiah*, 81 and 137.

[27] See Box, *Testament of Abraham*, 83. Von Nordheim ("Zitat des Paulus in 1 Kor 2,9," 118–20) suggests that the *Testament of Jacob* rather than Origen's *Apocryphon of Elijah* may have been the source for Paul's quotation in 1 Cor 2:9. This suggestion is rejected by Sparks ("1 Kor 2⁹"). For a complete listing of all the parallels see Stone and Strugnell, *Books of Elijah*, 41–73.

[28] James, *Philo*, 29–33, 157.

[29] Hennecke-Schneemelcher, *New Testament Apocrypha*, 2.320–21.

[30] ANF 7.471. See Resch (*Agrapha*, 110) for the text. Resch argues that Paul and Clement/*Apostolic Constitutions* have each drawn the saying from the same source.

[31] Hennecke-Schneemelcher, *New Testament Apocrypha*, 1.300; 2.144.

These are only two examples of a number of Thomas sayings that have parallels either as quotations, near quotations, allusions, or echoes in other ancient sources.[32] In most instances the position of Thomas in the sequence of the tradition-history of these logia is unclear. For example, Clement of Alexandria (*Strom.* 2.9.45; cf. 5.14.96)[33] attributes to the (early second-century CE[?]) *Gospel of the Hebrews* a saying that is paralleled in log. 2 of the *Gospel of Thomas* ("Jesus said: 'Let him who seeks not cease seeking until he finds, and when he finds, he will be troubled, and when he has been troubled, he will marvel and he will reign over the all' ": Guillaumont, *Thomas*, 3). Clement's two reports of the saying, the version in the Greek fragments of the *Gospel of Thomas* (P. Oxy. 654) and its Coptic form in the Coptic *Gospel of Thomas*,[34] are not identical. Their differences complicate the determination of priority between the *Gospel of the Hebrews* and Thomas, or perhaps one should say between their traditions. Actually the different versions of the saying suggest a rather lengthy tradition-history for Thomas as well as for the saying itself.

In the case just cited there is simply not enough evidence to argue for the priority of either text in the tradition. Thomas may have appropriated the logion from the *Gospel of the Hebrews,* or the *Gospel of the Hebrews* may have appropriated the logion from Thomas, or both independently may have drawn the logion from a common source. Any one of these options seems possible. However, when one considers that a number of Thomas's sayings are paralleled in ancient literature other than the canonical gospels, and that when used in other ancient literature these sayings are used independently of their context in Thomas (i.e., logia that precede and follow in Thomas are not used or alluded to), one is impressed that Thomas is not the original source to which all of these noncanonical sayings are to be traced. Rather, Thomas appears to be merely a transmitter of traditional material.

THOMAS DRAWS ON NON-CHRISTIAN "GNOSTIC" LOGIA

A rather large number of non-Christian, apparently "gnostic," logia appear in the *Gospel of Thomas* with no parallels in the Synoptic Gospels: logia 7, 15, 18, 29, 42, 49, 59, 60, 70, 74, 80, 83–85, 87, 110, 112, 114.[35] Did Thomas create all these sayings, or could they not be, at least in part,

---

[32] For partial lists of these parallels see Hennecke-Schneemelcher, *New Testament Apocrypha*, 1.297–307; Montefiore and Turner, *Thomas and the Evangelists*, 14–16.

[33] Hennecke-Schneemelcher, *New Testament Apocrypha*, 1.297.

[34] Fitzmyer, "Oxyrhynchus *Logoi*," 516–18.

[35] I have listed in this section only those sayings for which no parallel was found in the listing of parallels in the Guillaumont edition. This was verified in the critical edition of Layton, *NHC II*, 1:46–48.

traditional? The very diversity of literary forms represented in this group suggests that they are traditional: Blessings and curses—7, 49, 87; pronouncement stories—18, 60, 114; legal sayings—70, 110; exhortations—15, 42, 59; woes—112; aphorisms—29, 74, 80, 83, 84, 85. Indeed, one of the criteria for determining originality among the canonical sayings of Jesus (the criterion of multiple attestation) assumes that the likelihood of originality is increased where a similar motif is found in various literary forms,[36] since it is less likely that similar motifs are artificially produced in diverse literary forms. In this case the diversity of traditional literary forms in Thomas suggests that the sayings are found in the tradition rather than being created ad hoc by the "author" of the *Gospel of Thomas*.

IS THERE A SEMITIC BACKGROUND TO CERTAIN SAYINGS?

Guillaumont has discussed the evidence for a semitic background to the *Gospel of Thomas*.[37] Of course, he is not the first to make such claims for the tradition history of the *Gospel of Thomas*. Others have also noticed the presence of semiticisms in the text.[38] His approach is in part responsive to the criticisms of Dehandschutter,[39] who argues that alleged semiticisms in Thomas can be explained either as simple biblicisms or as being too superficial to be convincing. Guillaumont appears to agree with Dehandschutter's criticism of many of the semiticisms that have been identified in Thomas. He lists a number of examples of this kind of "Septuagint language": for example, "the man old in his days" (log. 4), "that which is before your face" (log. 5), "prostrate yourselves upon your face" (log. 15). Other Hebrew or Aramaic expressions could easily have derived from New Testament Greek: for example, the use of the word "sky" as a circumlocution for the divine name (log. 6; cf. Luke 15:18), the use of "son of man" as a designation for human being (log. 28). Such incidents of semiticisms in the Coptic text, in Guillaumont's view, do not demonstrate that Thomas has been directly influenced by Hebrew or Aramaic. Other seeming semiticisms, he argues, can be attributed to the conventions of the Coptic language: for example, in logion 61 the Coptic text reads: ⲠⲞⲨⲀ ⲚⲀⲘⲞⲨ ⲠⲞⲨⲀ ⲚⲀⲰⲚⲒ̄ ("the one will die, the one

---

[36] Perrin (*Rediscovering*, 45–47) is skeptical that this criterion may be used to establish specific *sayings* as original, although it "does have a usefulness in establishing the authenticity of motifs." However compare Stein, "Criteria for Authenticity." See also the discussion by Boring, "Criteria of Authenticity," 28–29. Crossan has argued for a new prime criterion in historical Jesus research: "Divine Immediacy."

[37] Guillaumont, "Sémitismes."

[38] Guillaumont, "Sémitismes," 190, n. 1.

[39] Dehandschutter, "La Parabole du Trésor caché," 207.

will live"). One might be led to understand this construction as a literal translation of the Aramaic (חַד ... וְחַד) or the Hebrew (אֶחָד ... וְאֶחָד) but in translating the Greek of Luke 17:34 ὁ εἷς ... ὁ ἕτερος the Coptic translator of the Sahidic New Testament employs an expression similar to Thomas log. 61 ΟΥⲀ ... ΟΥⲀ leading one to the conclusion that the expression derives from Coptic rather than from a semitic prototype.[40]

Guillaumont argues, however, that once one has discounted biblicisms and superficial semiticisms,[41] there remain a rather large number of semiticisms that in his judgment do seem to point to a semitic tradition level anterior to Thomas, particularly ones that have an affinity with the Syriac versions of the NT.[42] For example, log. 3 in the Coptic *Gospel of Thomas* reads ΝΕΤⲤⲰⲔ ϨⲎⲦⲐⲎⲨⲦⲚ ("Those who go before [or precede] you") whereas the Greek fragments (P. Oxy. 654) read οἱ ἕλκοντες ἡμᾶς ("those who draw [or drag] us"). Guillaumont argues that one can derive a satisfactory sense from the text only if one assumes that the Coptic ⲤⲰⲔ and Greek ἕλκειν are translations of the Aramaic נְגַד, "to lead."

In another example, he notes that the strange expression in log. 80, "to find the body," makes perfectly good sense if one assumes that it is a poor Coptic translation of an Aramaic original that read מְצָא, which often meant "to find" (the usual Hebrew sense) but frequently in Aramaic it meant "to have power" or "to master." If this explanation is correct, he argues, the *Vorlage* probably originally read "to master the body."

Some of the semiticisms noted by Guillaumont even seem to call into question the existence of a Greek *Vorlage* for the Coptic *Gospel of Thomas*. For example, in log. 13 one reads ΟΥⲔⲰϨⲦ ... ⲚⲤⲢⲰϨⲔ ("a fire ... will consume you") but in Coptic ⲔⲰϨⲦ is masculine gender and the pronominal prefix to the verb should have read ⲚϥⲢⲰϨⲔ. In the semitic languages (Hebrew, Aramaic, Syriac, and Arabic), on the other hand, the words for "fire" are regularly feminine. Hence, it appears to Guillaumont that in this instance a distracted translator has preserved a vestige of the semitic original.

Finally, he points to some linguistic peculiarities that appear to derive from Syriac influence. In the Coptic *Gospel of Thomas* log. 25 reads, "love your brother as your *soul*," while the parallel passage in the Greek Synoptic Gospels reads, "love your neighbor as *yourself*" (Matt 19:19; 22:39; Mark 12:31; Luke 10:27). But the reading "as your soul" is precisely what one finds for this saying in the Syriac versions of the New Testament and in the Peshitta of Lev 19:18 (the source in the Hebrew scriptures of the New Testament passages just cited above), although the Septuagint and the Hebrew read "as yourself."

---

[40] Guillaumont, "Sémitismes," 190–91.
[41] Guillaumont, "Sémitismes," 190–93.
[42] Guillaumont, "Sémitismes," 194–96.

Among those that Guillaumont lists as incontestably Syriacisms he discusses log. 14 where Jesus says, "if you give alms you will do evil to your spirits [πνεῦμα]." The sense of the text, he argues, suggests that the expression means "you will harm yourselves." It is characteristic of semitic languages in general to use a number of full expressions to express the reflexive (hence, "you will do harm to your soul" = "you will harm yourselves"). The most common of these expressions for the reflexive in semitic languages in general is the word "soul." The use of the word "spirit," however, is more peculiar to the Syriac. Based on his identification of semiticisms in Thomas, Guillaumont finds two semitic tradition levels prior to the present Coptic text of the *Gospel of Thomas*: A Hebrew Jewish-Aramaic (or Aramaic Jewish-Christian) level, barely identifiable in the Coptic text, and another level, more recent and hence more clearly discernible, that has fused with a Syriac stage of the tradition.[43]

Establishing the tradition history of Thomas is, of course, much more complicated than simply positing an Aramaic Jewish-Christian sublevel that finally emerges in a Coptic version. We also know of Greek versions[44] of Thomas whose differences from the Coptic text suggest that the Coptic version is not directly dependent on any of the Greek versions represented by the extant Greek fragments.[45] Hence one's explanation for the tradition history of Thomas must also include the Greek versions. It is entirely possible that there is an Aramaic substratum to Thomas. Although one might well be skeptical that an earlier semitic stage of the tradition would be discernible in Coptic after having passed through a translation into Greek and then into Coptic, all of the semiticisms that Guillaumont cites are at least possible when one compares the extant parallels in the Greek fragments.[46]

One would not have to conclude, however, that there is a semitic substratum to the compiled text of the *Gospel of Thomas* as it now exists, even though some sayings might reflect semitic characteristics. Thomas is probably a collection of collections and therefore Thomas constitutes in its Coptic version different tradition levels. Hence some sayings may be early (e.g., semitic) while others may be later (e.g., Greek and Coptic). But if there is a semitic substratum for at least *some* of the sayings in Thomas (as there appears to be), then one must keep an open mind with

---

[43] Guillaumont, "Sémitismes," 201.

[44] See Fitzmyer, "Oxyrhynchus *Logoi*," 510.

[45] See Fitzmyer's discussion ("The Oxyrhynchus *Logoi*," 501) for the differences between the sayings of the Greek fragments and the Coptic forms of the logia. Fitzmyer concludes that the Greek fragments and the Coptic text represent different versions of the *Gospel of Thomas* (pp. 552–53).

[46] Compare the following logia in Guillaumont (G) and Fitzmyer (F): 3 (G–p. 194; F–p. 520), 30 (G–pp. 194–95; F–p. 539), 33 (G–p. 195; F–p. 543), 36 (G–p. 200; F–pp. 544–45), 39 (G–p. 199; F–p. 551).

respect to the original tradition character of all the logia in Thomas. If Thomas betrays a semitic *Vorlage* at certain points, then it is entirely possible that Thomas has drawn on (an) independent source(s) reflecting semitic characteristics in other cases too, even though there no longer remains evidence of semitic character to a given logion in its Coptic version. Hence one must not exclude as late those sayings that do not reflect a semitic character.

DOUBLETS IN THOMAS

Finally the doublets in Thomas argue that its author used source materials other than the Synoptic Gospels. While some of the examples of doublets cited in the literature may be questionable, doublets do exist in the case of logia 3 and 113; 5 and 6 (in lines 33,21–23); 6 and 14; 48 and 106; 55 and 101; 56, 80, and 111b; 87 and 112.[47] Such data argue that it is more probable that a compiler did not recognize these materials as variant forms of the same saying than it is that an author/redactor duplicated in only a few select instances for some particular (although unclear) reason the same saying with variations. One can observe the same sort of phenomena in the Synoptic Gospels. See for example, Matt 12:38–39 = Matt 16:1–4; Matt 5:31–32 = Matt 19:9, but compare Luke 9:2–5 = Luke 10:4–11 where it does seem to be a conscious duplication.

CONCLUDING ARGUMENT

If Thomas did use the Synoptic Gospels as sources, it is clear that the compiler also drew on *at least* one other source. Whether it was oral or written is not certain, though it appears to have had a heterodox character. Hence, it probably included material acceptable to the authors of the Synoptic Gospels, as well as material unacceptable to those authors. Without limiting Thomas to only one source, this source (or sources) probably represented a type of heterodox Christianity whose theological character would have been similar to Thomas itself.

This is not an unusual phenomenon in the Nag Hammadi corpus. The *Apocryphon of James* (I,2) has also used a source or sources reflecting characteristics similar to the heterodox source(s) used by the *Gospel of Thomas*. Without question the author of the *Apocryphon of James* knew by name a collection of Jesus' parables, most of which may well be the parables preserved in the canonical tradition (e.g., I,2:7,1–8,10), but James also cites additional noncanonical parables, some of which appear to be on a tradition level with similar parables in the canonical tradi-

---

[47] Cf. Montefiore and Turner, *Thomas and the Evangelists*, 24.

tion.[48] And the *Dialogue of the Savior* (III,5), likewise, is comprised of traditional sayings of Jesus that were originally independent of their present literary setting.[49] Hence, one should not be surprised that Thomas is a composite text reflecting traditions of varying age.

Those who argue that Thomas depends only on the Synoptic Gospels must be prepared to give a plausible answer to the following question: On what basis do they decide whether a synopticlike saying derives from the Synoptic Gospels or from one of Thomas's other (non-canonical) sources? Or to put the question more precisely, how can they be certain that a given saying has *not* been derived from one of Thomas's other sources? Even if it could be convincingly shown that particular sayings in Thomas derive from the Synoptic Gospels, that does not prove that all such synopticlike material in the *Gospel of Thomas* comes from the Synoptic Gospels. Indeed, the lack of a synoptic sequence reflected in the order of the sayings in the *Gospel of Thomas* and the lack of any clear plan of organization to the sequence of sayings in Thomas, except primitive catch-word and motif associations,[50] tend to associate Thomas

---

[48] Hedrick, "Kingdom Sayings." See also the recent study by Cameron (*Sayings Traditions*), who finds that the text is composed out of originally discrete (traditional) sayings (pp. 125–31).

[49] See Koester and Pagels, "Introduction," 6–9.

[50] Dehandschutter, "Parabole de la Perle," 243–44 and n. 5 on 244. Dehandschutter explains the lack of a synoptic order to the sayings in Thomas as being due to the fact that Thomas has seen fit to "break up" the synoptic order so as to insert the synoptic material into a "particular thematic context." In support (in n. 5, p. 244) he indicates some of the (different) thematic arrangements that have been proposed for the organization of the *Gospel of Thomas*. (To this should also be added Davies, *Gospel of Thomas*, 49–155.) In Dehandschutter's view one can explain Thomas's break up of the couplet parables of a Merchant in Search of Pearls and the Hid Treasure on the basis of these themes. The "thematic" context weakens, he feels, the argument that Thomas as a "simple collection" of logia appears to reflect a more primitive stage of the tradition than does Matthew's "theological" arrangement of ch. 13.

That one is able to find in some instances thematic collections of logia in Thomas is clear, but caution must be exercised in the search for "themes" connecting the logia. It is an extremely subjective enterprise, and the interpreter does run the risk of self-deception as to the presence of a particular "theme" uniting several logia. "The broader the theme, the less convincing the thesis," is the safest rule to apply. The most convincing thematic arrangement would be one derived from concrete statements of the individual logia that are equally discernible on the various hermeneutical levels of the *Gospel of Thomas*. In any case, however, the fact that the parables of a Merchant in Search of Pearls and the Hid Treasure are separated into different thematic collections in the *Gospel of Thomas* does not automatically support the historical priority of their setting in Matthew. One could argue that the thematic arrangements of Thomas are prior to Thomas. Indeed, Thomas probably does represent a collection of collections of logia. In that case Thomas's collections would reflect the kind of source(s) from which Matthew drew to expand Mark and in that sense the Thomas arrangement of the parables is still logically prior to Matthew.

with a more primitive pre-synoptic level of the tradition like that represented, for example, by Q.

If one projects a scenario by which the author of the *Gospel of Thomas* used only the Synoptic Gospels as sources, what one is forced to assume is less than convincing. One is asked to believe that the author of Thomas has broken up a collection of parables like that in Matthew chapter 13[51] and has scattered them indiscriminately throughout the text of Thomas where they appear linked, if at all, with preceding and following sayings on the basis of catch-words and motifs (Matthew's order for the Thomas material = 9, 57, 20, 96, 109, 76, 8). This is, of course, not impossible. But why would Thomas break up this collection of parables and assemble them in smaller collections elsewhere scattered through the text (8–9, 20–21, 63–65, 96–98, 107, 109)? One is asked to believe that Thomas separates the synoptic sayings and scatters them throughout the text in what appears to be an indiscriminate way, or in a way that betrays no immediately clear and commonly agreed upon principle of arrangement for their new settings. Elsewhere, however, Thomas does transmit separately material that does seem to form well-integrated units in its synoptic setting, e.g., Luke 12:13–21 = *Gos. Thom.* II,2:46,1–6;44,2–10. But in cases such as these Thomas's sayings collection appears to reflect the original undifferentiated sayings tradition out of which the canonical evangelists constructed their narrative gospels, rather than the vestiges of the deconstructed canonical gospels.

If one assumes that the Synoptic Gospels are the only sources for Thomas, one must conclude that the author of Thomas has gone to a great deal of trouble to produce a text that lacks any identifiable principle of organization convincing to all. One must also account for a certain naiveté on the part of Thomas and a lack of theological sensitivity to synoptic sayings that correspond to the speculative tradition out of which "Thomas" has assembled the gospel. For example, Thomas lacks Matt 11:25–27 but uses Matt 11:29 (log. 90), and Thomas even lacks the Markan theory of the parables (Mark 4:10–13), even though both would fit the supposed theological perspective of Thomas quite well.[52] Indeed, it would have required a great deal of skill, expertise, and time to create the impression that the *Gospel of Thomas* was not derived from the Synoptic Gospels and that it represents instead a more primitive level of the tradition, since that is precisely the impression that an initial reading of the document produces. Any argument for the dependence of Thomas on the Synoptic Gospels must provide a plausible reason for this apparent attempt (under this thesis) to conceal the fact that the material was derived from the Synoptic Gospels.

---

[51] Cf., e.g., Garitte and Cerfaux, "Paraboles du royaume," 314.

[52] Montefiore and Turner, *Thomas and the Evangelists*, 73.

Recent work on the redaction-criticism of Matthew 13 argues that the design of the chapter is due to the author of the Gospel of Matthew;[53] that is to say, the author of the Gospel of Matthew used special traditional material to revise and expand Mark 4.[54] Very little is known about Matthew's special source(s). It is not known, for example, whether Matthew drew the material from oral tradition, or if the author had access to an early written parables collection. The latter is certainly possible, since it is known that such parables collections did exist.[55] That Matthew used some such parables source seems more probable than does the assumption that Matthew created all these special materials ad hoc. It appears then that Matthew 13 is not the only source from which Thomas could have drawn its parables. Indeed, the unsystematic arrangement in Thomas of those parables that Thomas shares with Matthew and Mark gives the impression that the *Gospel of Thomas* derived its parables from the oral tradition, or perhaps from Matthew's source or sources, rather than from Matthew itself.[56]

To demonstrate conclusively the influence of the Synoptic Gospels upon the *Gospel of Thomas* one will have to demonstrate that Thomas incorporated framework materials from the Synoptics or has clearly preserved distinctive synoptic redactional traits.[57] The framework and redactional traits constitute the evangelist's personal signature. And even if that could be shown conclusively in *some* instances, it would not thereby invalidate all of the material contained in Thomas as a later, revised version of the synoptic tradition, since it appears that Thomas

---

[53] Kingsbury, *Matthew 13*, esp. 12. See also Hedrick, "Treasure Parable."

[54] Kingsbury, *Matthew 13*, 12–16.

[55] Cf., e.g., Mark 4; *Ap. Jas.* I,1:8,4–10; see also Dehandschutter, "Parabole de la Perle," 243, n. 3.

[56] The fact that neither Matthew nor Thomas has transmitted the parable of a Sprouting Seed that was available to Matthew in Mark 4:26–29 is interesting. Kingsbury (*Matthew 13*, 64–65) argues that it is because it did not fit Matthew's theology; therefore, Matthew simply substituted in its place the Parable of Good Seed and Weeds (Matt 13:24–30). If that is the case one might argue that Thomas has omitted it since it was not in Thomas's source (i.e., in Matt 13). It is possible, however, that Thomas did not know the parable as parable but that it appeared in Thomas's source as logion; cf. *Gospel of Thomas* II,2:37,15–19 to Mark 4:26–29. It is possible that Mark has converted a logion into a parable and Thomas preserves the form of the tradition as it appeared in their (common) source. But see the observation in Funk, Scott, Butts, *Parables of Jesus*, 48.

[57] See Schrage, *Verhältnis*, 5. Schrage points out one instance in the *Gospel of Thomas* of synoptic framework material being preserved: log. 79—"A woman from the multitude said to him"—Luke 11:27. See also Dehandschutter ("Parabole de la Perle," 244, n. 4) who finds vestiges of narrative framework (somewhat less convincing in my opinion) in logia 22, 60, and 100. Compare Wilson, "Review of Schrage," particularly p. 120. Schrage's position that the *Gospel of Thomas* is dependent on the Coptic New Testament has been shown to be untenable by Patterson (*Gospel of Thomas*).

used sources other than just the Synoptic Gospels. Indeed, the conclusion that Thomas used the Synoptics must be hammered out in each individual instance of common material. Nor can it be assumed that synopticlike sayings capable of a "gnostic" interpretation must be understood exclusively in that way. Such an assumption proceeds on the basis that "gnostically inclined" writers (as many consider the author of Thomas to be) always corrupt the tradition whereas canonical writers always report it accurately. Indeed, by comparing the canonical Synoptic Gospels and the Gospel of John we know that the canonical writers freely adjust the tradition to suit their own theological bias. And at the same time, even the *Gospel of Thomas* reports sayings that are substantially the same as the canonical materials.[58]

I am convinced that our present Coptic version of the *Gospel of Thomas* was not originally dependent on the Synoptic Gospels. The evidence, in my opinion, leads inevitably to that conclusion. But at this stage of research, opinions have tended to polarize the discussion. What I have suggested is that we drop advocacy for dependence/independence of the compiled text of Thomas as it now exists in its Coptic and fragmentary Greek versions, and focus attention on individual logia. What is clear and beyond question is that if Thomas did use the Synoptic Gospels as sources, it also drew on an independent synopticlike source or sources. And it is that conclusion that forces one initially to treat every logion in the *Gospel of Thomas* as if it reflected an independent sayings tradition, since one cannot know a priori from which source the saying derives. Similarity does not mean dependency; therefore, each saying must be treated as independent tradition until each saying individually can be shown to be dependent on the Synoptic Gospels.

Hence it appears that Thomas must be brought into the discussion of the Jesus tradition on a level with the Synoptic Gospels. We must begin synoptic criticism with the assumption that Thomas in principle preserves a valuable independent witness to the early Jesus tradition. Thomas must be treated like Matthew and Luke. These gospels drew on Mark and Q as sources, but also they transmitted valuable material from their independent sources. In short, the discovery of the *Gospel of Thomas* has added new and exciting dimensions to the complexities presented by the similarity/diversity among the Synoptic Gospels. Since it shares a tradition common to the Synoptics, Thomas must become a part of that discussion[59] and of the attempt to recover the earlier levels of the Jesus tradition.[60]

---

[58] Higgins, "Non-Gnostic Sayings," 295–301.

[59] See a similar statement by Davies, "The Fourth Synoptic Gospel," 6–7, 12–14.

[60] Such a discussion would include also Papyrus Egerton 2, the Secret Gospel of Mark, and other early Christian literature. For the most recent collection of the pertinent texts see Miller, *Complete Gospels*.

Appendix B
The Stories Attributed to Jesus

Jeremias	Crossan Title/#	"L"	"M"	"Q"	Thomas Log/Pg & Ln	(Luke)	(Matt)	Mark	Source/Title
The Sower	The Sower #1				#9 34,3-13	8:5-8a	13:3b-8	4:3-8	A Sower
Patient Husbandman	The Harvest Time #16				#21d 37,15-18			4:26-29	A Sprouting Seed
The Mustard Seed	The Mustard Seed #3				#20 36,28-33	13:19	13:31b-32	4:31-32	A Mustard Seed
Wicked Husbandman	The Tenants #11				#65 45,1-15	20:9b-16a	21:33b-40	12:1b-9	A Vineyard
Return of Unclean Spirit	Ø			M 12:43-45a L 11:24-26a					The Unclean Spirit
The Doorkeeper	The Returning Master #17					12:36-38		13:34	A Man Going on a Journey
Going before the Judge	Ø			M 5:25-26 L 12:58-59					On Settling out of Court
Ø	Ø			M 7:24b-27 L 6:48-49					Two Houses
The Tares among the Wheat	The Planted Weeds #2	13:24b-30			#57 42,34-43,7				Good Seed and Weeds
The Leaven	The Leaven #4			M 13:33b L 13:21	#96 49,2-5				The Leaven
The Treasure	The Treasure #5	13:44			#109 50,31-51,3				The Hid Treasure
The Pearl	The Pearl #6	13:45			#76 46,14-18				Merchant in Search of Pearls
The Seine Net	The Fishnet #7	13:47-48			#8 33,29-34,2				A Net Thrown into the Sea
The Lost Sheep	The Lost Sheep #8			M 18:12-13 L 15:4-6	#107 50,23-27				The Lost Sheep

Jeremias	Crossan Title/#	"L"	"M"	"Q"	Thomas Log/Pg & Ln	(Luke)	(Matt)	Mark	Source/Title
The Unmerciful Servant	The Unmerciful Servant #9		18:23-34						A King Settling Accounts
The Good Employer	The Vineyard Laborers #10		20:1-15						The Wage of the Workmen
The Father's Love	The Prodigal Son #23	15:11-32							The Prodigal Son/ Elder Brother
The Two Sons	Ø		21:28a-30						The Two Sons
The Guest without a Wedding Garment	The Feast #12			M 22:2-10 L 14:16-23	#64 44,10-34				The Feast
The Ten Virgins	The Closed Door #14	[13:25?]	25:1-10						The Lamps of the Maidens
The Talents	The Entrusted Money #15			M 25:14-28 L 19:12b-24					The Entrusted Money
The Two Debtors	Ø	7:41-42a							The Two Debtors
The Good Samaritan	The Good Samaritan #13	10:30-35							The Samaritan
The Friend Asked for Help at Night	Ø	11:5-8							The Persistent Friend
The Rich Fool	The Rich Farmer #18	12:16b-20			#63 44,3-9				The Rich Man
The Barren Fig Tree	The Barren Tree #19	13:6b-9							The Barren Fig Tree
The Tower Builder	The Tower Builder #20	14:28-30							The Tower Builder
The King Contemplating a Campaign	The Warring King #21	14:31-32							The Warring King
The Lost Drachma	The Lost Coin #22	15:8-9							The Lost Coin
The Unjust Steward	The Unjust Steward #24	16:1b-7							The Dishonest Steward
The Rich Man and Lazarus	The Rich Man and Lazarus #25	16:19-31							A Rich Man and Lazarus
The Servant's Reward	Ø	17:7-9							The Servant
The Unjust Judge	The Unjust Judge #26	18:2-5							The Unjust Judge
The Pharisee and the Publican	Pharisee and Publican #27	18:10-13							The Pharisee and the Toll Collector
The Careless Woman	The Empty Jar #32				#97 49,8-14				The Empty Jar
The Slayer	The Assassin #33				#98 49,16-20				The Killer
Ø	The Palm Shoot #28								The Date Palm Shoot (Ap. Jas. 7,24-28)
Ø	Ear of Grain #30								The Ear of Grain (Ap. Jas. 12,22-27)

Appendix C: Comparative Literary Frames and Designations for the Stories in the Gospel Literature

X = HAS Ø = OMITS [—] = STORY LACKING	DESIGNATED AS A "PARABLE" IN THE INTRODUCTORY FRAME					HAS AN INTRODUCTION CALLING FOR A COMPARISON					HAS AN APPENDED INTERPRETATION				
"PARABLE"	Mk	Mat	Lk	Thos	Ap Jas	Mk	Mat	Lk	Thos	Ap Jas	Mk	Mat	Lk	Thos	Ap Jas
A Sower	X	X	X	Ø	[—]	Ø	Ø	Ø	Ø	[—]	Ø	Ø	Ø	Ø	[—]
A Sprouting Seed	Ø	[—]	[—]	Ø	[—]	X	[—]	[—]	Ø	[—]	Ø	[—]	[—]	Ø	[—]
A Mustard Seed	X	X	Ø	Ø	[—]	X	X	X	X	[—]	Ø	Ø	Ø	Ø	[—]
A Vineyard	X	X	X	Ø	[—]	Ø	Ø	Ø	Ø	[—]	X	X	X	Ø?	[—]
The Unclean Spirit	[—]	Ø	Ø	[—]	[—]	[—]	Ø	Ø	[—]	[—]	[—]	X	X	[—]	[—]
A Man Going on a Journey	Ø	[—]	Ø	[—]	[—]	X	[—]	X	[—]	[—]	X	[—]	X	[—]	[—]
On Settling out of Court	[—]	Ø	Ø	[—]	[—]	[—]	Ø	Ø	[—]	[—]	[—]	Ø	Ø	[—]	[—]
Two Houses	[—]	Ø	Ø	[—]	[—]	[—]	X	X	[—]	[—]	[—]	Ø	Ø	[—]	[—]
Good Seed and Weeds	[—]	X	[—]	Ø	[—]	[—]	X	[—]	X	[—]	[—]	Ø	[—]	Ø	[—]
The Leaven	[—]	X	Ø	Ø	[—]	[—]	X	X	X	[—]	[—]	Ø	Ø	Ø	[—]
The Hid Treasure	[—]	Ø	[—]	Ø	[—]	[—]	X	[—]	X	[—]	[—]	Ø	[—]	Ø	[—]
Merchant in Search of Pearls	[—]	Ø	[—]	Ø	[—]	[—]	X	[—]	X	[—]	[—]	Ø	[—]	X	[—]
A Net Thrown into the Sea	[—]	Ø	[—]	Ø	[—]	[—]	X	[—]	X	[—]	[—]	X	[—]	Ø	[—]
The Lost Sheep	[—]	Ø	X	Ø	[—]	[—]	Ø	Ø	X	[—]	[—]	X	X	Ø	[—]
A King Settling Accounts	[—]	Ø	[—]	[—]	[—]	[—]	X	[—]	[—]	[—]	[—]	X	[—]	[—]	[—]
The Wage of the Workmen	[—]	Ø	[—]	[—]	[—]	[—]	X	[—]	[—]	[—]	[—]	X	[—]	[—]	[—]
The Prodigal Son/ Elder Brother	[—]	[—]	Ø	[—]	[—]	[—]	[—]	Ø	[—]	[—]	[—]	[—]	Ø	[—]	[—]
The Two Sons	[—]	Ø	[—]	[—]	[—]	[—]	Ø	[—]	[—]	[—]	[—]	X	[—]	[—]	[—]
The Feast	[—]	X	Ø	Ø	[—]	[—]	X	Ø	Ø	[—]	[—]	X	X	X	[—]
The Lamps of the Maidens	[—]	Ø	[—]	[—]	[—]	[—]	X	[—]	[—]	[—]	[—]	X	[—]	[—]	[—]
The Entrusted Money	[—]	Ø	X	[—]	[—]	[—]	X	Ø	[—]	[—]	[—]	Ø	X	[—]	[—]

X = HAS / Ø = OMITS / [—] = STORY LACKING "PARABLE"	DESIGNATED AS A "PARABLE" IN THE INTRODUCTORY FRAME					HAS AN INTRODUCTION CALLING FOR A COMPARISON					HAS AN APPENDED INTERPRETATION				
	Mk	Mat	Lk	Thos	Ap Jas	Mk	Mat	Lk	Thos	Ap Jas	Mk	Mat	Lk	Thos	Ap Jas
The Two Debtors	[—]	[—]	Ø	[—]	[—]	[—]	[—]	Ø	[—]	[—]	[—]	[—]	Ø	[—]	[—]
The Samaritan	[—]	[—]	Ø	[—]	[—]	[—]	[—]	Ø	[—]	[—]	[—]	[—]	X	[—]	[—]
The Persistent Friend	[—]	[—]	Ø	[—]	[—]	[—]	[—]	Ø	[—]	[—]	[—]	[—]	X	[—]	[—]
The Rich Man	[—]	[—]	X	Ø	[—]	[—]	[—]	Ø	Ø	[—]	[—]	[—]	X	Ø	[—]
The Barren Fig Tree	[—]	[—]	X	[—]	[—]	[—]	[—]	Ø	[—]	[—]	[—]	[—]	Ø	[—]	[—]
The Tower Builder	[—]	[—]	Ø	[—]	[—]	[—]	[—]	Ø	[—]	[—]	[—]	[—]	Ø?	[—]	[—]
The Warring King	[—]	[—]	Ø	[—]	[—]	[—]	[—]	Ø	[—]	[—]	[—]	[—]	X	[—]	[—]
The Lost Coin	[—]	[—]	Ø	[—]	[—]	[—]	[—]	Ø	[—]	[—]	[—]	[—]	X	[—]	[—]
The Dishonest Steward	[—]	[—]	Ø	[—]	[—]	[—]	[—]	Ø	[—]	[—]	[—]	[—]	X	[—]	[—]
A Rich Man and Lazarus	[—]	[—]	Ø	[—]	[—]	[—]	[—]	Ø	[—]	[—]	[—]	[—]	Ø	[—]	[—]
The Servant	[—]	[—]	Ø	[—]	[—]	[—]	[—]	Ø	[—]	[—]	[—]	[—]	X	[—]	[—]
The Unjust Judge	[—]	[—]	X	[—]	[—]	[—]	[—]	Ø	[—]	[—]	[—]	[—]	X	[—]	[—]
The Pharisee and the Toll Collector	[—]	[—]	X	[—]	[—]	[—]	[—]	Ø	[—]	[—]	[—]	[—]	X	[—]	[—]
The Empty Jar	[—]	[—]	[—]	Ø	[—]	[—]	[—]	[—]	X	[—]	[—]	[—]	[—]	Ø	[—]
The Killer	[—]	[—]	[—]	Ø	[—]	[—]	[—]	[—]	X	[—]	[—]	[—]	[—]	Ø	[—]
The Date Palm Shoot	[—]	[—]	[—]	[—]	Ø	[—]	[—]	[—]	[—]	X	[—]	[—]	[—]	[—]	X
The Ear of Grain	[—]	[—]	[—]	[—]	Ø	[—]	[—]	[—]	[—]	X	[—]	[—]	[—]	[—]	X

Appendix D: Summary of Introductory Frames that Call for Comparison and the Use of the Term "Parable" in the Gospel Literature*

THE DESIGNATION OF STORIES AS "PARABLES" IN THE SYNOPTIC GOSPELS [THOMAS DOES NOT USE THE WORD PARABLE]

COMMON TRADITION

All three canonical evangelists designate the following as parable
A Sower
A Vineyard
Mixed designation in the introductory frame
A Mustard Seed (Matt, Mark = parable; Luke = not designated as parable)

MATTHEW'S SPECIAL TRADITION

Designated as parable
Good Seed and Weeds
Not designated as parable in the introductory frame
The Hid Treasure (but the broader context implies that it is parable)
Merchant in Search of Pearls (but the broader context implies that it is parable)
A Net Thrown into the Sea (but the broader context implies that it is parable)
A King Settling Accounts
The Wage of the Workmen
The Two Sons
The Lamps of the Maidens

---

*For texts see Appendix B.

LUKE'S SPECIAL TRADITION

Designated as parable
    The Rich Man
    The Barren Fig Tree
    The Unjust Judge
    The Pharisee and the Toll Collector
Not designated as parable in the introductory frame
    The Prodigal Son/Elder Brother
    The Two Debtors
    The Samaritan
    The Persistent Friend
    The Tower Builder
    The Warring King
    The Lost Coin
    The Dishonest Steward
    A Rich Man and Lazarus
    The Servant

MARK'S SPECIAL MATERIAL

Not designated as parable in the introductory frame
    A Sprouting Seed (but the broader context implies it is parable)

Q MATERIAL (MATTHEW AND LUKE)

Not designated as parable in the introductory frame
    The Unclean Spirit
    On Settling out of Court
    Two Houses
Mixed designation in the introductory frame
    The Leaven (Matt = parable; Luke = not designated as parable)
    The Lost Sheep (Matt = not designated as parable; Luke = parable)
    The Feast (Matt = parable; Luke = not designated as parable)
    The Entrusted Money (Matt = not designated as parable; Luke = parable)

INTRODUCTORY FRAMES THAT CALL FOR A COMPARISON

ALL EXTANT VERSIONS AGREE: STORIES THAT DO NOT CALL FOR A COMPARISON IN THEIR INTRODUCTORY FRAMES

    A Sower
    A Vineyard
    The Unclean Spirit
    On Settling out of Court
    The Prodigal Son/Elder Brother
    The Two Sons
    The Samaritan
    The Persistent Friend
    The Rich Man

The Barren Fig Tree
The Tower Builder
The Warring King
The Lost Coin
The Dishonest Steward
A Rich Man and Lazarus
The Servant
The Pharisee and the Toll Collector
The Two Debtors
The Unjust Judge

THE INTRODUCTORY FRAMES ARE DIVIDED ON WHETHER A COMPARISON IS CALLED FOR

A Sprouting Seed (Mark = comparison; Thomas = no comparison)
The Lost Sheep (Thomas = comparison; Matt, Luke = no comparison)
The Feast (Matt = comparison; Luke, Thomas = no comparison)
The Entrusted Money (Matt = comparison; Luke = no comparison)

IN ALL EXTANT VERSIONS A COMPARISON IS MADE BETWEEN THE STORY AND THE KINGDOM OF GOD/HEAVEN/FATHER

Good Seed and Weeds
The Leaven
The Hid Treasure
Merchant in Search of Pearls
A King Settling Accounts
The Wage of the Workmen
The Lamps of the Maidens
The Empty Jar
The Killer
The Date Palm Shoot
The Ear of Grain
A Mustard Seed

A COMPARISON IS CALLED FOR IN ALL EXTANT VERSIONS BUT TO SOMETHING OTHER THAN THE KINGDOM

Two Houses (Matt, Luke = to one who hears and does Jesus' words)
The Entrusted Money (Matt = to the return of the Son of Man)
A Man Going on a Journey (Mark, Luke = to the return of the Son of Man)

EXTANT VERSIONS DIFFER AS TO WHAT IS BEING COMPARED

A Net Thrown into the Sea (Matt = kingdom of Heaven; Thomas = the Man)

Appendix E
Classifying the Stories

One of the striking things about these stories is their generally accurate representation of first-century Palestinian village life. Using that as a clue, I have categorized the stories on the basis of their representation of the social, cultural, and economic facets of society. For text references, see Appendix B above. Some of these could reasonably fit into more than one category. For example, the Rich Man in Thomas, which I list under "Food Storage," could conceivably be listed under "Investment." And the Rich Man in Luke could be listed under "Food Storage."

NATURAL PROCESSES

FOOD PRODUCTION

Farming
   A Sower
   A Mustard Seed
   A Sprouting Seed
   The Ear of Grain
   The Date Palm Shoot

INDIVIDUAL HUMAN ACTION

BUSINESS

Real Estate
   The Hid Treasure
Merchandising
   Merchant in Search of Pearls

DOMESTIC ACTIVITIES

Marketing
   The Empty Jar
Cooking
   The Leaven

FOOD PRODUCTION

Fishing
   A Net Thrown into the Sea
Ranching: Livestock
   The Lost Sheep
Farming: Food Storage
   The Rich Man (Thomas)

CONSTRUCTION

   The Tower Builder

GOVERNMENT: MILITARY

   The Warring King

CRIME

Murder
   The Killer
Robbery
   The Samaritan

SOCIETY

BUSINESS

Banking
   A King Settling Accounts
   The Dishonest Steward
   The Two Debtors
Investment
   The Entrusted Money

LABOR RELATIONS

   The Wage of the Workmen

LANDLORD/TENANT

   A Vineyard

FEUD

   Good Seed and Weeds

FOOD PRODUCTION: ORCHARD/VINEYARD

The Barren Fig Tree

DOMESTIC

Servants
A Man Going on a Journey (only Luke)
The Servant
Household Activity
Lost Coin
Family Relationships
The Prodigal Son/Elder Brother
The Two Sons
Social Functions
The Feast (dinner party)
Lamps of the Maidens (wedding)
The Persistent Friend (hospitality)

LEGAL SYSTEM

Unjust Judge
On Settling out of Court

RELIGION

The Pharisee and the Toll Collector

CONSTRUCTION

Two Houses

MYTHOLOGICAL

A Rich Man and Lazarus
The Rich Man (Luke)
The Unclean Spirit

Index of Modern Authors

Index of Ancient Works and Authors*

---

*Shorter citations are incorporated into longer citations when they vary by only one or two lines.